the cyberspace lexicon

bob cotton and richard oliver

an illustrated dictionary of terms from multimedia **to** virtual reality

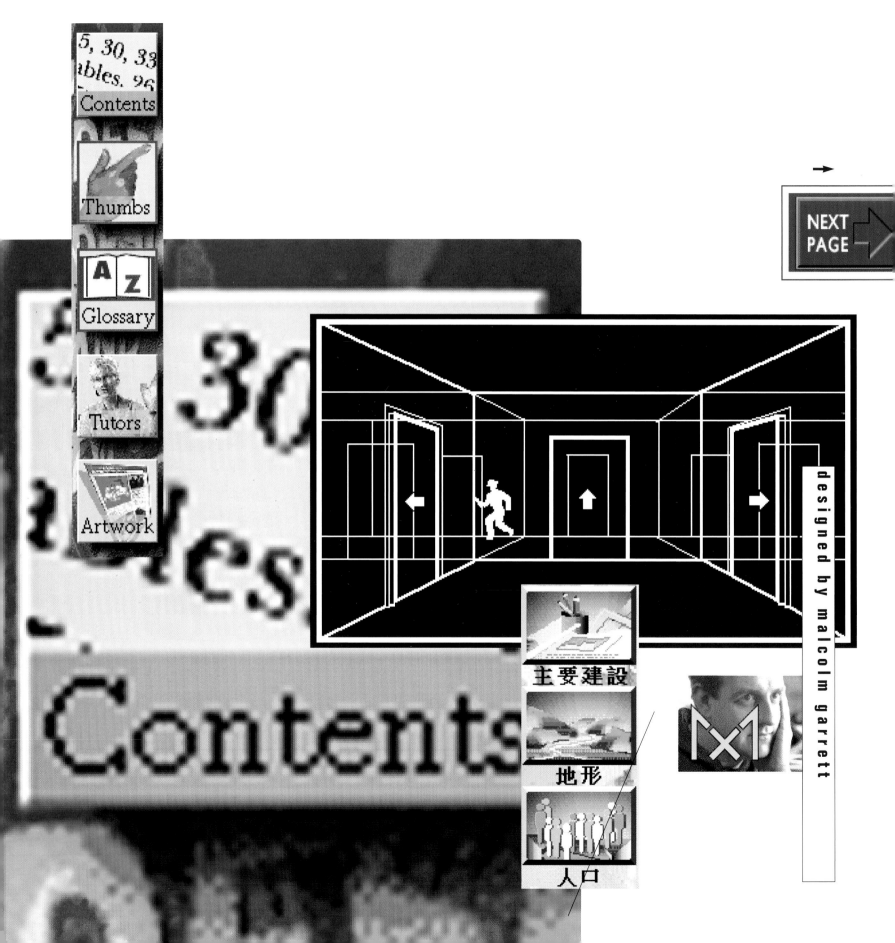

NEXT PAGE

Contents

Thumbs

Glossary

Tutors

Artwork

主要建設

地形

人口

designed by malcolm garrett

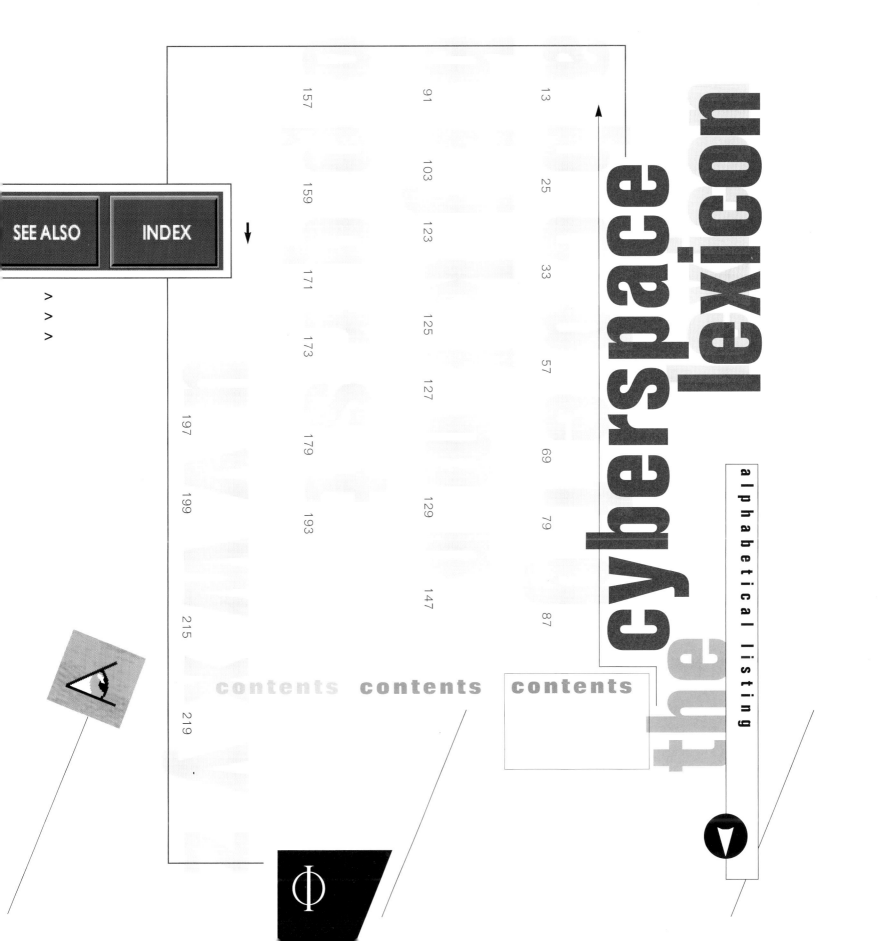

the cyberspace lexicon

alphabetical listing

contents contents contents

SEE ALSO   INDEX

13
25
33
57
69
79
87
91
103
123
125
127
129
147
157
159
171
173
179
193
197
199
215
219

Φ

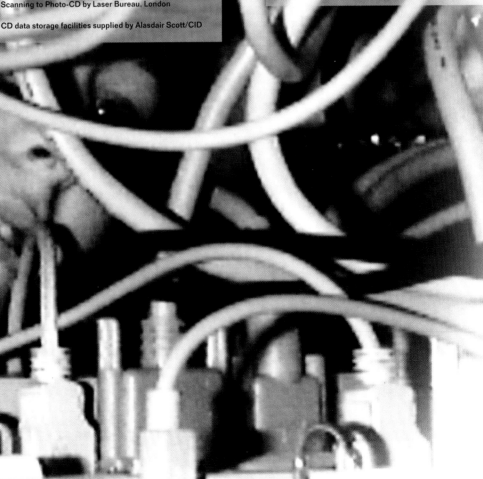

ACKNOWLEDGEMENTS

PHOTOGRAPHIC ACKNOWLEDGEMENTS

The publishers wish to thank the following for their assistance in providing images and permissions. While every effort has been made to ensure accuracy, the publishers cannot accept liability for any errors or omissions.

3DO 117, 161; **Ace Coin Equipment** 43; **Kumi Akiyoshi** 69; **Anglia TV/Westwood Studios** 178; **Apple Computer UK** 18, 45, 121, 129, 154, 163; **Atari** 205; **Autodesk** 13, 33; **Avid Technology** 86; **Mark Bowey** 29, 110, 111, 150; **Brilliant Adventures/Video Power/Swindon Cable/Acclaim** 204; **BSkyB** 115, 177; **BT Pictures** 80, 195, 208; **Cambridge Animation Systems** 47, 134; **Canon UK** 104; **Caplin Cybernetics Corporation** 196; **Carnegie Melon Engineering & Research Center** 22 (photograph of VuMan I ©Bill Redic, photograph of Future Navigator Concept ©Ken Andreyo); **Ian Cater** 140, 141; **CID/Alasdair Scott** 40; **Commodore UK** 40; **CompuServe** 46; **The Computer Lab** 72; **Bob Cotton** 7, 8, 9, 104, 114, 149, 150; **Bob Cotton/Mark Bowey** 54, 55, 120; **Cyan/Broderbund** 152, 153, 187, 198; **CytoVision** 122; **Digital Pictures** 48; **Digital Wisdom Publishing** 87; **Dimension International** 210; **Division** 209, 210; **Dorling Kindersley/Microsoft** 142, 143; **Electric Image** 48, 49, 50, 202; **Emigre** 63; **Empruve** 67, 68; **English & Pockett** 203; **EO Europe** 41, 160; **Evans & Sutherland** 91, 117, 183, 184; **Exos** 26, 83; **Fit Vision/Sophie Roberts** 166; **Fit Vision/WBSB** 115, 116, 177; **The Frame Store** 202, 203; **Fuse** 63; **Future Publishing** 70; **Malcolm Garrett/Assorted images** 9, 10, 15, 23, 24, 96, 97, 146, 172; **General Logistics** 105; **Genome Electronic Book Company** 32; **Joe Gillespie/Pixel Productions** 122, 169; **Patrick Glone/SCAD** 6; **GreatWave Software** 109; **Gremlin Graphics** 198, 199; **Gryphon Software** 135; **Hakuto International UK** 132; **HSC Software** 30; **Hughes Rediffusion Simulation** 82, 185; **Hulton-Deutsch Collection** 18; **IBM Multimedia** 103, 107; **IBM UK** 23, 33, 162, 165, 173, 194; **Infogrames** 94; **IN.form** 21, 167; **Informer/Mark Bowey** 110, 111; **Inmarsat** 106; **Jeff Instone** 71, 78, 99, 100, 101, 102; **Intel UK** 90, 133, 147, 186; **Interactive Network** 115; **Interplay Productions** 109; **Kagema** 39; **Peter Kennedy/Alistair Burns** 16; **courtesy The Kobal Collection** 53 (The Lawnmower Man First Independent); **Kodak** 124, 164; **Konami** 198; **William Latham/IBM UK Scientific Centre** 41, 48 (William Latham/Stephen Todd, Evolutionary Art & Computers, Academic Press 1992); **Jaime Levy** 72; **Logitech** 190; **Macromedia** 130; **Pete Maloney** 31; **Manga Entertainment** 52 ©1987 Akira Committee; **Maxis** 187, 207; **Media Design Interactive** 39, 74; **Microsoft** 200; **Microsoft/Cognitive Applications** 16, 168; **©MIT Media Laboratory** 19 (photograph of Seymour Papert ©Richard Pasley), 60; **Mondo 2000/Bart Nagel** 66; **Motorola** 126, 128, 180; **Namco Europe** 17; **NASA** 28, 175; **The Natural History Museum** 132, 147; **NEC** 39, 209, 215; **NextBase** 88, 98; **Nintendo UK Entertainment** 155, 156; **n.n.anonymous** 51; **Northern Telecom Europe** 200; **Ocean Software/DID** 206; **Octavo** 95; **Olivetti Research Lab** 197, 200; **Oxford University Press** 62; **Panasonic UK** 14; **Park Place Productions/3DO** 54; **Parsoft** 185, 191; **Peakash Patel** 89, 162, 194; **Philips** 35, 37, 60, 84, 85, 148; **Presto Studios/**

Gametek 151, 187; **Prospect Management** 42, 138, 139; **Quantel** 201, 202; **Raygun** 63; **Reactor Software** 212, 213; **Realworld/Brilliant Media/Steve Nelson** 144, 145, 187; **The Regency Town House** 168, 169; **Giles Rollestone** 101, 190; **Science Photo Library** 112 (Michael W Davidson), 127 (Eve Ritscher); **Sega UK** 131, 181, 182, 205; **The Shadow Robot Project** 176 (Johnny Millar); **Sony** 34, 57, 75, 93, 179, 188; **Sony Electronic Publishing** 39, 73, 74, 75, 206; **John Stevens** 108; **Studio DM** 71; **Tandy** 214; **Techex** 64; **Technology Applications Group** 176; **Tiger Media** 21; **Tomy UK** 26, 205; **Total Vision** 36; **Trip Media/David Collier** 34, 42, 99, 118, 119, 138, 139; **Virgin Interactive Entertainment/Cryo** 178; **Virtuality** 209; **Virtual Research** 104; **courtesy Virtual Technologies** 59 (Mitch Heynick); **The Vivid Group** 170, 211; **The Voyager Company** 27, 76, 77, 81, 137; **WCRS** 182; **Westminster Cable TV** 110; **Working Knowledge Transfer** 166; **Xerox Corporation** 218, 219, 220 (Brian Tramontana/Xerox PARC)

Scanning to Photo-CD by Laser Bureau, London

CD data storage facilities supplied by Alasdair Scott/CID

AUTHORS' ACKNOWLEDGEMENTS

Special thanks to Clive Richards of Infomart Ltd for his time and effort spent reading and commenting on an earlier version of this manuscript. Thanks also to Asif Choudhary of Newham College of Further Education for his patient, thorough explanations of some of the technical topics and to Andy Anderson of Anderson Public Relations for roaming the Net on our behalf. We would also like to express our very warm thanks to the team at Phaidon for bringing what turned out to be a very complicated task to a successful conclusion. Finally we would like to thank again all those from the hypermedia community who contributed pictures and information, and whose contributions are individually acknowledged in the photographic credits. Special thanks go to Graham Fletcher and George Scott of Fit Vision, Peakash Patel, Jill Monroe of Electric Image, and to Malcolm Garrett.

The authors can be contacted by E-mail at roliver@cix.compulink.co.uk
or
roliver@eudemony.demon.co.uk

Malcolm Garrett can be contacted via CompuServe 100121,131

THE CYBERSPACE VISION

> Men are suddenly nomadic gatherers of
> knowledge, nomadic as never before, informed
> as never before, free from fragmentary
> specialism as never before – but also involved in
> the total social process as never before; since
> with electricity we extend our central nervous
> system globally, instantly interrelating every
> human experience.
>
> HERBERT MARSHALL MCLUHAN, UNDERSTANDING MEDIA, 1964

At the end of the twentieth century we know a great
deal about information. We have learned how to
compress it digitally, how to pipe it into every
home via satellite communications and terrestrial
broadcasting, and how to package it in forms that
people understand: in words, pictures, diagrams,
films, print and music. We have developed
intimate systems such as the telephone and
videophone, the fax and the computer network,
enabling people to exchange information around
the world; we have invented machines that can
record changing weather, land-usage and other
global patterns from space; and with the digital
media revolution that is now upon us, we are
developing systems that will allow access to the
accumulated information and stored wisdom of
our entire history.

In the 1950s and 1960s, there was a widespread
concern about our ability to deal with the
'information explosion' that Marshall McLuhan,

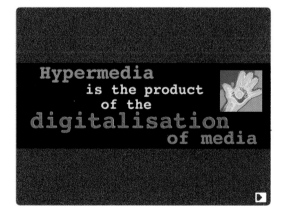

Hypermedia
is the product
of the
digitalisation
of media

Buckminster Fuller and others predicted. Since then, the development of systems such as the computer database, networks, hypertext, expert systems, hypermedia and 'knowledge-based systems' has gone hand-in-hand with a phenomenal acceleration of information processing technology. From the integrated circuit to the microprocessor, through the transputer and neural-network computing, to the development of fibre optics and digital-optical recording and a wide range of consumer electronics devices, we now have the means to confront the information explosion.

'We have the technology', as they say. We are bound up in an ever more powerful technological and commercial drive to perfect systems that will bring the means of receiving and transmitting information into every home, and even into every pocket. A large proportion of the planet's business is focused on the development of these new cyberspace markets. Industries that were previously quite separate, such as those involved in computing, consumer electronics, telecommunications, and the broadcast and

published media, find their interests converging – just as their means of production are converging in the binary code of digital information.

This book provides a kind of referential map of these 'trendings' – a guide through the maze of new and emerging technologies. One of the obstacles to action in this area is the words that are used, which span several previously quite different disciplines. As media and telecommunications converge with computing and with consumer electronics to create the cyberspace infrastructure, as concepts collide and catalyze, so the vocabulary needed to deal with this phenomenon becomes polyglot, even pidgin.

The Cyberspace Lexicon is a key to this vocabulary; a guide to the new medium of hypermedia and the new concept of cyberspace. Some of the words it includes are narrowly technical, such as **absolute disk address** or **timecode**. Many are acronyms, such as **TIFF** or **XCMD**. Some, like **bandwidth** or **digital**, are technical but with wider conceptual implications. Also included are companies and organizations (from **Apple Computer** to **Xerox PARC**) that have played an important part in developing and marketing

the technology that makes the new media possible, and the pieces of software and hardware (such as **CD-ROM**, **Sketchpad** and **Macintosh**) that have been significant.

Anyone who has read William Gibson will be only too aware that there can be a dark side to cyberspace. No doubt there will also be plenty of critics of the new 'smart' media, who will complain that it threatens accepted standards of literacy and numeracy, that it destroys our ability to think, that it usurps accepted practices of education. But this book takes a more positive angle. The authors see no real conflict between the older media and the new. All have their virtues, and their limitations. In the world of cyberspace, people will still read books printed on paper, listen to music in concert halls, and look at paintings and sculptures in galleries. But they will have a further choice: to become active participators in a worldwide matrix of media and telecommunications, to become 'nomadic gatherers of knowledge', or just to enjoy the new experiences of the largest entertainment and education machine yet devised.

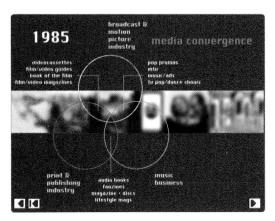

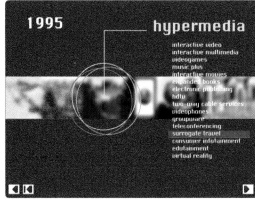

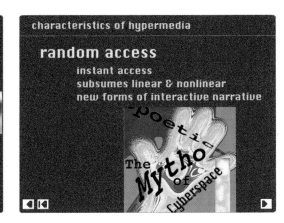

criteria for hypermedia software

simple, hot & deep
easy to get into
simple controls
just enough context

Deep in the Caribbean, hidden by an endless storm, lies LeChuck's fortress...

This book is organized as an A-Z dictionary.

Cross-references are indicated by **bold** type, and further entries of related interest are listed at the end of an entry [>].

Illustrated features on key terms and concepts supplement the dictionary definitions [•].

Further reading references [>>] are listed in full in the bibliography, page 221.

using the cyberspace lexicon

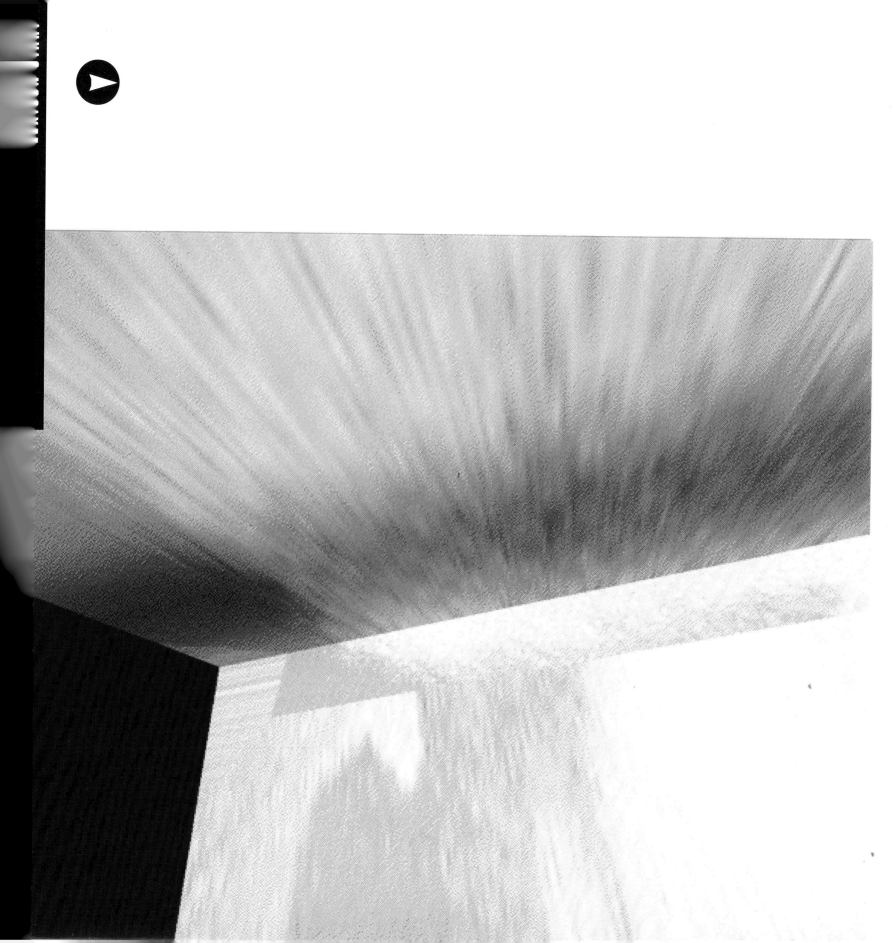

2½-D [TWO-AND-A-HALF DIMENSIONAL]

In computer graphics, describes a scene that creates the illusion of being in three dimensions, but which does not have the spatial data to generate different views of that scene.

> COMPUTER GRAPHICS

3-D [THREE-DIMENSIONAL]

In computer graphics, describes a model that exhibits breadth, height and depth and contains the spatial data to generate different views.

> COMPUTER GRAPHICS

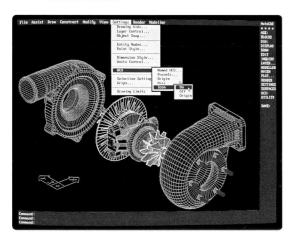

A turbo-charger unit in 3-d wireframe, designed using AutoCAD.

3-D SOUND

> BINAURAL SOUND

3DO

A consortium of videogame, consumer electronics, media and entertainment companies involved in the design and production of the 3DO Interactive Multiplayer, a RISC-based CD-ROM reader with powerful graphics and audio processors.

> • 3DO PAGE 14

6 DOF [SIX DEGREES OF FREEDOM]

In virtual reality systems, refers to the number of position and orientation inputs a sensor can measure. These typically include Cartesian (X, Y, Z) spatial coordinates, together with roll, pitch and yaw orientations.

ABSOLUTE DISK ADDRESS

The location of a particular sector on a computer disk or CD-ROM. In a CD-ROM it is specified in minutes, seconds and sectors, and contained in the sector header field.

> ADDRESS

ABSOLUTE RGB ENCODING

Method of picture coding. Pixels for an image are encoded using up to 8 bits each for the red, green and blue components of the pixel.

> RGB

ABSOLUTE SECTOR ADDRESS

The address component of the sector header field, whose value corresponds to the absolute disk address.

> ADDRESS

ABSOLUTE TIME

In compact disc audio (CDDA), the total time that the disc has been playing. This can be displayed during play by means of an LCD panel.

ACCESS CONTROLLER

In CD-i, a player component that retrieves drawmaps from RAM, and loads them to the video decoder.

ACCESS KEY

A password, number, or code that allows a user to gain access to a protected file. The use of access keys allows publishers to distribute large quantities of material – such as digital fonts or a range of applications programmes – on a single CD-ROM, with users selecting and paying only for those parts they require. A publisher could also make material available over a network on a similar basis. The massive storage capacity of CD-ROM makes this a very economic method of distribution for the supplier and of data access for the user.

ACCESS PROTECTION

Refers to techniques used to prevent unauthorized access to confidential data.

ACCESS TIME

The time taken to retrieve an item from memory, or to display a video frame from a laserdisc, or to locate a given sector address in a digital-optical recording medium.

ACOUSTIC COUPLER

A device that allows the computer to be connected to a telephone, and which converts serial digital data to a range of audio frequencies for transmission through a telephone network.

> MODEM

ACOUSTICAL CUE

In an interactive system, an audio signal designed to call the user's attention. Noises such as 'beeps' and 'bongs' provide essential feedback to the user, for instance by drawing attention to a dialogue box in which a positive response must be made before the program/programme can proceed.

> AUDIO FEEDBACK   > AUDITORY ICON
> EARCON

ACTIVE DISPLAY
That part of a video memory currently being displayed, in contrast to video memory held in **RAM** ready for display if needed.

ACTIVE LINE SCAN PERIOD
In a cathode-ray tube (**CRT**), the period of time necessary for an electron beam to pass across the **screen** phosphors and create a visible line of **pixels**.

ACTIVE MENU
A **menu** currently displayed in the **menubar**, and ready for the user to access.

ACTIVE REGION
The area of a **screen** display that will trigger an event (such as the revealing of a concealed **window**) when a **cursor** passes over it or when a **mouse** is clicked.
> BUTTON

ACTIVE WINDOW
The **window** to which **keyboard**, **mouse** or other input devices are directed. A variety of visual cues may be employed to distinguish the currently active window from any others. These include a highlighted bar at the top of the window, a flashing **cursor** within it, or the window appearing 'in front' of others on the monitor screen.
> INTERFACE   > MICROSOFT WINDOWS

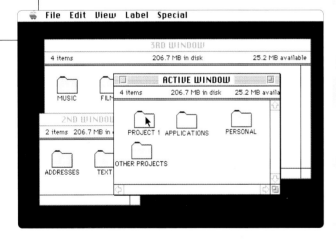

ACTOR
In Division's ProVision **virtual reality** system, 'Actors' are autonomous parallel processes that control different elements of the virtual environment. The visual Actor controls visualization, the audio Actor controls **audio feedback**, etc. Actors can be developed in **C** language, and reused in a variety of applications.

ACTV [ADVANCED COMPATIBLE TV]
A high-definition television (**HDTV**) system under development at the David Sarnoff Research Centre in the USA, which aims to provide varying levels of 'backward compatibility' to existing domestic (**NTSC**) broadcast systems.

Electronic Arts: 'World Builders, Inc.' combines superb computer graphics with complex strategy as players compete to 'terraform' new planets. With a claimed rendering performance of 64 million pixels per second and an ARM6 RISC chip capable of around six MIPS, 3DO have produced a standard-setting specification.

3DO
audio, video, 3DO

3DO is the brainchild of Trip Hawkins, the man behind software pioneers Electronic Arts and one of the formative figures in interactive media. 3DO's Interactive Multiplayer, an interactive media platform designed to play CD-ROM discs and link to a television monitor, is aimed at the home multimedia/games market also targeted by Philips (CD-i), Commodore (CD32), Sega (Mega-CD) and other electronic companies.

3DO has some undeniable advantages in the battle to establish a world standard for hypermedia. First of all there's the Multiplayer itself, which represents the first major innovation in interactive technology since CD-i was prematurely announced in 1986. The Multiplayer boasts a RISC (reduced instruction set chip) central microprocessor, promising very powerful and fast computing at 32-bit. Added to this is an impressive range of dedicated processors for animation and sound, as well as a double-speed CD-ROM drive that can also play CD-audio and read Kodak PhotoCD discs.

3DO's launch was a model of well thought-through planning, with incentives for hardware developers, distributors and software developers. The software development package, for example, included a complete range of programming tools and emulators based around the Apple Macintosh as well as over 100 gigabytes of copyright-free music, sound effects, video footage, clip art and photographs, supplied on CD-ROM.

There was also an impressive array of industrial might in the consortia backing the 3DO technology. Matsushita, the world's largest consumer electronics manufacturer (with brand names such as Panasonic, Technics and Quasar), will be the first to

The Software Toolworks: 'The Animals' is an interactive multimedia safari based on exhibits at San Diego Zoo. 3DO intends to encourage more edutainment and educational titles in the future.

produce an Interactive Multiplayer. AT&T, one of the world's leading computer and communications companies, will help in the development of network versions of the Multiplayer, as well as making Multiplayers of its own. On the software side, the media and entertainment giant Time Warner will be developing software titles and interactive cable applications for 3DO, while MCA, with a major presence on film, television, music, theatres and theme parks, will be developing interactive movie titles. Hawkins' own company, Electronic Arts, is also creating several interactive software titles for 3DO.

There are already several competing formats for the home interactive media system, as the computer, consumer electronics, media and telecommunications industries make their bid for a stake in a potential world market measured in billions of dollars. 3DO look as though they may have the right product and a winning strategy, but it is the combination of successful software with affordable hardware that will catalyse the market for hypermedia infotainment – and the consumer will decide when these conditions are met.

ADAPTIVE DELTA PULSE-CODE MODULATION
> ADPCM

ADDRESS
A particular location of a unit or area of memory that is uniquely identified, in **RAM** or **ROM** or within a storage medium such as a **floppy disk** or **CD-ROM**. In a **network**, a device, **node** or physical location within the computer network topology.

ADOBE TYPE MANAGER [ATM]
Adobe Systems software application for the Apple **Macintosh** and other **personal computers**. ATM works with any application using **PostScript** fonts, and ensures accurate screen representations of typefaces at any size. This is important for display typography (for example in titles or captions for **laserdisc** stills), because pre-**System 7** Macs had only a limited range of screen fonts, and represent non-screen font point sizes by enlarging the **bitmap** of the nearest available screen font – which resulted in some extremely jagged characters.

> ANTI-ALIASING　　　　> PAGE DESCRIPTION LANGUAGE

ADPCM [ADAPTIVE DELTA PULSE-CODE MODULATION]
Audio coding technique used in **CD-i**, which converts **analog audio** to a compressed **digital** format. ADPCM was developed so that CD-i could deliver a high-quality audio track at the same time as images and data. Compact disc audio uses **pulse-code modulation**, sampling analog audio at 44.1kHz, and can store about 72 minutes of top-quality stereo sound on a disc. CD-i uses the same size discs as CD audio (**CDDA**), and in order to accommodate pictures and program data, therefore, the audio data needs to be stored in a compressed form. ADPCM works by recording the changes in signal amplitude at every point, rather than by recording the actual amplitude (as is the case in pulse-code modulation).

Encoding all the audio tracks in ADPCM means that the CD can store over 300 megabytes of visual and program data as well as the audio data. ADPCM can deliver a range of audio quality, from Level A, 'hi-fi' quality (equivalent to a freshly pressed vinyl stereo LP), to Level C, 'speech' quality (equivalent to AM radio). Plotting optimal use of the different audio and picture modes on CD-i requires considerable ingenuity – the designer has to trade audio quality against the quality and complexity of images and other data. The designer is thus presented with a wide variety of options, such as using CDDA-quality audio to play over a still-frame graphic image, using hi-fi quality to play in synchronization with partial motion images, or using speech modes to carry a variety of tracks accessible through a highly interactive branching programme structure – or, indeed, any mixture of these.

> AUDIO SAMPLING　　　> BANDWIDTH
> CD-I DIGITAL AUDIO　　> COMPRESSION
> FULL-MOTION VIDEO

ADVANCED COMPATIBLE TV
> ACTV

AERIAL PERSPECTIVE
Atmospheric effect whereby distant objects appear to be dimmer than objects which are close to the observer (as a result of the dispersal of light by dust, water vapour etc). Aerial perspective is a device long used by artists to create the illusion of distance and space, and to separate foreground from background content. Graphics programmers have devised a system called 'intensity depth cueing' to create aerial perspective effects in computer-generated landscapes and cityscapes.

> COMPUTER GRAPHICS　　> PERSPECTIVE SYSTEMS

AGENT
In **hypermedia** programmes and software for **personal digital assistants**, a software entity – sometimes with an anthropomorphic visual 'characterization' on screen – that can perform simple and/or mundane tasks for the user, such as providing context-sensitive help when required, or retrieving information from a **database**. Alan Kay, inventor of the **Dynabook**, calls agents 'the next big direction in user-interface design', predicting that the next **interface** after the icon-based **graphical user interface** will be 'icons plus agents'. The idea of 'agents' was originated by John McCarthy in the mid-1950s and developed (and named) by Oliver G Selfridge (both at MIT). They envisaged a 'soft robot' that would be capable of carrying out computer operations to arrive at a given goal, and able to request human help or assistance when necessary.

> GUIDE　　　　　　　　> KNOWBOT
>> FURTHER READING: LAUREL ET AL 1990

AI [ARTIFICIAL INTELLIGENCE]
(Or 'machine intelligence'.) Software that enables computers to emulate the human abilities of learning and decision-making. AI research encompasses a broad range of activities, including **knowledge-based systems**, **expert systems**, decision-support systems, automatic program synthesis, parallel array systems and pattern-recognition systems.

The field of artificial intelligence is one of the most controversial areas in computer science. The AI project at its most extreme is an attempt to simulate human intelligence on a computer. Critics argue that this is intrinsically impossible, and that it is based on a conception of human intelligence that is fundamentally flawed. This argument is only going to be settled over time. Meanwhile, as a result of the ambitious goals of the project, a whole range of useful systems have been produced – such as expert systems, where the knowledge of experts in a particular field has been formalized and made more widely available. A further promising area is the development of **agents**.

>> FURTHER READING: BODEN 1991; HOFSTADTER 1979; KURZWEIL 1990; MINSKY 1988; WINOGRAD AND FLORES 1986

ALERT BOX
A type of **dialogue box** (often accompanied by an audio warning or **acoustical cue**) that warns the user of the implications of a desired action, and offers the choice of confirming or cancelling the action.

ALGORITHM
A procedure for solving a particular problem. Devising an algorithm in essence means formulating a method by which the solution to a problem may be found.

ALPHA CHANNEL
In **digital video** systems and **image-processing** software, the alpha channel is an extra set of **bits** that provide control information, mainly for special effects such as overlay and transparency.

> VIDEO GRAPHICS

ALPHANUMERIC
Describes systems that encompass both numerals and letters of the alphabet, such as the **qwerty keyboard**.

AMIGAVISION
A multimedia **authoring** system for the Amiga system. Released to coincide with the launch of **CDTV**, Amigavision is an **icon**-based application requiring no previous programming experience (although it supports **BASIC**).

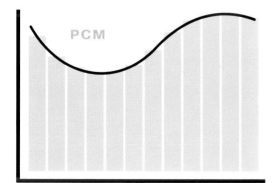

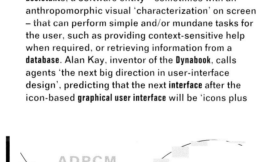

Pulse-code modulation records amplitude at each sample; ADPCM records only the changes in amplitude between successive samples.

AMPLITUDE

The strength and intensity of a sound (in terms of acoustics, the pressure level), determining the loudness or volume, and corresponding to the overall height of the sound wave.

> AUDIO SAMPLING   > DIGITAL AUDIO

ANALOG

Describes information that can be recorded, stored, processed and communicated in a form similar to its source. For example, the grooves on a gramophone record are similar in form to the soundwaves they reproduce, unlike a compact disc which is **digital** and describes sounds in terms of discrete binary numbers.

ANALOG AUDIO

The representation of sound by means of a continuously variable signal, such as an electric current. Analog signals are susceptible to **noise** and distortion, which are caused by imperfections in the electronic circuitry of the analog system, and by the failure of parts of the system to represent the original signal accurately. The shift from analog to digital modes of sampling and storing audio information took place in the early 1980s with the widespread adoption of the **CD** and other **digital-audio** recording techniques.

> DAT   > DCC
> • DIGITAL AND ANALOG MEDIA PAGE 61

ANALOG-TO-DIGITAL CONVERTER [ADC]

A device in a computer or a synthesizer that converts analog signals to digital code. ADCs work by taking regular samples of the continuous analog signal. For example, CD-quality audio is produced by sampling the analog sound signal 44,100 times per second.

> CDDA   > DIGITAL SIGNAL PROCESSOR

ANAMORPHIC LENS

In film-making, a lens that horizontally 'squeezes' light rays entering the camera. Used in wide-screen movie formats such as Cinemascope.

> ANAMORPHIC PROJECTION

ANAMORPHIC PROJECTION

A perspective projection in which the image can be seen in its correct form from one specific viewing position only. Perhaps the most widely known example of anamorphic projection is the painting The Ambassadors, by Hans Holbein the Younger (1497-1543), in which the central image in the lower third of the canvas only resolves itself into a readable image when viewed from a position a few inches in front of the painting, looking from the bottom right-hand side. (The image is of a human skull, an example of a device often used in painting at this time, called a 'memento mori' – a reminder of mortality.)

Anamorphic images such as this can be seen as a model for 'hyperspatial' devices – messages, images, diagrams and objects that only become readable when viewed from a specific position in the hyperspace of a **hypermedia** or **virtual reality** environment. The famous Ames Chair by Adelbert Ames only becomes a 'chair' when viewed from a singular perspective. From every other viewpoint it is apparently a random collection of components. Such anamorphic devices are set to become a regular feature of **role-playing games**, educational **courseware**, puzzles and quest-type **hypermedia** programmes, where the correct viewing position would be achieved as a reward to the user for drawing upon intelligence, observation or manual dexterity to solve a problem.

> COMPUTER GRAPHICS   > PERSPECTIVE SYSTEMS

ANIMATICS

Animations designed to demonstrate the viability of a storyboard before any live-action film or video is shot. Animatics are relatively quick and cheap to produce, and are used extensively by advertising agencies to test the effectiveness of ideas for commercials. Traditionally made by using a **rostrum camera** to film a succession of hand-drawn visuals, animatics can now be produced digitally using programs such as **Macromedia Director**, in which artwork or illustrations can be created or imported from specialist **paint programs** and then processed and sequenced to synchronize with an audio track. Simple animatics can also be produced in **HyperCard** and **SuperCard**, either by using the in-program drawing and painting tools to create a series of cards, or by importing a set of **PICS** images, and **scripting** them to display sequentially.

> COMPUTER ANIMATION

ANIMATION

The illusion of continuous motion produced by displaying a series of still images at rates of more than 15 frames per second.

> COMPUTER ANIMATION   > ROTOSCOPE

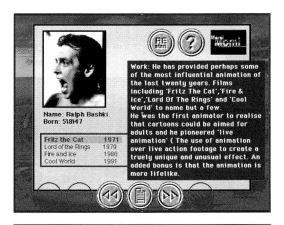

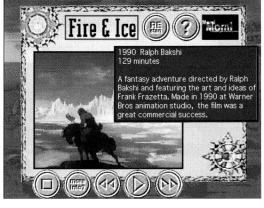

Peter Kennedy and Alistair Burns: Prototype point-of-information system for the Museum of the Moving Image, London. Animation provides both form and content in this dynamic system.

'The Ambassadors'

PAINTINGS

HOLBEIN 1533

Full title 'Jean de Dinteville and Georges de Selve' Signed lower left: ioannes/ holbein/ pingebat/1533. Wood (oak), 207 x 209.5 cm No. 1314. Purchased with contributions from Charles Cotes, Sir E. Guiness, Bt. (Lord Iveagh) and Lord Rothschild, 1890.

This picture memorialises two wealthy, educated and powerful young men. Left, Jean de Dinteville, the French ambassador to England during 1533. Right, Georges de Selve, Bishop of Lavaur. They are painted life-size and full-length - the most lavish style of portraiture.

The picture is underscored with reminders of their mortality. *NEXT PAGES... Dramatis Personae; Memento Mori; Anamorphosis; Cultural Setting; Identifying the Instruments; The religious background*

| Help | Find... | Go Back | 1 of 7 pages on 'The Ambassadors' 4 of 5 paintings from London 1300–1600 | Next Page | See Also | Contents |

Hans Holbein: The Ambassadors. The anamorphic projection across the bottom of the painting resolves itself into a human skull when viewed obliquely from lower right and close to. Image from Microsoft's 'Art Gallery' CD-ROM.

Namco: 'Ridge Racer' arcade console. Though still betraying their fairground origin, arcades are where future desktop consumer interactive media is tested, where new consumer-computer interfaces emerge, and where current technology is pushed to the limits. This console can texture-map onto 3-d polygons in realtime.

Namco: 'Ridge Racer'. This video-quality racing simulator is now available on domestic consoles. Simulators provide a dynamic and continuous free-form interaction that is quite different from 'beat-'em-ups' or 'shoot-'em-ups'.

ARCADE GAMES
from 'Space Invaders' to virtuality

Computer-based arcade games were the first media to exploit commercially the graphics and gaming potential of the earliest microprocessor chips (Intel's 4004 in 1971, and the 8-bit 8080 in 1972). Nolan Bushnell (one of the founders of Atari) introduced the first widely successful game, 'Pong', in 1972; and this was followed by other games classics such as 'Space Invaders' and Atari's 'Lunar Lander', 'Asteroids', 'Missile Command' and 'Centipede'. Since the 1970s, arcade games have grown in complexity, with both games and hardware designers exploring the leading edge of interface and software design to create fast, entertaining and responsive games.

Due to the limitations of the first chips, early arcade games were two-dimensional, using flat graphic bitmaps and moving sprites. After the introduction of the 68000 and 8086 microprocessors, the early 1980s saw the release of more complex games such as Sega's 'Turbo' (1982) and Namco's 'Pole Position' (1983) which exploited the third dimension by means of sprite expansion and compression. This technique provided a 3-d effect by enlarging and reducing sprites as they moved through the illusory space in front of the background plane. Other methods of creating a 3-d environment were also

adopted, including constructing computer-graphic 3-d models using wireframe graphics; drawing the games graphics in a 3-d perspective system such as isometric or axonometric; or using the pictorial illusion of vanishing point perspective in a fully painted or photographic backdrop, and super-imposing fixed or variable-size sprites. Early wire-frame or 'vector' games included 'Tailgunner' and 'Battlezone' (both launched in 1980), with solid-modelled (filled polygon) games appearing later in the same decade (Atari's 'I Robot' was the first). Isometric techniques were exploited in 'Zaxxon' (1982) and more recently in Atari's 'Escape from the Planet of the Robot Monsters'.

Photographic-quality illusions (which use sprite overlays) were first created using laserdisc-stored video images (Sega Laser's 'Mach 3', and 'Firefox'), while 'Dragon's Lair' utilized high-quality Disney-style animation, also stored on laserdisc. Accusations that arcade games were too violent led to the introduction in the early 1980s of games with a softer image, such as 'Pacman' which exploited the maze metaphor.

The future of arcade games is likely to see increasing realism in solid-modelled realtime graphics, greater use of composite games featuring full-motion video images with sprite and vector graphic overlays and

hi-fi stereo audio, and ever more spectacular virtual reality (VR) systems. Another development over the next few years could be the establishment of 'virtual theme parks'. The 'Battletech' centres that are becoming established in the USA have already begun to set the style for such parks, and the entertainment group Abrams/Gentile Entertainment has announced plans for a 'Total Virtual Reality' theme park in Osaka, Japan, featuring networked VR simulators. Arcade games are also on the move. In 1993, Peter Gabriel's Mind Blender trailers went on tour in the USA, with each 30-seat mobile offering an eight-minute audiovisual experience of 'heightened reality with music'.

The convergence of virtual reality and arcade videogames is well under way. And just as in the past arcades prototyped a variety of games that were later introduced into the home on console or PC, so in the 1990s arcades and theme parks look set to create markets for virtual reality products – products that will later be available to the home consumer via networks or in high-power standalone systems. The videogame industry has already invented a range of powerful and friendly interface styles for consumer interactive entertainment, and it is in the arcades and theme parks that we will see the next generation of 'cyberspace' interfaces emerge.

ANTI-ALIASING

Technique deployed in **imaging systems** to alleviate the jagged appearance of graphics produced on low-**resolution** devices such as computer monitors. Derived from techniques used in medieval tapestry, anti-aliasing involves the interpolation of a neutral colour between the edge of one colour plane and another.

> JAGGIES

not anti-aliased

anti-aliased

APPLE COMPUTER

Apple Computer, Inc. has a very special place in the development of **cyberspace**. Through an astute mix of product, image building and marketing, Apple, more than any other company, promoted the idea of the truly 'personal' computer – a computer that could even evoke emotions of affection. Founded by Steve Jobs and Steven Wozniak in 1976, Apple is notable for several major achievements, including Apple II, the first popular **microcomputer**, which can be credited with having launched the personal computer revolution, and the **Macintosh**, which brought many of the innovations developed at **Xerox Parc** (such as the **graphical user interface**, the **mouse** and **icons**) to a mass-market machine. The launch of **HyperCard** in 1985, and Apple's commitment to **interactive multimedia** and the

CD-ROM, established Apple as a major player in the emerging multimedia business of the early 1990s, while their **personal digital assistant**, the Newton, launched in 1993, is set to continue this trend.

>> FURTHER READING: LARSEN AND ROGERS 1985; SCULLEY 1988

Mac Classic: Apple led the way with computers for education, with a GUI that was sensible, useable and elegant; with DTP; with hypermedia, and with interactive multimedia. Thank you Apple.

APPLESCRIPT

A **scripting** language for Apple **Macintosh** computers running **System 7** that allows users to automate repetitive tasks. For example, a user could write an AppleScript program to find and delete specified files created before a particular date, or to cut and paste text from a number of different files into one continuous file. Scripting languages of this kind give the user with little programming experience the opportunity to customize their computer to suit the way they work – a facility that hitherto was only available to computer users experienced in handling a complex operating system such as **Unix** or **MS-DOS**.

APPLICATION PROGRAM

A computer **program** developed to perform 'real world' tasks, such as writing and drawing, as opposed to tasks related to the operations of the computer itself.

> OPERATING SYSTEM

ARC [AUGMENTATION RESEARCH CENTER]

Laboratory set up by Douglas Engelbart at the Stanford Research Institute, Stanford University, in the 1960s. The **mouse**, **windows**, **E-mail** and computer conferencing were all developed at ARC as part of Engelbart's NLS (oN Line System), several years before **personal computers** were invented. The laboratory's work also led to applications such as **hypertext** systems, **groupware** and networking.

ARCADE GAMES

Coin-operated games designed for use in arcades and other public entertainment areas. Produced for **dedicated** systems, arcade games integrate a **screen** or screens, a coin-op or **smart card** mechanism, and **input** or control devices such as **buttons**, **joysticks**, handlebars and steering-wheels. They can vary from

simple stand-up modules to lavish **consoles**, such as flight or driving simulators.

> COIN-OP MULTIMEDIA   > SIMULATION
> VIRTUAL THEME PARK   > • ARCADE GAMES PAGE 17

ARCHITECTURE MACHINE GROUP [ARCHMAC]

Originating from an idea by Nicholas Negroponte in 1964, the ArchMac (pronounced 'arkmac') group was founded in 1967 at the Massachusetts Institute of Technology (**MIT**). In the early 1980s the group metamorphosed into the **Media Lab**.

> • ARCHMAC TO MEDIA LAB PAGE 19

ARCHIVE

(1) A collection of records, images, graphic artefacts etc, generally for public or corporate use. New electronic technologies offer a convenient and safe form of storage and retrieval of archive material, and can also provide a 'user-friendly' front end.

> DATABASE

(2) In computing, a **file** or files that have been compressed for space-efficient storage. Many bulletin boards (**BBS**) store their files in this form.

ARCHIVING

The process of backing-up computer **files** for long-term storage. High-capacity storage media with slow **access time**s – such as **tape streamer**s and **WORM** systems – are often used for this purpose.

'Hulton Picture Finder': the huge Hulton-Deutsch photographic archive is now being made available on CD-ROM, with a suite of innovative search tools and browsers to assist the user in finding exactly the right image.

ARCHMAC TO MEDIA LAB

ARCHMAC TO MEDIA LAB
the silicon Bauhaus

As Stewart Brand pointed out in the preface to his book The Media Lab: Inventing the Future at MIT, the Media Lab is as much a metaphor for the worldwide media situation as it is a particular building in Massachusetts. Indeed, the multimedia, intermedia and new media research and development carried out there prefigure the profound changes that are occurring in the world at large, as telecommunications converge with entertainment and information media. As well as gathering truly world-class scientists and designers together in a hot-bed of creative research, the Media Lab also focuses the corporate interests of the most innovative media businesses in the United States. The span of Lab activities stretches from holographic projections to Lego/Logo toys, from full-body virtual reality tracking suits to high-definition television (HDTV), and includes disciplines as diverse as artificial intelligence (AI) and typography, music and electronic engineering.

The Media Lab has been called the Bauhaus of the late twentieth century, and like the Bauhaus, it is fronted by an architect (or at least a former student of architecture), Nicholas Negroponte. In the 1920s, the Bauhaus became the focus for the newly emerging Modernist movement in art, architecture and design. And just as the Bauhaus used the new industrial technologies of plastic, steel and electricity, so the Media Lab uses the new information technologies of AI, silicon chip microprocessors and fibre optics.

The Media Lab emerged from the coming together of several departments at the Massachusetts Institute of Technology (MIT), the largest of which was the Architecture Machine Group (ArchMac), formed by Negroponte in 1967. The name denoted one of Negroponte's driving concerns since his student days some four years earlier: he wanted to build a machine that would help architects produce better architecture. The ideas in his 1968 book The Architecture Machine became a nexial component of the Media Lab's self-image. The central idea was that of a partnership and dialogue between the designer (architect) and an 'intelligent' computer – an 'architecture machine' that would learn from its human interlocutors, analyse their design and working methods, and predict their requirements. Such a machine would enter into a collaboration with the human architect:

> Imagine a machine that can follow your design methodology and at the same time discern and assimilate your conversational idiosyncrasies. This same machine, after observing your behaviour, could build a predictive model of your conversational performance... The dialogue would be so intimate – even exclusive – that only mutual persuasion and compromise would bring about ideas, ideas unrealizable by either conversant alone.
>
> NICHOLAS NEGROPONTE, THE ARCHITECTURE MACHINE, 1970

Spatial Data Management System. Spatial mnemonics help orchestrate memory in cyberspace. The SDMS screen displayed a calculator, calendar and telephone – all of which are now commonplace tools in desktop computing.

Seymour Papert of MIT: the inventor of Logo and author of Mindstorms.

The early work of the ArchMac group involved seminal research in computer-aided design for architects, followed by the development of the Spatial Data Management System (1977), an important contribution to the evolving 'desktop' metaphor for graphical user interfaces on PCs, and the Movie Map project (1978), an historically important step in the history of interactive media.

The Movie Map was a pioneering example of what could be done by integrating the newly available videodisc technologies (Philips' Laserdisc had been launched earlier in 1978) with computer-mediated interaction. Movie Map was made by filming all routes through and around the city of Aspen, Colorado, and loading these sequences onto videodisc. Software was written that allowed users to control the sequencing and display of these stored images – effectively 'travelling' around the city, turning left or right, or going straight ahead, at any junction. Movie Map was thus the first 'surrogate travel' programme utilizing high-resolution video images.

In 1979 the ArchMac group demonstrated how Spatial Data Management techniques could be used in a voice-directed computer interface. The 'Put That There' prototype used position-tracking and voice-recognition to allow users to point at a wall-sized computer display screen and manipulate images, icons and files. Again, this was ground-breaking work in the field of 'projected' virtual reality, where users become participants in a life-size computer-generated environment.

During the early 1980s ArchMac linked up with other MIT departments, and by 1985 it had become the Media Lab. Its range of activities expanded to embrace R&D in the various electronic media, including electronic publishing, speech, TV, movies, computer animation, digital music, spatial imaging, visible language, computer entertainment, education, and human-machine interface. These Media Lab activities are sponsored by some of the largest and most forward-looking multinationals operating in the consumer electronics, telecommunications, media and computing businesses – companies that are corporately shaping the global media scene now, and are building the technological and industrial base for the new cyberspace 'hypermedia' of the twenty-first century.

>> FURTHER READING: BRAND 1987; NEGROPONTE 1970

Aspen Movie Map: the first interactive video, the first surrogate travel, the first 'city simulator' – seminal 1978 cybermedia from ArchMac.

Electronic Publishing Group: 'Newspeek'. The ideas of broadcatching, customized news and 'tell-me-more television' were embodied in this working demo in the mid-1980s.

Today

The New York Times
U.S. SAYS BOTHA SPURNED APPEAL FROM REAGAN TO RESCIND DECREE
By GERALD M. BOYD
White House officials said today that President P. W. Botha of South Africa had defiantly rejected a personal appeal from President Reagan for restraint andan end to the nationwide state of emergency decree.
The officials said Mr. Botha, who was told that the Administration's "patience was wearing thin," had reacted in a manner they described as "obstinate" and had indicated tha"

↓

ARCHMAC
> ARCHITECTURE MACHINE GROUP

ARPA [ADVANCED RESEARCH PROJECTS AGENCY]
Agency funded by the US Government Department of Defense and created in response to the USSR Sputnik launch in October 1957, with a brief to fund high-technology research and development projects. ARPA beneficiaries included Douglas Engelbart's Augmentation Research Centre (**ARC**), and MIT's **ArchMac** group. But perhaps its most significant initiative was the **ARPAnet**, an experimental **packet-switching network** that has been called 'The mother of **Internet**'. Through the funding of centres of excellence, ARPA exerted a major influence in the development of the enabling technologies for personal computing and networking. In the early 1970s ARPA was renamed DARPA (Defense Advanced Research Projects Agency), and limited by statute to funding weapons-related research.

ARPANET [ADVANCED RESEARCH PROJECTS AREA NETWORK]
One of the earliest computer **networks**, established by the Advanced Research Projects Agency of the US Government Department of Defense (**ARPA**) in 1972. ARPAnet was the prototype for **packet-switching networks**, and was designed to link computer scientists at universities and other research centres to distant computers (computers were scarce in the early 1970s). One of ARPAnet's features was an **E-mail** service.
> DATA SUPERHIGHWAY   > INTERNET

ARROW CURSOR
The standard **cursor** used on the **Macintosh** and **Microsoft Windows** interface: a black arrow pointing to the 'eleven o'clock' position.

ARTIFACT
The degradation in an image caused by processing or compressing data. Artifacts can take the form of **pixels** or groups of pixels of the wrong colour, or, in **full-motion video** and other forms of digital video compression, of clumps of pixels of the same colour, known as 'blockiness'.
> COMPRESSION
> FULL-SCREEN FULL-MOTION VIDEO
> MPEG   > NOISE

ARTIFICIAL INTELLIGENCE
> AI

ARTIFICIAL REALITY
Essentially the same as **virtual reality**. Artificial reality was the term used by virtual reality pioneer Myron Krueger to describe the illusion of reality created in computer-orchestrated video environments. From 1969 onwards, Krueger developed a series of interactive environments that emphasized physical and multi-sensory participation in computer events. Using pressure-sensitive floor pads, infrared light beams, **lasers** and other **feedback** and control mechanisms linked to a computer and to videotape

or videodisc players and display monitors, Krueger developed his 'Videoplace' environments, in which participators could freely move around, and by their movements and gestures effect the display of various video and computer images.
> PROJECTED REALITY
>> FURTHER READING: KRUEGER 1983, 1990, 1992

ASCII [AMERICAN STANDARD CODE FOR INFORMATION INTERCHANGE]
A standard scheme for encoding **alphanumeric** characters so that they can be stored in the computer. Each character input from the **keyboard** is represented by 7 bits.

ASPECT RATIO
The ratio of width to height of **screen** images or **pixels**. In TV this is 4:3; in 35mm transparency film, 3:2. The consideration of the correct aspect ratio for the framing of images within a given medium is of crucial importance for the designer. Even from first rough storyboard stage, **frames** should be drawn up in the correct aspect ratio for the intended final screen or image window proportion. The ideal pixel is square (as on the **Macintosh**), but some systems display a rectangular pixel, and this causes distortions that are particularly noticeable in images that are intended to display perfect squares or circles. Image processing techniques can be used to compensate for variations in **pixel aspect ratio**.

ASSEMBLER
A computer program that translates a program written in an **assembly language** into **machine code**. Programmers often talk of writing software in 'assembler' rather than in 'assembly language'.

ASSEMBLY EDITING
Video editing technique where shots are re-recorded one after the other, from start to finish, to create a coherent sequence.
> TRANSITION

ASSEMBLY LANGUAGE
In computer **programming**, any low-level symbolic **language** that must be translated by an assembler to produce the **machine code** with which the computer operates. Assemblers operate by converting programme instructions to machine code on a one-for-one basis, which makes the code produced extremely compact and fast. However, writing a program in an assembly language is very difficult and time-consuming, and a **high-level language** such as **C**, which has many of the advantages of an assembly language, is now generally preferred.

ASSETS
The **copyright**-owned (or copyright-cleared) properties, such as text, music, video, graphics, games etc, that form the basis of a **multimedia** production.

ASSOCIATIONAL BROWSING
The act of moving through a **hypermedia** programme by means of cross-referenced links to associated items of information.

ASYNCHRONOUS
A process in a computer that, once triggered, executes independently of the main clock.
> SYNCHRONOUS

ASYNCHRONOUS COMMUNICATION
Data communication where the **bits** of data are not synchronized by a clock signal but are sent one after another using a start bit and a stop bit to mark the beginning and end of the data unit. Most communication between personal computers – such as **E-mail** or bulletin boards – uses asynchronous communication **protocols**.
> NETWORK

ATARI CORPORATION
Formed by Nolan Bushnell, Al Alcorn and Ted Dabney in 1972, Atari leapt into prominence in the coin-op arcades with 'Pong' – the first arcade **videogame** – which sold over 100,000 units. Atari was bought by the giant Warner Communications in 1976, and in the first wave of home videogame mania in the late 1970s and early 1980s, Atari was enormously successful, with sales of up to US $1.7 billion in 1982. During this period Atari's Sunnyvale Laboratory, run by Alan Kay (developer of the **Dynabook**), became a major R&D centre for games and related software, with software stars of the calibre of Jaron Lanier, Scott Fisher, Warren Robinett, Brenda Laurel, Kristina Hooper, Thomas Zimmerman and many others working there. Atari still has a major presence in the videogame market, and in 1993 announced the **Jaguar**, a **RISC**-based multimedia system with optional **CD-ROM** drive.
> ARCADE GAMES

ATM
> ADOBE TYPE MANAGER

ATM [ASYNCHRONOUS TRANSFER MODE]
A fast **packet-switching** technology for carrying large volumes of data of different types (such as voice, video, **fax** and computer data) on wide-area **networks**. ATM is one of three systems (including X.25 and Frame Relay) that are competing to be the leading technology for data networking in the late 1990s. Unlike **Ethernet** and **FDDI**, the performance of ATM does not deteriorate as the number of on-line users increases.
> X-SERIES RECOMMENDATIONS

ATM [AUTOMATIC TELLER MACHINE]
Cash and account information dispenser operated by a customer's plastic **magstripe** or **smart card** and personal identification number (PIN). The card carries account identification codes and credit limit information, stored as up to 226 **alphanumeric** characters in three linear tracks within the magnetic stripe. ATM machines read this data, check the customer's PIN against the coded magstripe data, and link to a central computer at the particular bank or finance company to check credit availability and worthiness and to record details of the transactions performed by the customer.

'Paris Interactive': the future shape of ATMs? Design for Exact Change by Andrew White, Giles Rollestone and Studio DM, programmed by Paul Booth and produced by the London-based design company IN.form.

ATTACK

In music, the rate of increase in strength and intensity (**amplitude**) that characterizes the beginning portion of a sound.

> MIDI

AUDIO BLOCK

A data block of 2304 bytes in a **CD-i** audio **sector**. The audio block is itself comprised of 18 sound groups of 128 bytes each, encoded in sequential order.

> CD-I DIGITAL AUDIO

AUDIO CHANNEL

Audio data from one source. **CD-i**, for example, supports up to 16 channels of audio data.

> CD-I DIGITAL AUDIO   > CONCURRENT AUDIO

AUDIO FEEDBACK

In computer **software** and **interactive multimedia** programmes, a sound that signals confirmation of a user's action, draws attention to an 'alert' **dialogue box**, or reinforces the user's action. This can range from a simple 'beep', warning the user that he or she has done something wrong, to audio metaphors such as the sound of paper pages being turned to signify changing screens of information, or the sound of rubbish being dumped into a metal dustbin to signal the deletion of a file.

> AUDITORY ICON   > FEEDBACK

AUDIO SAMPLING

The practice of digitizing or digitally copying passages of music, spoken narrative or sound, in order to mix them together to create new musical pieces or soundtracks.

> SAMPLING RATE

AUDIO TRACK

In CD audio, an individually addressable section of the disc, usually containing a complete song or musical piece. In audio 'multitrack' recording, a discrete track can be used to carry the audio signal or data recording a single musical instrument.

> CDDA

AUDIOVISUAL [A/V]

A term applied to presentations and shows incorporating both photographic slides and audio tape recordings. A/V techniques have become increasingly sophisticated since the mid-1960s when 35mm slide projectors with carousels or trays first became available. At the time, projectors could only display slides in the order in which they were loaded into the carousel, and were controlled either manually or by electronic timers and faders. Today, a large number of projectors can be controlled simultaneously by **microcomputer**, or via audio pulses on a spare track of a multi-track audio tape recorder. In this way, multiple projections, screens and audio sources can be synchronized to create complex A/V displays. With the availability of (**random access**) CD audio and **digital-audio** processors in microcomputers, and a wide variety of control and **feedback** devices, A/V environments will become increasingly interactive.

The 35mm slide has been the standard unit of A/V presentations. In the early 1980s, the production of graphics for slides became one of the first commercial applications of **dedicated** graphics computer systems ('paintbox' systems). These were the first to provide 'designer friendly' interfaces, driven from a **digitpad**, that controlled a wide range of graphics, painting, **image processing** and typographic software. Video images could be input directly from videotape, or through a **frame grabber**, and manipulated by the designer. Finished **screen art** could be output to 35mm film and then incorporated into conventional A/V presentations. A natural extension of this production technique was to use the computer itself as a frame store, **sequencer** and display medium, using either high-resolution monitors or videobeam projectors. This in turn led to an increased use of **realtime animation** within presentations (using **CLUT** manipulation to make barcharts 'grow', for example, or sequentially to reveal the bullet-points of a speaker's address), and to the development of sophisticated presentation software providing a wide range of digital **transition** effects.

While the 35mm slide projector remains the best way of displaying very high resolution images on the multi-projection systems and large screens required for some A/V applications, desktop computer systems are rapidly gaining ground for more intimate presentations.

AUDITORY ICON

An **icon** that provides additional information about its functions or actions through the use of sound. For example, in a **graphical user interface** (GUI) incorporating auditory icons, file size could be related to pitch of note – the larger the file, the deeper the note. While GUIs such as the **Macintosh** do already use sound to alert the user to problems, such as the need to respond to a **dialogue box**, the use of true auditory icons has only been explored experimentally up until now. But as the audio capabilities of PCs are increasingly exploited, it seems probable that such innovations in the use of sound will move from being interesting experiments to part of the mainstream of **interface** design.

> ARC

AUGMENTED REALITY

Display system using transparent glasses or head-up displays on which information can be projected. This allows the user to view data such as maps and alphanumerics as images superimposed upon his or her 'real world' view. Applications of such systems include engineering (for example, enabling electricians to refer to wiring diagrams while actually working on a circuit board), security (checking IDs), navigation (in-car route finding), and medicine (diagnostic information).

> IMMERSIVE VR   > PROJECTED REALITY
> VIRTUAL REALITY
>> FURTHER READING: PIMENTEL AND TEIXEIRA 1993; RHEINGOLD 1991

Carnegie-Mellon Engineering Design Research Centre: VuMan Wearable Computer, controlled either by fingerpad or speech recognition. The monocular 'Private Eye' head-up display provides data where the user needs it – right in front of the eyes.

AURAL PERSPECTIVE

An illusion of three-dimensional space created by sound cues. In audio recording/mixing, 'distant' sounds are recorded at a lower level of volume than those sounds which are to appear 'close' to the listener. Spatial illusions in audio playback can be enhanced by increasing the number of separate speakers, and by using multiple sound sources (such as tape recorders) to address them, or by channelling the audio signal through different speakers in turn. This latter technique has been used in large auditoria to create the illusion that the audience is in the centre of a dynamic 'performance'. Aural perspective techniques are also being developed for **virtual reality** environments.

> CONVOLVOTRON

AUTHORING

The process of designing an **interactive** programme. The term derives from early **software** systems for computer-aided learning (**CAL**) that were designed for use by trainers and teachers who were not computer programmers; it is now used generically to describe the design process for **hypermedia**.

> • AUTHORING AND PRODUCTION PAGE 23

AUTHORING LANGUAGE/TOOL/SYSTEM

A very **high-level language** or applications package (a toolkit of graphics, sequencing and linking devices) for the production of **interactive** programmes, designed for use by non-programmers. Authoring packages include **HyperCard**, Authorware Professional, **Macromedia Director**, **Guide**, **Linkway** and **SuperCard**.

> AUTHORING   > DESIGN STAGE

AUTOMATIC SPEECH RECOGNITION

> SPEECH RECOGNITION

AUTOPLAY

Mode of play of a disc when no user **input** is made (akin to the **default mode**), or when the programme is intended to run automatically (ie to display a linear or looped sequence).

AUTOSTOP

In interactive **CD** authoring, a programmed instruction that will automatically stop a player when a certain point has been reached on the disc.

> CD-I

AUTOTRACE

A function of some **draw programs** that automatically creates a set of vectors to represent the outline of a bitmapped image. Autotrace can be used to create **EPSF** (PostScript) files from (scanned) bitmapped images, ensuring high-resolution scaling and resizing of the resultant draw-type image.

> BITMAP

AUXILIARY DATA FIELD

In **CD-i** and **CD-ROM**, the final 288 bytes of a **sector**, available for additional error detection and correction, or in some modes as an area for user data.

A/V

> AUDIOVISUAL

AVATAR

In **virtual reality** environments and games, the virtual construct that represents the human user. The appearance and attributes of an avatar can be 'off the peg', or customized by users to optimize their chances of success. Currently avatars are low-resolution, rendered in simple **solid modelling** with little or no smooth shading. With more powerful processors, avatars will become more lifelike, with smoother movements, more expressive body language and more subtle personal characteristics.

AUTHORING AND PRODUCTION
the new dream factory

Making interactive media programmes, like making video, can be split into three main stages: pre-production, production and post-production. The first stage is often called the 'design stage' or 'authoring stage', and includes a variety of creative, research and organizational tasks. The original idea of authoring grew out of computer-aided learning (CAL), where the design and production stages may have been handled by two or three individuals – generally a subject expert, an instructional designer, and a programmer. With the advent and growth of multimedia technologies in the late 1980s, and the establishment of consumer interactive media, the three key individuals became the hypermedia designer, the programmer and the information designer. These key personnel formed the creative nucleus around which grew a much larger infrastructure of researchers, picture researchers, graphic designers, animators, film-makers and production personnel.

The pre-production phase involves several stages, and several different disciplines. The original idea for the programme must be fleshed out in detail, and a prototype developed, while at the same time researchers get to work sourcing the 'programme assets' – the information, text, pictures, graphics, sound and video resources required. Production planning also takes place during this time, with the producer and production manager devising schedules and preparing budgets.

As far as the hypermedia designer is concerned, the pre-production stages include: working with the subject expert on the research, and acquiring an overview of the subject material; making a list of desired functions for the intended programme; selecting suitable applications software for programme and prototype development; designing an overall structure for the programme, for example by producing a branching flowchart; designing and/or specifying the design for the graphical user interface, including an overall design grid, backgrounds, text panels, image and video windows, buttons, etc; producing a test programme or prototype that models the desired structure and contains enough content material to gauge the effectiveness of the programme structure and user interface; assisting the production manager and accountant in devising schedules and budgets for the production stage and, finally, supervising the selection of the creative team required for the production. The design stage will culminate with a full paper specification of the programme, prepared in consultation with the chief programmer.

Much of the production phase is 'platform independent' (ie not limited to one particular platform). This phase includes the scanning of images, the digitizing of video, the digital sampling of sounds and the creation of computer animation and graphics for titles, interface and other programme components. Once in digital form, these assets can easily be converted to the formats required for the intended delivery system. About 70 per cent of most

production work is independent of the final delivery platform. This is one of the advantages of digital technology, meaning that to a large extent work on multimedia programmes is 'future proof' – these digital assets can be formatted to create software that will run on any digital system. Of course, in the final stage of production – the creation of software that contains these digital assets and runs on a particular delivery system – it is crucial that the particular features and strengths of the delivery system are exploited to the full. Depending on the system, the actual assembly of the programme will generally be carried out by a team headed by the hypermedia designer, a senior programmer, and the production manager, and which will also include computer animators, graphic artists and video, audio and subject specialists. A disc is then created using CD-R or WORM technology, and the programme will be extensively tested during a validation period before final debugging. A period of user-testing usually follows, and this can occasion some re-design before final mastering.

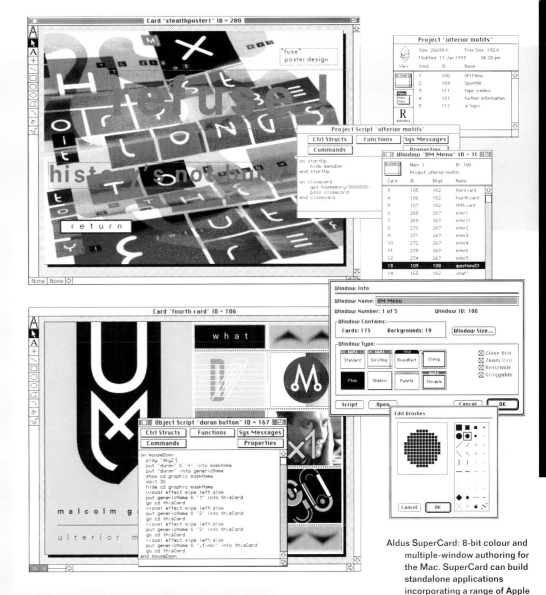

Aldus SuperCard: 8-bit colour and multiple-window authoring for the Mac. SuperCard can build standalone applications incorporating a range of Apple interface tools.

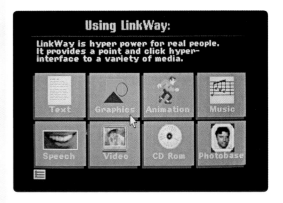

IBM's LinkWay authoring for MS-DOS computers, one of many authoring tools available for PCs.

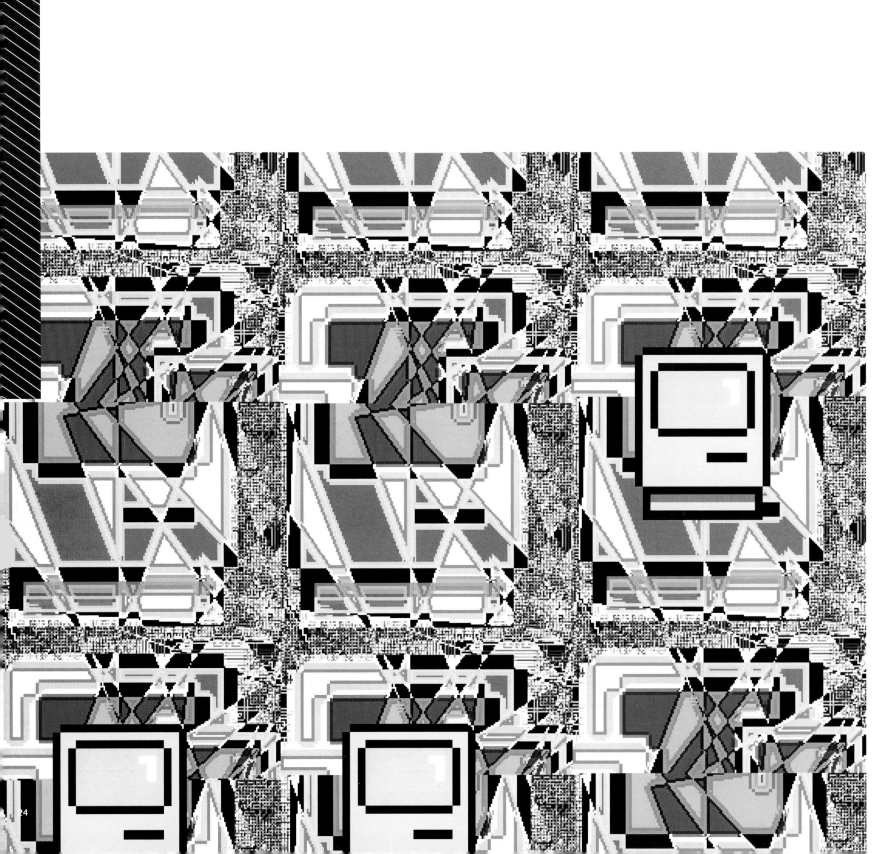

B-ISDN [BROADBAND INTEGRATED SERVICES DIGITAL NETWORK]

An extension of **ISDN** that supports data rates of up to 600 megabits per second, and is able to support motion video and digital audio as well as a range of other data types including voice, **fax** and computer data. B-ISDN is not likely to be generally available until the first decade of the next century.

>   BANDWIDTH

BACK PROJECTION

(Or 'rear projection'.) The technique of projecting an image onto the rear side of a translucent screen. It is frequently used in **audiovisual** presentations, and specifically in animation rostrums, where back-projected images can be combined with foreground imagery and recorded onto film through the **rostrum camera**.

>   ROTOSCOPE

BACKDROP

(Or 'background plane'.) In **interactive multimedia** systems, the image plane that is left visible when all superimposed planes are made transparent. In a 'virtual world' (the software environment of a **virtual reality** system), 'backdrop' refers to the stationary background that provides the virtual environment's underlying structure and defines its boundary. Backdrops provide the visual context for a virtual world, and generally cannot be changed, moved or resized, mainly to avoid distracting or disorientating participants involved in navigating through or manipulating 'foreground' objects.

BACKGROUND

In **animation**, the image on which the cel animations are overlaid. The background may be a drawn, painted, photographic or computer-generated image; it may be produced to the same dimensions as the cels, or as a larger image which can be scrolled horizontally or vertically between shots so as to give the impression of movement.

>   MOTION PARALLAX

BACKGROUND PATTERN

The pattern (or solid colour) used for erasing lines or shapes drawn in a **bitmap** 'painting' application.

>   PAINT PROGRAM

BACKGROUND PLANE

An alternative term for **backdrop**, used particularly in **CD-i**. In CD-i players equipped with an FMV cartridge, the background plane is reserved for digital **full-motion video**.

BACKUP

The duplication of data **files** on an external memory device for safety, recording and archive purposes. **Multimedia** applications are particularly demanding of memory, and storage capacities of at least 600 megabytes are required for the development of **CD-ROM**, and **CD-i** programmes. There are a range of options for the storage of backup files, including **hard disks** (available in a range of capacities from 20 megabytes to over 1 gigabyte), **WORM** and **WMRM** drives (typically 900 megabytes to 1 gigabyte) and **tape streamer**s.

>   ARCHIVE   >   ARCHIVING

BANDWIDTH

Defines the capacity of a communication channel: the wider the bandwidth, the greater the volume of information that can be transmitted within a given time. For example, conventional television images require a bandwidth of 6 MHz; voice and data transmissions are classified as broad band (over 3,000 Hz), voice band (300-3,000 Hz) and narrow band (below 300 Hz). The higher the resolution to be transmitted, the broader the bandwidth must be so as to accommodate the high frequencies required to convey the information.

Bandwidth is more than simply a technical consideration: it determines the very nature of the communications infrastructure, and is thus a matter of considerable political and economic importance. Decisions by regulatory bodies as to whether cable TV and **telecommunications** companies should be providing **fibre-optic** or **copper cable** networks may seem narrowly technical, but in fact will determine what services can and cannot be provided over those networks. The argument extends to the economic sphere in that the investment required to lay down a fibre-optic network is immense. For private companies to profit from such an investment, the network would have to be allowed to carry a wide range of services.

Currently in most countries telecommunications companies are only allowed to carry a narrow range of services, as prescribed by their regulatory bodies. It is argued that these restrictions are necessary to promote proper competition between the wide variety of companies offering network services. Advocates of electronic **data superhighway**s argue that these restrictions, far from promoting competition, are in fact inhibiting the development of a whole new range of information-based industries which require an appropriate infrastructure if they are to flourish. They point to the crucial role in the industrial revolution of the transport infrastructure of rail, roads and canals, and argue that a high-bandwidth communications infrastructure will make a similar contribution to the information revolution. This ongoing argument has its parallel in similar debates about the division of the **broadcast** frequency spectrum to accommodate new cellular networks (**cell-nets**) and new channels for television and **digital** radio.

>   COMPRESSION

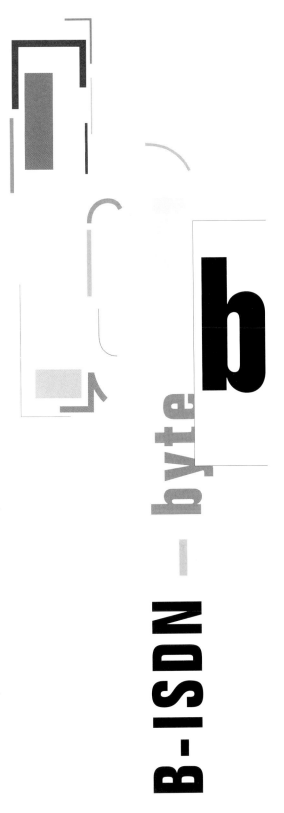

B-ISDN – byte

→

BAR CODE

Pattern of vertical lines in varying thicknesses that encodes data in a form readable by a special scanner or bar-code reader. Examples are the European Article Numbering (EAN) Code and the American Universal Product Code (UPC). The UPC was adopted by the grocery industry in the US in 1973; the EAC is a variant of the UPC, standardized for use in Europe.

Apart from their use in packaging and other product labelling, bar codes have been used successfully in other applications such as the production of large visual **databases**, where many thousands of images have to be recorded and identified for easy retrieval. And in 1993 Tomy launched a **videogame** console with a built-in bar-code scanner, the Barcode Battler; bar codes from all types of products are scanned by the user in a search for the key codes that will help play the game.

> EDI

>> FURTHER READING: BAR CODE SYSTEMS INC 1988

Barcode Battler: a videogame from Tomy.

BASE CASE

Describes a system that conforms to minimum **standard** specifications.

BASIC [BEGINNERS ALL-PURPOSE SYMBOLIC INSTRUCTION CODE]

Programming **language** created in 1964 by John Kemeny and Thomas Kurtz of Dartmouth College to allow novice computer users to become programmers as quickly as possible, and widely used in schools and colleges in the late 1970s and 1980s. The first version of Basic for **microcomputers** was written in 1976 by Paul Allen and Bill Gates (later founders of **Microsoft**). Their Basic interpreter eventually became Microsoft Basic, one of the most widely used versions of the language. In the early 1990s Microsoft's Visual Basic became the leading **software** development environment for **Microsoft Windows** applications.

>> FURTHER READING: BARON 1988

BAUD

In **digital** systems, the serial communications data unit (one baud equals one **bit** per second). It was devised by the French scientist Baudot, a pioneer of telegraphic communications. The baud rate is effectively the number of bits per second that can be transmitted between compatible systems.

> BANDWIDTH

BBS [BULLETIN BOARD SYSTEM]

The electronic equivalent of a notice or bulletin board, in which anyone can display information for others to read. Bulletin board systems are incorporated into most commercial **networks** (along with features such as **E-mail**), in the form of general notice boards or boards for special interest groups. They are also used for the distribution of copyright-free or inexpensive software (**shareware**).

BEZIER

A curve or spline defined by adjustable control points. It is used in 'draw'-type graphics programs, in computer-aided design (**CAD**) and in the specification of font outlines.

> DIGITAL FONTS   > DRAW PROGRAM

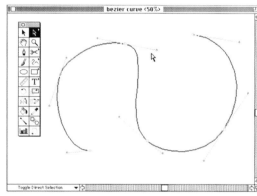

Bezier splines in Adobe Illustrator.

BIBLIOGRAPHIC DATABASE

A bibliography organized as a **database**, ie in such a way that the user can search not merely by author, but by title, subject, level of complexity, publisher, date, ISBN number or any other predetermined parameter.

BIG ROOM, THE

Hackers' slang for 'outdoors'. The big room is the one that is very well lit with a blue ceiling in the daytime, and dark with a black ceiling at night.

BINAURAL SOUND

(Or '**3-d sound**'.) The recording of sound in such a way that it generates an illusion of **3-d** space when played back through headphones. Binaural sound techniques are used in the development of **virtual reality** systems. Working at NASA in the 1980s, Scott Fisher pioneered the development of 3-d sound, notably with the **Convolvotron** system devised in collaboration with Elizabeth Wenzel.

BIOFEEDBACK

Describes the use of **sensors** to provide information on the functioning of the body or brain. Biofeedback methods can be used to monitor the activity of the brain, for instance, via signals represented as waveforms on a computer screen.

BIOSENSOR

A bracelet, headband, pair of glasses or other special apparel containing electrodes to monitor muscle activity, temperature, eyeball movements etc, providing **biofeedback** and data input for **virtual reality** systems.

> DATAGLOVE   > DATASUIT
> HEAD-MOUNTED DISPLAY   > SENSOR

Exos: Force ArmMaster. Linking force-feedback techniques with biosensor input brings real-world physics into the 'reality' of virtual systems.

BIT [BINARY DIGIT]

The smallest unit (valued either 0 or 1) of computer data.

BIT ERROR RATE

A measure of the average number of errors to be expected in the storage and transmission of data from a particular storage medium. The bit error rate is expressed as the number of bits that a system can store or transmit with only one bit in error. In **CD-ROM**, which has three levels of error correction, the bit error rate is one in 1,000,000,000,000,000,000 (1 in 10^{18}).

BITMAP

A computer **monitor** screen image comprised of dots of colour that correspond directly to data bits stored in memory. Bitmap editors (or **paint programs**) are the most intuitive and easy to learn of the computer graphics tools, and range from simple black-and-white packages such as **MacPaint** to fully-featured 32-bit colour programs such as Pixel Paint Professional and Studio 32. In bitmap programs, the artist has control over each individual **bit** (represented as a screen **pixel**). The disadvantage is that bitmap images cannot be resized without loss of quality.

> DRAW PROGRAM

BITMAPPED TEXT

Text that is defined in terms of a pattern of pixels, rather than as a scalable set of vectors.

> DIGITAL FONTS   > MULTIPLE MASTER
> POSTSCRIPT

KEYBOARD

An input device for entering text and numbers into a computer or computer-based system, when an alphanumeric character or other symbol is depressed.

Keyboards are a very efficient input device if you have the necessary 'keyboard skills' – the ability to type or at least to use two fingers rapidly. Keyboards generally use the QWERTY layout which evolved with the typewriter, but other configurations exist such as the DVORAK layout which is easier to use.

BITS PER SAMPLE

In the conversion of **analog** to **digital** data, the number of **bits** used to represent the numerical value of a sample.

> AUDIO SAMPLING   > SAMPLING RATE

BIX (BYTE INFORMATION EXCHANGE)

A worldwide computer conferencing system established by Byte magazine. BIX is a subscriber service for computer users, and offers access to **microcomputer** industry news and to special-interest 'exchanges' for information, news and views on **IBM** and **Macintosh** platforms (including much free, downloadable **software**). BIX also offers **BBS** and **E-mail** services to its customers.

> COMPUSERVE   > INTERNET
> NETWORK

BLANKING

A loss or removal of a video signal that results in a blank screen. This problem is encountered when the time taken by a system (for example a **videodisc** player) to locate, retrieve and display an image exceeds the screen refresh time. To avoid screen blanking, **interactive video** applications that include a variety of simultaneous **branching** options have to ensure that the relevant video sequences are recorded onto the disc in close proximity to each other (ie interleaved), or that some other device is used to disguise the blanking period. Many videodisc players now offer 'instant jump' facilities of up to 250 frames at a time, so that with good design the **interleaving** of quite complex branching sequences and stills can be performed without blanking.

> REFRESH RATE   > SEEK TIME

BLITTER

In computer systems such as the Amiga series, a custom **chip** (a graphics **co-processor**) designed to work with the direct memory access (**DMA**) channel, and used for high-speed **data** movement in bitplane animation. Blitter functions are used in **videogames** to display and control graphics **sprites** and other high-speed pictorial effects.

BLOCK

In computer systems generally, groups of data that are treated as a logical unit. In **CD-ROM** and **CD-i** systems, 'block' refers to that part of the data sector which contains the user data.

BOOKMARK

A facility in **hypermedia** programmes that allows the user to record frames or sequences for easy and speedy subsequent retrieval.

BOOKS PLUS

Term given to books in **digital** form that utilize extra features and interactive techniques derived from the areas of **database** design, **computer graphics**, hypertext and **hypermedia**.

> ELECTRONIC BOOK   > ELECTRONIC PUBLISHING
> EXPANDED BOOKS

BOOLEAN OPERATORS

Symbols used in Boolean algebra to denote logical relations of inclusion and exclusion. The logic circuits of a computer process a series of instructions (the **program**) and the information to which the program is to be applied (the data), by applying the rules of Boolean algebra, which uses the binary code (0 or 1) to represent a 'true' or 'false' condition. The three main operators – 'and', 'not' and 'or' – each have a corresponding logic (switching) circuit called a 'gate'. Simple gates take one or two **inputs** and produce one **output**. For example, the 'and' gate comprises two switches wired one after the other, and produces a 'true' output only if both the inputs are true.

Boolean operators are also used for searching **databases**. For example, the enquiry 'Find Richard Burton and Elizabeth Taylor' in a database of films would retrieve only those titles in which they both appeared. The enquiry 'Find Richard Burton or Elizabeth Taylor' would retrieve all the titles that either of them had appeared in, while 'Richard Burton not Elizabeth Taylor' would retrieve all the films in which Richard Burton had appeared except those with Elizabeth Taylor.

> RELATIONAL DATABASE

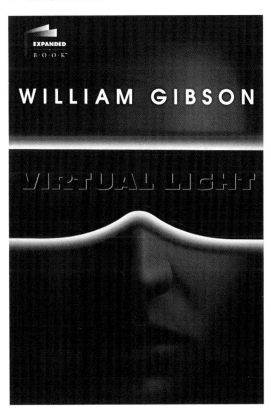

The Voyager Company is a pioneer in electronic publishing. First with 'expanded books' of both Crichton's Jurassic Park and Gibson's Virtual Light, Voyager is aiming at the expanding Powerbook market with a growing range of novels and textbooks.

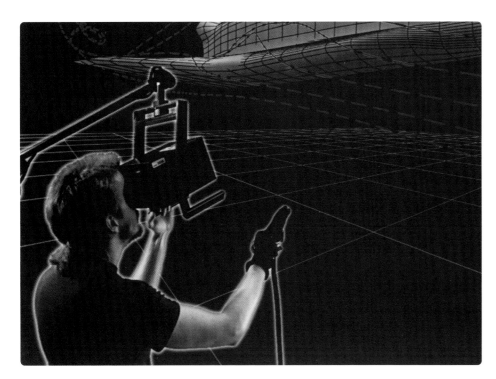

Fake Space Labs: BOOM system – high-resolution mobile VR. Shown here is a composite image, demonstrating the view the user would see in the monitor.

BOOM-MOUNTED DISPLAY

In **virtual reality** (VR) systems, a 3-d display device mounted on a counter-weighted arm (boom) that can be manipulated in space by the VR participant. An alternative to **head-mounted displays** or **EyePhones**, boom-mounted displays can carry heavier, higher-resolution **CRT** monitors. With **position sensors** attached to the shafts of the boom itself, **latency** or 'frame-lag' (the disparity between the participant's movement and a corresponding movement of the virtual world) can be kept to a minimum. Boom-mounted VR displays provide a useful halfway-house between desktop VR and full sensory immersion.

BRANCHING

A basic **authoring** strategy for interactive programme design, where the different options available to the user are represented schematically as a branching 'map' or **flowchart**. The points at which the user is given a choice of how to proceed through the programme are called 'nodes'. Nodes are decision points that may contain two or more options; they may offer a free choice to the user or direct him or her along a particular path as a result of a response given to some form of question. Such 'conditional' nodes, for example, can route students along a particular branch depending on their cumulative score in a questionnaire, or on the number of **cards** or **buttons** that they have accessed in the preceding sequence.

Branching flowcharts are a good way of sketching out the initial design of an **interactive** programme. Main nodes (such as a main menu and subsidiary menus) can be defined first, then further hierarchical choices indicated by drawing connecting lines to the relevant programme modules. While branching flowcharts such as this are an effective way of approaching the design of simple interactive programmes, they are limited in their ability to indicate the wide range of cross connections possible in true **hypermedia**.

> CONDITIONAL BRANCHING   > CONTINUOUS BRANCHING

BROADBAND CHANNEL

A high-speed, high-capacity transmission channel. 'Broadband' is a loosely defined term, generally used to refer to **telecommunications** channels that have a wider **bandwidth** than conventional telephone lines. This includes systems such as **ISDN** and **B-ISDN**, as well as full **fibre-optic** systems.

> FDDI

BROADCAST QUALITY

Video of a standard acceptable to public **broadcasting** organizations. Due to rapid improvements in video technology, the definition of 'broadcast quality' now includes consumer formats, such as **Hi-8**.

> TELEVISION STANDARDS

BROADCASTING

The transmission of electromagnetic signals from one source to many receivers. The regular broadcasting of radio programmes began in the early 1920s, and by 1921 there were 564 newly licensed transmitting stations operating in the US.

Although television was first broadcast by the British Broadcasting Corporation (BBC) in 1931, this used Baird's mechanical system, which was a technological cul-de-sac. The first 405-line all-electronic broadcasting service was launched by the BBC in late 1936. In the USA, regular colour television broadcasting began in 1954 (in Japan it

BROWSING AND NAVIGATION
exploring the electronic frontier

Cyberspace is big. Cyberspace media will give the user access to hundreds of channels of entertainment and a plethora of online information and telecoms services offering vast databases of multimedia information. In order to exploit these new media, the user will need software tools for 'navigating' in cyberspace and tools for browsing through the range of options, much as a bibliophile wanders through a library or bookstore.

While many navigation tasks will eventually be performed for the users by 'intelligent' software agents, easy-to-use browsing and navigation tools will be a central feature of successful cyberspace media. Browsing allows the user to survey all or part of a hypermedia programme by using some form of abbreviated overview (a menu), or via devices such as buttons linking items of information together, or simply by looking at items in a sequential or random order. Browsing is closely related to 'navigation', but generally implies the more active involvement of the user in choosing the information he or she wants, whereas navigation tools provide the user with 'trails' or 'maps' of where they have been, as well as indications of where they might go to and (sometimes) how to get there.

Browsers are commonly devised to provide an overview or 'contents list' of the programme from which the user may choose an item of interest and call it directly to the screen, or call up a sequence of text and/or image displays that progressively elucidate a particular aspect of the information base. So, from an outline description of the entire programme, the user may select a particular area and metaphorically 'zoom into' it, accessing increasingly detailed information on a subject of interest, or following a particular line of enquiry.

Navigation tools provide a more structured level of information access. Most people know how to 'navigate' around a book (or even a library of books) to find the information they require. All of us are familiar with three main methods for information retrieval that have emerged from the Gutenberg revolution: the table of contents, the alphabetical ordering of entries in a reference book and the index. All three methods are used in the ordering of information in cyberspace, supplemented by new navigation tools made possible by the power of the microprocessor. These include string-searching, where the user types in a word or phrase (a 'string' of letters) and the computer searches through a text or series of texts held in its memory in order to find a match for that word. A second method of information retrieval is the automation of cross-referencing that we know as 'hypertext'. Hypertext gives us the facility for following up 'associative links' between items of related information. Navigating around an information base in this way can of course reveal all kinds of new associations that may or may not entice the user along new pathways. Hypertext may be used for casual browsing, focused casual reading or

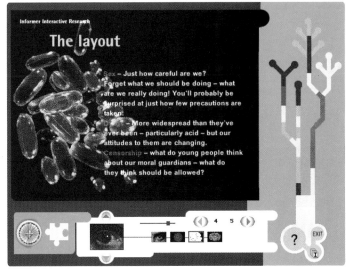

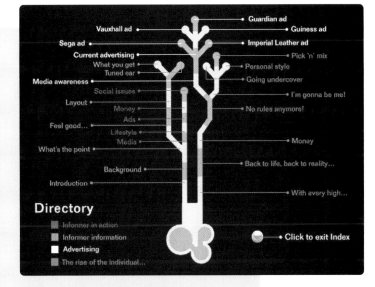

'information grazing', or for the intensive 'trawling' of data related to a particular subject. Items discovered in any of these three modes can of course be recorded by printing the entry, by copying it to a word processor or to another database, or by using an electronic 'bookmark' – effectively a list of references for future study.

A third navigation technique employed in hypermedia involves software that keeps a record of the user's track through the programme. 'Tracking' records each frame or module of the programme that the user has accessed, and stores these as a list which the user can access on demand – to check his or her progress, or to trace an item of information they wish to review. Some systems are programmed to compare the user's track against a model of the entire programme, so that users can be provided with a list of what they have not yet seen. Simple 'inference engines' can use these lists to prompt the user to view items that are contextually relevant.

In interface terms, the programme designer must provide graphic buttons or icons that allow for a variety of different navigation features. Most common are the familiar 'arrows': an electronic surrogate for 'turning the page', ie displaying more text or images. Arrows allow the user to navigate forwards, and backwards, through the information stored within (or accessible through) the hypermedia system. Other buttons or icons may be provided for string-searches, for tracking, for bookmarks, and often for 'fast forward/backward' navigation.

In the virtual world of cyberspace, navigation techniques are being continuously developed and tested to accommodate the three- and four-dimensional nature of the new 'telecosm'. In virtual reality, the participant's position can be established and tracked by means of position sensors, but so far only a small amount of work has been done on information retrieval in this VR cyberspace. Systems currently being developed include allowing the user to 'fly' over or through three-dimensional representations of data, navigating through successive 'sub-spaces' of data to locate the required information.

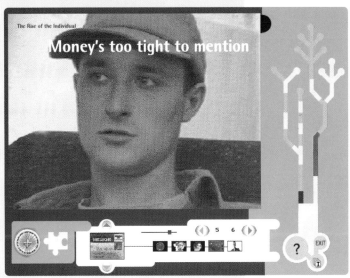

Mark Bowey, Mindbath Design Associates: Informer CD-ROM. This is a periodical CD-ROM carrying advertising and marketing research. Bowey has developed a 'branching tree' diagram that indicates the user's position in the programme and the sections that have been viewed.

Informer CD-ROM: Designers Mark Bowey, Colin Taylor and Mike Worthington worked with programmer Jonathan Taylor on this examplary CD-ROM from the London-based advertising research agency, Informer.

It is increasingly recognized that people tend to learn more quickly and more effectively if information is presented from a variety of different perspectives (ie in a variety of different media, and at a number of different levels), and if they are in direct control of the information base. Hypermedia theorists have long argued that interactive multimedia is the perfect educational tool, in that it can closely model both the way in which we think and the means by which we 'naturally' learn from our environment. These notions are receiving more and more support from the findings of cognitive psychologists. Just as young children learn to speak by physical trial and error while being immersed in an environment which uses speech and language in a variety of different ways and at different levels, so too should the users of hypermedia programmes 'learn' by performing actions while being immersed in a multimedia information base accessible in many different ways. Successful hypermedia programmes provide both structural navigation and free-form browsing tools to facilitate information retrieval, learning and the intelligent management of entertainment.

Kai Krouse & HSC Software: Kai's Power Tools, a seductive, dynamic interface with animated cuecons. Kai's Power Tools provides a range of exotic and innovative image-processing tools that extend the functionality of Adobe Photoshop.

CID: The Creative Image. Photographers & Illustrators Portfolio Directory, a cool and extremely functional image-browser for easy access to a large database of creative images.

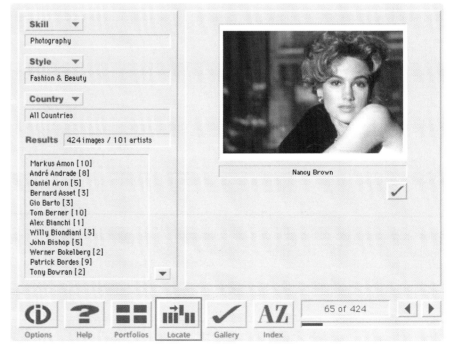

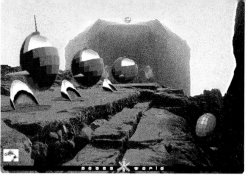

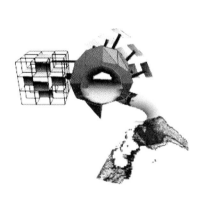

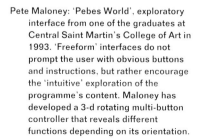

Pete Maloney: 'Pebes World', exploratory interface from one of the graduates at Central Saint Martin's College of Art in 1993. 'Freeform' interfaces do not prompt the user with obvious buttons and instructions, but rather encourage the 'intuitive' exploration of the programme's content. Maloney has developed a 3-d rotating multi-button controller that reveals different functions depending on its orientation.

started in 1960, and it had reached the UK and the rest of Europe by 1967).

Broadcast media (both radio and TV) have dominated the twentieth century, and only in the late 1980s and 1990s do they face any significant challenge from narrowcast (cable), and disc and tape-based media, such as **VHS** videocassettes and **CD-ROM**. How broadcasting will adapt to this reconfiguration of media has been the subject of considerable speculation. According to Nicholas Negroponte of the **Media Lab**: 'Broadcast spectrum is scarce, whereas fiber, like computing power, is something we can just keep making more of. Those facts mean that the channels for distributing different types of information, as we know them today, will trade places. Most information we receive through the ether today – television, for example – will come through the ground by cable tomorrow. Conversely, most of what we now receive through the ground – such as telephone service – will come through the airwaves.' This so-called 'Negroponte switch' would allow the broadcast spectrum to be used for communicating with things that move – such as people and cars, boats and planes, while information and entertainment would be delivered to the fixed location of the home by means of the virtually infinite **bandwidth** of **fibre-optic** networks. Whether or not this switch takes place, the broadcast media – especially television – will face considerable upheaval as a direct result of the new technologies.

> BROADCATCHING   > DAB
> HDTV   > INTERACTIVE BROADCAST TV
> NARROWCASTING   > NETWORK
>> FURTHER READING: NEGROPONTE 1991

BROADCATCHING
Expression coined by Stewart Brand to describe the potential for 'intelligent' interactive network systems to scan and select information on specific subjects. The idea is that users will be able to customize special software (**agents**) automatically to search and retrieve ('catch') information on specialist subjects from many different sources.

> ARCHMAC   > NARROWCASTING
>> FURTHER READING: BRAND 1988

BROWSE MODE
The facility for a user to choose their own path through a **database** or **hypermedia** programme without having a predetermined structure imposed on them.

> BROWSING

BROWSER
A front end to a **database** that allows the user quickly to scan the content headings.

> BROWSING

BROWSING
The process of moving through a **database** or **hypermedia** programme in an unstructured manner.

> • BROWSING AND NAVIGATION PAGE 28

BUFFER
In computer systems, an area of memory reserved for temporary data storage. **CD-i** and **CDTV** systems, for example, allocate one megabyte of memory for the temporary storage of images, program data or digital audio sequences.

BULLETIN BOARD SYSTEM
> BBS

BUMP-IN/BUMP-OUT
In **animation**, terms used to describe the effect of making an object appear or disappear within one frame.

BUS
The pathway or channel along which electronic signals flow from one part of a computer system to another. In **microcomputers**, the bus consists of parallel paths through which data is carried between the computer's central components (for example, between the memory and peripheral interfaces). In **networks**, bus topology is a configuration in which all the networked devices are connected to a single continuous channel.

BUTTON
Area of the **screen**, or an object displayed on the screen, that reacts to some form of user **input**, such as the presence of a **cursor** or the click of a **mouse**. Buttons contain **scripts** (programs) defining what actions or behaviours will follow when the button is activated. One of the most interesting areas of research in **hypermedia** is the design of buttons: the challenge is how to ensure that the user can distinguish between 'non-active' graphics and 'active' buttons.

> GRAPHICAL USER INTERFACE   > HOTSPOT
> HYPERTEXT

Genome Electronic Book Company: 'Browser info' from 'When God makes God', one of the many ingenious trips through probability and games theory from innovative hypermedia writer/designer Peter Small.

BYTE
A set of **bits** considered as an individually addressable unit in the computer memory. In personal computers, a byte normally equals eight bits and can represent a single character such as a letter of the alphabet, a number from 0 to 9, or a punctuation mark.

> KILOBYTE   > MEGABYTE

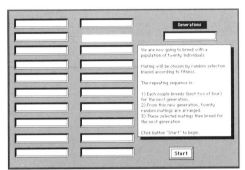

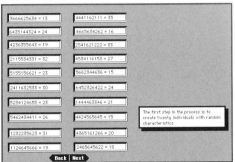

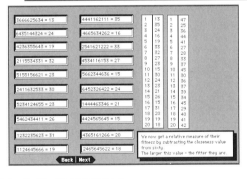

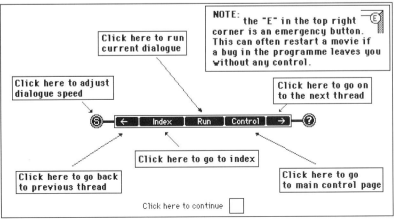

C

A very powerful programming **language** combining many of the advantages of an **assembly language** with the readability of a **high-level language**. It was developed at Bell Laboratories by Donald Ritchie in 1972 as the programming tool used for the development of the complex **Unix** operating system. Now a general-purpose programming language used for a wide variety of applications including **videogame**s and **hypermedia** programmes.

C++

An object-oriented extension of **C** language, C++ has been adopted as the standard programming language by companies such as **Apple Computer** and many of the major software developers. C++ combines the power and efficiency of C with the strengths of an object-oriented language such as the ease of adapting and reusing code.

CABLE INTERACTIVE TV

> INTERACTIVE CABLE TV

CAD [COMPUTER-AIDED DESIGN]

A term generally restricted to the use of computer systems and **software** in engineering and architectural design. Now somewhat misleading because many other design professionals, such as graphic designers, fashion designers and textile designers, use computers as part of the design process.

> DTP

CAI [COMPUTER-AIDED INSTRUCTION]

> CAL

CAL [COMPUTER-ASSISTED LEARNING]

The use of computers to deliver instructional material and to test the user's grasp of that material in education and training. Other closely related terms include computer-aided instruction (CAI), computer-based training (CBT) and computer-managed instruction (CMI).

> DISTANCE LEARNING

IBM: LinkWay. This popular package for the PC provides a powerful multimedia authoring tool for the development of computer-aided learning software.

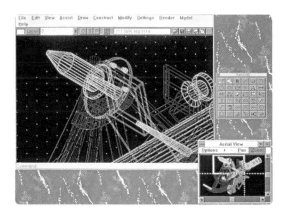

Autodesk: AutoCAD, the definitive CAD interface, works within the Windows graphical user interface and features a floating toolbox of the most frequently used commands.

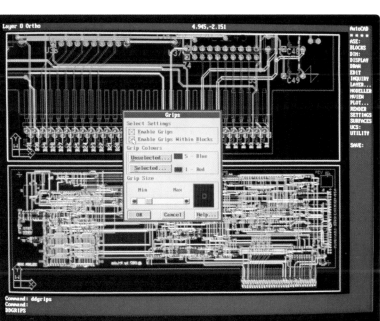

CAMCORDER

Video camera with built-in videocassette recorder and microphone. Camcorders use **VHS**, **SVHS** or **Hi-8** tape formats, and combine ease of operation and portability to provide excellent 'video sketchbook' facilities for **hypermedia** designers and film or video makers. They can be used as tools for test shots and sequences; for recording '**surrogate travel**' visuals, interviews, or training sequences; or for planning video sequences that are to be shot later onto **high-resolution** systems. Images recorded in camcorders can be transferred to another videotape or videocassette recorder for editing, or into a **frame grabber** or video digitizer for incorporation into **multimedia** programmes.

> IMAGING SYSTEM   > STILL-VIDEO CAMERA

Sony Video 8 Handycam camcorder.

CAPTION GENERATOR

A system that allows text captions and titles to be added to video, either in-camera or during post-production using keying or **chromakey** techniques. The combination of caption and image can then be recorded to tape.

> VIDEO GRAPHICS

CARD

The basic unit for building programmes in **authoring** programs such as **HyperCard** consisting of a single **window** or **screen**. Typically, cards contain four different types of object: text fields, **buttons**, draw graphics and paint graphics, so that bitmapped images such as digitized photographs or freehand drawings can be combined with precise diagrams, text and typography in colour, and buttons/icons. The cards themselves, as well as the objects and text within each card, can be linked together to form a hierarchical structure or matrix of interconnections.

CART [CARTRIDGE]

Method of distributing computer games, based on solid-state memory (**ROM** or **EPROM**). A precursor of **memory cards**, carts can be encrypted to protect software from illegal copying, but they are a much more expensive medium than **floppy disk** or **CD-ROM**.

CARTESIAN COORDINATE SYSTEM

(Or 'X,Y,Z coordinate system'.) The standard method of representing the relationship between two or three variable quantities, by means of a series of points plotted between axes (coordinates). Thus two-dimensional data, such as a line graph or bar chart could be plotted onto two axes – the X-axis (the horizontal, 'abscissa' axis) and the Y-axis (the vertical, 'ordinate' axis). Cartesian coordinates are an essential element in **computer graphics** and computer-aided design (**CAD**), both for two-dimensional drawing and image manipulation, and for three-dimensional **modelling**, which uses three coordinates, X, Y and Z, at right angles to each other. Computer graphics software uses algebraic transformations to alter the position, size and shape of the objects within the coordinate system.

> COMPUTER ANIMATION

CATHODE-RAY TUBE

> CRT

CAV [CONSTANT ANGULAR VELOCITY]

A mode for reading data from a **disk**, in which the disk rotates at a constant speed. Retrieval of data is faster when the read/write head is nearer the centre of the disk, slower as it moves towards the perimeter. This is the mode used for **floppy disks** and **hard disks**. It is also the mode used for **laserdisc** formats. CAV allows fast **frame** retrieval, with maximum seek time of around one second for any one of 54,000 frames. As these frames are stored as 54,000 concentric circular tracks (ie one frame or two fields of video per track), perfect still frames can be displayed. CAV laserdiscs are thus a favoured medium for **interactive video** applications, and are still the best medium for interactive programmes that need **high-resolution** still frames and, importantly, near-**broadcast-quality full-screen full-motion video**.

> CLV   > LASERVISION

CBT [COMPUTER-BASED TRAINING]

> CAL

CCD [CHARGE-COUPLED DEVICE]

A **chip** consisting of a number of capacitors that can be charged up (by exposure to light for instance) and the pattern of charges read out. CCDs are widely used in **camcorders**, electronic news gathering (**ENG**), and other portable video camera systems, where they have replaced the bulky and much heavier vidicon tube.

> STILL-VIDEO CAMERA

CCIR 601

The specification for a world **standard** for **digital video** recording, established in 1987 by the Consultative Committee for International Radio (CCIR), the Society of Motion Picture and Television Engineers (**SMPTE**) and the European Broadcasting Union. CCIR 601 is a component system, combining the red, green and blue TV signals into one **luminance** (black-and-white) signal and two **chrominance** (colour)

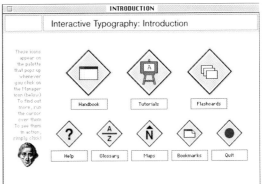

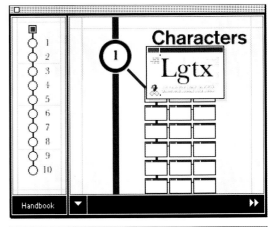

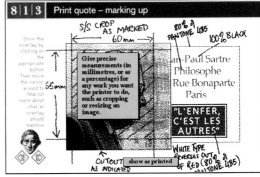

Trip Media: 'Intertype'. Produced by David Collier and Ian Martin, this multimedia CD-ROM aims to present an interactive guide to producing work of the highest typographic quality on a desktop computer.

CD-i

consumer digital video comes of age

The launch of Philips' Compact Disc Interactive (CD-i) system in 1992 marked the start of the race to create a market for the kind of interactive programmes previously only available to dedicated games players and personal computer/CD-ROM users. In 1992, the only competition faced by Philips was from Commodore (who had recently launched their CDTV system), but within a year several other television-based interactive media systems had been announced or launched, including Tandy's Video Information System (VIS), and rival CD-ROM-based systems from Sega and 3DO. Philips have something of a head start in the race, however, and their careful groundwork in promoting CD-i as a potential world standard may yet pay off.

CD-i grew out of Philips' innovations in the development of optical (laser-read) discs both for the professional and consumer sector, starting with research and development in the 1960s and marked by the release of the LaserVision videodisc system in 1978, compact disc audio in 1982, CD-ROM and LV-ROM in 1986, and compact disc video in 1988. This 'systems family' developed by Philips also includes the data capture and storage system 'Megadoc', as well as CD-ROM XA, and WORM and WMRM discs. CD-i is an all-digital medium, storing video, graphics, text, computer and audio data as interleaved data, all of which is under the direct interactive control of the end-user. CD-i is also a system specification and, importantly, looks set to become a major contender in the battle for a world standard for consumer interactive multimedia. CD-i discs can be played on CD-i systems anywhere in the world, regardless of local differences in broadcast TV standards.

A CD-i player is essentially a computer with an onboard memory of 1 megabyte of RAM and an integral CD drive, and is designed to be plugged into a standard TV set and an audio hi-fi system. The system can be used to play ordinary CD audio discs and PhotoCD, as well as CD-i programmes, all of which are operated by a hand-held remote control pad. CD-i offers sophisticated image manipulation facilities, with pictures displayed on as many as four image planes. Furthermore, CD-i provides a variety of digital visual effects that can be used for switching between one or more of the image planes. These include facilities for scrolling, dissolves, wipes, cuts and granulation.

When launched, CD-i could only offer motion video in a window about one-third the size of the screen, but in 1993 Philips launched a full-motion video (FMV) cartridge that could be plugged into a CD-i player, offering a maximum of 72 minutes of full-screen full-motion video (FSFMV), which can be either linear or interactive. As well as FMV, the CD-i system offers high-resolution still images, computer animation, games, text, and a number of channels of audio (voice and music) – from AM radio quality right up to near-CD quality.

One of the main problems in launching systems such as CD-i is that the sophisticated – and fairly pricey – hardware is useless without a wide range of attractive software titles. Such titles must be simple enough for first-time users with no experience of interactive systems, yet sophisticated enough to attract children and adults accustomed to highly interactive, but graphically much cruder, videogames. Philips' response to this challenge was to launch CD-i with around one hundred titles, covering a wide spectrum from education to games. These include a highly successful golf simulator for the adult market and programmes such as 'Sesame Street' and 'Face Kitchen' for children. At the launch of the FMV CD-i player at least one interactive feature film, 'Voyeur', was available, together with the promise of over 50 linear feature films, and a variety of other titles to cater for a wide range of interests.

CD-i has begun to create a new market for consumer multimedia, a market that will increasingly demand further innovation and ever greater levels of realism. With their globally established standard, full-motion video technology, and a wide range of consumer entertainment programmes, Philips currently dominate the burgeoning consumer multimedia market. To maintain this lead in the face of growing competition, however, will require constant innovation in terms of both hardware and software, and the full exploitation of existing strengths.

Philips: CD-i player. This bland black box may become the world's first digital multimedia standard. The plug-in FMV cartridge adds an extra 1.5 megabytes of RAM.

Philips: 'Video Speedway', a racing car simulator with high-resolution motion-video footage. Philips were the first to launch MPEG digital video into the mass consumer market, some 16 years after the launch of the LaserVision videodisc.

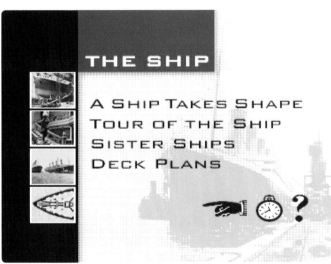

Total Vision: 'Ski Aspen', 'Horse Racing' and 'Titanic', a suite of very different programmes from this Los Angeles-based production company. The Philips CD-i titles catalogue now spans almost the complete range of publishing, including programmes for children, videogames, strategy and board games, sport, music, movies, Photo-CD, reference works and documentaries.

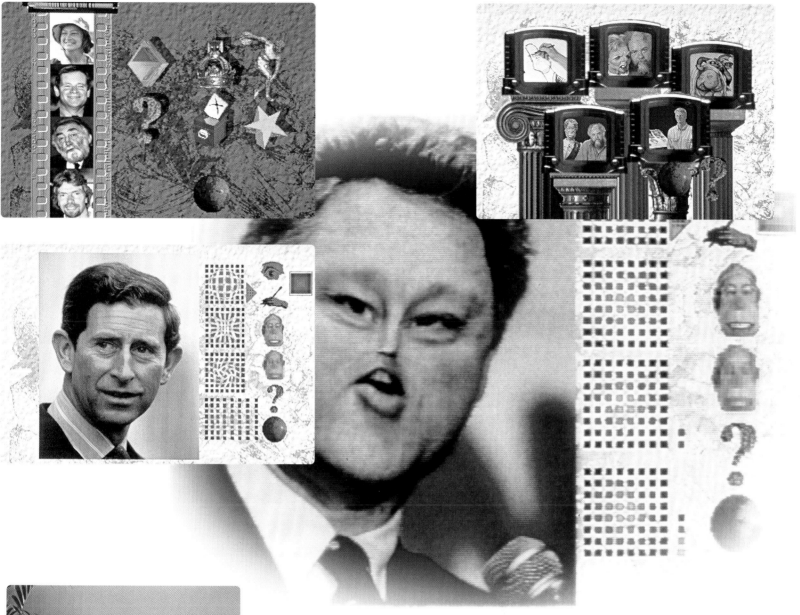

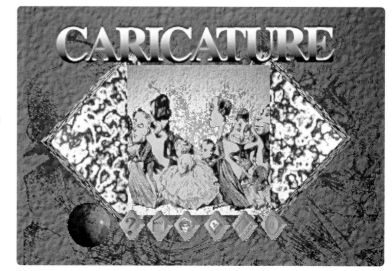

Philips IMS: 'Caricature with Spitting Image'. A CD-i disc with over one hundred celebrity portraits for the user to bend, twist and drag into photo-realistic caricatures. 'Caricature' transforms the bland CD-i player into a powerful image-processing package, with thousands of tool combinations to experiment with. The programme is also designed to use images from Photo-CD discs – so users can lampoon members of their own family. Finished caricatures can be downloaded to videotape. Non-linear programmes like this combine both re-playable and documentary elements, extending use-time far beyond that of single-viewing linear media.

signals. Such **digital** recordings can be copied and recopied many times more than equivalent analog tapes without a significant loss of quality – important in special-effects editing, where the same tape may need to be processed on numerous occasions to add extra layers of imagery. CCIR 601 provides a standard method for encoding digital pictures that allows (for example) easy transfer of images between edit suite and paintbox.

>   QUANTEL   >   SAMPLING RATE

>   VIDEO GRAPHICS

CCITT
[COMITÉ CONSULTATIF INTERNATIONAL TELEGRAPHIQUE ET TELEPHONIQUE]

Consultative Committee on International Telegraphy and Telephones: the international committee set up by the world's **telecommunications** authorities to establish **standards** for telephone, telegraph and data communications.

CD [COMPACT DISC]

A digital-optical storage medium jointly developed by Philips and **Sony**. Originally launched in 1982 as medium for carrying recorded music, but now used for storing all kinds of **digital** data, such as text, video, **hypermedia** programmes and application programs. CD is a read-only storage medium that can store up to 650 megabytes of digital data, though this may increase in the future (see **CD2X**).

CDs consist of a polycarbonate disc usually 120mm (5 inches) in diameter and 1.3mm ($1/20$ inch) thick. On one side of the disc there is a spiral of small pits and spaces between pits which represent the digital data. The spaces between pits are called land. A '1' bit is represented by the transition between pit and land or land and pit. A '0' bit is represented by a constant pit or constant land. In order for the stretches of land or pit to be recognized as a constant, and therefore '0' bit, the disc has to contain timing information as well as the user data. The disc is coated in gold or aluminium to increase reflectivity and then coated in a clear lacquer to protect the surface.

Encoding digital information in this way gives the CD two significant advantages over other storage media. Firstly, it is effectively a permanent storage medium. This is because the discs are read by a non-contact optical head and are not prone to mechanical damage and wear. Nor are they subject to electromagnetic disturbance, because they are essentially a physical medium.

Secondly, being a physical medium they can be cheaply reproduced. The pits are produced by a high-powered **laser**, and on short runs all of the discs can be produced this way. However, this makes each disc relatively expensive. For mass production, a **master disc** is prepared from which moulds can be made and the discs produced either by injection or compression-moulding of heated polycarbonate.

Up until the early part of the next century CDs seem likely to be the dominant storage and distribution medium for hypermedia programmes. While currently limited to a capacity of 650 megabytes, it seems probable that a combination of advances in compression techniques and increases in the physical capacities of the discs themselves will enable them to store significantly more data than at present. By the turn of the century, competition in the form of high-bandwidth **Data Superhighways** – which offer the user access to effectively unlimited storage – may begin to pose a significant threat to the CD's dominant position.

>   CD-i   >   CD-ROM

CD AUDIO

>   CDDA

CD-BRIDGE

An extension to **CD-ROM XA** that specifies the means by which additional information can be added to a CD-ROM XA track, so that it can be played on a **CD-i** player. All data tracks on CD-Bridge must be in **Mode 2**. Kodak's Photo CD is an example of a CD-Bridge application.

CD GRAPHICS

(Or 'CD+G'.) A technique available (but not widely used) in compact disc audio (**CDDA**) that utilizes the subcode **channels** R-W to store graphics data such as song titles and lyrics. CD+G is mainly used for karaoke discs.

CD+G

>   CD GRAPHICS

CD-i [COMPACT DISC INTERACTIVE]

An **interactive multimedia** compact disc-based system developed jointly by Philips and **Sony**. CD-i players plug straight into a standard TV set, and are activated by a remote hand-held controller that allows the user interactively to manipulate the information and games content via a **graphical user interface**. Professional CD-i players were launched in 1990, consumer players in 1992. In 1993, the CD-i **standard** was enhanced by **full-motion video**.

>   CD-i DIGITAL IMAGES   >   FULL-SCREEN FULL-MOTION VIDEO

>   • CD-i PAGE 35

CD-i DIGITAL AUDIO

In **CD-i**, digital audio tracks can be recorded at four different levels of audio quality in either mono or stereo. At the highest level, in stereo, one second of sound requires 171.1 kilobytes of storage giving a maximum play time of 74 minutes with no space for any other data, such as images or text. At the lowest level, Level C Mono, one second of sound requires only 10.6 kilobytes of storage which translates into a maximum capacity 1,040 minutes of sound. The designer of a CD-i programme has to weigh the level of sound quality required against the requirements to include other data, such as images, animations and text, within the overall storage capacity of the medium. With up to 16 parallel audio channels, CD-i programmes can have several alternative voice-over commentaries, or different language versions.

>   ADPCM

>> FURTHER READING: PHILIPS 1992; HOFFOS, SHARPLESS, SMITH & LEWIS 1992; PRESTON 1987

CD-i DIGITAL IMAGES

CD-i can store images using a variety of **compression** techniques, and this facility offers the designer the option of trading image size and **resolution** against storage space. Obviously, the higher the resolution and the larger the image, the more memory is consumed on the disc. A full-screen image encoded in **PAL** using **Delta YUV** (DYUV – the best mode for photographic images) fills a 384x280 **pixel** matrix. Each pixel (at 8 bits/pixel) needs 1 byte, thus 107,520 bytes (104.74 kilobytes) of memory are required to store the complete image.

Using the entire disc space of 650 megabytes, then, some 6354 full-screen images of DYUV quality can be stored. **RGB 5:5:5** images, best for graphics and user-operated 'paintbox' applications (offering a range of 32,768 colours), require 210 kilobytes per image for PAL (170 kilobytes for **NTSC**), and are available in double resolution only. Two other methods of encoding graphics are available: **CLUT** compression restricts the number of colours available to 256 or fewer at normal resolution, or only 16 colours in double resolution; 8-bit CLUT images require 104.74 kilobytes of disc space, and 4-bit CLUTs need 52.5 kilobytes. Disc space for **run-length encoded** images depends on how complex the images are. For example, a full screen of two colours needs only about 500 bytes, while a cartoon-style image with flat colour-fills might need around 25 kilobytes.

>   FULL-SCREEN FULL-MOTION VIDEO

>   JPEG   >   MPEG

>   • CD-i PAGE 35

CD-i READY

A **CDDA** disc with additional features that can only be accessed when the disc is used in a **CD-i** player. Such discs are primarily **digital audio** discs, with added visual data. CD-i data is stored within the first 'pre-gap' track on the CDDA disc (normally this is only two to three seconds in duration and is used to store disc identifiers, track address data etc), which can be extended to accommodate a CD-i track of any length (providing of course that sufficient digital-audio tracks are left). The CD-i track will only be read by a CD-i player – not by a CD player.

CD-i SECTOR

A data unit on **CD-i**, comprising 2,352 bytes.

CD-M

>   CD-MIDI

CD-MIDI [CD-M]

A **CD** system that connects to electronic musical instruments. The disc carries two types of information: **MIDI** data to control the musical instruments, and graphic displays related to instrumental functions such as tempo, tone and timing. Introduced by JVC in 1989, CD-MIDI requires a specially adapted **CD-ROM** player. It enables professionally prepared MIDI musical scores (stored on the disc) to be reproduced 'live', with the user taking interactive control, adding or removing tracks, changing tempo and tone etc.

CD-ROM

the laserdisc
information machine

Compact disc read-only memory (CD-ROM) was the uninspiring title given by Philips in 1986 to a quite inspired adaptation of the technology of the audio compact disc. Since then, CD-ROM has blossomed far beyond even the most optimistic expectations of the technologists and computer scientists at Sony and Philips who together devised the format. In the 1990s it has become the central medium for the distribution of multimedia software.

The first CD-ROM applications mirrored the command-line interface then still dominant in personal computers (remember the C:> prompt?), but gave access to databases that previously would have been stored on giant hard disks and administered by mini-mainframe computers. CD-ROM technology made these databases available to anyone with a personal computer attached to a suitable drive.

But the plain green text on a black screen that was a hallmark of the early CD-ROM applications indicated little of the multimedia potential that was to emerge within two or three years. The fact that CD-ROMs were cheap to produce, could store data of any type – including text, images and sound – and also store computer programs (applications), made the growth of multimedia inevitable. By the late 1980s, multimedia interactive encyclopedias had become available, featuring extensive text databases – with search engines that offered the user quick and easy access to information – as well as sound, music and still pictures.

The first multimedia products could only show motion video at low frame rates, and in small windows on the screen. The problem stemmed from CD-ROM's data transfer rate (the speed at which data is read off the disc and transferred into the controlling computer for display on the screen). In order to maintain compatibility with CD-audio discs, CD-ROM disc drives delivered data at around 150 kilobytes per second. This may sound fast, but when one considers that a broadcast-quality TV image requiring, say, 2 megabytes of data, would take over 13 seconds to appear on the screen, it becomes obvious why the 25 frames per second necessary for motion video was a problem. By the early 1990s, this problem had been solved by advances in compression – squeezing more pictures onto the disc – and by the development of new chips for decompressing these images in realtime before displaying them on the screen.

There is now a proliferation of CD-ROM-based products (including the 3DO Interactive Multiplayer, CD-i, and DVI) that can offer motion video at various frame rates and levels of image quality. Kodak has adopted an extended version of the CD-ROM format (CD-ROM XA) for their PhotoCD discs, which have started a mini-revolution in photographic archiving, reprographics and publishing, as well as for consumer digital snapshots.

CD-ROM discs and drives are available for every major make of computer, and with millions of drives already in use, and forecasts of continuing growth, the CD-ROM market appears to be flourishing. Portable CD-ROM drives, such as NEC's personal computer add-on and Apple's self-contained PowerCD (which just needs to be plugged into a TV to show PhotoCD discs), point the way to a greater variety of corporate and consumer applications.

Kagema: PhotoLib photographic library CD-ROM. It features Aldus Fetch, an image database offering fast search, retrieval and display of any of the disc's four thousand 24-bit images, stored using JPEG compression. Reprographic-quality 3000x2000 pixel images can be ordered from the CD-ROM library; these are delivered to the client on Kodak PhotoCD discs.

The Voyager Company: 'Learn to Speak Spanish' and 'The Bible Library'.

Media Design Interactive: 'London, The Multimedia Tour'.

NEC: Portable CDR-25/CD-Express. With interactive multimedia CD-ROM players for linking to notebook and laptop PCs, enormous databases can be made available to professional users in remote locations or on the move.

CD-MOVIE
> VIDEO-CD

CD-R [CD-RECORDABLE]
A 'write-once', recordable **CD-ROM** format, with affordable desktop drives, launched in 1993. CD-R is perfect for prototyping interactive multimedia titles before conventional disc pressing (for design development and for test marketing); for archiving **data**, pictures and backups; and for limited-edition runs of presentations, **multimedia** and other applications. CD-R makes the regular updating of archives and **point-of-information** systems possible as an in-house operation. At launch, drives were available from several manufacturers including Philips, **Sony** and JVC. With a high-power laser, CD-R 'burns' data into a blank, pre-grooved **CD-ROM**. A low-power laser is used to read data.

CD-ROM [COMPACT DISC READ-ONLY MEMORY]
A laser-read 120mm (5-inch) disc that stores up to 640 megabytes of **digital** data, and which has become the most popular carrier of **database**, **hypermedia** and **interactive multimedia** programmes. CD-ROM is a very dense storage medium, with a capacity the equivalent of 1500 **floppy disk**s, or 200,000 pages of A4 text, as well as media of different types, such as audio, images, **animations**, **videogames** and graphics.
> CD-R   > • CD-ROM PAGE 39

CD-ROM XA [CD-ROM EXTENDED ARCHITECTURE]
An extension of the **CD-ROM** specification that allows the CD-ROM to play audio information at the same time as retrieving other types of data – such as text, images and graphics. This facility is made possible by **interleaving** graphics, text and image data with audio data that has been compressed using **ADPCM** techniques. A CD-ROM XA disc requires a CD-ROM XA-compatible disc-drive linked to a PC with CD-ROM XA board. The XA drive will play ordinary CD-ROMs, but has extra data-handling logic and an ADPCM decoder.
> CD-BRIDGE   > CD-i
> PHOTO CD

CD2X
A non-standard development of the **CDDA** format, by Nimbus Technology and Engineering, that doubles the playing time of a compact disc to 150 minutes and enables it to store digital **full-motion video** for a feature-length film. On CD2X, the pits that store the digital data are reduced in size and increased in frequency, and the speed with which they are read from the disc is diminished in a ratio of 1:4. Nimbus have also developed a special video adapter unit to play CD2X discs that plugs into a standard CD player and connects it to a television set.

CD32
A combined computer/**CD-ROM** system announced by Commodore in 1993, comprising a 32-bit Amiga A1200 with a built-in CD-ROM drive. The CD32 will run games, CD-audio discs, CD-ROMs and the Karaoke format CD+G. Targeted at the multimedia games market, the CD32 will compete with systems from 3DO, Sega and Atari, as well as Philips' **CD-i**.

CDAD [COMPACT DIGITAL AUDIO DISC]
> CDDA

CDDA [COMPACT DISC DIGITAL AUDIO]
Launched in 1982 as the result of a joint development between Philips and Sony, CDDA was the first audio medium to use **digital-optical recording**. CDDA is a read-only medium using compact discs (**CDs**) to store sound in the form of **digital** data, effectively eliminating the sound disturbances common to earlier recording systems such as background noise, wow and flutter. Digital audio data is recorded as a spiral track of tiny pits, each 0.9 – 3.3 microns long and 0.6 microns wide. A full 72 minutes of audio on the standard 120mm (5-inch) disc results in a track of 5 billion pits that is around 5 kilometres (3 miles) long, and some 60 times finer than the track of a vinyl record.
During CD mastering, digital data from an original recording is encoded in CDDA format and used to drive a high-power laser which burns the pits into the surface of the disc. In playback, a lower power laser is used to illuminate the track as the disc is spinning, and reflected light is directed to a photo-sensor. Because more or less light will be reflected depending upon whether the light is reflected from the optically flat surface or from a pit, different signals can be interpreted by the sensor and converted to an electrical signal for amplification. The track is read at a constant linear velocity (**CLV**) of 1.25 metres (4 feet) per second, which means that the disc must be made to rotate at a variable speed. While vinyl records are read from the outside inwards, the CDDA track is read in the opposite direction, and the disc speed gradually reduces from 500 rpm to about 200 rpm as the music is played.
CDDA data is structured into a main program area (storing the hi-fi music or sounds), lead-in area and lead-out area. These areas contain the main **data channel** and eight subcode channels. The main control and display information is contained in the **Q channel**.
> CD-i DIGITAL AUDIO   > CD-i READY
> DIGITAL AUDIO

CDRTOS [COMPACT DISC REALTIME OPERATING SYSTEM]
The **multi-tasking**, **realtime operating system** developed by Philips for **CD-i**, based on the OS-9 operating system.

CDTV [COMMODORE DYNAMIC TOTAL VISION]
The first commercially available consumer multimedia **CD-ROM** player. CDTV was launched by Commodore in 1991 and subsequently abandoned.

CDV [COMPACT DISC VIDEO]
A compact version of the **laserdisc** developed by Philips and **Sony** and launched in October 1988. CDV stores video as an analog signal.

CELL-NET [CELLULAR RADIO NETWORK]
A network of radio transmitters organized into cells – areas covered by each transmitter – used for mobile communications. The geographical area covered by the service is divided into hexagonal cells, each serviced by a low-power antenna. Adjacent cells broadcast on different frequencies. As mobile-phone users move around in the area, their calls are switched to the frequency of the new cell, and the previous cell reallocates the frequency. The advantage of cellular radio is that a limited number of frequencies can service a large area. Digital cell radio uses **data compression** techniques to squeeze even more calls into the same frequencies. Because of compression, digital cell phones offer the user privacy and security – their calls cannot be accidently overheard.
> • CELL-NETS AND WIRELESS-NETS PAGE 41

CELL RADIO
> CELL-NET

CELLULAR AUTOMATA
Simple mathematical systems (described by Stanislaw Ulam as 'recursively defined geometric objects') that operate within a cellular structure such as a grid. Cellular automata can be used to devise models of

Commodore Amiga CD32.

the real world that start from very simple premises, but are capable of reproducing very complex phenomena. The mathematician John Von Neumann used cellular automata to prove his hypothesis that self-reproducing machines are possible.

Cellular automata work on the principle that a particular cell in a grid will either be filled with colour or not ('on' or 'off') depending upon a set of simple rules, such as those invented at Cambridge University in 1970 by the mathematician John Horton Conway. Conway prescribed a set of rules for a game he called 'Life', which was to be played out on a large grid of graph paper (or by using the **pixel** screen of computer monitors), and the progress of the game governed by **digital** time (that is time indicated as a succession of discrete 'ticks' or 'generations'). The rules are very simple. The state of each cell is governed by what is happening in the eight cells surrounding it. For example, if a cell has two neighbours that are 'on' (ie filled), then in the next generation, the status of the cell remains the same (if it is on, it stays on, and vice-versa). If the number of adjacent 'on' cells is three, the cell itself will be 'on' in the next generation, regardless of its current state. If the neighbouring 'ons' number zero, one, four, five, six, seven, or eight, then the cell will be 'off' in the next generation. The player's role is also simple: to decide on which cells are 'on' or 'off' at the beginning ('time zero') of the game. From then on the rules of Life govern the entire game scenario.

Cellular automata demonstrate that complex and sophisticated structures can develop from very simple entities following a limited number of simple rules. These principles have been applied in many different ways by programmers to create abstract patterns and computer animations.

> FRACTAL IMAGES

>> FURTHER READING: DAWKINS 1983; LEVY 1992; POUNDSTONE 1985

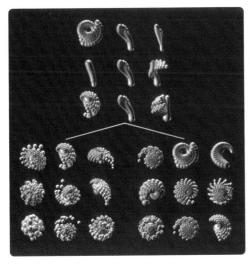

William Latham: In his work at the IBM UK Scientific Research Centre, Latham uses a specially developed genetic program called Mutator, with which he selectively 'breeds' new images based on aesthetic 'natural selection'.

CELL-NETS AND WIRELESS-NETS
inter-personal information networks

Fifty years ago the wristwatch-sized two-way radio existed only in the Dick Tracy cartoons of artist Chester Gould. By the mid-1980s, the portable phone had shrunk to something approaching pocket-size, and had become an unexceptional, if expensive, adjunct to business life. By the mid-1990s, the next step in the fulfilment of Chester Gould's vision is well under way. The establishment of personal communications networks has introduced not just low-cost, pocket-sized portable phones, but portable communications systems that transmit and receive data as well as voice messages.

Two driving forces are behind the development of wireless networks: firstly, the phenomenal success of cellular radio as a method of optimizing the limited bandwidth of radio frequencies available for personal communications; and secondly, the development of digital compression techniques for squeezing ever more information into these frequencies.

Cellular radio works by limiting the power of each transmitted signal to the absolute minimum necessary. This means that only a small range of frequencies is required to service transmissions in a city-wide area. By dividing the geographical coverage of the network into hexagonal cells, each serviced by an antenna, and avoiding the use of the same frequency in adjacent or nearby cells, interference is kept to a minimum, and the system is expandable merely by subdividing the cells and adding more antennas. Alternatively, new digital compression techniques can be used to pack more transmissions into the existing cells.

Wireless personal communications have grown from one-way systems such as paging and messaging, to two-way carriers offering both voice-and-data and data-only transmission. There is also strong potential for LEO satellite-based paging and messaging (one-way) systems, such as that operated by SkyTel (from Washington DC) and the Florida-based Embarc/Motorola system (see Satellite Communications). Such systems could eventually provide blanket worldwide coverage, and by linking the satellite paging service to E-mail networks could also offer two-way services.

Receivers for such satellite communication systems can be embodied on 'smart cards' (using the PCMCIA-2 format), for insertion into laptop or palmtop computers or personal digital systems. Such personal communications systems have become a practical possibility only relatively recently, and are the product of technologies that pack ever greater power and memory into portable computers and that allow these computers to talk to each other by means of cellular radio networks and other 'wireless' systems.

Cell-nets and wireless-nets thus harness two of the dominant trends in the use of computers over the last decade: portability (freeing the computer user from the necessity of working at a desk), and connectivity (providing an individual with remote access to other computers). Portability and connectivity open up the possibility of a number of computer users in different locations working together on the same project (a teleworking technique using 'Groupware' software applications), or having their individual local decisions informed and coordinated by a central computer, database or expert system. Where wire-based communications depend on the sender and receiver both having access to a phone and modem, wireless networks offer the freedom of truly portable communications, as direct and as efficient as mobile telephones.

Until recently a strange situation has existed whereby two-way communications between people (who are often on the move) have been handled by inflexible, hard-wired systems like the telephone network, while one-way broadcast television has been available anywhere, to anyone with a TV set. Nicholas Negroponte, of MIT's Media Lab, predicts a major switch between these two modes of communication. According to Negroponte, the radio spectrum will come to be used for inter-personal, mobile two-way communication, while the wired network will be used for the delivery of television and other 'infotainment', including interactive services, straight into the home. The personal communications networks that are currently being established are but the first step in the 'Negroponte Switch', and herald a development in personal communications as revolutionary as the introduction of the telephone system itself.

EO Personal Communicator: penpad datacoms.

CELLULAR RADIO NETWORK
> CELL-NET

CGA [COLOUR GRAPHICS ADAPTER]
This was IBM's first colour graphics standard for the personal computer. CGA supported two colours at 640x200 pixels, and two palettes of four colours at 320 pixels x20 lines. In text mode, CGA supports 25 lines of 80 characters, with 16 text (foreground) colours and 8 background colours.

> EGA   > VGA
> XGA

CHANNEL
A path along which data is transmitted. This may be a cable, an optical fibre, a frequency for broadcast transmissions, etc. The size (**bandwidth**) of the channel determines the amount of information that can flow through it. For example, **CD-ROM** has a channel bandwidth of between 150 and 170 kilobytes per second.

CHAPTER SEARCH
A method of searching through an interactive programme chapter by chapter, ie by accessing each self-contained segment (chapter) of the programme.

> BROWSING

CHECK DISC
A test disc that is produced to verify the quality and performance of a **hypermedia** or **interactive video** programme. Check discs are relatively cheap, and provide a final **validation** and **debugging** test bed before final masters are made and quantity replication begins. Many pressing facilities offer glass or plastic **videodisc**, **CD-R** or **WORM** check disc services for programme developers.

> GLASS DISC

CHIP
> MICROCHIP

CHROMAKEY
A video system that enables two or more video images to be combined into a single, composite image. Used in the production of video and broadcast television programmes, chromakey employs the principle of colour keying – effectively rendering one or more colours 'transparent', so that a second image may be displayed in their place. Chromakey and related techniques such as Ultimatte and CSO (colour separation overlay) offer a relatively cheap method of combining video shot in the studio with painted or photographic backdrops from a second video source or from a computer 'paint' system. Thus, for example, actors can appear to walk about in a cartoon-style set, fly across a landscape or walk across the sea. Multiple layers of chromakeyed imagery result in rich mixes of image-types. One of the earliest examples of the creative use of chromakey (integrating paintbox, tape and studio video) was produced in the early 1980s: 'The Adventures of Frank', a surreal television drama by John McGrath.

Video boards now make chromakeying possible for **desktop video** producers, allowing video sources from tape or **laserdiscs** to be seamlessly integrated with graphics and text data stored on hard disk. In these 32-**bit** systems, three bytes describe the red, green and blue components of each **pixel** in the colour image, while the fourth byte (called the **alpha channel**) can be used to control the extent to which the video signal can be mixed with **RGB** computer graphics.

> VIDEO GRAPHICS

CHROMINANCE
The **colour** component of a video signal, which defines the colour's richness or intensity (ie both the hue and saturation).

CISC [COMPLEX INSTRUCTION SET CHIP]
A **CPU** designed to execute a large number of instructions, enabling it to carry out most computations directly. Computers such as the Apple **Macintosh** and **IBM** and **IBM-compatibles** use CISCs, and can deal with over one hundred different instructions. The penalty for this is a reduction in processing speed compared to **RISC** processors.

CIX [COMPULINK INFORMATION EXCHANGE]
A electronic **teleconferencing** system (**network** service) that allows multiple users to participate in debates and discussions set up by individuals or companies on a wide range of topics.

CLIP ART
Collections of (generally **copyright**-free) graphics, illustrations and photographic images that can be used within **DTP** documents and **multimedia** productions. Clip art can be bought in book form, or stored digitally on **floppy disk** or **CD-ROM**, and is often classified by subject.

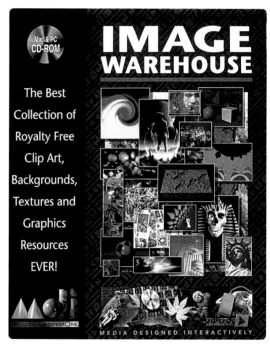

Image Warehouse provides clip art on CD-ROM.

Prospect's 'Virtual Nightclub' by Trip Media uses chromakey techniques to full effect.

CLIPBOARD

In Apple **Macintosh** computers, the area of temporary memory that holds objects (data such as text or images) that have been 'cut' or 'copied'.

CLUT [COLOUR LOOK-UP TABLE]

An array of data (or 'table') containing values for all the colours represented in an image. CLUTs are a means of compressing colour images, so that instead of storing the **RGB** values for each **pixel**, only the relevant CLUT address (a much smaller amount of data) is actually stored.

> COMPRESSION

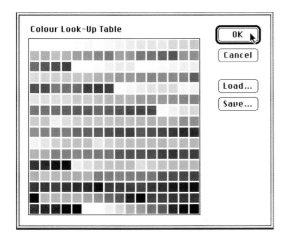

CLUT ANIMATION

(Or 'colour cycling'.) A method of redefining some or all of the values in a colour look-up table (**CLUT**) as a function of time. CLUT animations only operate on a single image – an image in which the colours have been carefully disposed to achieve the desired effect. For example, it is possible to use CLUT animation to make bar charts 'grow' in **realtime** by painting the bar in horizontal stripes using a range of palette 'cells' that have been defined to the same colour as the background. The bar will be invisible until the colours in the CLUT are redefined one at a time, when the bar will appear and start to grow. Several 'latent' images or text characters can be stored in the same screen graphic and made to appear or disappear at will, thus creating interesting titling and captioning effects.

> COMPUTER ANIMATION

CLV [CONSTANT LINEAR VELOCITY]

A mode of reading data from a compact disc (**CD**) where the speed that the disc rotates varies so that the speed at the read head remains constant. CLV allows the maximum amount of information to be stored on disc, but is not as efficient as **CAV** for **random-access** retrieval.

> LASERVISION   > VIDEODISC

CMY [CYAN, MAGENTA, YELLOW]

A colour-generation system where any colour is produced by mixing combinations of cyan, magenta

and yellow. It is the basis of many printing systems, where a fourth colour black (K) is added to provide greater depth of contrast. Images in such printing systems are often referred to as CMYK.

CODEC [CODER-DECODER]

A circuit or unit that converts analogue video or audio information into digital form (and back again). Commonly used in **videophone** and **video conferencing** systems, where video signals are sent via telephone lines.

COGNITIVE SCIENCE

The branch of science that concerns itself with how we acquire knowledge, and how we remember it and use it. Cognitive science has focused on two main issues of relevance to the **hypermedia** designer working in the education or 'infotainment' fields. The first concerns cognition itself: how we acquire, arrange, classify and interrelate information in our minds, how what we know in turn helps us to learn more, and how this new knowledge can restructure existing knowledge. The second issue relates to the process of 'metacognition': how we become aware of how we learn, and how we remember and utilize what we learn in order to make the process of learning more efficient and more reliable in the future.

Because hypermedia from its very conception was intended to be a device that would echo our own human cognitive powers – and that would extend them by adding extra (machine) memory – it is not surprising that there are many similarities between how hypermedia works, and the views that cognitive scientists have put forward on how we learn and interrelate new facts. Facts in themselves are not knowledge. It is the process of classifying new facts, and the process of cross-connecting them to other things that we know, that constitutes the beginning of 'knowledge'. Vannevar Bush with his **Memex** system, envisaged a 'memory extension' that would employ **hypertext**-like linking techniques to allow users to develop tools for the correlation of large amounts of information. Subsequent evangelists such as Ted Nelson (who invented the term hypermedia) also stress its importance as a method for locating, storing and cross-referring information: in other words, as a tool for thinking.

> CAL   > INTERACTIVE MULTIMEDIA

COIN-OP MULTIMEDIA

Coin-operated **quiz games** using a **multimedia** interface. Very much a growth area in arcades, pubs and clubs, the two sectors which are of most interest to **hypermedia** designers are AWP (amusement with prizes) and SWP (skills with prizes). AWP games are largely based on chance, and thus fall under the UK gaming laws which restrict stakes and jackpots. SWPs, because they are defined as games of skill, do not come under this restriction. Most SWPs are quizzes, and offer questions that are graded according to difficulty, and answered by selecting from a multiple-choice list, often playing against the clock. Multimedia technologies such as **CD-ROM** and **DVI** confer several advantages on coin-op manufacturers. The use of sophisticated multimedia

Ace Coin Console, a DVI-equipped pub quiz game.

mixes of video, **stills**, **animations** and **sprites** attracts more custom, and the storage capacity of CD-ROMs means that **databases** of questions can be much larger than **hard-disk** storage.

> ARCADE GAMES

COLOUR

Colour, or 'hue', describes the various wavelengths of light that are visible to the human eye, from ultra-violet (390 nanometres) to red (700 nanometres). Within this tiny 'visible light' spectrum, the average human is able to perceive around 1000 different modulations of about 200 hues. In colour classification systems, such as those by Mansell and Ostwald, colour is ordered in terms of hue, **saturation** (colour intensity) and brightness or **luminance** (the tonal value of the colour). The problem with colour classification systems is that they can only be applied under a set of 'ideal' conditions, when all colours are equally illuminated by the same pure light source. They do not take into account the everyday fluctuations that may be subjective, environmental or atmospheric – for instance the difference between seeing a red poppy in a green field in strong sunlight, and seeing the same poppy laid on a mahogany table in the half-light of evening. While the human eye is very adept at adjusting and adapting to different viewing conditions, mechanical **imaging system**s are not. So while our perception of the colour of the poppy will remain fairly constant, the actual colour information of the same scene recorded by the imaging system will not.

Artists and designers who use colour imaging systems (such as oil paints, cameras and computer **paint programs**) have to learn how colours interact with each other, how colours are perceived by different people under different conditions, and how the imaging system they are using can in turn modify and distort colour. For instance, it is well known by designers working in television that very saturated colours bleed badly into surrounding areas, so they purposely restrict their working palette to non-saturated or more 'pastel' colours. In **video graphics**, the best colours for text are of low saturation and high luminance, and text works best with a dropped shadow or outline in a darker, neutral colour.

> **CMY**
> **RGB**
> **HSV**

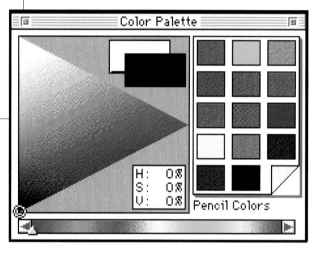

Palette from Fractal Design's Painter.

COLOUR CODING

The use of colours to separate and classify items of information, such as sections of a report, or types of road signs. One of the first and most successful examples of colour coding applied to information graphics was Henry Beck's map design for the London Underground system in 1933, which has influenced the design of transit maps around the world. The colours that Beck used – black, red, yellow, green, mauve, and light and dark blue – were arbitrary, but were rapidly 'learned' by the travelling public. Equally effective was Beck's codification of the route lines into a rigid grid of horizontals, verticals and diagonals – indeed the two devices worked together synergetically.

This use of colour coding as a device to aid navigation is an important pointer to the solution of **browsing** and **navigation** problems in **hypermedia**. Colours can be used to denote main classifications of information, while important issues within each classification can be denoted by an increase in colour **saturation**, and so on. Colour can also be used in terms of its 'hot' and 'cold' emotive connotations as a metaphor for getting closer to an item of information, or the target of a game. If the user is doing well, navigational icons would probably become more 'hot' (red or orange), whereas if the user is doing badly, the icon would become 'cool' (blue/green).

COLOUR CYCLING
> **CLUT ANIMATION**

COLOUR LOOK-UP TABLE
> **CLUT**

COMBI PLAYER
'Combination' disc player introduced by Philips and Pioneer in 1988. It will accept 300mm (12-inch) laser **videodiscs**, 120mm (5-inch) **CDV** (compact disc video), and **CDDA** (digital audio) discs.
> **LASERVISION**

COMMENT
In **programming** and **scripting**, a statement inserted in plain English to identify the function of a piece of code or an instruction. Comments are ignored by the compiler (ie they do not interfere with the running of the program), and are especially important where an application (such as a **Hypermedia** programme) is to be worked on by more than one programmer.
> **LANGUAGE**

COMPACT DISC
> **CD**

COMPACT DISC VIDEO
> **CDV**

COMPILER
A **program** that translates code written in a **high-level language** into **machine code** that can be executed by a computer.

COMPONENT VIDEO
A professional-quality video system in which the **luminance** and two **chrominance** signals are recorded onto separate tracks on the videotape. The colour information is contained in the two chrominance signals (R-Y and B-Y), in such a way that that can be converted back into **RGB** with minimal loss.
> **COMPOSITE VIDEO**

COMPOSITE VIDEO
The most common standard of video signal. It is used in consumer **VCR**s and video cameras and television, where the red, green and blue signals are mixed together.
> **COMPONENT VIDEO**

COMPRESSION
The reduction of the amount of data required to store and transmit information. Various techniques are used for the compression of audio and visual data.

IMAGE COMPRESSION
> **DELTA YUV**
> **FULL-SCREEN FULL-MOTION VIDEO**
> **JPEG**
> **DVI**
> **FRACTAL COMPRESSION**
> **MPEG**

AUDIO COMPRESSION
> **ADPCM**
> **PULSE-CODE MODULATION**
> **• COMPRESSION PAGE 45**
> **CD-I DIGITAL AUDIO**
> **STILL-FRAME AUDIO**

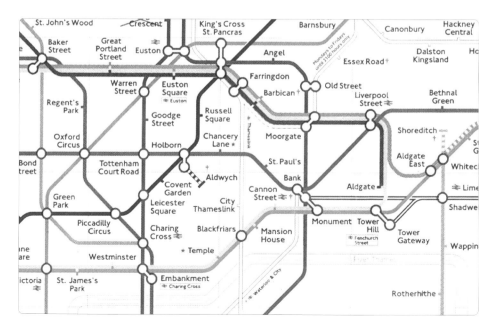

Colour coding: Henry Beck's seminal London Underground map.

COMPRESSION
if it's digital,
squeeze it

Compression techniques are crucial to the successful development of cyberspace multimedia systems, for both data storage and data transmission. Several different methods exist for compressing images, audio and other computer data: still-image compression standards are well established (see JPEG), and compression standards for motion video are now formalized as the MPEG standard.

The problem of motion picture compression is not a trivial one. Without compression, a digitized broadcast TV picture requires about 1 megabyte of storage. As at least 25 frames are displayed every second to provide full-motion video (FMV), the storage and transmission of digital movies would require not only a massive hard disk (at least 1.5 gigabytes for every minute of video) but also a yet-to-be-invented desktop computer that could deliver the required display rate of 25 megabytes per second (current hard disks can only manage a maximum of 2 megabytes per second). In the early 1990s, other communications and consumer electronics media were also hampered by the log jam of motion video data. The future of broadband networks, videophones, video conferencing and ISDN all hinged on this problem being resolved.

The answer, of course, was to compress the image data, and to store only the differences between successive frames, not entire images. MPEG is the standard that has evolved for motion video compression and offers a rate around 1.2 megabits per second (146.5 kilobytes per second) which, although within the data transfer rate for CD-ROMs, does not leave much room for the accompanying audio data. However, Philips and Matsushita have developed a new audio compression technique for their DCC (digital compact cassette) called PASC (precision adapted sub-band coding), which can squeeze high-quality audio into between one-quarter and one-eighth of the bits needed for compact disc-quality sound. Audio compression techniques similar to PASC have been incorporated into MPEG, and are now widely used by Philips and others in FMV programmes.

Still images can be compressed using a variety of industry-standard techniques such as those endorsed by the Joint Photographic Experts Group (JPEG), and fractal compression, a technology developed by Dr Michael Barnsley of Iterated Systems. Fractal techniques can deliver compression ratios up to about 150:1, squeezing a 1 megabyte image (over one million bytes of data) down to just 6500 bytes. Using this technology some 80,000 images could be stored on a CD-ROM. Fractal compression is also suitable for use in motion video.

In 1993 the US company Total Multimedia launched their fractal-based 'producer-video' compression software, offering full-motion video in a screen window of 320x200 pixels on a standard PC with no additional hardware. In contrast, non-fractal technologies such as Microsoft's Video for Windows and Apple's QuickTime can currently run at rates of between 15 and 22 frames per second in much smaller screen windows. Moreover, these latter two technologies are inexpensive, and users have the choice of a wide range of editing software, and can even include movies in word-processing files for multimedia electronic mail.

Compression techniques are changing the face of the multimedia CD-ROM market. Now that full-motion video and interactive video can be combined within hypermedia programmes, a whole range of new products becomes possible, including Music Plus, interactive drama-documentaries, interactive movies, videogames, surrogate travel discs, virtual shopping malls, and much more. But it is not just disc-based media that rely on data compression. Cable and wireless networks use similar data compression techniques in order to speed up the transfer of data. Even broadband networks using fibre-optic cables (which have a capacity in the region of 100 megabits per second) will use compression techniques to provide fast and cost-effective two-way transmissions.

>> FURTHER READING: BARNSLEY AND HURD 1993

QuickTime Movie, Apple's software-only compression/decompression system extension. QuickTime was one of the key steps towards the Mac becoming a true multimedia machine.

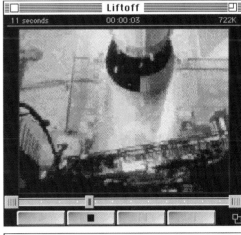

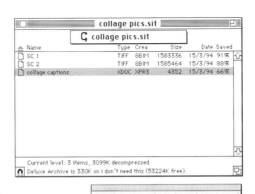

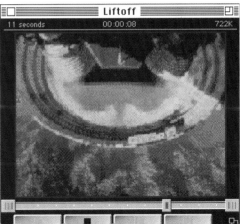

Aladdin Systems: 'Stuffit'. This is a shareware compression/decompression utility for the Mac, used to compress data files for archiving or distribution, or merely to save valuable hard-disk space.

COMPRESSION RATIO

The factor by which **digital** data can be compressed. The **JPEG** algorithm, for instance, compresses images by a maximum of 50:1, compressing an 800-kilobyte 24-bit **PICT** colour image to just 16 kilobytes.

> COMPRESSION

COMPUSERVE

A worldwide computer conferencing, information and electronic mail (**E-mail**) **network** for personal computer users. CompuServe has more than 750,000 subscribers, and offers over a thousand services, including an E-mail service with 72 channels, and 175 forums for special interest groups. Other services include electronic editions of computer periodicals; news services compiled from agencies such as Reuters and UPI; games and quiz shows; travel information and flight-booking services; and 'Rocknet', a rock music forum. Subscribers need a personal computer and **modem** connection to the telephone. They pay an initial fee for a membership kit, and usage charges for their time on the network.

> INTERNET

COMPUTER ANIMATION

The display of a series of computer-generated images in sequence at a speed where the **persistence of vision** creates an illusion of continuous movement. Most commonly refers to computer-generated three dimensional images. May also refer to computer systems that mimic conventional cel animation, or the simple diagrammatic animations that can be produced using authoring packages such as **HyperCard** or **SuperCard**.

> • COMPUTER ANIMATION THIS PAGE

COMPUTER GRAPHICS

Describes the generation of images using computer systems. Most commonly refers to the creation of three-dimensional images, but also refers to the creation of two-dimensional images using **paint** or **draw program**s. Computer graphics are the quintessential art of the late twentieth century, providing a successful synergy of art and science, perspective and technology.

> • COMPUTER GRAPHICS PAGE 49

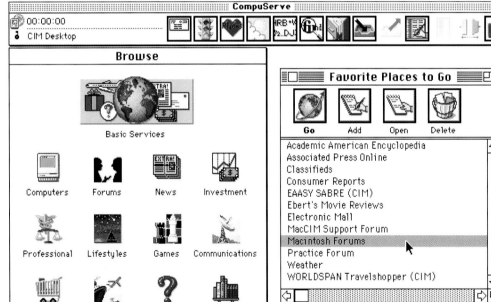

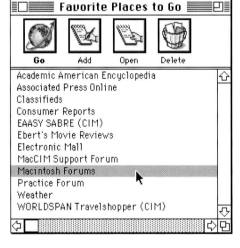

Typical Macintosh interface screens for CompuServe, the popular E-mail, conferencing and BBS network. The CompuServe Magazine features news and reviews of cyberspace developments.

COMPUTER ANIMATION

movies from the dream machine

The use of computers in animation stems from the experimental work of John Whitney and his sons in the 1950s and 1960s. The period between Whitney's experimental films and the first commercial application of computer-aided animation in Walt Disney's Tron (1982), spanned a revolution in the world of computers. In the 1950s, Whitney worked with analog, electromechanical computers – based on ex-US Artillery gunsights – but by 1979 infinitely more powerful digital machines were available, costing only a few thousand dollars. This period also encompassed the great pioneering work of computer graphics: Ivan Sutherland's invention of the Sketchpad program, and his subsequent development of realtime animation techniques.

The two main methods of computer animation are frame-by-frame, where each frame of the animation is individually rendered to a storage medium (either disk or directly to videotape or film) before viewing at 25 frames per second (30 frames per second in the US), and realtime animation, where the computer generates images directly at the viewing speed. Frame-by-frame techniques are used for the bulk of animation work where high resolution and detailed, realistic images are required, such as television idents, adverts and feature film work. Realtime animation is used where a high degree of interactivity is required, but powerful mainframe or supercomputers are needed to achieve high resolution. Such realtime applications include flight simulation, and other vehicle simulators, and walkthroughs for large architectural projects.

With frame-by-frame animation it is possible to produce photographically realistic sequences, with very high resolution images that appear 'super-real' (such as images of landscapes with every near and distant detail in sharp focus). The downside of this level of resolution is the processing time needed. At the top end of computer animation – for lavish commercials and feature movies – highly realistic images may require both supercomputer power and several minutes of processing time for every frame of video or film recorded. A 60-second animation will require 1500 frames, or some 125 hours (at 5 minutes per frame) of expensive supercomputer time. With slower processors this 'time debt' can extend production times considerably. Desktop computers such as the Macintosh may need several hours of processing time to render a complex model realistically. For this reason, computer animation is still an expensive process.

However, computers can produce frame-by-frame effects that are impossible in conventional animation. In computer animation, the camera, lens, rostrum, baseplate, lighting, optical effects unit and model itself exist as digital software, directly under the interactive control of the director and animator. 'Camera' movements can be plotted through the computer model while the camera lens is changed frame by frame from wide-angle to telephoto.

Cambridge Animation Systems: Animo, professional animation software that is closely modelled on conventional cel animation, with full in-betweening and line tests. Animo brings the professional tools of the animator to the desktop, offering complete workstation control of the entire animation process. Cambridge Animation has developed a system that complements the human animator, thus allowing precise artistic control as well as the semi-automation of repetitive tasks.

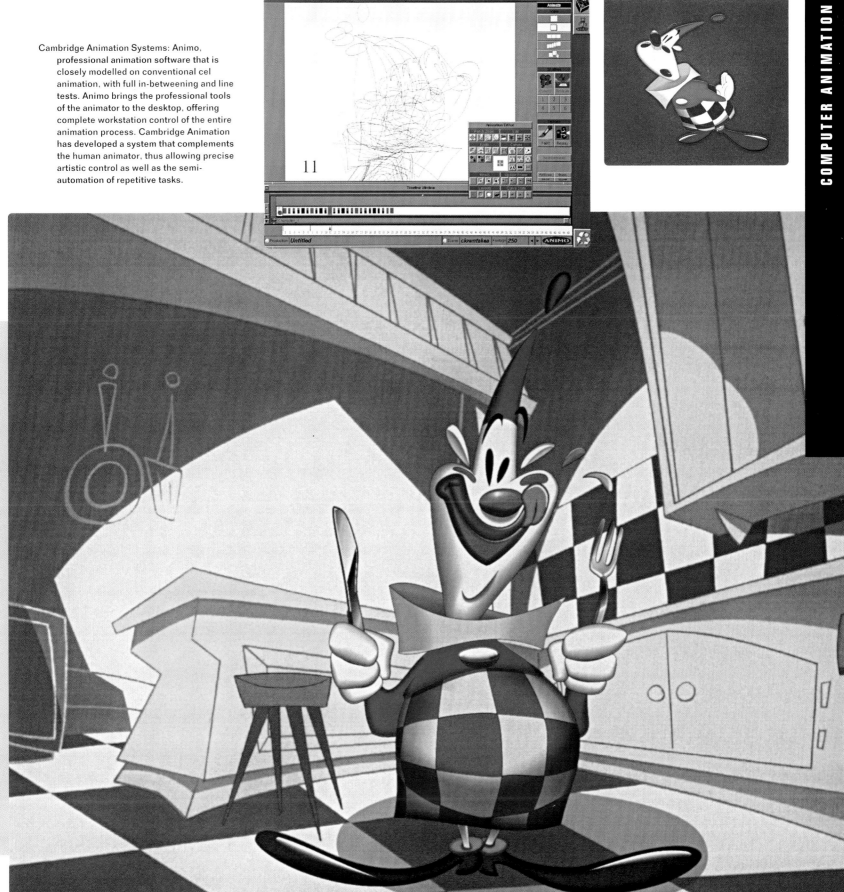

Furthermore, computer cameras are not bound by the physical constraints of reality. 'Soft' cameras can 'fly' through walls, or zoom from the height of a satellite orbit down to a single sand fly on a beach. Movement, colour, lighting, and atmospheric effects can all be programmed to change subtly over a series of frames, exactly as the animator requires. Lighting can be controlled to set the ambient illumination, and to represent spotlights or local sources of light of any intensity or colour. Algorithms have been developed that will calculate the subtle reflections and refractions from a wide variety of solid and liquid materials, translucent and opaque surfaces and textures.

But this level of realism is really only possible if the images are pre-computed, and recorded frame-by-frame to a storage medium. Such sequences are linear, and the degree of interaction is limited to simple branching options into other linear sequences. Realtime animation, on the other hand, is highly interactive. Realtime animation involves the construction of a virtual 3-d model (for instance of an airport and its surrounding countryside, for a flight simulator), and the development of software that will input the observer's location and speed, and the direction and field of his or her view. This input determines the 'view' of the virtual landscape that the computer then processes at very high speed. The image is then projected onto a suitable wide-angle screen, or (in the case of virtual reality systems) two stereoscopic images are displayed on small screens in front of each eye, projected at realtime rates of 25-30 frames per second.

Low- to medium-resolution realtime animation is possible on desktop computers, and is used for a variety of hypermedia, videogame and virtual reality applications. Authoring packages such as HyperCard can be scripted to create realtime animation – by manipulating objects (text, graphics and images) on each card, by playing a set of PICS files or a QuickTime movie, or by scripting cards to display sequentially at speeds over 10 frames per second. Most realtime work is produced in custom animation programmes such as Macromind Director, where 2-d and 3-d sequences can be built up, synchronized with sound, and scripted to operate under the interactive control of the user. However, the realtime animation of photographically realistic images is very demanding on processing power. The processing units employed for military and commercial flight simulators are mainframe or mini-mainframe computers, while lower-resolution model animations for VR require powerful workstations or very fast desktop machines.

High resolution, photographically realistic animated images of real and virtual scenes have demonstrated that the computer can truly become a 'dream machine', a cornucopia capable of entertaining, informing and educating us as no other medium has done before. Just as the photographic camera pictorialized the real world, so the computer pictorializes the world of the imagination and the human intellect.

>> FURTHER READING: DEKEN 1983; GREENBERG ET AL 1982; JANKEL & MORTON 1984

Digital Pictures: 'Carpet Mite' from a Turkish TV commercial. Computer graphics is a dynamically developing science and art. New algorithms continually improve the photographic realism of digital images, including the ability to simulate the 'realism' of electron photomicrographs.

William Latham: Latham's work at the IBM UK Scientific Centre breaks new ground in computer art. The product of a synergy of mathematics, programming and creative talents, Latham 'breeds' his images using artificial genetic algorithms.

Electric Image: 'John's Dragon'. 3-d computer-generated models bring photographic realism and dynamism to creatures of fantasy and fable. The computer is easily the most sophisticated illustration tool available.

Digital Pictures: Opening titles for London Weekend Television's 'Blind Date'. Since the early 1980s, computer graphics have become ubiquitous features of television commercials, news graphics, station idents and programme titles sequences.

Electric Image/Lintas: 'Dubro Doekje'. Computer animation doesn't have to look computer generated. Electric Image creates images that have the aesthetic control of fine illustration.

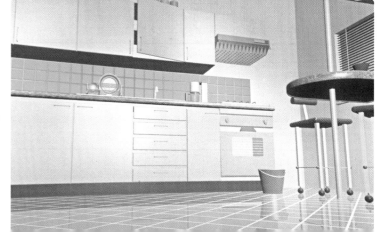

COMPUTER GRAPHICS
the algorithmic image

Three-dimensional computer graphics now play a vital and creative role in a wide range of applications. In industry, computer-aided design is used for product and packaging, and it is increasingly used by architects and interior designers. Computer graphics are now commonly used in scientific research, flight simulation, corporate presentations, advertising and the broadcast entertainment industry. All these applications use either realtime 3-d animation or frame-by-frame photo-realistic graphics, techniques which developed from Ivan Sutherland's work at the Lincoln Laboratory in the 1960s, and later at the University of Utah.

At Lincoln, Sutherland developed his seminal 'Sketchpad', an interactive graphics program running on the first transistor computer, the TX2. Although Sketchpad was constrained to two dimensions (because of the limited processing power of the TX2), Sutherland went on to work with one of his PhD students, Danny Cohen, on the development of 3-d flight simulation software. This first flight simulation program was a 'wireframe' model – ie the shapes delineated by lines or 'vectors' (as opposed to 'solid-modelled' graphics that are 'rendered' with realistic surfaces). Wireframe images can be processed much more quickly than 'solid-modelled' graphics, and in flight simulation, it is essential that images are displayed in realtime (ie responding with no discernible delay to the pilot's joystick and instrumentation). By the 1980s, the software and hardware for flight simulators had developed to the point at which solid-modelled realtime animation was possible. Companies such as Evans and Sutherland in the US and Rediffusion Simulation in the UK now produce flight simulators capable of highly realistic realtime animation. Such techniques are also central to virtual reality – a spin-off from flight simulation technology that promises to provide powerful visualization tools for scientists, as well as hyper-realistic entertainment, sports and 'infotainment' scenarios and simulators.

Photo-realistic 3-d computer graphic images require lengthy processing times, even when using powerful supercomputers. Animations cannot be produced in realtime, but instead are generated frame-by-frame, and then recorded to film or video. These are the computer graphics that can be seen at the movies or on television: beautifully rendered, photographically real images of spinning chromium logotypes, breathtaking animations through Manhattan skyscrapers, or fictional battles in space.

Early solid-modelling involved breaking the surfaces of objects down into polygons, and then devising algorithms that enabled the computer to determine which surfaces were visible from a particular viewpoint. Treating the model as a collection of polygons made 'hidden-surface removal' much easier to compute, but these early models were not very realistic. Various smooth shading techniques were devised (notably by Henry Gouraud and Bui Tong Phong) to improve the look of polygonal surfaces, but the breakthrough in photo-realistic

Electric Image/TVP Norway/Statoil: Gullfaks oil rig. Computer models like this can be used in presentation, training and publicity programmes.

graphics came in 1974, with the invention of bicubic surface patching techniques by Ed Catmull of the University of Utah. Using a process called 'recursive subdivision', Catmull was able to render smooth, realistic surfaces using surface patches as small as a single pixel. Catmull also devised the concept of the 'Z-buffer' to solve the problem of hidden-surface removal, 'alpha-blending' to simulate transparency, and texture mapping – a method by which 2-d images can be 'mapped' onto 3-d objects and surfaces. Catmull went on to form the Computer Graphics Lab at the New York Institute of Technology, and started his own company, Pixar.

Two key developments in photo-realistic 3-d modelling were 'ray-tracing', a technique devised by Turner Whitted, which allows objects with shiny surfaces to reflect other objects in the model, and fractal geometry, which enables subjects such as mountain ranges, lakes and forests to become more detailed and realistic as the virtual 'computer camera' approaches them. The most recent development in photo-realism happened in the mid-1980s. A group working at Cornell University, under the leadership of Don Greenberg, developed a technique called 'radiosity', that modelled the interaction between lighting and the virtual environments created in computer graphics. Using radiosity algorithms, programmers and designers could achieve the subtle lighting effects observable in the real world, such as

direct and ambient light reflected from walls and objects within a room.

With every step taken towards photo-realism, more and more processing power, or longer periods of processing time, are needed. Efforts are being made to integrate ray-tracing and radiosity techniques (both very computation-intensive). To speed up the rendering process, special computer systems ('rendering engines') that use arrays of processors are being developed. These new processing architectures and chips have implications that go far beyond computer-graphics applications. Devices like these could provide the central processing engine for the kind of digital high-definition television (HDTV) systems envisaged by Nicholas Negroponte of MIT and Jim Clark of Silicon Graphics – 'smart' HDTV systems, capable of storing the images, sounds and program codes of linear and interactive programmes in compressed form, then decompressing material as and when required by the eventual user.

>> FURTHER READING: VINCE 1984; FOLEY & VAN DAM 1982; NEWMAN & SPROULL 1979

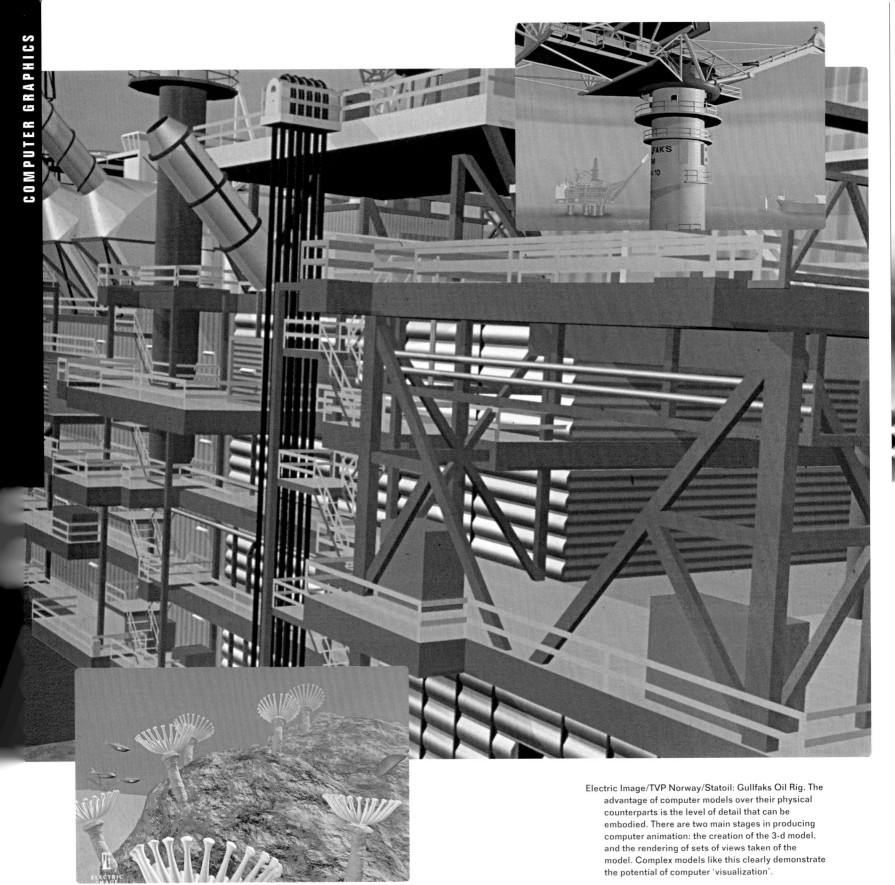

Electric Image/TVP Norway/Statoil: Gullfaks Oil Rig. The advantage of computer models over their physical counterparts is the level of detail that can be embodied. There are two main stages in producing computer animation: the creation of the 3-d model, and the rendering of sets of views taken of the model. Complex models like this clearly demonstrate the potential of computer 'visualization'.

COMPUTER ROTOSCOPING

A technique that involves the computer manipulation and processing of digital film or video images. Computer rotoscoping techniques include automatically **frame grabbing** an image or sequence of images, colouring or recolouring the image, digitally **matt**ing-in or **chromakeying** a different foreground or background image, or retouching the image. A more ambitious use of computer rotoscoping is in the creation of **soft actors**, and the creation of special effects sequences – for example, where live footage of present-day actors is combined with silent movie footage for humorous or dramatic effect. To create virtual performances of this kind, a mix of different **computer graphics** effects are used, including **morph**ing, distortion, 3-d modelling, and **texture mapping**.

> COMPUTER ANIMATION

CONCURRENT AUDIO

The technique of recording separate audio **channels** on to a disc so that the same visual material can be accompanied by a commentary in different languages or expressing a different point of view. In **CD-i**, for example, up to 16 audio channels can be recorded concurrently.

CONDITIONAL BRANCHING

A technique used in computer programming in which the alternative courses of action available to the user are conditional on past performance. Choices may be conditional upon the answer to a test question, or upon more complex conditions, such as the number of **frames** the user has accessed on a particular subject, or the user's success in negotiating a maze or puzzle.

> CONTINUOUS BRANCHING

CONSENSUAL

Describes **hypermedia** programmes and 'information environments' that may be defined or customized by their users. **Cyberpunk** author William Gibson describes his fictional **cyberspace** as a 'consensual hallucination shared by millions'.

> CYBERPUNK

CONSOLE

A control panel or unit for electronic or computer systems; now frequently used as a generic term for **videogame** hardware. Videogame consoles can be hand-held (with a built-in colour or monochrome screen), but more generally the term is applied to hardware designed to be plugged into a television monitor. These consoles include a processor, random-access memory (**RAM**), a slot for games cartridges and control devices for user interaction. Principle videogame console manufacturers include **Nintendo**, **Atari** and **Sega**. The videogame console may provide a better model for the future of home-based consumer multimedia machines than that offered by the predominantly office-based PC.

CONSOLE METAPHOR

The use of a **hardware** 'console' as an **interface** metaphor. Because users are broadly familiar with the kinds of controls available in hardware devices (such as TV sets, **VCRs** and hi-fi equipment), many videogame and **hypermedia** interfaces are designed to give the appearance of these 'hard' controls. Flight simulator software, for example, presents the user with a software replica of the plane's cockpit, complete with **analog** and **digital** dials and readouts, a **joystick** and **head-mounted displays**, etc. In hypermedia development applications, such as video-editing and sequencing **software**, the control panel is modelled on familiar VCR edit-suite controls.

CONTENT PROVIDER

The owner or licensee of the source contents (audio, stills, video, text or data) for a **multimedia** programme.

> ASSETS

CONTINUITY

The smooth **transition** from one shot to another, so that there are no unwanted discrepancies between contiguous sequences. This is very important in film and video production, where scenes may be shot in quite a different sequence to that of the final edit.

CONTINUOUS BRANCHING

A style of **interactive** programme design in which the user can interact at any point within the programme, rather than just at pre-specified nodes or menu frames, or upon occasions that are conditional on previous performance.

> BROWSING   > CONDITIONAL BRANCHING

CONVERGENCE

In stereoscopic viewing, the fusing together of left-eye and right-eye images to create a single, three-dimensional image.

> INTEROCULAR   > STEREOSCOPE
> VIRTUAL REALITY

CONVOLVE

The process of filtering sounds so that they appear to have a specific spatial location in a virtual environment.

> CONVOLVOTRON   > VIRTUAL REALITY

CONVOLVOTRON

A system for the spatial location of up to four different sound sources, developed by Scott Foster and Elizabeth Wenzel for NASA's VIEW **virtual reality** system. Systems such as this add a great depth of realism to the **3-d** visual environment, allowing users walking through a 'virtual' city, for example, to receive the same kind of auditory stimulation that they would experience walking through a real city, ie with both moving and fixed sound sources.

CO-PROCESSOR

A **microprocessor** that operates in conjunction with the main processor (the **CPU**). Co-processors are usually dedicated to specific tasks, such as digital signal processing, graphics handling or video **compression** and decompression. By relieving the CPU of these time-intensive tasks, the computer can work more efficiently.

COPPER CABLE

The main transmission medium for **telecommunications** and cable TV, despite the growing importance of **fibre optics**. There are two main types of copper cable: 'twisted pair' and 'coaxial'. Although both have a limited **bandwidth** compared to fibre-optic cables, new developments in data **compression** and **packet-switching** techniques are considerably improving performance. Two services introduced in 1993, the HDSL (high bit-rate digital subscriber line) and ADSL (asymmetrical digital subscriber line) can transmit large amounts of data over twisted-pair copper. HDSL, for example, can transmit 1.544 megabits per second.

> NETWORK

COPYRIGHT

Laws relating to authorship and intellectual property, designed to give authors some control over the use of their work, and authors and other copyright owners the exclusive right to print, publish and sell their material.

'Information wants to be free', wrote Stewart Brand in The Media Lab. He went on, 'Information also wants to be expensive. Information wants to be free because it has become so cheap to distribute, copy and recombine – too cheap to meter. It wants to be expensive because it can be immeasurably valuable to the recipient. That tension will not go away. It leads to endless wrenching debate about price, copyright, 'intellectual property' and the moral rightness of casual distribution, because each round of new devices makes the tension worse, not better.'

Disc pack from n.n.anonymous, an interactive magazine 'with work from musicians, artists, writers, composers, designers... all anonymous and copyright-free'. Also available on CompuServe and other bulletin board systems.

CYBERPUNK
the low-life,
high-tech
millennium

'Cyberpunk' was originally the name given to the work of a group of science fiction writers who emerged in the 1980s. Specializing in 'low life/hi-tech' subject matter, they were also known as the Movement, the Mirrorshade Group, Radical Hard SF, the Eighties Wave, the Outlaw Technologists, and the Neuromantics. Cyberpunk takes many of its preoccupations and themes from the fusion of two previously distinct realms: the world of high technology and the modern pop underground.

Two themes are constantly probed in cyberpunk writing: the technological invasion of body and mind – prosthetic limbs, implant surgery, genetic alteration, artificial intelligence, neurochemistry – and the dislocation of time and space through the action of electronic global networks and the machinations of multinational corporations. Above all, cyberpunk explores and celebrates the eclectic use and misuse of the products of high technology on 'the Street' – the place where hi-tech meets pop underground – and extrapolates from that into possible futures.

The term is gradually broadening its meaning to describe a lifestyle and an aesthetic sensibility – a sensibility expressed in popular movies such as <u>Blade Runner</u>, <u>Mad Max 2</u>, and <u>Robocop</u>. Elements can also be found in graphic novels, videogame arcades, virtual nightclubs, rave parties and VR theme parks. This eclectic, aesthetic mix of the archaic and primitive with the hi-tech has been a recurrent theme in youth culture, which is rapidly becoming the dominant global culture. As Peter Schwartz reminds us: 'Barring widespread plague or other catastrophe, there will be over two billion teenagers in the world in the year 2001. That's five hundred times the number of teenagers in America in the peak years of the baby boom' (<u>The Art of the Long View</u>, 1991).

Manga Video: 'Akira'. Manga created a new and influential style of cyberpunk animation with 'Akira'. Characters are fully shadowed and set in realistic 3-d environments, while plots are mythic, fast-paced and gripping.

The majority of those teenagers live in Asia or Latin America. For most, the Walkman and the games console are familiar, desirable objects.

Youth culture has consistently celebrated the marriage of technology and lifestyle: from the electric guitar, through the jukebox, the light-show, the ghetto-blaster and the Walkman, to designer drugs, Lycra sportswear, video arcades and hand-held games machines. Cyberpunk takes this theme, and projects a distopian future beyond the year 2000 AD.

But as one of the most influential of the cyberpunk writers, William Gibson, points out, the cyberpunk vision is not merely a futuristic fantasy; it is also about a present that many of us cannot see. As he said in a 1989 interview with The Face magazine: 'I think a lot of the things I wrote about – rebel hackers, cyberspace, virtual reality – were already there in a larval sense. I just came up with a few buzz words.' Gibson would like his work to be read as critical fiction which makes people ask questions about the kind of future they want, but doubts whether this is how it is actually read: 'I was delighted when scientists and corporate technicians started to read

me, but I soon realized that all the critical, pessimistic, left-wing stuff just goes over their heads. They read me and just take bits, all the cute technology, and miss about 15 levels of irony.' While the science fiction of the mid-twentieth century mapped out a multiplicity of possible futures, cyberpunk analyses the 'future' we are actually living through.

First Independent: 'Lawnmower Man' – virtual reality reaches the big screen. The cross-marketing of film and videogame product has been a hallmark of the early 1990s, with videogame rights now an important source of additional income for the movie-makers.

GET INFO: A CYBERPUNK READING LIST

BESTER, ALFRED GOLEM 100. LONDON: PAN BOOKS, 1981.
BLANKENSHIP, LOYD GURPS CYBERPUNK: HIGH-TECH/LOWLIFE
    ROLEPLAYING SOURCEBOOK. STEVE JACKSON GAMES INC., 1990.
GIBSON, WILLIAM NEUROMANCER. LONDON: GRAFTON BOOKS, 1986.
    (FIRST PUBLISHED 1984.)
    COUNT ZERO. LONDON: GRAFTON BOOKS, 1987.
    MONA LISA OVERDRIVE. LONDON: GRAFTON BOOKS, 1988.
    BURNING CHROME. LONDON: GRAFTON BOOKS, 1988.
RUCKER, RUDY SOFTWARE. NEW YORK: AVON BOOKS, 1982.
    WETWARE. LONDON: NEW ENGLISH LIBRARY, 1989.
SHIRLEY, JOHN ECLIPSE. NEW YORK: BLUEJAY, 1985.
    ECLIPSE PENUMBRA. NEW YORK: POPULAR LIBRARY 1987.
    ECLIPSE CORONA. NEW YORK: POPULAR LIBRARY, 1990.
SIMMONS, DAN HYPERION. NEW YORK: DOUBLEDAY, 1989.
STIRLING, BRUCE (ED) MIRRORSHADES: A CYBERPUNK ANTHOLOGY.
    LONDON: PALADIN BOOKS, 1988.
STIRLING, BRUCE ISLANDS IN THE NET. NEW YORK: LEGEND/ARROW
    BOOKS, 1988.
    SCHISMATRIX. NEW YORK: ACE BOOKS, 1985.
STEPHENSON, NEAL SNOW CRASH. NEW YORK: BANTAM BOOKS, 1992
VINGE, VERNOR TRUE NAMES AND OTHER DANGERS. NEW YORK:
    BAEN BOOKS, 1987.
    ACROSS REALTIME. NEW YORK: BAEN BOOKS, 1991.

RELATED SCI-FI

BRUNNER, JOHN THE SHOCKWAVE RIDER. LONDON: METHUEN,1988.
    STAND ON ZANZIBAR. NEW YORK: BALLANTINE, 1969.
    JAGGED ORBIT. NEW YORK: ARROW,1979.
BURROUGHS, WILLIAM S NOVA EXPRESS. NEW YORK: GROVE PRESS, 1964.
    THE SOFT MACHINE. NEW YORK: GROVE PRESS, 1966.
DICK, PHILIP K DO ANDROIDS DREAM OF ELECTRIC SHEEP? LONDON:
    GRAFTON BOOKS, 1968.
    THE SIMULACRA. LONDON: METHUEN,1977.
MOORCOCK, MICHAEL THE JERRY CORNELIUS QUARTET: THE FINAL
    PROGRAMME. LONDON: FONTANA, 1965.
    A CURE FOR CANCER. LONDON: FONTANA, 1968.
    THE ENGLISH ASSASSIN. LONDON: FONTANA, 1972.
    THE CONDITION OF MUZAK. LONDON: FONTANA, 1976.
NIVEN, LARRY RINGWORLD. LONDON: VICTOR GOLLANCZ, 1972.
    THE RINGWORLD ENGINEERS. LONDON: VICTOR GOLLANCZ, 1980.
POHL, FREDERICK BEYOND THE BLUE EVENT HORIZON. LONDON:
    VICTOR GOLLANCZ, 1980.
SHECKLEY, ROBERT MINDSWAP. LONDON: VICTOR GOLLANCZ, 1966.

CYBERSPACE
the new world game

> Cyberspace: a consensual hallucination experienced daily by billions of legitimate operators, in every nation, by children being taught mathematical concepts... A graphic representation of data abstracted from the banks of every computer in the human system. Unthinkable complexity. Lines of light ranged in the nonspace of the mind, clusters and constellations of data. Like city lights, receding.
>
> WILLIAM GIBSON, <u>NEUROMANCER</u>, 1984

Park Place Productions: '3-d Adventures' for 3DO, an interactive movie that lets the viewer assume the role of a movie-style action hero. The viewer controls his or her own actions and ultimately determines the plot outcome. Using full-motion video, 3-d graphics and digital audio, '3-d Adventures' also features this 'world-game'-like globe.

This is cyberspace in the futuristic fiction of William Gibson. But as Gibson has pointed out, his cyberpunk novels are concerned with the very real changes in communications infrastructure that are happening right now.

Cyberspace is the virtual space of computer memory and networks, telecommunications and digital media. In the words of John Barlow, journalist and 'Grateful Dead' lyricist: 'Cyberspace is where your money is.' It is an emerging environment created, on the one hand, by the global network of telephone, satellite communications, and computer networks, interactive cable TV and ISDN, and on the other by the internal quantum space of the microchip, and electromagnetic and digital-optical storage technologies.

The foundations of the cyberspace infrastructure were established as long ago as the 1830s with the development of the electric telegraph, a network that carried its own binary information in the form of the dots and dashes of Morse code signals. Telegraph networks rapidly expanded and coalesced to form an international communications web, spanning the English Channel in 1851, and the Atlantic Ocean in 1870. This proto-cyberspace was enormously expanded after the invention of the telephone and 'wireless telegraphy' (the 'rear-view mirror' label for 'radio'). From the 1920s, radio waves were also being used to broadcast the human voice and music, and by the 1930s both radio and

cables were carrying television signals.

The most recent developments in cyberspace stem from the linking of computers to the telephone system. Originally, these links provided scientists with better access to software and databases through terminals at remote sites. However, computer networks soon developed autonomous lives, acting as conduits for electronic mail, bulletin board systems and a great variety of conferencing, information and messaging services. From the 1960s onwards, with the computerization of financial services (banking and stock trading), the world's money became bits of digital data inhabiting the cyberspace of networks and computer memory.

With the ongoing development of fibre-optic networks, the establishment of high-bandwidth data superhighways, and the development of inter-personal communications based on personal digital systems, radio cell-nets and satellite communications, cyberspace will become the place where we spend an increasing amount of our business and leisure time. Cyberspace is set to become the 'electronic extension of our central

nervous system' that Marshall McLuhan wrote about (in <u>War</u> <u>and</u> <u>Peace</u> <u>in</u> <u>the</u> <u>Global</u> <u>Village</u>) some 30 years ago, the interconnecting web of telecommunications that he predicted would inevitably break down barriers of distance, language and time, creating a new and instantaneous 'global village'.

Cyberspace could become a global village in more than the McLuhan sense, however. Timothy Leary has claimed that cyberspace will be the virtual real estate of the twenty-first century, an 'electronic frontier' which will accommodate virtual townships and cities, as well as telecottages and the millions of individual 'telematic nomads' that will be an increasing feature of the next decades. Inhabitants of the electronic frontier would of course have a new range of problems to deal with: problems such as personal privacy, and the security of personal data records. Problems of copyright protection in an era when copying is as easy as a single keyboard command, and problems such as computer crime, digital pornography, and data sabotage and espionage. And the problems of the power that

will be increasingly wielded by the State and the large corporations controlling the media and telecommunications infrastructures.

Optimistically, cyberspace technologies could also create an environment where the kind of 'World Game' envisaged by Richard Buckminster Fuller could be played. Fuller's original idea involved creating a vast computer simulation of the planet's resources, which would be used to establish the best way of making the world work. A cyberspace World Game would take this to its ultimate extreme: an electronic repository of the planet's physical and information resources, it would enable us to simulate global problems, and harness the capabilities of the entire human race in the course of searching for their solution.

The idea of a globally-distributed cyberspace World Game, accessible to all through personal computers and home multimedia players linked together by fibre-optic cables, may seem absurdly futuristic. But with world experts in every conceivable subject on tap for information, with realtime satellite pictures providing the visual datum for resources and weather, with supercomputers to process the enormous datastream and advanced computer graphics to visualize competing strategies, all the components for world gaming are available now. Such a system would have immediate practical applications – not only in education, but in the monitoring and management of draught, famine, disease and pollution; in shepherding threatened species and in assessing longer-term problems such as population growth, sea-level changes and ozone depletion. Cyberspace could thus become the ideal forum for the 'global village', providing the means by which many millions of people could participate in shared experience and activities.

>> FURTHER READING: BENEDICT 1992; FULLER 1971; GIBSON 1986; LEARY 1990; MCLUHAN 1968

Panther Science Fiction

WILLIAM GIBSON
NEUROMANCER

WINNER OF THE HUGO AWARD, THE NEBULA AWARD AND THE PHILIP K. DICK MEMORIAL AWARD

William Gibson: Neuromancer – cyberspace is defined.

Mark Bowey and Bob Cotton: frames from 'Digital Dracula'. Cyberspace is embodied in metaphor – the 3-d constructs of CAD mix with the hyperlinks and narrative branching of interactive multimedia. The 'Digital Dracula' prototype combines an animated graphic treatment of Bram Stoker's classic, surrogate travel sequences, text and voice-over, and a multimedia glossary of cross-references.

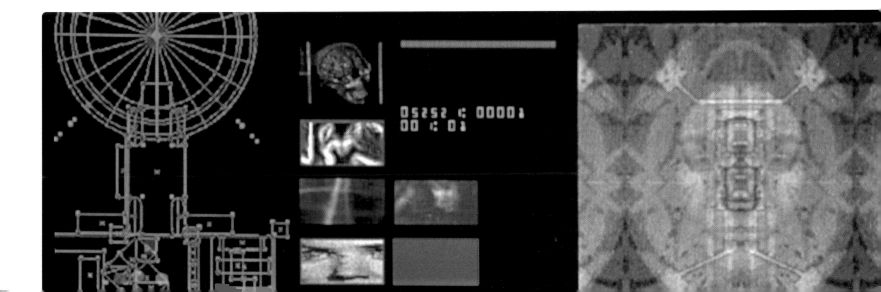

The emergence of **digital** media (which makes both copying and the modification of existing material extremely easy) and of electronic **networks**, makes the distribution of information virtually cost-free. This situation raises crucial issues about the legal protection of the rights of the owners of intellectual property, and the rights of users of information. On the one hand, the investment of time, knowledge and creativity in a design, a book, an applications program or any other information product should clearly be rewarded. On the other hand, digital media provide the means for easy use and reuse of data, information and programs, encouraging a new generation of information users to quote from, reconfigure and elaborate upon published work. Current legislation fails adequately to address this dilemma because its roots rest in the old media, such as print, and give considerably more weight to the rights of the owners of intellectual property than to the users of their creative works. As a result, the law is increasingly ignored, to the eventual cost of property holders. This problem will continue to worsen as informal networks of exchange grow and flourish.

> PUBLIC DOMAIN SOFTWARE   > SHAREWARE

COURSEWARE

Originally used to describe **software** containing learning materials for computer-assisted learning (**CAL**) or computer-based training systems. Now more generally used to describe the many materials (software, **audiovisual** aids, **multimedia** programmes, books, manuals etc) that have been originated, collected together and structured to form part of an educational or training package.

CPU [CENTRAL PROCESSING UNIT]

The part of a computer system that controls and coordinates its operations and performs the arithmetic and logical processes applied to data.

> MICROPROCESSOR

CROSS-FADE

> DISSOLVE

CROSS-TALK

An electromagnetic phenomenon that occurs when signals from one channel interfere with signals in another channel that is physically close to it.

> NOISE

CRT [CATHODE-RAY TUBE]

The standard technology used in computer **monitors** and television sets, comprising a glass vacuum tube with an electron gun at one end (the cathode), and a **screen** (the anode) at the other. The inside surface of the screen is coated with phosphor. A concentrated beam of electrons is emitted by the electron gun and accelerated by a high voltage towards the screen. The electron beam is modulated and focused by an electrostatic or magnetic field, so that the electrons are made to strike the phosphor and cause it to glow. The brightness of the screen depends on the density of the electron beam, which is made to scan the entire screen in a series of horizontal lines from top to bottom. In video monitors, the electron beam makes two passes over the screen, creating two 'fields' (one of which contains all the evenly numbered scanlines, the other all the odd-numbered lines), that are 'interlaced' to create a video 'frame'. In the **PAL** system the creation of a two-field frame takes 1/25 of a second, in **NTSC** 1/30 of a second. Aided by the human eye's **persistence of vision**, and the fact that the phosphors glow briefly as they are hit by the electron beam, this process creates the illusion of seeing complete images.

CUECON

A form of **icon** that prompts the user to further exploratory action. The notion of cuecons grew out of the desire to call users' attention to specifics on a graphically dense screen, where it was necessary to demarcate areas that were 'hot' and active (ie **button** areas), without necessarily producing a standard or even recognizable iconic 'button'. It is possible to devise cuecons that are context-sensitive, inferring from the user's previous actions which kind of information he or she might prefer, and highlighting those particular items on the screen. Such cuecons could also interlink, guiding the user through an extensive **database**. In this scenario, other button areas would remain hidden unless the user passed the **mouse** pointer over them, thus providing a free choice of manoeuvre for the user while at the same time encouraging him or her to take a particular route through the information base.

> INTERFACE

CURSOR

In computer interface and **multimedia** systems, the symbol that represents the screen position of the pointing device (ie the **mouse**, **joystick**, **digitpad**, **infrared controller** etc).

Cursor icons: text insert, paint bucket, pencil.

CURSOR PLANE

In **CD-i**, a small graphics **image plane** that is moved by the pointing device and can be positioned over other image planes. The cursor plane is 16x16 **pixels**, single colour, and can be made transparent.

> CD-I

CUT

In film- and video-making, an abrupt change of scene from one shot to the next. In **windows**-based interfaces, a menu command that removes the selected text or graphics to the **clipboard**.

> TRANSITION

CUT AND PASTE

A feature of some computer **software** applications that allows the user to specify a section of data (eg a paragraph in a word-processing application) and remove it ('cut') then reposition it elsewhere ('paste') within the document.

CUTTING COPY

In film-making, the name given to the print that is used for editing.

CYBERNETICS

Term coined by Norbert Wiener to describe the science of control and communications in animals and machines. The word is derived from the Greek kubernétés ('steersman'). Cybernetics is concerned with the study of any system – it is sometimes referred to as systems theory – not simply computer systems. While as science it has yielded a wide range of insights, its major practical impact has been in engineering and in the design of large, complex computer systems. In popular usage, the prefix 'cyber' has tended to be used very loosely to mean something related to computers.

> CYBERSPACE
>> FURTHER READING: WIENER 1948

CYBERPUNK

A genre of science fiction that emerged during the 1980s. Characterized by 'low-life, high-tech' subject matter, the cyberpunk ethos was crystallized in William Gibson's trilogy Neuromancer, Count Zero and Mona Lisa Overdrive. The cyberpunk 'movement' (also known as the Eighties Wave, the Mirrorshades Group, the Outlaw Technologists, Radical Hard SF and the Neuromantics) has many literary precedents and a wide range of current practitioners. Also related to the wave of post-apocalyptic movies such as Blade Runner and Mad Max the term 'cyberpunk' is increasingly being used to characterize a lifestyle and aesthetic sensibility associated with the new pop underground.

> • CYBERPUNK PAGE 52

CYBERSPACE

Term coined by William Gibson referring to the interconnected web of **databases**, telecommunication links and computer **networks** which perceptually seem to constitute a new space for human communication and action.

> • CYBERSPACE PAGE 54

CYBORG

A human that is part-machine. The expression was coined in 1960 by research scientist Manfred Clynes to describe the implications of advances in biomedical engineering, such as prosthetic limbs, heart pacemakers, drug-dispensing implants and synthetic body and organ implants. The exploration of the notion of the man-machine has been a theme of **cyberpunk** novels over the last ten years or so, and has its origin in myth and in the stories of Mary Shelley, Karel Capek and, more recently, Isaac Asimov and Philip K Dick.

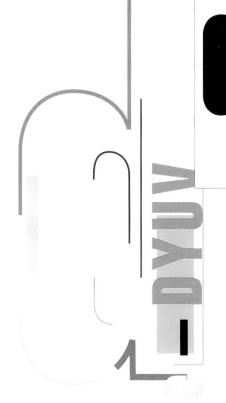

D1 VIDEOTAPE
19mm **digital** videotape format used for professional **broadcast-quality** video production.
> VIDEO FORMATS

DAB [DIGITAL AUDIO BROADCASTING]
A **broadcasting** system intended to provide high-quality **digital** stereo of near-**CD** quality across the airwaves. Because of the demand for available radio frequency space, European Community Eureka-funded DAB researchers are developing several **compression** systems to allow the broadcasting of digital music within a narrow **bandwidth**. In 1990 two compression systems, Musicam and Aspec, were being developed for DAB. Both split the **analog audio** signal into frequency bands, and in each band only audible sounds are digitized. The bandwidth saved by not having to convert inaudible sounds can be transferred to other bands with a high audio content, enabling the transmission of a wide dynamic range. Aspec and Musicam use similar methods to compress the data stream, but differ in their use of techniques to analyse and digitize the original audio signal.

The combination of a digital-audio radio with a digital compact cassette (**DCC**), digital audio tape (**DAT**) or **mini-disc** recording system, would make it possible to record CD-quality music off-air. The establishment of DAB would open the way for a truly mobile pocket record store service: radio/recorders with a built-in **LCD** screen, **alphanumeric** keypad, and some cell-networking capability would allow users to select from the entire range of music and electronically order their tracks directly from a central databank service, paying by credit card. The only reason to visit high street record stores would be for the social interaction, and to look at the sleeve covers.
> CDDA   > DIGITAL AUDIO

DAC [DIGITAL TO ANALOGUE CONVERTER]
A device which converts digital signals to analog values.
> DIGITAL SIGNAL PROCESSOR

DARK FIBRE
Popular term for a fibre-optic network provided by a telecommunications company, in which the users of the network provide the services. (As opposed to 'lit fibre', where the telecommunications companies also supply the network services.)
> DATA SUPERHIGHWAY   > FIBRE OPTICS

DARPA [DEFENSE ADVANCED RESEARCH PROJECTS AGENCY]
> ARPA

DAT [DIGITAL AUDIO TAPE]
An internationally agreed standard for **digital** audio tape recording. Tapes can record up to two hours of

continuous **CD**-quality digital sound with CIRC error correction, offering options of 32 kHz, 44.1 kHz and 48 kHz sampling. DAT is now the standard format for the digital audio components of **interactive multimedia** programmes.
> DAB   > DCC

DATA ACQUISITION
In **multimedia**, the digitization of original (**analog**) text, images and sounds. Data acquisition can involve several different **peripheral** systems, such as **OCR scanner**s for text; **flatbed scanner**s or **frame grabber**s for images; and **DAT**, **MIDI** or other audio input/recording techniques for sounds. Motion sequences on film can be **telecine**d to video and grabbed (digitized), processed and **compressed** as partial-motion or **full-motion video**.

DATA DISCMAN
Portable, hand-held **CD-ROM** reader launched by **Sony** in 1990. Some models have built-in **LCD** screens (for reading **electronic books**); others just have a port for connecting to a computer and monitor. The original DD1 model includes a drive for an 80mm (3¼-inch) diameter CD-ROM (housed in a rigid plastic casing, like a large **floppy disk**) that can store 200 megabytes of data (equivalent to 100,000 pages of A4 text), and a 3½-inch LCD screen. The screen is configured to display 10 lines of 30 characters in monochrome only. By 1992, Data Discman had been launched in Japan, the US and the UK, and a variety of electronic books were available, including encyclopedias, the official <u>Scrabble</u> book and a guide to Europe's golf courses. Sony also markets the Electronic Book Authoring System (**SEBAS**), an authoring package for electronic publishers that produce or are interested in material for this system.

Sony: Data Discman, a portable electronic book player.

DATA-DRIVEN ACTION TAGGING

In **CD-i**, the process by which events on the different data streams (video/audio/text etc) are identified ('tagged') in order that they can be synchronized by the application program.

DATA HIGHWAY

> DATA SUPERHIGHWAY

DATA INTEGRITY

The protection or preservation of data against theft, corruption or loss.

DATA PREPARATION

The conversion and formatting of **digital** images, sound and video for a particular **interactive multimedia** system. Programme contents may be produced in native file formats on a wide range of computer graphic, digital audio and digital video equipment. They must therefore be converted to **file formats** suitable for **CD-i**, **DVI** etc during programme production.

DATA SUPERHIGHWAY

A national and international high-**bandwidth** communication **network**. Various proposals for such networks exist, and advocates argue that Data Superhighways will play the same role in economic development that canals, railways and roads have done in the past.

> • DATA SUPERHIGHWAYS THIS PAGE

DATABASE

A structured collection of data: information that has been organized in such a form that it is retrievable through a computer system. Many **hypermedia** programmes (such as encyclopedias and illustrated dictionaries) use sophisticated database techniques to store the information content. **Interactive multimedia** techniques can be used to make database access extremely 'user-friendly'.

> DATABASE MANAGEMENT SYSTEM

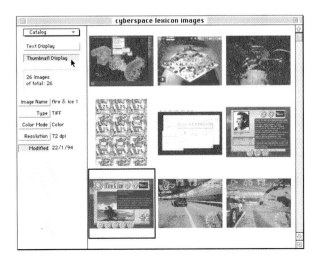

DATA SUPERHIGHWAYS
roads to the future

Society is on the verge of an information revolution. It is a revolution that will transform global society in the same way that the first industrial revolution transformed the West, and in the same way that automation and electronics transformed the economic status of the Pacific Basin. As information moves towards becoming the key commodity of the twenty-first century, the technologies used to store, process and disseminate information are becoming increasingly important. New industries are being created through the synergy of digital media, digital telecommunications and computers. And in the same way that new industries grew up around the network of canals and railways in the eighteenth and nineteenth centuries, these new digital industries look set to flourish around the infrastructure of communications networks based on fibre-optic cables. In the USA, this concept of infrastructure has been dubbed the 'Data Superhighway'.

The idea of a high-speed, high-bandwidth computer network spanning the United States, linking every citizen's home to the nation's centres of learning and archives of information, has recently graduated from being a Utopian fantasy to becoming a realizable, and potentially highly profitable, national objective.

The American computer pioneer Vannevar Bush was probably the first person to guess the potential of an information network that would link centres of research and learning. As early as 1945 he speculated on the possibility of a television network that would link his 'Memex' machines, allowing scientists and researchers to share information as text, pictures and drawings. Later, in the 1960s, Ted Nelson expanded this idea into a general, global system for information sharing. Nelson called his scheme 'Xanadu', and imagined a networked hypermedia system linking drive-in Xanadu stands – electronic founts of knowledge as accessible as McDonalds' burger bars.

By the 1980s, these visionary ideas had gained technologically respectable mass; they began to snowball when (the then Senator) Al Gore promoted the High Performance Computing Act, to facilitate the creation of a high-speed network based on fibre optics. Gore explained his vision in the September 1991 special issue of <u>Scientific American</u>, in which he argued that just as the transportation infrastructure had once determined a nation's economic success, so will the communications infrastructure determine success in the twenty-first century. Gore has successfully campaigned for federal funding to ensure direction and coordination in the laying down of this 'infostructure'.

The driving vision is of a networked society in which everyone would have access to libraries of digital books, museums of multimedia information, degrees and diplomas from universities of distance learning, and schools where tele-homework would be as common (and as enjoyable) a pastime for children as videogames are today. The data superhighway would be capable of squirting the 5 gigabytes required digitally to store an average movie down a fibre-optic cable and into the memory of a 'smart' HDTV set in around five seconds. In fact, an entire evening's entertainment and infotainment could be pre-selected from a menu of movies, general news, customized news, documentaries, plays, soaps etc, and downloaded in just 30 seconds.

These programmes could then be browsed through and viewed at will. Some of the documentary and news material might be interactive, offering access to further levels of information in the form of text, commentary and pictures. Other forms of entertainment could be just as easily available, with the network home shopping service (open 24 hours a day) allowing you to sample the latest releases, place your order by credit card, and five seconds later have the latest videogame or CD-quality music stored on your hard disk or digital audio tape.

The establishment of data superhighways, like the motorway networks and rail networks before them, would have a profound effect on our lifestyle. Just as transport networks gave us the suburb and the commuter, so data networks will give us the 'telecottage' and the 'telecommuter'. The concept of teleworking has many advantages: individuals may plan their own work day, for instance, using the hours of commuting time they have saved to stagger their work load throughout the day. An increased use of videophones and video conferencing facilities would also save further hours of travel time.

The combination of commercial and strategic pressures means that the data superhighway will not be confined to the US alone. Similar initiatives in both Europe and the Pacific Rim promise to bring super-computing power to large areas of the industrialized world by the first decade of the new century. The data superhighway network could eventually span the globe, spurring a third revolution of cyberspace technologies.

The data superhighway network looks likely to have as powerful an impact on national and international economies as the race to put man on the moon did in the 1960s. After all, the personal computer was a spin-off from President Kennedy's commitment to the R&D necessary for the Apollo Mission. What effects the Clinton/Gore administration's commitment to the infrastructure of data superhighways will have, we can only guess. However, Bill Clinton has already been dubbed 'The electronic Roosevelt' by John Sculley (the then CEO of Apple Computers), so perhaps the Data Superhighways will herald a 'digital new deal' for the twenty-first century.

Cumulus is a picture database manager designed for the administration of picture archives. It stores catalogues of records in which images are represented as thumbnails, with references to their stored location.

DATAGLOVES AND POWERGLOVES
hands on in cyberspace

Developed in the 1980s, the DataGlove presented a breakthrough in human-computer interface. Why breakthrough? Look at what people do when they are talking to each other: they use their hands. Gesture is a component of natural language, codified now for all those who 'speak' one of the sign languages for the deaf. And because of the DataGlove and similar devices, a new gestural language is emerging for use in cyberspace.

In fact, Thomas Zimmerman was thinking about another kind of gesture when he conceived the DataGlove. His idea was to invent a virtual guitar – some way of making sound emerge from the imitative strumming action that many of us make when we listen to rock music guitar solos. We're still waiting for that gizmo, but the DataGlove has much broader applications, in that it lets us talk more naturally to computers. The ideal interface between humans and computers would be spoken language, supplemented (as in real life) by gesture, facial expression, eyeball contact and so forth. The DataGlove is one more step towards that ideal.

The DataGlove, and similar position sensors such as Mattel's Powerglove, are important because they allow people literally to 'handle' intangible computer data. Virtual reality systems, coupled with the all-important sensor glove, imbue data with apparent form and mass. The sensor glove enables the position of the user's hand and fingers to provide a constant stream of input data for the VR system. This data is used to provide the coordinate information for the position of a computer model of the glove in cyberspace. As the user flexes his or her fingers, the computer model echoes the user's actions, flexing in response. In this way, virtual objects can be grasped and moved in computer space. Using techniques such as 'force feedback', these objects can be given apparent mass, and can be made subject to friction and inertia.

Sensor gloves, coupled with the appropriate VR software, represent a major phase shift in human computer interface design. For the hybrid multimedia and virtual reality entertainment and information software of the twenty-first century, the DataGlove and its offspring, the Powerglove, provide the means to usurp the ubiquitous mouse, and allow the user to 'pass through' the screen and into cyberspace itself.

The notion of 'directly' manipulating computer data in a virtual space – reaching out and 'grabbing' data that appears to have shape and weight – is quite revolutionary. It creates the possibility of simulators for manually critical tasks (such as surgery); for surrogate travel, entertainment and games; for science visualization and research; and for new kinds of computer programming. Further to this, such systems could be used to control remote robotic systems – in space, on the seabed, or deep underground.

The DataGlove provides us with a tool for the magical ability to act at a distance, to enter realms of the

imagination and to explore virtual environments that span the microcosm and macrocosm. Gloves are already used as interfaces with videogames that allow you to spar with boxers and karate experts, and they offer a much more natural alternative to the ubiquitous infrared controllers for consumer VCRs and multimedia products such as 3DO and CD-i. The development of other articles of 'data clothing' also has an obvious application as a central component in remote control systems for the disabled. It could be that DataGloves are too unaesthetic, too clumsy for mass appeal; but what VPL and Mattel have done is prove that physical gesture and action will play a central role in our interaction with the new cyberspace media.

Virtual Technologies: CyberGlove, a lightweight and flexible second-generation interface glove. It contains 22 sensors for monitoring hand and finger movement and position. The CyberGlove is available with several software features, including GestureGlove, which uses neural network technology to recognize gestures (for example by converting finger-sign language to synthesized speech) and CyberForce, which provides programmable grip-force feedback to the user.

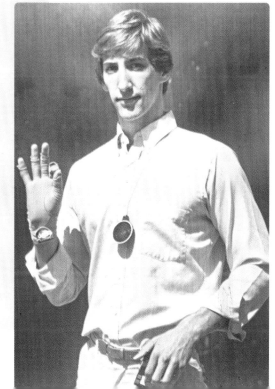

Full-body optical tracking suit from the MIT Media Lab.

DATABASE MANAGEMENT SYSTEM

A set of interrelated **program**s for the **input**, retrieval, formatting, modification, **output**, transfer and maintenance of information in a **database**.
> BOOLEAN OPERATORS > HYPERTEXT
> KNOWLEDGE-BASED SYSTEM

DATACOM

Colloquial term referring to a telecommunications channel dedicated (or partly dedicated) to data transfer, such as **ISDN**.

DATAGLOVE

A data input device developed by Thomas Zimmerman and Jaron Lanier of VPL Industries, designed to translate the movements of the hand and fingers into code that is readable by a computer. The DataGlove has absolute position sensors attached to it, and is lined with **fibre-optic** cables that run along the glove fingers. These transmit light from an electronic light source at one end of the cable, which is read by an electronic photosensor at the other end. When the hand is flexed, light is released from precisely calibrated incisions at each knuckle. The amount of light released corresponds to the degree that the finger is crooked. The DataGlove and similar products such as Mattel's **PowerGlove** open up the possibility of a whole new range of **gestural interface**s for **interactive multimedia** and **virtual reality** products.
> DATASUIT > NATURAL LANGUAGE
> • DATAGLOVES AND POWERGLOVES PAGE 59

DATASUIT

A full-body version of the **DataGlove** introduced in 1987 by VPL Industries. Similar optical-tracking suit techniques have been developed at the **Media Lab**, while techniques for 'whole body' interaction are also being developed by Myron Krueger's Artificial Reality Corporation and the Advanced Telecommunications Research Institute in Japan. VPL's DataSuit resembles a diver's wet-suit and incorporates a network of **sensor**s that monitor around 50 body movements, enabling a wide range of gestural interaction.
> VIRTUAL REALITY > VIRTUAL SEX

DCC [DIGITAL COMPACT CASSETTE]

A digital audio tape (**DAT**) cassette system developed by Philips and launched in 1992. DCC is the same size as the **analog audio** compact cassette introduced by Philips in the 1960s, and DCC tape decks also have a pair of conventional (analog) stereo heads for recording and playback of compact cassettes, making the system 'backwardly compatible'. DCC uses a new coding technique called precision adaptive sub-band coding (PASC) originally developed for broadcasting digital stereo over radio channels. PASC is an efficient coding system, which reduces the number of bits per second required for **CD**-quality digital stereo by using fewer bits to encode the signals that would normally be inaudible to the human ear.
> DIGITAL AUDIO > MINI DISC

DCC600 Player from Philips, a recordable digital tape drive, backwardly compatible with the analog compact cassette.

DEBUGGING

The process of identifying and correcting errors in a computer **program**.
> VALIDATION

DECISION POINT

A part of an interactive programme where the user must make a choice between two or more options.
> MENU > NODE
> SEGUE

DEDICATED

Describes **hardware** or **software** that can only perform a particular function or task. For example, a 'dedicated' word processor is a computer that can only be used for word processing, as opposed to a general purpose computer, which may be used for word processing as well as a variety of other tasks.

DEFAULT

In computer systems, the state that the system will assume in the absence of any action by the user. Many programs allow the user to set the defaults; thus, for example, a page makeup application may be set to default to a certain user-specified typeface, size and style.

DEFAULT MODE

In **interactive multimedia** programmes, the term 'default mode' is used generally to describe that part of the programme that is enabled if the user does nothing. For example, a **point-of-information** system may default to a looped sequence which advertises the system's features, while inviting users to interact by

prompting them to use the **mouse**, keypad, touchscreen or other **input** device.
> AUTOPLAY

DELAY
In **digital audio** recording systems, an effect that slows the incoming audio signal to create reverberation or echoes.

DELIVERY SYSTEM
In **multimedia**, the computer system through which the programme reaches the end user, as opposed to the development platform. Until the arrival of **DVI** and **CD-i**, the most cost-effective method of delivering full-motion interactive programmes was **interactive video** (IV). The delivery system for IV includes a **personal computer**, **laserdisc** player and some form of **input** device. **DVI** delivery systems include a large **hard disk** or CD-ROM drive attached to a PC with additional DVI chipsets or expansion boards, again with a suitable input device. Integrated computer/CD drives such as CD-i and **3DO**'s Interactive Multiplayer are the cheapest delivery systems, since they are mass-produced for a global consumer market, are networkable and use readily available output devices such as domestic television sets and hi-fi systems. Other delivery systems include specialized **touch-sensitive screen** or coin-op consoles for **point-of-information** or entertainment purposes; touchscreen window displays; personal computer/CD-ROM systems; and portable and hand-held multimedia systems such as Sony's **Electronic Book** format (**Data Discman**).

DELTA MODULATION
A differential form of **pulse-code modulation**, used in data communications. Delta modulation uses only one bit for each sample.
> ADPCM

DELTA YUV [DYUV]
In **CD-i**, an efficient image-coding system for 'natural' (photographic quality) images. DYUV encodes only the differences between adjacent YU and YV **pixel** values along each line of the display.
> YUV   > YUV ENCODING

DESIGN STAGE
In **interactive multimedia**, the phase in pre-production when the programme is defined and specified. The design stage will normally include the working-up of an outline or 'overview' of the programme from the original concept or motivating idea; the preparation of detailed **flowcharts** and **storyboards**; the specification of a **graphical user interface** (including indications of the style of **icons** and screen typography, and graphic styling); the production of a prototype or programme sample, and the production of a complete specification of the finished programme: the 'design document', ready for scheduling, budgeting and other essential pre-production planning.
> AUTHORING SYSTEM

DIGITAL AND ANALOG MEDIA
quantizing media

Information can be stored, processed and communicated in two forms: digital and analog. For most of this century the familiar form has been analog. Print, photography, radio, recorded music, film, television and video were all analog media. An analog medium, as the name suggests, is one that is like its source. For example, the grooves on a gramophone record are similar in form to the sound waves that they reproduce.

Analog media are continuous, and because of this subject to 'noise'. (Think of the scratches, pops and hisses of the gramophone record.) They are also imprecise in an important way: they are to do with quantity as opposed to number. Imagine a bowl full of eggs. Most of us would have little difficulty in counting the number of eggs, but asked to rank those same eggs in terms of size or weight would be a more difficult task because we would be dealing with quantity.

Analog systems are always dealing with more or less, higher or lower, heavier or lighter, thicker or thinner, and so on. There are no discontinuous jumps in analog coding, just different points on a curve. In contrast, digital media are discontinuous, and their form is unlike the signal they are reproducing. Digital processing reduces everything to patterns or ons and offs, or yes or no, or zeros and ones. For example, in digital audio recording, the analog signal is sampled at over 44,000 times per second, and each of these 44,000 values is stored as a discrete unit of digital code. There are none of the continuous in-betweens of an analog system.

This has some very important consequences. It virtually eliminates the problem of noise. It effectively removes the problem of the degradation of information content when copying. In principle, in a digital system a copy of a copy should be exactly the same as the original master, whereas in an analog system the further from the master, the greater the information loss. (In digital video editing, for example, there is none of the gradual deterioration or 'generation loss' associated with analog video.) And, perhaps most importantly, reducing any medium to the same computer code – whether image, sound, text or video – makes possible the new interactive medium of hypermedia.

In the 1990s, all the familiar media mentioned above have either gone digital, or are in the process of going digital. The fact is that all the information resources of the planet can now be encoded in digital form. This opens up the possibility of computer-mediated education, entertainment and information services carried around the world by digital broadcasting and by digital telecommunications networks.

One of the ironies of the digital revolution is that as more and more media go digital, the means by which people interface with these media are becoming increasingly analogic in form. The desktop metaphor, the rooms metaphor, digital gloves and body suits, the increasing sensory mix of how we interact with digital systems: all are movements towards a powerful user illusion based on an analogy with a familiar world of objects located in space. Cyberspace is digital, but the way we interface with the digital computer systems that mediate our use of cyberspace still depends on analogy.

>> FURTHER READING: BATESON 1979

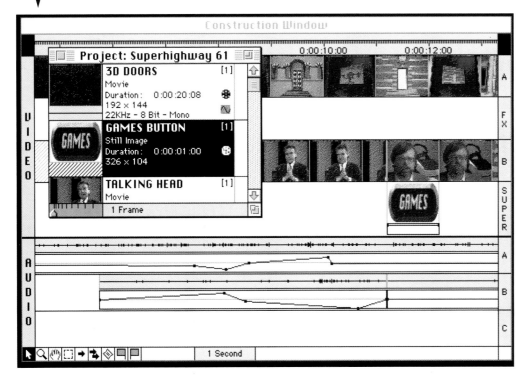

Adobe Premiere: digital video editor, one of the key software components of desktop video. Premiere offers full video editing, soundtrack dubbing, graphics and titles, and digital transition effects.

DESKTOP PUBLISHING
> DTP

DESKTOP VIDEO [DTV]
A desktop computer system with the ability to process and edit video. DTV systems may include video inputs from tape or disc; a digitizing board; **hard-disk** storage; **image processing** and graphics software; editing and 'sequencing' software; soft controls for remote video tape recorders (**VTRs**); and a device for output to VTR.
> VIDEO GRAPHICS

DEVICE DRIVER
Software that enables a host computer to communicate with an external device, such as a **laserdisc** player or **CD-ROM** drive.

DIALOGUE BOX
In a **multimedia** system or **windows**-based computer **interface**, a small box or window that asks the user to choose from a number of options, or to verify an action they have taken.
> ALERT BOX

DIFFERENTIAL PCM
A version of **pulse-code modulation** (PCM) which encodes the difference in value between a sample and the preceding sample. Differential PCM thus uses fewer **bits** than standard PCM.
> ADPCM

DIGITAL
Describes the use of discrete signals to represent data. Digital telecommunications and computer systems use binary digits (0 and 1) which are grouped together to represent numbers or alphabetical characters. The advantage of digital signals over their **analog** ancestors is that it is much easier to ensure a clean interference-free signal using digital encoding. Digital signals can also be compressed for efficient storage and rapid transfer via **copper cable**, fibre-optics (**FDDI**) or radio.

The media revolution of the final decade of the twentieth century is a direct result of the digitalization of media. For the first time, all of the principal elements of media – graphics, text, music, video, animation, photographs and so forth – were available in digital form, ie they could all be stored on optical **discs** (such as **CD-ROM**) or electromagnetic (**hard** and **floppy**) **disks**, and processed by a 'multimedia' computer. The **random-access** nature of computer and disc memory, already explored in software such as **computer graphics** and **hypertext**, opened up the possibility of highly interactive control by the user. In broadcasting and telecommunications, developments for digital **HDTV** and broadband integrated services data networks (**B-ISDN**) were already well advanced by the early 1990s.
> COMPRESSION > TELECOMMUNICATIONS
> • DIGITAL AND ANALOG MEDIA PAGE 61

DIGITAL AUDIO
The representation of sound by means of discrete signals. **Analog audio** signals are sampled at a rate at least double the highest frequency to be reproduced. Sampling rates of 44.1 kHz are used in **CDDA** (with 16 bits per sample), while the CD-i designer is able to choose from four digital audio levels, ranging from level C (sampled at 8.5 kHz and using 4 bits/sample); level B (37.8 kHz, 4 bits/sample), level A (37.8 kHz, 8 bits/sample) to full stereo CD Audio.
> DCC > MIDI
> MINI DISC

DIGITAL AUDIO TAPE
> DAT

DIGITAL COMPACT CASSETTE
> DCC

DIGITAL DICTIONARY
Dictionary stored in **digital** form, most commonly on **CD-ROM**. By storing the contents of a dictionary in this form, and providing powerful **software** for searching, locating and retrieving information, digital dictionaries offer many 'value-added' functions compared with their printed ancestors. **Multimedia** dictionaries not only provide the user with **random-access**, search and **browsing** facilities, but can supplement the text content with illustrations, photographs, spoken pronunciation (with regional accents), sound effects, music, animations, video clips and simulations.
In the mid-1980s, Philips produced a demonstration digital dictionary on **CD-i**, which supplemented text definitions with pictures and spoken 'pronunciation'

Digital dictionary: the OED on CD-ROM.

samples. Most current applications, however, are text-only, such as the Oxford English Dictionary (OED) on **CD-ROM**. First published in 1988, the digital OED combines the contents of the entire 16-volume dictionary (which includes over 450,000 entries and sub-entries) with many illustrational quotations. This information is organized as a structured **database**. Roughly one-half of the OED CD-ROM's storage capacity of 650 megabytes is used to store the dictionary contents, with much of the rest of the space devoted to the database index, tagging information and controlling software.

> ELECTRONIC BOOKS   > INTERACTIVE ENCYCLOPEDIA

DIGITAL FONTS

The complete range of type characters that make up a font encoded in digital form. Digital fonts for professional typesetting have been around since the launch of the Digiset typesetter in 1965, but it is only since the introduction of the **PostScript page description language** in the mid-1980s that many thousands of fonts have been made available in digital form for desktop publishing (**DTP**) systems as well as for **personal computers**.

Digital fonts for DTP have to perform three main functions: they must be able to print to the highest **resolution** possible on whatever printer or typesetter is being used (effectively, at resolutions of 150–3000 **dpi**), and look as good as or better than photo-typesetting; they must look good on screen, at resolutions of around 72 dpi, showing enough of their particular characteristics (such as serifs and stroke-weight) for a **WYSIWYG** design layout to be possible; and they must be scalable – available in all of the sizes that the designer may want – both on-screen and for print.

Fonts encoded in PostScript, and competing digital formats such as **Apple**'s TrueType, store letterform shapes as code that describes the **bezier** curves, line weight, fill, shadow and other characteristics of the font. When this data is sent to the laserprinter or imagesetter, that machine decodes the font data and prepares a **bitmap** for printing by means of a raster image processor. The bitmap can be produced to the highest resolution available in the printing device.

Early digital fonts handled screen display with sets of screen fonts – ie bitmaps that were specially drawn to appear on screen. These screen fonts were available in half a dozen of the most commonly used sizes – generally 9pt, 10pt, 12pt, 14pt, 18pt and 24pt – but any other sizes would be scaled up or down from the nearest available screen font. This did not produce satisfactory results, and Adobe introduced Display PostScript and then **Adobe Type Manager**, systems which ensured fidelity between screen and printer outputs by using the same digital format (PostScript) for both. Nowadays, digital fonts for both screen and printer can be created or modified using special applications. Many new fonts created initially on desktop computers have been released by major type manufacturers, all of whom now supply fonts in digital form for personal computers and DTP systems, as well as professional graphic design **workstations**.

➡

Digital fonts from David Carson's <u>Raygun</u> magazine, Zuzana Licko & Rudy Vanderlans' <u>Emigré</u> and Neville Brody's <u>Fuse</u> magazine.

DIGITAL-OPTICAL RECORDING [DOR]

Describes read/write techniques that use lasered light to encode/decode digital information on a plastic or metal substrate, either permanently (CD-R and WORM discs) or for short-term storage (WMRM discs). Pioneered by Philips with their LaserVision system (which encoded analog video signals as a series of pits in the disc surface), and developed through CDDA, CD-ROM, CD-i and CD-R, DOR provides a long-lasting medium for storing digital (and analog) data that is safe from electromagnetic corruption.

DIGITAL PAPER

A digital-optical data-storage medium developed by ICI, consisting of a sheet of polyester coated with polymer dye, which can absorb infrared light from a laser. The laser heats the dye, changing its reflective characteristics, thus enabling it to store data bits. Digital paper is much cheaper than other storage substrates. ICI have supplied Canada's Centre for Remote Sensing with digital paper-tape drives for storing the immense quantities of data from the ERS1 satellite. Each drive takes 300mm (12-inch) spools, each of which can hold about 1 terabyte (1000 gigabytes) of data. Disc-based systems using digital paper are also being developed.

> BACKUP

DIGITAL RECORDING

The recording of audio or video signals in digital form. Audio sampling must take place at a rate at least twice that of the highest frequency to be reproduced, so that for CD-quality audio, for example, large hard disks of at least one gigabyte capacity are required to store the digital audio files.

> CDDA
> DAT
> DIGITAL AUDIO
> CD-R
> DCC

DIGITAL SIGNAL PROCESSOR [DSP]

A powerful microprocessor designed to perform complex operations on digital data representing digitized waveform signals. DSPs are used in addition to the central processor in a microcomputer (or in a CD audio player, digital video player, music synthesizer or HDTV set), in order to speed up the processing of sounds and images. The Motorola DSP 56001 (the DSP used in the NeXT computer), for example, uses a 24-bit data path, and operates at 20 MHz to deliver a performance of 10 million instructions per second.

DIGITAL-TO-ANALOG CONVERTER [DAC]

Device in a computer or digital synthesizer that converts digitally encoded signals to analog values.

DIGITAL VIDEO

Video systems that record and store information in digital, as opposed to analog form.

> DESKTOP VIDEO
> FULL-SCREEN FULL-MOTION VIDEO
> HDTV
> FULL-MOTION VIDEO

DIGITIZER

Device for converting an analog measurement into digital code.

> DIGITPAD
> SCANNER
> FRAME GRABBER

DIGITIZING TABLET

> DIGITPAD

DIGITPAD

(Or 'digitizing tablet'.) A tablet resembling a drawing board that converts a freehand drawing into digital signals. The artist uses an electronic stylus (pen) and the tablet records the X and Y positions of the stylus tip. The resulting image is displayed on a computer monitor.

> SKETCHPAD

DIN CONNECTOR

A round connector made to DIN (German industry) standards. It is widely used on computers, tape recorders, video cameras and MIDI equipment.

DIRECTOR

The person responsible for the design and overall artistic direction of an interactive multimedia programme. The hypermedia director's role is analogous to that of the film or video director. It is his or her responsibility to act as the creative executive in charge of all the various production specialists, guiding and coordinating their efforts in the production of a programme that satisfies the functional and aesthetic criteria established by the designer.

> AUTHORING

DIRECTOR™

> MACROMEDIA DIRECTOR

DISC LABEL

(1) In CD discs, the information contained within track 1 of the disc, which describes disc type and format and contains a description of all the files on the disc, the location of any software files that are to be loaded into the system, and a path table (an index of the directory structure of the disc) to allow access to those files.
(2) The graphic information printed onto the disc itself, identifying the programme and carrying the publishers logotype.

DISC MAP

The organization of data on the CD tape master, prior to disc mastering.

DISC MAPPING

In interactive video, the process of listing the frame numbers pertaining to motion sequences and stills stored on the videodisc, ready for incorporation within the authoring (control) program. The pictorial contents are listed by frame number, and sequences by start-frame and end-frame. Frame numbers provide the address content of buttons and functions within the user interface.

Techex desktop digital video editor.

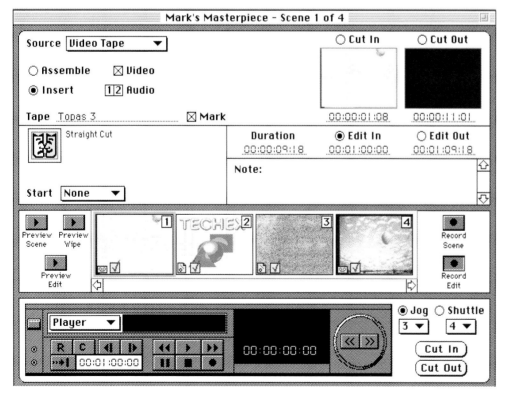

DISK DRIVE

In computer systems, an integral or **peripheral** unit for
reading data from or writing data to an
electromagnetic disk or optical disc.

> CD-ROM   > HARD DISK

> FLOPPY DISK   > WORM

DISPLAY POSTSCRIPT

An extension of Adobe's **PostScript page description language**
designed to describe all the graphic elements on a
screen, thus providing a true **WYSIWYG** display. (Page
description languages were originally developed to
perform this function on printers.) Like PostScript,
Display PostScript is device-independent. This
means that it will automatically use the maximum
colour capability and resolution of the **display system**
being used. Output to a PostScript printer will match
what is displayed on the screen.

DISPLAY RESOLUTION

A measurement of the sharpness of an image on a **monitor**
expressed in terms of the number of **pixels** (dots) per
inch. For PCs this is typically 72 dots per inch.

> DPI   > RESOLUTION

DISPLAY SYSTEM

Refers to any **hardware** used to show images. Includes
domestic television sets, video and computer
monitors, **HDTV** and large **flat-screen** displays, **LCD**
displays and overhead projectors.

> DELIVERY SYSTEM

DISSOLVE

(Or 'cross-fade'.) In film and video, a **transition** effect
wherein one scene is faded out while the following
scene is simultaneously faded in.

DISTANCE LEARNING

Study by students not in direct contact with tutorial staff,
via specially designed educational materials and
courseware. Such materials may be conventional
books and printed materials, but can also include
interactive training programmes available on **floppy
disk**, **CD-ROM** or through cable and telecommunication
networks. Such **software** can provide self-assessment
facilities, and distance learning may use telephone
tutorials and assessments.

> CAL   > EDUTAINMENT

DITHERING

A technique for mixing two or more **colours** together to
create the illusion of extra colours; used in computer
systems that have limited colour **resolution**. As with
colour printing techniques or Pointillist painting,
dithering uses the idea of employing dots (**pixels**) of
colours and mixing them on screen so that new
colours are perceived by the observer. Dithering
(using various black-and-white patterns) is also used
in the representation of **greyscales** on systems that
only support one **bit** of tonal information. Such
dithered images can be aesthetically pleasing in
their own right.

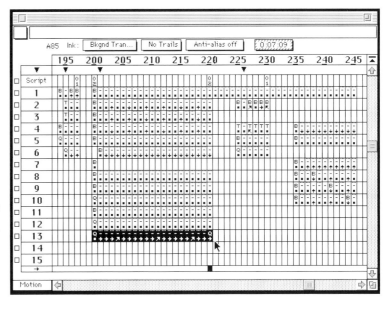

Macromedia Director's 'score'
window is based on the
traditional animator's dope
sheet. Time is represented
horizontally by the number
of frames, and the images,
graphics and text 'sprites'
can occupy any of 24
channels (vertical scale).

DMA (DIRECT MEMORY ACCESS)

In computer systems, the process of 'reading to' or
'writing from' data storage devices (such as a **hard
disk** or an optical drive) directly, ie without utilizing
the central processor (**CPU**). This technique provides
faster data transfer rates.

DOCUMENTATION

The printed or digital user's **manual** for a computer
program or application.

DOLLY

A trolley on which a camera with accessories may be
mounted. Used in film and **animation** for tracking
shots.

> MOTION CONTROL   > ROSTRUM CAMERA

DOPE SHEET

In traditional (cel) **animation**, a 'camera exposure' chart
used to provide the rostrum cameraman with frame-
by-frame instructions as to camera movement,
background movement etc. **Macromedia Director** uses
an analogy to the dope sheet in its 'score' window.

> ROSTRUM CAMERA

DOR

> DIGITAL-OPTICAL RECORDING

DOS (DISC OPERATING SYSTEM)

> MS-DOS

DOTS PER INCH

> DPI

DOUBLE-FREQUENCY SCANNING

In **CD-i**, a method of improving the vertical **resolution** of an
image by scanning at twice the normal frequency, to
produce double the number of horizontal lines within
one frame.

Dithering: the computer attempts to display
continuous tones by 'dithering' a limited range of
colours, or by creating tones with patterns of
black and white pixels.

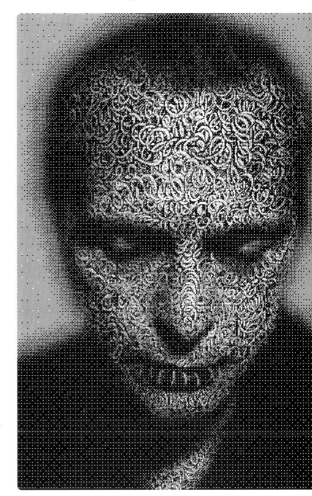

DOWNLINK

Describes the telecommunications radio or **microwave** link between a satellite and a ground station.

> REMOTE SENSING   > SATELLITE COMMUNICATIONS

DOWNLOAD

Originally used to describe the movement of information from a large computer to a smaller one. Now used to describe the process of transferring data from one computer system to another, or from a **network** or bulletin board to a personal computer, or from a computer to an **archiving** storage device.

> BACKUP

DPI (DOTS PER INCH)

A measure of the **resolution** of an image. Dpi is the number of individually addressable points that constitute an image. In a black-and-white image each point is encoded with one **bit** (either 0 or 1). In an 8-bit image, up to 256 **greyscale** or **colour** values can be encoded. Dpi is used as a measure of resolution for a wide range of imaging technologies, including **screen** displays (mostly around 70 dpi), laserprinters (300–600 dpi) and imagesetters (800–3000 dpi).

DRAMATIC METAPHOR

The use of ideas and approaches drawn from the theatre in the design of **hypermedia** programmes and other **software**. Many of these ideas are derived from formal theories of drama developed in classical Greece. Brenda Laurel, in her book <u>Computers as Theatre</u>, describes how she has used such ideas in her work in **interface** and application design. As a new medium, hypermedia has no tradition of its own on which practitioners can draw, and its early years are likely to be marked by many such borrowings from other traditions.

> INTERACTION   > INTERFACE
> NARRATIVE   > VIDEOGAMES
>> FURTHER READING: LAUREL 1991

Brenda Laurel, software design guru and author of <u>Computers as Theatre</u>, featured in <u>Mondo</u> <u>2000</u>.

DRAW PROGRAM

Generic term describing image-making software applications that utilize object-oriented graphics techniques, and use **bezier** editable lines and shapes. Draw programs produce graphics that are 'device independent', ie they will print to the highest **resolution** available on the printing device (unlike 'paint' or bitmap graphics programs, that have a resolution fixed at around 72 dots per inch). Examples of draw programs are Aldus Freehand; Corel Draw; MacDraw and Adobe Illustrator, which are used by professional illustrators.

> DIGITAL FONTS   > PAGE DESCRIPTION LANGUAGE
> PAINT PROGRAM

DREAM MACHINES

Term coined by Ted Nelson and used to describe computers/hypermedia systems. <u>Computer Lib</u>/<u>Dream</u> <u>Machines</u>, Nelson's 'two-books-in-one' magnum opus on the potential of computers, hypertext and hypermedia is required reading for hypermedia designers and enthusiasts. Jon Palfreman and Doron Swade used the title <u>The Dream Machine</u> for their book accompanying the BBC/WGBH television series of the same name, covering the history of computers and computing from the abacus to artificial intelligence (**AI**).

> XANADU
>> FURTHER READING: NELSON 1987; PALFRENAN AND SWADE 1991

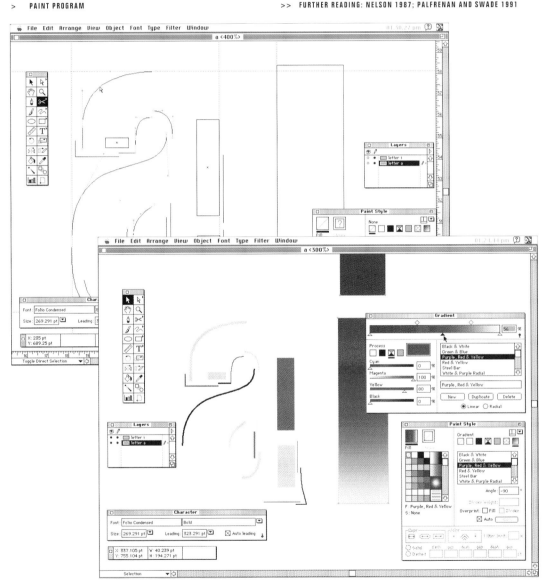

Screen shots from Adobe Illustrator 5.0.

DRIVER
> DEVICE DRIVER

DSP
> DIGITAL SIGNAL PROCESSOR

DTP [DESKTOP PUBLISHING]
Generic term referring to systems that comprise a
desktop (personal) computer, scanner, laserprinter
and software for graphics and page layout. The first
popular DTP system was launched by **Apple** in 1986,
comprising an Apple **Macintosh** (Mac) computer, an
Apple LaserWriter and 'bundled' software: Aldus
PageMaker and Adobe PostScript. Although all
these technologies were already available in one
form or another in professional typesetting and
reprographic facilities houses, the Apple system
was the first to bring them together at a generally
affordable price, and in a convenient 'desktop'
format that could be operated by one person.
DTP heralded a revolution in personal publishing, for the
first time putting the tools of the graphic designer,
typesetter and printing press together into the hands
of a single user. DTP technology had a radical
impact on traditional publishing – first in graphic
design studios, where the Mac became the dominant
graphics **workstation**, then in reprographics, with the
Mac linked to high-resolution scanners and
electronic page composition systems (such as those
produced by **Quantel** and Scitex), and finally in
publishing itself. It was the DTP concept, and
its software and hardware components, that
established a new interactive style of design
practice, thus laying the foundations for the design
revolution that was to link together many different
media into an integrated suite of **multimedia**
presentation and **hypermedia** tools.
> DTV
>> FURTHER READING: COLLIER AND COTTON 1989

DTV
> DESKTOP VIDEO

DUBBING
From French <u>doubler</u> (to copy), a term generally used to
describe the process of adding sound effects, music
or commentary to a video or film. Used variously to
describe: (1) the process of copying sound or video
from one source to another; (2) the process of
copying sounds onto a videotape; (3) the mixing
of a number of sound tracks into a single track.

DUBBING SCRIPT
The commentary script marked with **time code** (or film
footage and frame number) references, so that it is
ready for the actor or presenter to read during a
videotape or film dub.

DV CART [DIGITAL VIDEO CARTRIDGE]
A cartridge that is designed to add **full-motion video**
functionality to **CD-i** and other **CD-ROM**-based **multimedia**
systems that conform to the **Video-CD** 'White Book'
standard agreed by Philips, Matsushita, Sony and
JVC in 1993.

DVI
digital video for the PC

Digital Video Interactive was the first compression
technology that allowed personal computers to
display full-motion video (FMV), finally realizing the
true potential of the computer as a hypermedium,
a medium that could simulate all other media.
Currently DVI-equipped personal computers are in
widespread use in the development and delivery of
software for training, education, point of information
(POI) and point-of-sale. It has been prototyped as
a key component in consumer products, most
successfully in Empruve's 'Cornucopia' machine,
and looks set to play a substantial role in the
development of consumer video and interactive
media, personal digital information systems and
telecommunications developments.

Why? Because DVI is a powerful chip (the Intel i750)
that allows compressed data to be decompressed
in realtime. This means that more data can be
squeezed onto a floppy disk or CD-ROM, or through
a cable network, and that it can be displayed on a
monitor screen at frame rates of 25-30 frames per
second. DVI is important because it is a generalized
technology – it is designed to work with any
computer-based system that includes a DVI chip. It
processes compressed data stored on floppy disk,
hard disk, CD-ROM, memory card, in fact any digital
optical or electromagnetic medium.

DVI was conceived by Larry Ryan at the RCA
Laboratories in 1983 as a solution to RCA's attempt
to make their analog videodisc system interactive.
Ryan proposed an all-digital system, which was
demonstrated four years later at the 1987 CD-ROM
Conference. Intel acquired the DVI Technology
Venture in 1988, and by 1989 had already begun
to market DVI development tools (the Pro750
Application Development Kit and End-user Kit).
These kits were marketed as expansion boards
for the IBM (or compatible) PC, but by 1991 the
Californian company New Vision had launched their
DVI expansion board for Apple Macintosh.

The DVI chip provides efficient compression and very
fast decompression of digital video information. The
chip will itself compress video to a presentation-
level standard Intel call Real Time Video. This is
useful for programme development, prototyping,
presentation and courseware applications. The best
quality production-level video is achieved by the
mainframe compression of digital video data (a
service provided by Intel). In this sense, DVI is an
'asymmetrical' compression system – it will
decompress in real time, but is not powerful
enough to compress images of very high quality.
This is not surprising, as video compression is very
computation-intensive, requiring very powerful
machines that are too expensive for any single
programme developer. Currently DVI can compress
about 60 minutes of full-screen FMV onto a
CD-ROM (640 megabytes) and decompress this
in realtime.

Empruve's prototype DVI system is
ergonomic and stylish, with FMV
colour and paper-white A4 screen.

Since DVI was launched, several competing video
compression and decompression systems have
appeared on the market (most of which conform
to the MPEG standard), including hardware and
software for personal computers, and FMV systems
for dedicated platforms such as Philips CD-i and
CD-Movie, and 3DO's Interactive Multiplayer, but
DVI is a well-established, mature technology, and
will play an important role in both corporate and
consumer interactive media.

THE DYNABOOK
the 25-year-old blueprint of the future

For over 25 years the computer industry has been inspired by the idea of a portable computer that is easy to use, powerful, networkable and inexpensive. The idea was first proposed in 1968, by a young computer scientist and part-time jazz musician called Alan C Kay. He wanted his 'dream machine' to be as ubiquitous as a book, and to have all the dynamic power of a computer, so he called it the Dynabook. It is only now, with the recent introduction of personal digital assistants, that the Dynabook has become a practical proposition.

Kay intended the Dynabook to take a number of forms, accurately foreseeing the range of portable machines, palmtops and notepads that we have today. The best known version was a notepad-sized system, with a full-page graphics display of 'pen on paper' clarity. Kay's prototype Dynabook was designed to have a flat-screen display, a graphic interface and the capability of handling several megabytes of text. It was to be a read/write medium, designed with children in mind and to include an easy-to-use 'development environment' or programming language (which Kay called 'Paintbrush') that children would use to create and animate pictures. Kay proposed that the Dynabook would link to other Dynabooks and to 'digital library' resources (via phone lines and/or wireless), and that it should be produced for under US $500 so that it could be made available to every child of school age.

Kay joined the Xerox Palo Alto Research Centre (PARC) in the early 1970s, and his first paper was on the Dynabook. The research and development work carried out by Kay and his colleagues at Xerox PARC profoundly influenced the direction of computing, creating working models of the kind of personal computers we now take for granted. By the mid-1970s, PARC researchers had developed a coherent graphical user interface, which went on to inspire Steve Jobs, the co-inventor of the Apple personal computer. The Mac, launched in 1984, brought the graphical user interface to millions, and effectively mapped out the future of personal computing for the 1980s and 1990s.

Much of Kay's research work (at PARC, and from 1984 as an Apple Fellow) has been focused on creating the tools that will be needed for the Dynabook. This includes his work on Smalltalk – one of the earliest object-oriented languages, which influenced Apple's HyperCard scripting language HyperTalk – and his work on software agents.

Kay sees the emergence of the Dynabook as a parallel to the process that began with Gutenberg's invention of printing, progressed with the idea of the portable, legibly printed book, and ended with the modern paperback. Just as books evolved from being desktop-sized with Gothic typefaces to pocket-sized with modern Roman faces, so will the Dynabook evolve into a personal (and individualized) information resource, one that would be as easy to use as a book. And just as the availability of mass-produced books helped to create the individualism and personal perspective that spurred the Renaissance, so could the Dynabook and 'intimate computing' initiate profound social changes in the twenty-first century.

Much of the enabling technology needed for the Dynabook is now in place: hardware such as high-resolution flat screens, powerful processors and cheap, compact memory; software tools such as object-oriented programming, knowledge-based systems, hypermedia and agents; and digital communications networks (cell-nets). Neatly put together, and marketed at an affordable price, these components would provide more than an approximation of what Kay has in mind. It is not surprising that Apple, IBM and many other computer manufacturers and consumer electronics companies have recently launched their own personal digital systems. These hand-held computers/communicators have begun to provide some of the functionality of the Dynabook, but for the real, globally networked item, we may have a few more years to wait.

DVI [DIGITAL VIDEO INTERACTIVE]
A computer microchip developed by Intel, and specially designed for the compression and decompression of video images. Multimedia systems use DVI chips so that they can display full-motion video. For production-level video, images are compressed on a mainframe computer, stored on a CD-ROM or hard disk, then decompressed in realtime by the DVI-equipped delivery platform.
> WORM
> • DVI PAGE 67

DYNABOOK
A concept developed by Alan Kay in 1968 for a small portable computer that could recognize handwriting and communicate with large databases over wireless networks. The Dynabook, while never built, was nevertheless a very powerful concept and one which can be seen as playing an important role in the development of the personal computer as we know it today. The concept is now beginning to be realized in the form of the personal digital assistant.
> • THE DYNABOOK THIS PAGE

DYNAMIC LOADING
A technique available in CD-i, whereby the contents of the colour look-up table or CLUT (up to four colours) can be updated during the horizontal retrace period (the time it takes for the electron beam in the monitor to reposition for another scan line). Up to 256 colours can be updated during the vertical retrace period (the time it takes for the electron beam to reposition for a new field scan).

DYNAMICS
In virtual reality systems, the rules which simulate the physical laws – such as gravity, inertia and friction – that govern all the actions within the virtual environment, as well as the deviations that suspend or alter natural laws – such as slowing time, changing scale, instant travel, and other effects.

DYUV
> DELTA YUV

Empruve's revolutionary Cornucopia prototype combines style and functionality. With a paper-white screen for text and graphics and colour screen for DVI-compressed full-motion video, and internal CD-ROM, Cornucopia comes close to the Dynabook ideal.

E-MAIL (ELECTRONIC MAIL)

A system that allows messages to be sent from and received by **personal computer**s via a computer **network** or telephone connection. E-mail users need a **microcomputer**, a **modem**, a telephone and a subscription to an electronic mail service. Messages are keyed into a word-processing **program**, then converted via an E-mail application and modem into signals suitable for transmission via the telephone. The E-mail service's host computer is dialled and a 'welcome' screen appears, into which the user's box number and password is typed. This effectively logs the user into the central host computer, from where messages can be sent to other subscribers' 'mailboxes' – ie the memory areas that store the message until the recipient is ready to collect it (copy it to his or her own computer).

Companies providing E-mail services include **CompuServe**, **BIX**, British Telecom (Telecom Gold), Microlink, and the **WELL**. These networks also offer services such as 'bulletin boards' (**BBS**) and electronic conference forums for special interest groups.

EARCON

A screen **icon** which triggers a **digital** sound or soundtrack.

> AUDITORY ICON

EDAC
(ELECTRONIC DETECTION AND CORRECTION)

In **telecommunications**, **digital-optical recording** and computing, a code that is designed to detect an error in a character or word, and after identifying the incorrect **bit**, replace it with a correct one.

EDGE, THE

A metaphor, drawn from biology, for the place where mutations develop and flourish, now applied to the fringes of mainstream society where new ideas are likely to develop and innovations, such as **hypermedia**, to be adopted first. Used to describe the pop underground and the design communities at the core of the **videogames**, **virtual reality**, **AI**, **network** and **simulation** industries.

> • THE EDGE PAGE 70

EDI (ELECTRONIC DATA INTERCHANGE)

A networked **telecommunications** service allowing institutions and commercial corporations to transact routine business in the form of electronic documentation. EDI allows subscribers to exchange orders and invoices much more quickly and reliably than traditional paper-based methods, enabling fine-tuning of stock inventory control and contributing to the automation of the transaction chain. EDI opens up the possibility of a much closer match between supplier and customer, saving time and money for both. Pioneered in the US, EDI services are also growing rapidly in Europe, especially in the UK, where by the early 1990s around 300 of the top 1,000 companies used EDI.

> VIRTUAL PRIVATE NETWORK

EDTV (EXTENDED-DEFINITION TV)

A 'wide-screen' television format that replaces the 4:3 image ratio of conventional television with a 16:9 ratio. This allows greater use of wide-angle shots in sports and news coverage, etc, as well as enabling wide-screen movies to fit the screen, rather than being shown reduced size, cropped or 'squeezed'. EDTV is seen as a possible stop-gap before high-definition (**HDTV**) systems become widely available.

One of the main problems with EDTV systems is that viewers watching EDTV broadcasts on conventional televisions will see a 'letterbox' shape, with broad black bands above and below the image. Whether consumers will tolerate the letterbox format before upgrading to EDTV remains to be seen.

EDUTAINMENT

A composite word combining 'education' and 'entertainment', created to identify **interactive multimedia** products that present educational material in an entertaining manner.

> INFOTAINMENT

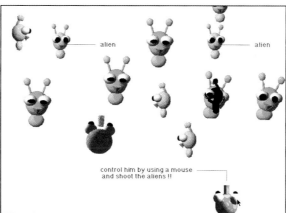

Kumi Akiyoshi: 'Kumitronics'. Educational software should be 'simple, hot and deep' – and as entertaining as the best videogames. The Kumitronics prototype combines digital media and digital processing to create exciting edutainment.

EFF (ELECTRONIC FRONTIER FOUNDATION)

A US-based, non-profit-making organization concerned with civil liberties and individual rights and freedoms in the emerging electronic technologies of **software**, **networks** and **cyberspace**. Founded by Mitchell Kapor in 1990, EFF has a broad agenda, including the sponsorship of a range of projects designed to educate and inform the public on these issues.

→

EFFECTOR
In **virtual reality** systems, an **input**/output device or sensor (such as a **head-mounted display**) that carries positional data and commands from the user to the computer, and images, audio and other sensory stimulation from the computer to the user.

EFM [8-14 MODULATION]
In CD audio (**CDDA**), a method of formatting the pulse-code-modulated signal to maximize the amount of data that can be stored on a CD, and to provide an efficient synchronization pattern.

EGA [ENHANCED GRAPHICS ADAPTOR]
A display standard for personal computer **screens** (and also an **expansion board** to implement the standard). EGA has three graphics modes: 4 colours at 320x200 **pixels**; 16 colours at 640x200; and 16 colours at 640x350 pixels.

> CGA   > VGA
> XGA

ELAPSED-TIME RECORDING
(Or 'time-lapse recording'.) The film and video technique of recording a live-action sequence as a sequential series of images separated by units of time ranging from a few seconds to several minutes or hours. When the elapsed-time sequence is projected or displayed at normal film or video rates, the result is an enormous speeding-up of the natural movements that have been recorded. Elapsed-time techniques are used to reveal natural movements that are too slow to be perceived naturally, such as the growth of animals and plants, or the formation of clouds, and as such are valuable explorative techniques for scientific purposes. They have also been used dramatically, notably by John Boorman in his films Point Blank and Excalibur. (In the latter, a scene of knights riding out of the wasteland is accompanied by a carefully matted time-lapse sequence of flowers budding and flowering.)

> STOP-FRAME RECORDING

ELECTRONIC ARTS
The largest publisher of interactive consumer software, Electronic Arts is the leading third-party provider of **videogame** cartridges, with interests in PC entertainment software, and games and edutainment for **CD-ROM**. Electronic Arts was founded and is still chaired by Trip Hawkins, whose philosophy 'Software should be Simple, Hot and Deep' has since become the company motto.

> 3DO   > SOFTWARE DESIGN

ELECTRONIC BOOK
A term used to describe a book that has been converted into **digital** form to be displayed on a computer screen or a **hypermedia** programme based on the metaphor of a book.

> • ELECTRONIC BOOKS PAGE 73

ELECTRONIC MAIL
> E-MAIL

THE EDGE
exploring the electronic frontier

'The Edge' is a cyberpunk metaphor for the place where 'the New' develops. The idea is that the extreme edge of a habitat is the place where mutations flourish and become established. Applying this metaphor to human society, the New is likely initially to establish itself on the fringes of respectable, mainstream social activity – places such as the pop underground, the demi-monde of artists, designers and intellectuals, and the wilder world of techno-freaks, hackers and cyberpunks.

Much of what we have talked about in this book is far from the Edge. The vocabulary of cyberspace is drawn from the world of big multinational corporations and prestigious research institutes, who drive forward the revolution in hypermedia and cyberspace technology in an attempt to develop new markets. The computer and the consumer electronics industries desperately need new products and new markets. The markets for existing products are relatively mature and so companies in this sector can only compete on price, resulting in smaller profit margins. The entertainment, information and telecommunication industries are also hungry for the profits which they believe can be made by exploiting the new technologies. Research institutes also need big bucks to pay for their investments in the latest technology: what better way to attract interest from industry than by tempting offers of even more powerful money-making machines that will bring the consumers running again?

But new markets cannot be created by marketing alone. As Terry Winograd and Fernando Flores point out in Understanding Computers and Cognition (1986), the significance of an innovation or invention depends upon its capacity to find its place within, or change, a complex network of human activities and equipment. People don't just sit down at a computer without a purpose. They might do so for any number of reasons: to write a letter, to design a book, to do some spreadsheet calculations, to write a computer program. All those activities only make sense within a context, which is much more complicated and extensive than it might at first appear: there is no point in writing a letter if there are no postal services, or if the person you are sending it to cannot read. Postal services and reading both rest on a web of interconnected human activities involving institutions, equipment, conventions, economic behaviour, social practice and so on.

Winograd and Flores go on to make a distinction between the minor innovations that simply improve some aspect of an activity within a social network, and those which change the structure of the network itself, inventions that 'open up whole new domains of possibilities for the network of human interactions'. They continue: 'Just as the automobile had impacts on our society far beyond speeding up what had been done with horses, the use of computers will lead to changes far beyond those

of a fancy typewriter. The nature of publishing, the structure of communication within organizations, and the social organization of knowledge will all be altered, as they were with the emergence of other technologies for language, such as the printing press.'

The question is: Who is doing the altering? Is it the multinational corporations and prestigious research institutes? They will certainly be providing the means, but the real energy and momentum is coming from elsewhere. As Peter Schwartz explains in The Art of the Long View (1991): 'People and organizations often organize knowledge concentrically, with the most cherished, vital beliefs at the protected centre...The structure, the power, and the institutional inertia all tend to inhibit innovative thinkers and drive them to the fringes. At the social and intellectual fringes, thinkers are free to let their imaginations roam, but are still constrained by a sense of current reality.' And at the Edge people do more than let their imaginations roam – they start to live the New, working within the spaces and gaps of organized society to create their own room for movement and self-expression.

The people of the Edge seize upon those inventions and innovations that open up new possibilities, that free them to be the people their imaginations tell them they are. To do so they may twist, appropriate, misuse and distort those inventions from their original purpose. Much of the story of our century has been of a movement of ideas and activities from the Edge to the Street and finally into our official versions of reality. The story of hypermedia and cyberspace is likely to be the same.

>> FURTHER READING: SCHWARTZ 1991; WINOGRAD AND FLORES 1986

Edge is one of the UK's leading interactive media and videogame magazines, covering all aspects of disc-, cart- and network-based gaming and infotainment, as well as developments in arcades, simulation and virtual reality.

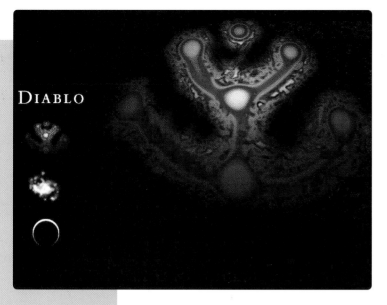

YOU CAN'T LEAD
A BALD MAN
TO A COMB

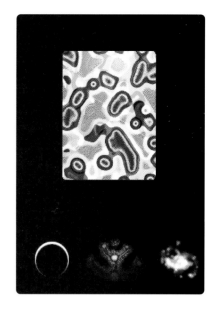

DIABLO

Diablo: an interactive 'decision-advisor' desk-accessory for the Mac, from leading digital typographers Studio DM, who are in the forefront of pushing new interactive technologies to the limit.

Experimental pieces by Jeff Instone. Exploring the leading edge of digital textworks, Instone's work is stylish, insightful and witty, and a major contribution to the evolution of future 'art interfaces'.

ELECTRONIC PUBLISHING

Term used to describe 'non-print' publishing, often in **digital** form. Electronic publishing includes **hypermedia** and **database** publishing on **CD-ROM** and disk, and 'on-line' **publishing** through **telecommunications** networks such as **ISDN** (in the US the publisher Random House already make their World Classics series available 'on-line').

> ELECTRONIC BOOK

EMERGENCY RESPONSE SYSTEM [ERS]

A system designed to facilitate immediate and effective response by emergency services (fire brigade, police etc). **Multimedia** emergency response systems can take several forms, based on diagrams, **simulations**, maps, **flowcharts** or any other model suitable for the particular application.

As an illustration, consider a map-based ERS designed to provide emergency management facilities for an offshore oil field. Such a system would feature full-colour, high-resolution frames of nautical charts and Ordnance Survey maps stored at a variety of scales, which could be accessed via a multimedia **interface** capable of displaying video, photographs, satellite images, pipeline schematics, terminal layouts and so on, as well as **windows** of **database** information. Using this hypothetical system, the emergency response team would be able to locate and 'zoom into' the location of an emergency at the required scale within one or two seconds (compared with a paper-based ERS, in which the process of finding the correct chart, map or photograph might take a several minutes). On-screen **icons** would give access to any stills, aerial or satellite photographs, or motion-video sequences available for the area, as well as giving the team the ability to overlay the location of rescue teams and services such as the fire brigade and police.

The system interface could be configured to include windows for telecommunications, **network** access and database access; software for 'blast effect' simulation; tidal-flow animations for oil slick tracking and prediction. An emergency response system similar to this, the MERMIS system, has recently been developed by BP Exploration and Synergy. Systems like this can also be used to simulate emergencies and are therefore invaluable for training the emergency response team.

> GEOGRAPHICAL INFORMATION SYSTEM
> GPS   > KNOWLEDGE-BASED SYSTEM
> MANAGEMENT INFORMATION SYSTEM

EMULATION

The process of using a computer to model the behaviour of another computer-based system. For example, in preparing a **CD-i** programme, special add-on boards and **software** can be used to 'emulate' the performance of a CD-i player on a personal computer or **workstation** such as an Apple **Macintosh** or **IBM** PC. The Mac platform is widely used for programme design and development, and systems such as Philips' CD-i Author 850 can provide the hardware and software necessary to convert Mac image, graphics and audio **files** to CD-i formats, in order to construct or 'build' CD-i discs.

Jaime Levy: 'Electronic Hollywood', Issue 3 1992, a desktop electronic fanzine. The early 1990s saw a spate of experimental electronic publishing as artists, designers and programmers explored the potential of the new hypermedia. These are examples from the West Coast.

The Computer Lab: 'Beyond Cyberpunk', 6 megabytes of high-tech low life.

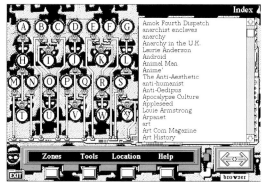

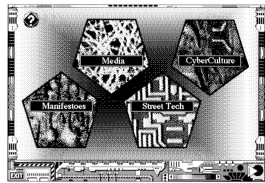

ELECTRONIC BOOKS
the soft printing press

The transition from 'print on paper' to electronic publishing presents an opportunity to add considerable value to the black-and-white text-based information carrier invented by Gutenberg and Aldus Manutius in the fifteenth century. Books published in digital form are not limited by constraints of printing and bookbinding. CD-ROMs can store vast amounts of data in text form, as well as in digital images, animations, video sequences, spoken commentary, music and sounds to supplement this text.

The cost of replicating a compact disc is only a fraction of that of printing and packaging a book. While it is certainly necessary to have a suitable 'reader' or player to view an electronic book, these have already come down to affordable price levels. The added software features of hypermedia (its ability to perform text searches, provide hypertext links, expert guides, online glossaries and marginal notes, and so on), is certain to create a growing demand for 'books' in this form.

Many of the first generation of electronic books simply featured digital text, perhaps with a string-searching function for finding words, phrases and illustrations. For today's second-generation electronic books, publishers are able to employ a much wider range of options, 'extending' the text with multimedia facilities and providing extra tools for the 'reader'.

It is an area rich in possibilities. Consider, for example, a hypothetical encyclopedia of soul music, to be adapted for CD-ROM. To the complete text of the original book, one would first of all add database and/or hypertext search and retrieval tools. These would allow random access to entries through instant search and 'rapid browsing' facilities, enabling the user to select a particular entry or speed search through all the entry headers. Hypertext and database methods would allow for extensive cross-referencing links and 'associational browsing', offering the user an overview of potential

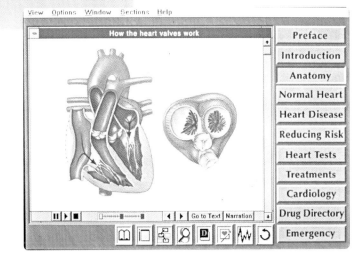

Sony Electronic Publishing: 'Mayo Clinic Family Healthbook', a 1300-page home medical reference, with 90 minutes of audio, extensive video, 45 animated illustrations and over 500 colour illustrations and photographs.

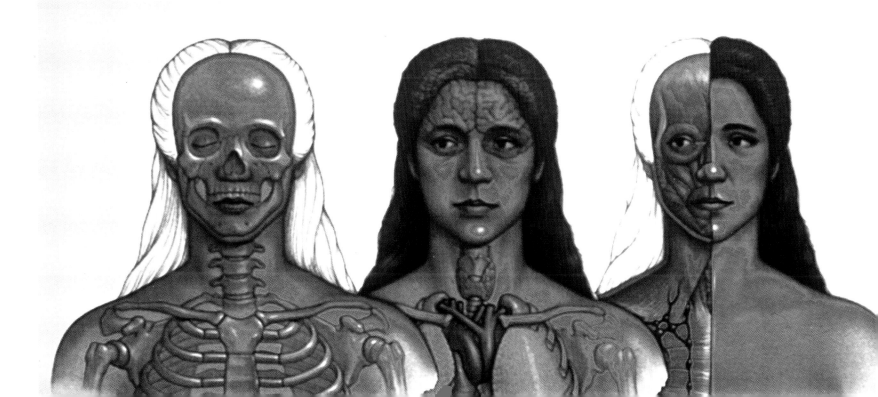

links. Reading an entry on James Brown, for example, the user would be able to follow a cross-reference to Chess Records and browse through the list of artists on the label, then follow cross-references to another artist or manager, and so on.

Another method of accessing information from the encyclopedia would be through multiple-criteria searches, allowing the user to isolate particular entries satisfying the search criteria (assessing, for example, a list of all the records by a particular artist in a particular year). Information could also be 'layered', with glossary and footnote icons that would provide instant access to a window of additional information on technical terms, recording techniques, sheet music or artists biographies.

Unlike a printed book, information on CD-ROM can be 'customized' by the user in a number of other ways, such as accessing entries chronologically so that historical surveys are possible. Entries in the encyclopedia could be called up in chronological order, with extra 'current affairs' panels on what was happening in the wider music scene. Another feature might be an icon for accessing discographies as separate items – this function could produce information for selected individual artists, publishers or record labels, or the user could compile his or her own discography from the database. Other features might include a week-by-week 'animation' of the soul charts: for a rapid search to find your favourite tracks, you would 'tag' them in another colour and watch their progress up and down the charts as the weeks go by. The publisher might also decide to include previously unpublished background text and the writer's research notes on many entries.

So far we have only occupied a fraction of the storage space on the CD-ROM – perhaps 40-50 megabytes for text, indices, interface graphics, audio material, titles animation and music, and of course the controlling software. The multimedia elements – comprising perhaps 200 or so photographs of artists, graphics of album sleeves, single labels, posters, etc would each take up around 500 kilobytes, adding another 100 megabytes to the 'book'. The all-important music – in hi-fi quality digital stereo – would include track clips, interviews and voice-over commentaries. Twenty to 30 minutes of sound would occupy another 200 megabytes, making our total so far around 350 megabytes – just over half the storage capacity of a CD-ROM. Some CDDA (full CD-audio) tracks, QuickTime video clips or full-motion video sequences such as interviews, promo videos or live concert recordings could also be included, depending on the intended delivery system.

By bringing entertainment and information into the locus of today's major communications medium – the television – the new generation of electronic books may be able to tap a much wider 'readership' than paper books ever did. And as the convergence of television, computers and telecommunications gathers pace, more and more consumers will be using a hybrid 'teleputer' (combined television and computer), to 'read' these new 'books', alongside other more conventional TV programmes.

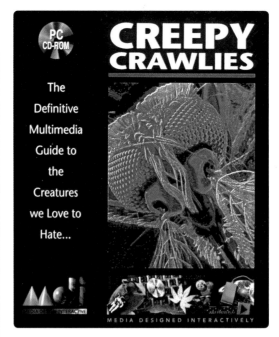

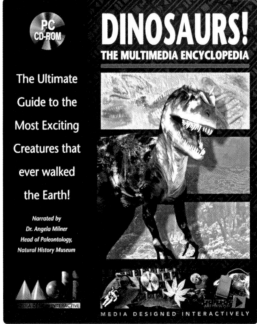

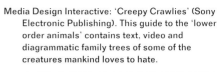

Media Design Interactive: 'Creepy Crawlies' (Sony Electronic Publishing). This guide to the 'lower order animals' contains text, video and diagrammatic family trees of some of the creatures mankind loves to hate.

'The Best of Both Worlds' (Sony Electronic Publishing). Sony publishes CD-ROM titles for the Mac and the PC, as well as for videogame platforms, Philips CD-i and the Amiga.

Media Design Interactive: 'Dinosaurs' (Sony Electronic Publishing). This interactive book provides 90 minutes of video, 200 illustrations and photographs, and special animated narrative sequences on the evolution of dinosaurs.

'Last Chance to See' (Sony Electronic Publishing).
Sci-fi novelist Douglas Adams and zoologist
Mark Carwardine survey the endangered
species of the world in a double CD-ROM set.

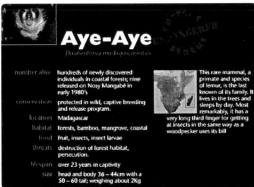

ENCODER
A **hardware** unit or system that accepts a **component video**
signal (such as **Hi-8** or **SVHS**, or **RGB**) and converts it to
a corresponding **composite video** signal.

ENCODING
The process of converting information to computer- or
machine-readable (**digital**) form; used especially to
refer to **full-motion video** encoding.
> DIGITIZER

ENCRYPT
The process of scrambling data to protect it for security
purposes. Encrypted data is decrypted by the
authorized end-user.

ENG [ELECTRONIC NEWS GATHERING]
Describes a highly portable, professional-standard
camcorder system used for television news coverage.

ENVELOPE
The sound characteristics of timbre, frequency or
amplitude over time, 'envelope' refers to the time of
attack, decay, sustain and release of sound.

ENVIRONMENT METAPHOR
A variety of metaphors of physical 'environments' are
being developed by **software interface** designers.
These include the 'desktop' environment of personal
computers; the 'rooms' environment of personal
computer interfaces from **Xerox PARC**; and space/time
metaphors that provide the environments for

surrogate travel, **flight simulation** and so on. Currently,
most of these environment metaphors are
represented through the monitor **screen** (sometimes
with additional soundtracks), but the technology to
'break through' the screen barrier and seemingly
enter the **cyberspace** of the program is already
available. By furnishing the user with **eyephones** and
datagloves, and by **tracking** their position and gestures
in high-resolution **3-d** computer models, such
systems can situate the user within a virtual
environment in which the metaphor is fleshed out
to become a reactive, 360-degree **virtual reality**.

EPOS [ELECTRONIC POINT OF SALE]
Systems designed digitally to capture the details of
transactions at sales points such as supermarket
checkouts. EPOS systems generally comprise a
cash register and a **bar-code** scanner.

EPROM
[ERASABLE, PROGRAMMABLE READ-ONLY MEMORY]
A solid-state memory cartridge that can be 'written to' up
to its memory capacity, 'read from' many times, and
when full can be either stored or erased and written
to again.
> CART   > MEMORY CARD
> READ/WRITE MEDIA   > ROM

EPSF [ENCAPSULATED POSTSCRIPT FORMAT]
A picture file format that depicts **PostScript** output
accurately on a computer **screen** display, and
provides high-resolution output. EPSF consists of

CCD ENG camera from Sony.

Sony publishes a wide range of electronic books
for its Data Discman including directories,
guides and general travel information for
major cities. Language dictionaries and
phrase books can even pronounce the
translations you are looking for.

two files: a **bitmap** file for screen display, and the
PostScript code for output.

> PAGE DESCRIPTION LANGUAGE

ERASABLE OPTICAL DISC

A laser disc that can be 'written to' until full, then erased
and written to again.

> DIGITAL-OPTICAL RECORDING

> READ/WRITE MEDIA　　　> WMRM

ERROR CORRECTION

> EDAC

ERS

> EMERGENCY RESPONSE SYSTEM

ETHERNET

A local area network (**LAN**) system developed in the early
1970s by **Xerox PARC**. Ethernets work at 10 million bits
per second with transmission times (for a **network** of
1.5 kilometres/1 mile) of less than 10 microseconds.
The signals, transmitted via **copper** (coaxial) **cable**, are
heard by all receivers, which 'listen' and wait for a
suitable access time before themselves transmitting
on the network. This technique, called 'carrier sense
multiple access' (CSMA), minimizes the network
collisions and problems caused by simultaneous
transmissions. Ethernets covering an area larger
than 1.5 kilometres would be likely to suffer much
higher incidences of message collisions.

> WAN

EVALUATION

The assessment of the effectiveness of **hypermedia**
programmes as they are used. Evaluation is
conducted with a representative sample of end-
users and may include a measure of consumer
satisfaction; an assessment of the effectiveness of
the various media used; and a judgement on how
'user-friendly' the programme is. Evaluations are
made with a trial or 'beta' version of the programme,
and often result in some level of redesign before the
final ('alpha') version is released.

> AUTHORING　　　　> VALIDATION

EVENT HANDLER

> HANDLER

EVENT LOOP

In computer systems, the sequence of events that the
computer cycles through in order to maintain and
run a **program**. In **virtual reality** systems, for example,
the event loop will include a check of all **input**
devices, such as **position sensors**; the sending of this
data to the computer, and the computer's response
to this data, for instance by changing viewpoint and
lighting. This in turn will determine the view the user
has of the model, thus completing the 'loop'. To
create a sense of realism, this loop must occur at
rates of at least 20 times per second.

EXECUTIVE INFORMATION SYSTEM

> MANAGEMENT INFORMATION SYSTEM

EXPANDED BOOKS

Electronically published books developed by The
Voyager Company for distribution on **floppy disk**.
'Expanded' books include not only the complete text
of the featured book, but several additional features
such as searching tools, text annotations and
animated illustrations (such as in their expanded
book version of The Annotated Alice by Martin
Gardner, which includes all the original Tenniel
drawings). Designed for use with the Apple **Powerbook**
(a laptop portable with backlit LCD screen), other
launch titles included Douglas Adams' Hitch-hikers'
Guide to the Galaxy and Michael Crichton's Jurassic
Park. Voyager also markets **software** for publishers to
create their own expanded books.

> ELECTRONIC BOOK　　　> ELECTRONIC PUBLISHING

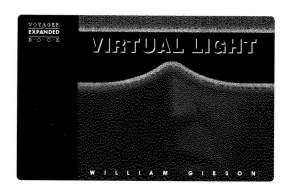

The Voyager Company has been a seminal influence
on electronic publishing with it
books' format. With Virtual Light , rumours
persist that the text deletes itself when the reader
has finished the expanded book.

Type in your own
margin notes.

Hold mouse down
for list of
chapters.

Move cursor to the top
of the screen to
display menu bar.

Go to marked pages.

Find any word or phrase in text
or margin notes.

Go to other chapters.

Read page-by-page or
access page by number.

Dog-ear [mark] page.

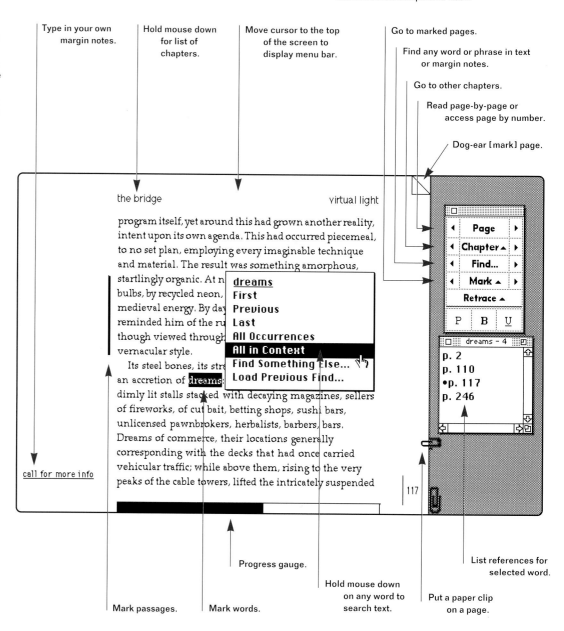

the bridge　　　　　　　　　　　　　　virtual light

program itself, yet around this had grown another reality,
intent upon its own agenda. This had occurred piecemeal,
to no set plan, employing every imaginable technique
and material. The result was something amorphous,
startlingly organic. At n...
bulbs, by recycled neon,...
medieval energy. By day...
reminded him of the ru...
though viewed throug...
vernacular style.

Its steel bones, its str...
an accretion of **dreams**...
dimly lit stalls stacked with decaying magazines, sellers
of fireworks, of cut bait, betting shops, sushi bars,
unlicensed pawnbrokers, herbalists, barbers, bars.
Dreams of commerce, their locations generally
corresponding with the decks that had once carried
vehicular traffic; while above them, rising to the very
peaks of the cable towers, lifted the intricately suspended

dreams
First
Previous
Last
All Occurrences
All in Context
Find Something Else...
Load Previous Find...

Page
Chapter
Find...
Mark
Retrace

P　B　U

dreams – 4
p. 2
p. 110
•p. 117
p. 246

117

call for more info

Mark passages.　　Mark words.

Progress gauge.

Hold mouse down
on any word to
search text.

Put a paper clip
on a page.

List references for
selected word.

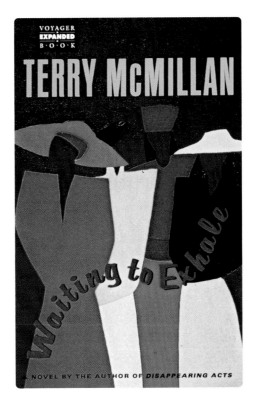

Expanded books from The Voyager Company. Such titles offer complete text for reading, with very fast text-search and retrieval software, and often include monochrome illustrations and additional commentary by authors.

EXPANSION SLOT

A place inside the computer for connecting additional circuits – such as **video board**s – that expand the capability of the machine.

EXPERT SYSTEM

(Or 'rule-based system'.) **Software** that enables a **database** of expert subject knowledge to become available to non-expert users. Expert systems are characterized by their ability to reason by logical inference, starting with a problem set by the user. The 'rules' that govern the way in which such systems operate is extracted or 'knowledge-mined' from human experts by a question-and-answer process.

Expert systems are a branch of artificial intelligence (**AI**), a scientific discipline that attempts to model human intelligence by means of computer software. Expert system techniques have been successful in a number of spheres including medical diagnosis, prospecting for oil and minerals, the design of **microchips** and the configuration of **telecommunications** networks. They are also used within **hypermedia** programmes for training, fault diagnosis and emergency management.

> KNOWLEDGE-BASED SYSTEM

EXTERNAL DEVICES

Peripheral hardware connected to a computer, such as a disk drive, keyboard, digitpad, etc.

EYEBALL TRACKING

The use of light-emitting diodes and infrared light to detect and 'track' the movement of a human eye, for the purpose of controlling a computer, **virtual reality** system or telematic device. Eyeball tracking is playing an important role alongside **speech recognition** and position tracking in the development of '**natural language**' and **gestural interface**s for computer systems. During the 1970s and 80s, eyeball-tracking techniques were developed for the control of weapons systems and flight controls in military fighter planes, and by the mid-1980s such devices were being developed for integration within virtual reality systems at both **MIT** in the USA and at the Advanced Telecommunications Research Institute in Japan.

> EYEPHONE   > HEAD-MOUNTED DISPLAY

EYEPHONE

A **head-mounted display** device developed by VPL Industries for interfacing with a **virtual reality** system. The VPL EyePhone incorporates stereo display **screens**, stereo headphones and a **position sensor** that responds to head movements and determines the view the wearer enjoys of the virtual world.

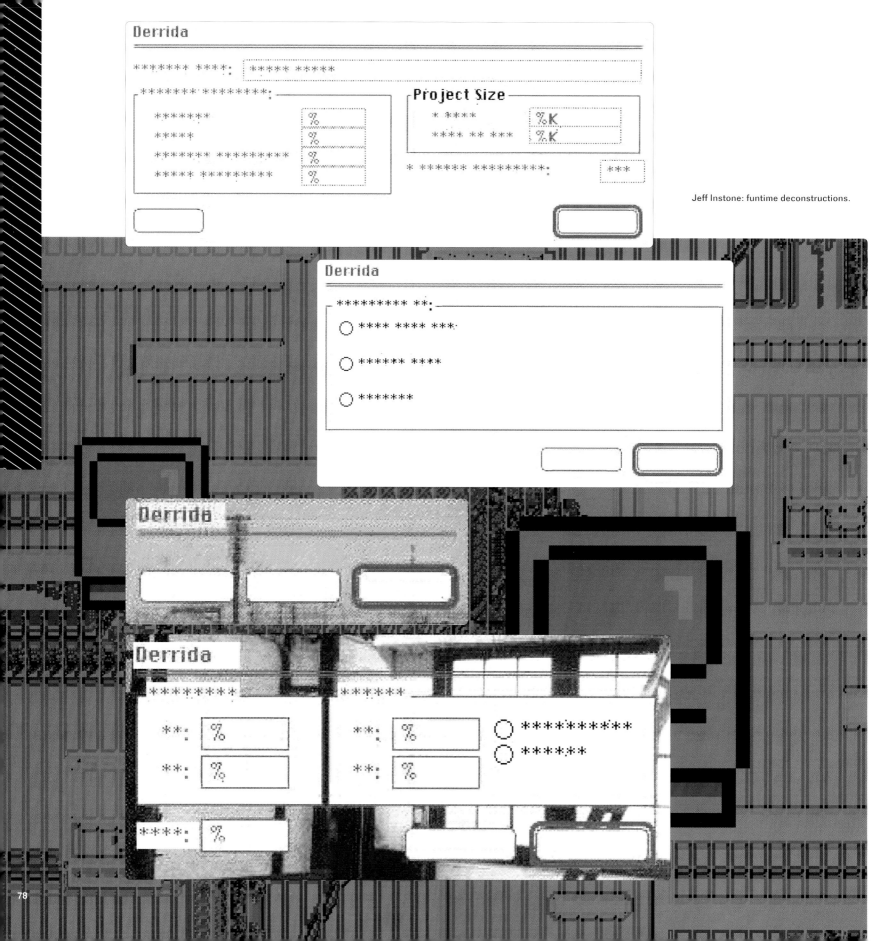

Jeff Instone: funtime deconstructions.

FADE IN/OUT

A **transition** effect where the **screen** begins as a solid black, or some other dark colour, and lightens in a series of graduated steps to reveal an image ('fade in'), and ends with the reverse of this process ('fade out'). First developed in film and then adopted by television and video, it is now extensively used in computer presentations and **hypermedia** programmes.

FAX (FACSIMILE TRANSMISSION)

A method of 'photo-telegraphy' for transmitting images, writing and text via telephone cables. Fax technology is over one hundred years old, but present-day fax machines are a development of the systems introduced in the early 1970s in Japan (where the need for facsimile transmission was driven by the difficulty of transmitting ideograms). By 1989, over 10 million fax machines were in use around the world. By the early 1990s, **digital** versions of the fax were available, allowing **personal computer** users to become the senders and receivers of fax transmissions.

>   TELECOMMUNICATIONS

FDDI
(FIBRE-DISTRIBUTED DATA INTERFACE)

An International Standards Organization (**ISO**) **standard** for the connection of communication devices to **networks**, using **fibre-optic** cables. The FDDI standard calls for a data rate of 100 megabits per second, operating over a 100-kilometre (62-mile) area. Such fibre networks will connect smaller local area networks (**LANs**) or metropolitan-area networks, providing the basic infrastructure or **data superhighway** for national and even international networks.

FEEDBACK

Technically, the return of part of a system's output to its **input**, which is thereby changed. Positive feedback takes an increase in output back to increase the input; negative feedback takes an increase in output back to decrease the input.

This term is often used more loosely to describe the process by which a program or system informs users of what it is doing so that they can take appropriate action. In **interactive** systems, such as **computer graphics** and 'paintbox' systems, feedback is more or less instantaneous. The user makes a gesture by moving a stylus across a **digitpad**, and the system 'paints' this line across the monitor screen.

Conversely, a program or system can be modified by a user's actions. It is possible to create software that not only 'learns' from the user's actions (and past performance), but is able to store a record of these past actions and gradually build up a model of the user's tastes and preferences. Such a program could then make inference from this record, so that for instance in a 'news filtering' role it could select

items from the broadcast news datastream that it 'knows' are of special interest to the human user, store them, and present the user with a customized 'news' programme.

>   AUDIO FEEDBACK   >   CYBERNETICS
>   FORCE FEEDBACK   >   INTERFACE
>>   FURTHER READING: NEGROPONTE 1991; WIENER 1948

FIBRE OPTICS

Thin strands of highly transparent glass or plastic, that carry data in the form of pulses of laser light energy.

>   • FIBRE OPTICS PAGE 80

FIELD

(1) In video, half the scan lines (every other line) necessary to complete a video scanning cycle. Two interlaced fields produce one video **frame**. Interlaced frames reduce image flicker.

(2) In **hypermedia authoring**, an area in which text can be created, edited or displayed. 'Read-only' text appears in a 'locked' text field.

(3) In computer **databases**, the subdivision of the database that contains a particular type of data.

FILE

A unit of information stored in a storage medium such as a **floppy** or **hard disk**. Files may contain programs, data, text, images, or any other information. While a file is a constant unit that can be retrieved or copied, the elements from which it is composed may be physically dispersed over the disk.

>   FILE MANAGEMENT

FILE FORMAT

A defined structure in which data is organized for storage or transmission. A **file** created using one program cannot usually be read by another without a special program (called a filter) to translate one file format into another.

FILE MANAGEMENT

The efficient management of computer **files** as they are updated and revised. While this is an essential, but often neglected, aspect of running any computer system or project, it is particularly important in **hypermedia** production.

A typical hypermedia production can involve several different designers and programmers working together over a period of several weeks. During this time large numbers of graphics, text, audio, animation, video, image and program files will be created, processed, edited and reworked by different people working at different times. The file management system must ensure that only one designer or programmer is working on a file at any particular time (to avoid duplication of effort and the creation of files that mutually conflict, each having been updated in a different way); that files are

→ →

FIBRE OPTICS
high-bandwidth
gossamer

The transmission of large quantities of information over long distances through tiny glass fibre cables is a triumph of doing more with less technology. Fibre optics are a key element in the emerging cyberspace of hypermedia and telecommunications. With their vast bandwidth, they promise to carry all kinds of new services and entertainment – including home shopping, videogames, videophones and teleworking facilities as well as the familiar terrestrial, satellite and cable television channels – all piped directly into the home. Fibre-optic networks are 'future proof', with enough capacity for all currently conceivable media developments

Optical fibres are fine strands of high-transparency glass which act as 'waveguides' for the transmission of single-frequency light beams. Fibre-optic communication systems require a light source (emitter), an optical fibre, a light detector, and connectors and couplers to link these components together. The message (ie the picture or audio signal) is encoded digitally and converted to pulses of laser light energy by the emitter. The optical fibre provides a 'guide' which the light energy follows until it is 'received' by an optical detector. This detector converts the pulse back into electronic pulses and restores the signal to match the original information. At first, optical signals could only be sent a short distance without amplification, but advances in engineering gradually increased the range from 30 kilometres (18 miles) in 1981 to 400 kilometres (250 miles) in the early 1990s. A new generation of fibre optics being developed at the University of Southampton (UK) will enable signals to be sent hundreds of miles.

Fibre-optic technology stems from research on waveguides by G C Southworth and others in the 1920s. Their research resulted in the development of the coaxial cable (1928) followed by hollow-tube wave guides for electromagnetic radiation. In 1960, the first LASER (Light Amplification by Stimulated Emission of Radiation) was produced. In the late 1960s, researchers at ITT's Standard Telephone Laboratories in the UK established a framework for the design of optical fibres that would allow the practical transmission of information using laser light beams as data carriers. By 1980, the technologies necessary to make this a reality (in the form of solid-state laser emitters and light-emitting diodes) were in place.

At 120 microns, fibre-optic cables are about the thickness of a human hair, with a glass core of about 7 microns in diameter. Operating at very high frequencies of infrared, they can support an almost unlimited bandwidth and can be used to carry large volumes of low-band multiplexed signals (such as telephone calls) or wide-band signals for television and video conferencing. According to communications expert John Alvey (former chief engineer at British Telecom), fibre-optic cables can carry a thousand times more signals than can be

Finer than a human hair, these strands of glass gossamer have a bandwidth that exceeds that of the entire broadcast spectrum. And when the limit is reached? You simply add more fibres.

transmitted over the entire radio bandwidth. 'In this way', states Alvey, '350 million phone calls could be carried over a single fibre optic at any one time…or over 50,000 HDTV signals.' (D H Mellor (ed.), 'Communications and Technology', <u>Ways of Communicating</u>, 1990)

Fibre optics are 'future-proof' because they have enough bandwidth for any conceivable developments in communications. They are thus set to play an important role in the growing trend towards integrated multimedia. George Gilder has pointed out that within ten years – the time it might optimistically take to establish a Data Superhighway infrastructure – personal computers will have more power than present-day supercomputers. This is not a wild prediction: in 1993, top-of-the-range PCs have more power than the CRAY 1, the first supercomputer. The combination of optical-fibre networks and supercomputing power in the home will provide sophisticated and revolutionary consumer 'infotainment' technology, opening up the possibility of high-resolution realtime experiences such as virtual reality, interactive movies, and more.

In the USA, the Clinton administration has committed itself to supporting the establishment of the infrastructure for such a data superhighway network. In Japan, US $12 billion has been committed to a plan to create a nationwide fibre network by the year 2015. In the UK, British Telecom has a nationwide fibre-optic trunk grid and Mercury a much smaller grid, but currently neither has a licence to supply fibre-optic links into the home. Neither Britain nor Europe have yet developed a coherent strategy for this kind of national and pan-European infrastructure. Elsewhere, such networks are widely seen as essential to post-industrial success.

>> FURTHER READING: MELLOR 1990

labelled according to a planned programme structure; that they are dated and/or labelled with a version number; that the many 'incidental' files that are created (such as working graphics) are kept separate from the 'production' files; and that all production files are regularly backed-up on a storage device that is housed quite separately from the development platforms.
>   AUTHORING

FILM PLUS
The concept of making films (especially classics) more attractive to consumers by including additional information or means of analysis. 'Films Plus' are released on disc-based media such as **laserdisc** or **CD-ROM**. Additional information might include critical commentaries by film practitioners, critics and historians, details of the actors, locations, production methods and special effects and so forth. The film therefore becomes the central narrative within a **branching**, **interactive** programme, with users able to access contextual information as they want, to listen to extra commentary when they would like to, or to consult the script, **treatment** or **storyboard** as text and graphics.

In these kinds of ways, Film Plus can add value to a whole range of film product. The Voyager Company in the USA has already released 'Film Plus' titles on laserdisc. Advances in **compression** techniques, and increases in the capacity of the discs themselves, mean that by the mid 1990s CD-ROM-based systems will be able to store full-length feature films and the additional data required for Film Plus.
>   INTERACTIVE MOVIE   >   MUSIC PLUS

FILM RECORDER
A computer-controlled output device or 'camera' that takes signals from the host computer and generates an image independent of the main **monitor screen** image before recording it onto film. It is widely used in the preparation of slides from **computer graphics software**, and in the production of animated sequences from high-resolution **modelling** and **animation** software. Film is still the highest-resolution medium for recording computer-generated images, and has the advantage that it can easily be converted (**telecined**) to any **video format** or international broadcast standard.

FIRMWARE
In computers and **hypermedia** systems, the regularly used **software** that is permanently stored in the system in some form of **hardware** (such as a **ROM**). All or part of a **microcomputer** or consumer **multimedia** player operating system may be 'firmware'.

FLASH MEMORY CARD
A **PCMCIA memory card** produced by companies such as Intel and Mitsubishi. Designed for use in **personal digital assistants** and **palmtop** computers, these standard-interface cards can hold up to a maximum of 64 megabytes, and boast access times of around 200 nanoseconds. Flash memory cards are essentially **EPROMs**, but unlike EPROMs they do not

A HARD DAY'S NIGHT

CONTENTS

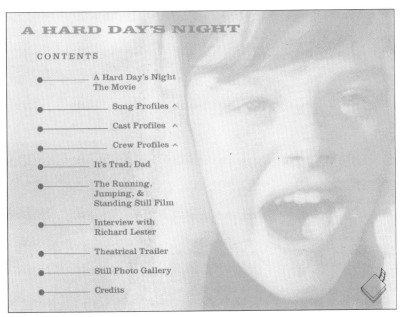

- A Hard Day's Night The Movie
- Song Profiles ∧
- Cast Profiles ∧
- Crew Profiles ∧
- It's Trad, Dad
- The Running, Jumping, & Standing Still Film
- Interview with Richard Lester
- Theatrical Trailer
- Still Photo Gallery
- Credits

A HARD DAY'S NIGHT

FORMAT CONTENTS ‹ MARK ›
QUIT ? CONTROLS ‹ FIND ›   ◄ Photo Gallery – 6 of 25 ►

A HARD DAY'S NIGHT

years before there were satellite shots of the Earth on the news every night); *The Naked Kiss*, which opens with a bald prostitute beating up a man. That's just about how unusual this sequence was for audiences in 1964.

A Hard Day's Night is just as daring as these other films in its technique and in the structure of its opening – and it applies those techniques to rock 'n' roll. So if it's the best rock 'n' roll movie ever made, then it's because it respected the intelligence of its audience, and challenged that audience in a way no rock 'n' roll movie, and precious few popular films, ever has.

Although no one realized it in 1964, *A*

FORMAT CONTENTS ‹ MARK ›
QUIT ? CONTROLS ‹ FIND ›   ◄ Commentary – 6 of 166 ►

A HARD DAY'S NIGHT

WILFRID BRAMBELL

"John McCartney" (Paul's grandfather)

B. Dublin, 1912.
D. 1985

Originally a journalist, Wilfrid Brambell entered the acting profession in his early '20s and worked the boards in vaudeville and travelling shows before joining the Abbey Theatre company in the mid 1930s. He made his London debut soon after. A character actor who specialized in playing sometimes comical, sometimes sinister eccentrics, as well as dirty old men, Brambell was elevated to stardom in 1964 with his

MARK ›
FIND ›   ◄ Wilfrid Brambell – 1 of 3 ►

FORMAT CONTENTS ‹ MARK ›
QUIT ? CONTROLS ‹ FIND ›   A HARD DAY'S NIGHT

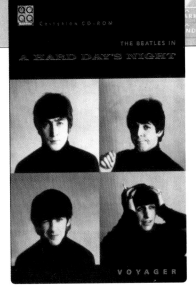

The Voyager Company: 'A Hard Day's Night', maybe the first entire feature film on CD-ROM. A QuickTime movie with cast information, 160 pages of text and hypertext, and biographies on the cast and director, it even includes the cinema trailer.

have to be removed from the host computer and placed in a special device to be reprogrammed. The term 'Flash' means that the card can be erased 'in-circuit' (ie while still in the host device). Like EPROMs, flash memory cards are 'non-volatile' – they do not require power to retain data that is held in memory.

FLAT SCREEN

Describes cathode-ray tube television monitors with flat display screens; also the **LCD** flat screens used in **laptop** computers and hand-held portable colour televisions, or the 'Flatter Squarer Tubes' (FSTs) made popular by Toshiba, Mitsubishi, Philips and other manufacturers.

FLATBED SCANNER

A digitizing **scanner** rather like a photocopier, with a flat glass platen or bed (as opposed to a 'gravity fed' scanner or rotary scanner). Flatbed scanners deliver resolutions of around 300-800 **dpi**, and are used for digitizing 'flat art', ie photographs or illustrations on paper, images from books, etc. Flatbed scanners are available for black-and-white (line), greyscale (tone) or full-colour image digitizing.

> DIGITAL

FLIGHT SIMULATION

A system for training pilots that allows them to practise the actions they would take while flying, in a model of the cockpit they would use and within a recreation of many of the conditions they would meet. The roots of modern flight simulation technology lie way back in the 1930s when the first flight simulator, the Link Trainer, was introduced. The Link was the first in a long line of training simulators for aircraft pilots. From a simplified full-scale model of a fuselage and cockpit, mounted on a platform that could rotate and move up and down, with the bare minimum of audio and visual cues to help the trainee pilot suspend disbelief in the 'reality' of the experience, simulators grew into immensely sophisticated machines employing hydraulics, wrap-around video screens, and powerful computers using state-of-the-art **'realtime'** animation software.

In early machines the only visual illusion of flight was that provided by the instruments in the cockpit. Later simulators used back-projected film to give the trainee the illusion of being airborne. The current generation of flight simulators employs powerful computers to generate the images, which are projected onto 200-degree-wide screens using the latest **monitor** and videobeam technology.

> SIMULATION   > VIRTUAL REALITY

FLOPPY DISK

A removable, electromagnetic-disk storage medium. Originally made in 8¼- and 5¼-inch diameter sizes and mounted in flexible plastic envelopes, modern floppies are 3½-inch diameter and mounted in rigid plastic, with a metal sliding cover to protect the disk surface. Typical capacity is 1.4 megabytes.

> FLOPTICLE   > HARD DISK

Rediffusion Simulation: Concept 90 simulator for Alitalia with Novoview WIDE visual system and ACCESS instructor station. Simulators such as this are used extensively for both military and commercial flight training.

FLOPTICLE

A removable, electromagnetic-disk storage medium that uses laser technology to increase its capacity. For example, while a 3½-inch **floppy disk** can hold up to 1.4 megabytes, the equivalent floptical can store up to 21 megabytes.

> CD-R   > WMRM

FLOWCHART

A graphical representation of a series of events or a system. In **hypermedia** programme design, a combination of **storyboard** and flowchart can be a useful way of representing all of the different media elements that make up the programme and the variety of routes that the user may take through it.

> AUTHORING   > DESIGN STAGE

FM TOWNS MARTY

A **CD-ROM**-based **multimedia** player manufactured by Fujitsu. The Marty has a 32-bit processor rated at 16 MHz, 2 megabytes of **RAM** and a graphics 'sprite engine' capable of supporting up to 1,024 sprites. Although highly rated in Japan for its 16.7 million colours and impressive sprite-handling ability, Marty does not yet support double-speed CD-ROM or **full-motion video (Video-CD)**.

FMV

> FULL-MOTION VIDEO

FOCAL LENGTH

In cameras, the distance from the lens to the recording device (eg the **CCD** chip) when a very distant object is brought into focus. The longer the focal length of the lens, the larger the image that is recorded. Thus, a wide-angle (short focal length) lens will give a small image size with a wide view of the scene, whereas a telephoto lens will give a large image size within a much narrower view of the scene. In **computer graphics** and **computer animation**, the software 'lens' is fully programmable, and the focal length of the lens can be changed frame-by-frame through the extremes of fish-eye to telephoto.

FOLDER

In the **Macintosh** 'desktop' **interface**, a collection of **files** or other folders represented on-screen by an **icon**.

> GRAPHICAL USER INTERFACE

FORCE FEEDBACK

A technique deployed in **flight simulation**, telepresence and **virtual reality** systems whereby the controlling device (eg the **joystick**, **DataGlove**, boom or remote manipulator) provides a form of physical response to the user that corresponds with the physical mass of the real or virtual object being manipulated. Thus in virtual space, as in the real world, a feather will be easier to move than a brick. Force feedback, along with automatic **speech recognition**, stereo imaging, position tracking, **eyeball tracking** and so on, will undoubtedly form part of the all-encompassing multi-sensory interfaces of tomorrow's information and entertainment systems.

> POSITION SENSORS   > SKETCHPAD
> VIRTUAL REALITY

FORTH (FOURTH-GENERATION LANGUAGE)

A **high-level language** and **operating system** originally developed for the **realtime** control of technical equipment. Invented by Charles Moore in 1970 to help him control the equipment at the Kitt Peak National Radio Observatory, it is not a popular language, but has some very enthusiastic advocates. While it is capable of being used as a general-purpose language, Forth tends to be employed for specialized applications. These include machine control, **robotics**, laboratory data acquisition, automation, interfacing with musical instruments, **arcade games** and **videogames**.

FORTRAN (FORMULA TRANSLATION)

A **high-level language** developed in the 1950s by John Backus at IBM, for scientific and engineering applications. At one time one of the most widely used languages in this field, most of the early work in **computer graphics** was written in it. It has now largely been supplanted by **C**.

>> FURTHER READING: BARON 1988

Fractal images produced on a PC.

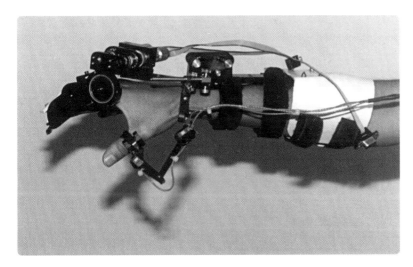

Exos: SAFire (Sensing And Force reflecting exoskelton) provides joint torque feedback to human fingers and motion commands to the simulated model.

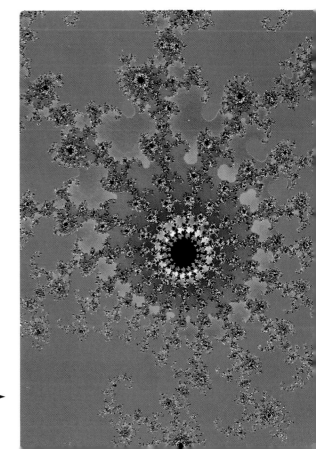

FRACTAL COMPRESSION

Compression techniques used to reduce the amount of data required to store and transmit a **digital** image, based on equations developed in fractal **geometry**. Fractal compression gives satisfactory results with very high **compression ratio**s (up to 200:1), and in theory this means that a two-hour feature film delivering VHS-quality **resolution** could be stored on a **CD-ROM** disc (currently CD-ROMs can store 72 minutes of **MPEG**-compressed full-motion video, or 25 seconds or so of uncompressed video images).

Fractal compression techniques will increasingly be used in **archiving** and **telecommunications** (videophones, **video conferencing**, image libraries and so forth). They will prove invaluable in the compression and decompression of motion pictures.

> JPEG > MPEG
> VIDEO-CD
>> FURTHER READING: BARNSLEY & SLOANE 1988

FRACTAL IMAGE

An image that is generated from an equation, yet can be zoomed to very high degrees of detail, effectively allowing an infinite amount of visual information to be encoded in a finite formula. Fractal formulas are used to generate the image by an iterative (repetitive) mathematical process, and can be used to generate natural-looking forms such as trees and lakes, and (with NASA astrological data) equally natural-looking images of planets. These techniques are used in film special effects, **computer graphics** and **computer animation**.

> FRACTAL COMPRESSION

FRACTAL TRANSFORM

A **fractal compression** technique developed by British mathematician Dr Michael Barnsley in 1987. Fractal transform techniques are used to break an image down into a grid of large blocks called 'ranges' and small units called 'domains'. Domains are then compared to each of the larger ranges to see if there is any similarity between them (regardless of orientation, position or size). The more complex the image, the more likely it is that self-similar domains will occur, and a single domain may describe the components of several larger 'ranges'. Domains are stored as fractal equations that describe qualities such as colour, pattern and intensity, and their mapped relationships within the image. In this manner fractal transform techniques developed by Barnsley can produce several thousand fractals per image, each stored as a mathematical equation. The string of equations is further compressed using standard data-compression techniques (such as Huffman **encoding**), and the result is that a typical 24-bit 768 kilobyte image file can be stored in 10 kilobytes. Images are reconstructed from the fractal information by processing the equations and mapping domains into larger regions.

Currently, Barnsley's company Iterated Systems markets fractal transform compression software for personal computers, and these compression techniques will find an extensive range of applications in **cyberspace** media, including **archiving**, **digital video**, **videophone** and video conferencing.

> FRACTAL IMAGES
>> FURTHER READING: BARNSLEY & SLOANE 1988

FRAME

(1) A single, individual picture in a film strip or movie.

(2) Two interlaced **field**s, or a single non-interlaced field, of a video image.

(3) In **CDDA**, a unit of $^1/75$ of a second, containing 2352 **byte**s of data.

(4) A single page or screen display of videotext.

(5) A unit of instruction in computer-based training.

CD-i digital video cartridge. The Philips ER9141 plug-in cartridge for CD-i players adds 1.5 megabytes of player RAM and decompresses MPEG data in realtime.

FRAME BUFFER

In **video graphics** or **computer graphics**, an area of memory that stores one or more **frame**s of video or computer-generated images.

FRAME GRABBER

An add-on board for the computer that allows single **frame**s to be digitized from a video source.

FRAME RATE

The rate at which video or film is projected or displayed. **Full-motion video** can be achieved at rates of around 25 **frame**s per second, and this is the television broadcast system (**PAL**) standard frame rate in the UK. In the US, the **NTSC** standard displays video at 30 frames per second. Film is projected at 24 frames per second.

> FREEZE FRAME > STOP-FRAME RECORDING

FREEZE FRAME

In film or video, a single **frame** from motion footage that is held motionless on **screen**. Not to be confused with 'still frame', which is an image originally intended to be shown on its own as a still.

> STILL-FRAME AUDIO

FRONT END

The visible part of a computer **program**, **database** or **hypermedia** programme, that the user interacts with directly.

> INTERFACE

FULL-MOTION VIDEO [FMV]

Describes a computer system or **multimedia** player capable of displaying **digital** video at a rate of not less than 25 frames a second. Until the early 1990s full-motion video was generally displayed in a small window measuring no more than a quarter of the full **screen** size.

> DVI
> FULL-SCREEN FULL-MOTION VIDEO
> MPEG > VIDEO-CD
> • FULL-MOTION VIDEO PAGE 85

FULL-SCREEN FULL-MOTION VIDEO [FSFMV]

Describes a computer or multimedia system that is capable of displaying digital video at rates of 25 frames per second or over, with images at full-screen size. FSFMV depends on **compression** and decompression techniques that have only become a practical reality in the early 1990s. The advances in these techniques open up the potential for **CD-ROM**-based systems to compete directly with video as a means of distributing films for home viewing.

> CD-i > DVI
> FULL-MOTION VIDEO > INTERACTIVE MOVIE
> MPEG > VIDEO-CD
> WHITE BOOK

FUNCTION HANDLER

> HANDLER

FULL-MOTION VIDEO

welcome to the digital cinema

Moving pictures are the vehicle through which most of our entertainment, news and information reaches us. At 16 years of age the average child will have watched some 12,000 hours of television – about the same amount of time that they have spent at school. The average adult spends around 35 hours a week watching the box. Motion pictures are part of our way of life. From the age of three or four we have all been covertly educated in the art of video and cinematography, so much so that when children are given video cameras at school, teachers are surprised by their seemingly innate knowledge of the techniques of panning, zooming and tracking.

Moving pictures are so important to us that the provision of 'full-motion video' (FMV) is of major concern to the developers of digital entertainment systems like Philips' Compact Disc Interactive (CD-i) and 3DO's Interactive Multiplayer. The acronym 'FMV' distinguishes video quality from slow frame rates of (typically) 10-15 frames/sec (so-called 'partial-motion video') and describes a system capable of displaying motion video at rates of 25 frames per second or over. FMV systems may or may not be full-screen (FSFMV). Developers of systems that support FMV know that they have to produce digital motion pictures of a quality that at least matches that of consumer-quality VHS videotape.

For several years FMV has been a 'holy grail' for the designers of compact disc-based interactive multimedia systems, such as CD-i. A system with FMV capability opens up the possibility of marketing films, videos, music, videogames and interactive multimedia programmes all on the same kind of discs. Such a system would replace several separate items of hardware, and provide the consumer with an integrated entertainment system. For the publisher, discs are much cheaper to manufacture, replicate and distribute than tape cassettes.

Any system that is going to be 'backwardly compatible' with audio CDs must read data from the disc at a (maximum) rate of 170 kilobytes per second. The trouble is that at this rate an average television-quality image takes just under a second to load from the disc to the display screen. Motion video requires at least 25 such frames to be displayed every second. Initial attempts to provide motion pictures on compact disc focused on small windows of video, less than one-quarter of the screen area, that could be displayed at rates of around 15 frames per second. Real full-screen motion video required breakthroughs in image compression and decompression, first achieved by the inventors of Digital Video Interactive (DVI), a computer microchip that can decompress VHS-quality video in realtime. DVI is now available as a chip-set (Intel i760) for IBM PCs and an expansion board for Macintosh computers.

Philips CD-i, the first consumer interactive system to offer digital full-motion video, uses a compression/decompression system based on a chip co-developed by C-Cube Microsystems and Philips. CD-i offers full-screen FMV of a quality slightly better than VHS tape. Other consumer products offering quality full-motion video include the 3DO Interactive Multiplayer. At its launch in late 1993, the Interactive Multiplayer could deliver around 60 minutes of FMV from a CD-ROM, with plans to offer feature films by means of an extra plug-in decompression cartridge.

High-quality full-motion video is so important that its presence or absence will make or break a consumer interactive media system. FMV can be used to encode movies for distribution on disc, it can provide TV-quality interactive multimedia, highly realistic videogames or interactive movies, and all kinds of top quality 'edutainment' programmes. Consumer electronics manufacturers have agreed on a standard defined by the Motion Picture Experts Group (MPEG) for FMV. This holds the promise of several otherwise incompatible multimedia systems being able to play a common digital movie standard for non-interactive films. MPEG FMV could be the beginning of the set of world standards that will define the multimedia technologies of the twenty-first century.

Philips: 'Voyeur' CD-i. Early versions of 'Voyeur' incorporated smooth partial-screen motion video. Later versions make full use of the MPEG FMV cartridge. With a budget of US $750,000, a nine-day film shoot, and Hollywood actors of the calibre of Robert Culp, 'Voyeur' broke new ground in interactive entertainment.

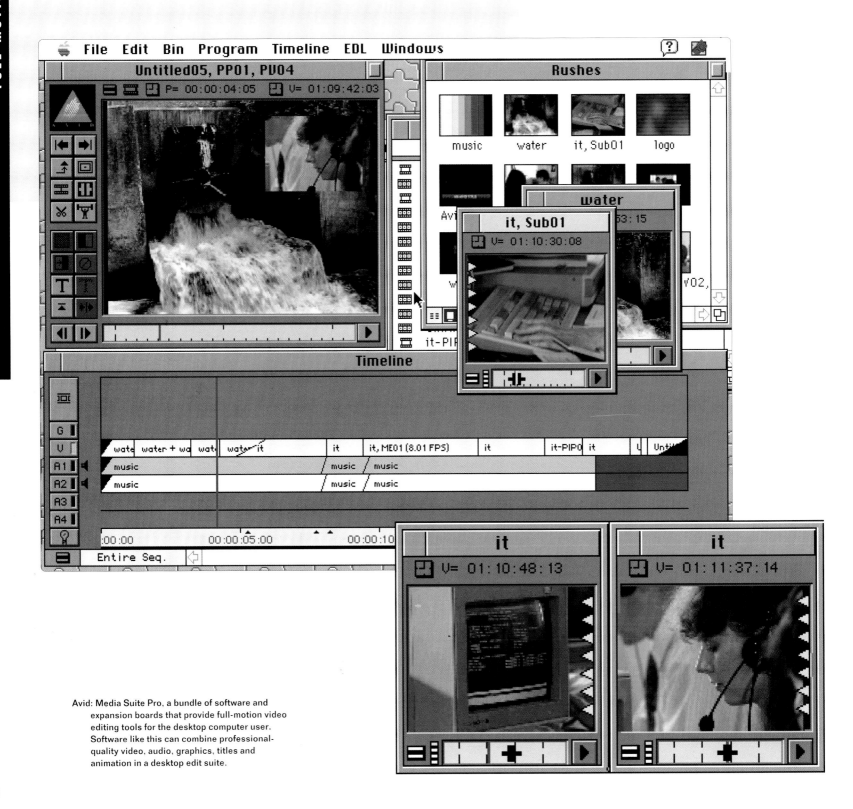

Avid: Media Suite Pro, a bundle of software and
expansion boards that provide full-motion video
editing tools for the desktop computer user.
Software like this can combine professional-
quality video, audio, graphics, titles and
animation in a desktop edit suite.

GAMES
> ARCADE GAMES > QUIZ GAMES
> VIDEOGAMES

GAMES NETWORK
System for linking games machines. When fully
established, games networks will encourage multiplayer games, tournaments and games forums, and
will facilitate the previewing, sampling and ordering
of games **software**. In 1993 **Sega**, in alliance with
Telecommunications Inc. and Time Warner, had an
experimental games network available through cable
TV coaxials linking 350,000 households in 13 major
cities in the USA. In Japan, **Nintendo** has been running
a games and information network since 1989,
offering Super Famicom owners services such as
electronic banking, share-trading and teleshopping
as well as games network facilities. Nintendo has
also announced the St Giga 'Message Information
Broadcast Service System', providing information,
music and games services, through which Super
Famicom owners can play against each other via
satellite links. In the UK, the telecoms giant BT
is developing its Project ICE (Information,
Communications and Entertainment), a scheme
that will give **videogames** distributors access to 26
million households. Although BT is banned from
'broadcasting' on its network, it argues that this is a
grey area and that the 'one-to-one' interactive nature
of ICE does not constitute broadcasting.

GENERATION LOSS
In analog video, the degradation of image quality in video
editing, caused by the multiple copying of video
signals. The original tape is described as 'first
generation', a copy of this is 'second generation',
and so on. There is no 'generation loss' in **digital**
media, where copies are exact replicas of the
original image.

GENLOCK
The automatic correction of the timing of video systems
to match the timing of an external signal (such as
that from a computer controlling a video edit deck).
Genlock is necessary in video-graphic and **desktop
video** systems in order smoothly to combine **computer
graphics** and video images.
> VIDEO GRAPHICS

GEOGRAPHICAL INFORMATION SYSTEMS
[GIS]
A computer-controlled, map-based information system.
Such systems use the familiar **interface** of the map or
chart to provide the user with information that is
linked to cartographical features. They may also
include other geographical information such
as satellite remote images, aerial photographs,
sidescan radar images, panoramas, geological data,
and so forth.
Paper maps can contain a wide range of information on
terrain, topography, communications, land use, and

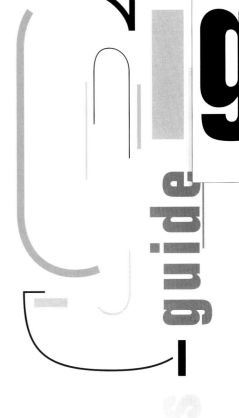

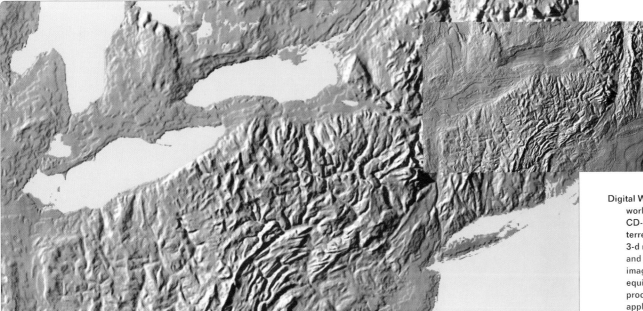

Digital Wisdom Inc: 'Mountain High Maps',
world topographical information on
CD-ROM. Compiled from satellite and
terrestrial survey data and embodied in
3-d models that have been photographed
and digitized for CD-ROM, these relief
images provide clearer information than
equivalent satellite images. They can be
processed in a variety of graphics
applications on the PC and Mac,
including Photoshop, Freehand and
PageMaker.

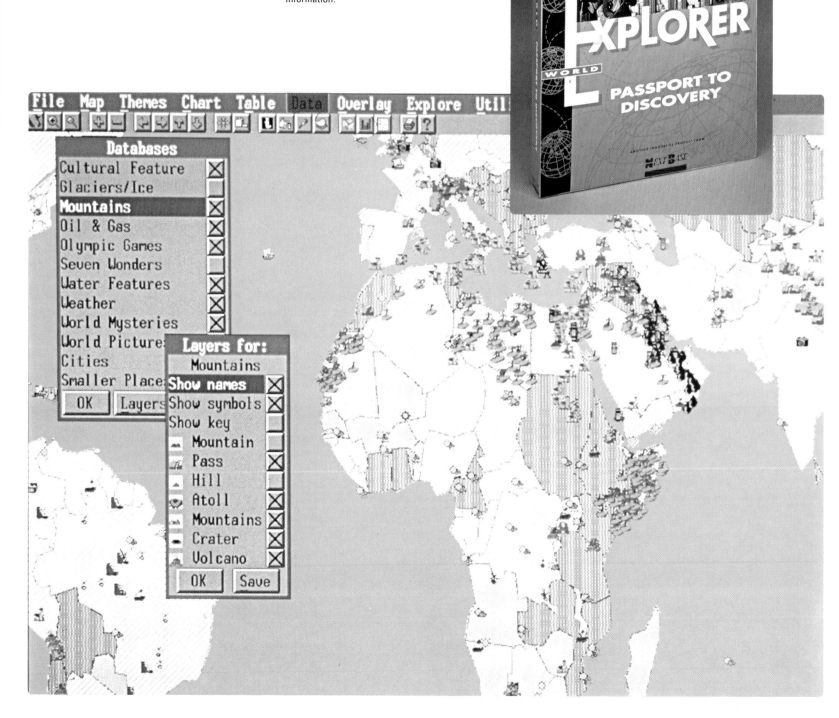

NextBase: 'World Explorer', a consumer geographical information system. Here, maps become menus for a wide range of geophysical and cultural information.

so forth. **Hypermedia** or **database** GIS systems can use map symbols and place names as **icons** or **buttons** to provide the user with additional information in **multimedia** form. Maps can also be stored digitally in several scales, allowing the user to overview a wide area and to 'zoom' into the area of interest. GIS techniques are being applied to a wide range of products including route-planning **program**s for PCs, tourist **point-of-information** programmes, holiday planning guides and **surrogate travel** experiences, as well as in-car navigation systems, ship management systems and military intelligence systems.

> EMERGENCY RESPONSE SYSTEM
> GPS
> MANAGEMENT INFORMATION SYSTEM

GEOS [GEOSTATIONARY SATELLITE]

A satellite that orbits at an altitude of 37,500 kilometres (23,300 miles), at a speed enabling the satellite to maintain a relatively stationary position above a particular area of the Earth's surface. Three such satellites together can provide global satellite communication services.

> SATELLITE COMMUNICATIONS

GESTURAL INTERFACE

The use of significant movement of a limb or other part of the human body to communicate with a computer system. This kind of interaction with computer systems goes back to the development of the light pen and stylus/**Sketchpad** invented by Ivan Sutherland in the early 1960s, and to the development of the **mouse** by Douglas Engelbart in 1965. With the innovations in gesture-sensing apparatus made by Myron Krueger in the 1970s, and the invention of 'touchscreen' monitors in the early 1980s, VPL's **DataGlove** (1988), consumer digital gloves like Mattel's '**PowerGlove**' (1990), VPL's **DataSuit** (1990), the '3-d mouse' and 'wand' **input** devices, gestural communications have become increasingly three-dimensional and fluid. These kinds of gestural interfaces are pointing the way towards computer-mediated or 'intelligent' (real or virtual) environments for work, study or play, where every aspect of our body language would be tracked by **sensor**s to provide responsive feedback.

> FORCE FEEDBACK   > PROJECTED REALITY
> VIRTUAL REALITY

GIF [GRAPHICS INTERCHANGE FORMAT]

A bitmapped colour graphics **file format**, developed by **CompuServe** in 1987 for the transmission of colour images over a **network**.

GIGABYTE

One thousand **megabyte**s. Some WORM and WMRM discs and some **hard disk**s have capacities of one gigabyte.

GIS

> GEOGRAPHICAL INFORMATION SYSTEMS

GLASS DISC

Recordable **videodisc** used for short runs of **interactive video** programmes, or as a test or 'check' disc before disc

mastering and replication. Glass discs follow the same format as Philips' **LaserVision** videodisc (holding 54,000 individually addressable video **frame**s), and comprise a polymeric recording medium on a glass/acrylic substrate coated with aluminium. For very short runs glass discs are much cheaper than conventional videodisc pressings, since no master is involved and they can be produced within much shorter turnaround times.

> INTERACTIVE VIDEO

GOURAUD SHADING

In **computer graphics**, a technique devised by Henry Gouraud for the smooth shading of polygonal surfaces. This rendering or smoothing technique averages the 'light intensity' at the vertexes of polygons, effectively disguising the edges of adjacent polygons.

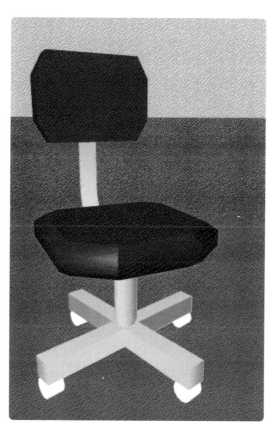

Gouraud shading: example by Peakash Patel.

GPS [GLOBAL POSITIONING SYSTEM]

A computer-based navigation system that uses signals from a number of satellites to calculate precise locations on the Earth's surface. A by-product of US government investment in a highly accurate military position-fixing navigation system, GPS delivers an accuracy of a few metres in a longitude/latitude position, as well as altitude readings. A GPS navigation system works by measuring the time difference between signals from three or more of the

20 or so GPS satellites orbiting the Earth, calculating the position of each satellite, and then calculating its own position. Such GPS data can be input into **microprocessor**-based navigation systems where position can be plotted on an electronic chart, or fed to a personal computer running suitable navigation software.

> GEOGRAPHICAL INFORMATION SYSTEMS
> IN-CAR INFORMATION SYSTEM

GRANULARITY

A term used to describe the smallest unit of **interaction** in a **hypermedia** programme. A hypermedia programme with high granularity would have an extremely large number of decision points and correspondingly large number of different routes through it. One with low granularity would have relatively few decision points and a limited number of routes through it.

GRAPHICAL USER INTERFACE [GUI]

A human-computer **interface** that uses screen graphics to display **windows**, **icons** and **menus**, and uses a **mouse** or similar pointing device to select them. Typical examples of GUIs are the Apple **Macintosh**, and **Microsoft Windows**.

> WIMP

GRAPHICS OVERLAY CARD

A computer expansion board that enables computer-generated graphics to be displayed over a video image from tape or **videodisc**. Used for titling, captioning, diagrams and other text/image combinations in **interactive video**, **desktop video** and **hypermedia** programmes.

> VIDEO BOARD

GREEN BOOK

The document specifying **CD-i standard**s. Philips publish the standards for their digital-optical disc formats in a set of books, the others are: **Red Book (CDDA)**, **Yellow Book (CD-ROM)**, Orange Book (recordable **CD**s) and **White Book (Video-CD)**.

GREYSCALE

A method of representing monochrome continuous-tone (contone) images in **digital** form. Greyscale scanned images represent the continuous tones of photographs, watercolours, ink-wash and airbrush drawings as a number of levels or 'scale' of greys – for example, using 16, 64 or 256 levels of grey from black to white. Greyscale images are best saved in **TIFF**, **RIFF** or **PICT2** formats for archiving or if they are to be edited at any future date, as these formats retain all the scanned data, and can be re-edited.

GROUPWARE

Software designed to assist individuals at different locations to collaborate and work together in small groups via a computer/**telecommunications** network. Although pioneers such as Douglas Engelbart had been working on groupware since the early 1960s, it only became a major focus of activity among **software** developers in the late 1980s. In the 1990s we are likely to see a growing emphasis on groupware as

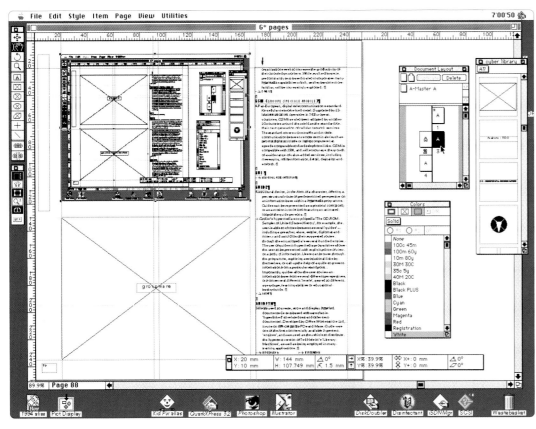

The Mac interface: QuarkXPress with a production
spread from <u>The Cyberspace Lexicon</u>.

DVI in Windows running Lotus Notes, a powerful groupware network
application through which users from different locations can
participate in the same virtual workspace.

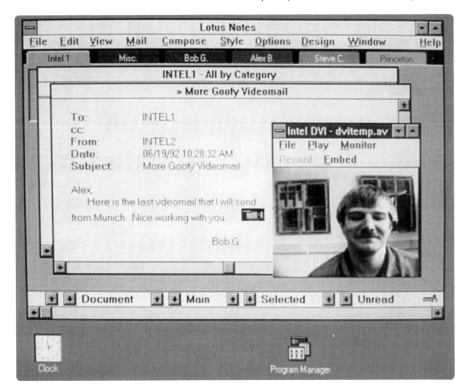

organizations seek to increase the productivity of
their knowledge workers. While such software is
predominantly text-based it also incorporates many
hypermedia capabilities which, as they become more
familiar, will be increasingly exploited.

> E-MAIL

GSM [GROUPE SPECIALE MOBILE]

A Pan-European, digital **telecommunications standard** for
cellular networks (**cell-nets**). Supported by 23
telecommunications operators in 16 European
countries, GSM has also been adopted by another
20 countries around the world as the standard for
their next generation of cellular network services.
The standard covers voice traffic and mobile
communication between remote terminals (such
as **personal digital assistants** or **laptop** computers) at
speeds comparable to fixed telephone links. GSM is
compatible with **ISDN**, and will encourage the growth
of many value-added services, including messaging,
online information, **E-mail**, digital **fax** and so forth.

GUI

> GRAPHICAL USER INTERFACE

GUIDE

A structural device, in the form of a character, offering a
pre-structured route and predetermined perspective
on an information base within a **hypermedia**
programme. Guides can be represented as a
pictorial **icon** (**picon**), or as a motion icon (**micon**)
featuring an animated loop of the guide persona.
In Grolier's hypermedia encyclopedia 'The CD-ROM
Sampler of United States History', for example, the
user is able to choose between several 'guides' –
including a preacher, slave, settler, diplomat and
miner – and can follow their suggested routes
through the encyclopedia's several hundred entries.
The use of guides in hypermedia programmes allows
the user to be presented with explicit points of view
on a body of information. Users can browse through
the programme, exploring associational links by
themselves, or call up the help of a guide to
present information from a particular standpoint.
Importantly, guides allow the user to view an
information base from several different perspectives,
or from several different 'levels', geared to different
age groups, learning abilities or educational needs.

> AGENT

GUIDE™

Software used to create, store and display **hypertext**
documents (ie text-based software that is
'hyperlinked' to related text and other text
documents). Developed by Office Workstations Ltd,
it runs on **IBM-compatible** PCs and Macs. Guide was
one of the first commercially available hypertext
'engines', and was used as the vehicle to distribute
the hypertext version of Ted Nelson's 'Literary
Machines', as well as being employed in many
training applications.

> HYPERCARD   > HYPERMEDIA

HACKER

A programmer obsessed with mastering the most arcane details of a computer system. Now most popularly used to describe programmers who gain access to a system without authorization.

> VIRUS

>> FURTHER READING: HAFNER AND MARKOFF 1991; STOLL 1989

HAM [HOLD AND MODIFY]

Image display mode for the Amiga and the Commodore **CDTV** multimedia system. HAM mode can display up to 4096 colours, and is useful for colour photographic (continuous tone) images.

HANDLER

In a **scripting** language, such as HyperTalk, a **script** embedded in an **object** that intercepts user-initiated actions. For example, a **mouse** click on an object (such as a button) would be intercepted by a handler, and a procedure (such as moving to another card or launching an animation sequence) thus initiated.

HAPTIC

In a **virtual reality** system, describes the physical **sensors** that provide the user with a sense of touch at skin level, and that provide the **force feedback** information from the user's muscles and joints.

> BIOSENSOR

HARD DISK

Electromagnetic storage medium made up of one or several rigid disks mounted in a single unit. Each disk has an independent read/write head. Hard disks range in capacity from around 20 megabytes to over 1 gigabyte, and may be housed within the case of the computer (internal hard disk) or within its own case (external hard disk).

HARDWARE

The electronic components and other equipment that make up a computer system. Hardware for **multimedia** typically includes a computer and disc storage medium for the delivery platform, plus a **scanner**, video **frame grabber** and audio **digitizer** for the development system.

> DELIVERY SYSTEM   > PLAYSTATION

> SOFTWARE   > WORKSTATION

HDTV [HIGH-DEFINITION TELEVISION]

A broadcast television or video system capable of displaying more than 1200 lines on the **screen**. There have been a variety of different initiatives around the world to produce HDTV systems. Many of these have been based on **analog** systems, but since the early 1990s the emphasis has switched to **digital** systems as part of a general movement towards digital communications and storage media.

> • HDTV PAGE 93

HEAD-MOUNTED DISPLAY [HMD]

A stereoscopic screen mounted in a helmet or visor, used for creating three-dimensional computer graphic displays.

The first head-mounted display, developed by Ivan Sutherland in 1966-7 at **MIT**'s Lincoln Laboratory, was binocular but not stereoscopic, and relied on a mechanical 'head-tracking' system to provide the movement of images necessary to sustain the illusion of three-dimensionality. Later improvements of the HMD, made during Sutherland's stay at the University of Utah in the late 1960s and early 1970s, incorporated stereoscopic **vector displays**, with sophisticated **software** for the representation of 3-d imagery. In the 1980s, HMDs were developed at NASA for flight and spaceflight simulation, and at Jaron Lanier's company VPL, whose 'EyePhone' became the first commercially available **virtual reality** (VR) head-mounted display. In the early 1990s, a British company, W Industries, produced an HMD called Visette for use in VR arcade simulators, and by 1993 **Sega** had announced an HMD for their games machines, including the **Mega-CD** system.

Evans & Sutherland: Nite-View head-mounted display, offering fully immersive virtual reality with stereo opticals and audio.

HELP SYSTEM

Software that provides information on the use of a particular application or **program**. Although applications software generally comes with a printed instruction manual or manuals, many people prefer an **online help** system so that they do not interrupt the flow of their work. Help systems can be accessed by means of a **keyboard** command or a **dedicated** 'function' key, or from an **icon** or a **menu** selection, and may be in **database** or **hypertext** form. The most sophisticated help systems are those that track the user's activities within the software application and provide 'context-sensitive' help or advice.

```
┌──────────────────────────────────────────┐
│ □         QuarkXpress™ Keys              │
├──────────────────────────────────────────┤
│ ●●●●●●●●●●●●●●●●●●●●●●●●●●●●●●●●●●●●●●● ⬆ │
│       ● QuarkXpress™ Command Keys ●       │
│ ●●●●●●●●●●●●●●●●●●●●●●●●●●●●●●●●●●●●●●●    │
│           FOR USE WITH TEXT               │
│ ●●●●●●●●●●●●●●●●●●●●●●●●●●●●●●●●●●●●●●●    │
│ ● Font Size                               │
│   √Increase font size:                    │
│     Preset range...........CMD-Shift->    │
│     In increments of 1 pt...CMD-OPT-Shift->│
│   √Decrease font size:                    │
│     Preset range...........CMD-Shift-<    │
│     In increments of 1 pt...CMD-OPT-Shift-<│
│ ●●●●●●●●●●●●●●●●●●●●●●●●●●●●●●●●●●●●●●●    │
│ ● Leading                                 │
│   √Increase leading:                      │
│     In increments of 1 pt...CMD-Shift-"   │
│     In increments of 1/10 pt...CMD-OPT-Shift-"│
│   √Decrease leading:                      │
│     In increments of 1 pt...CMD-Shift-:   │
│     In increments of 1/10 pt...CMD-OPT-Shift-:│
│   √Baseline Shift                         │
│     Increase by 1 pt......CMD-OPT-Shift-+ │
│     Decrease by 1 pt......CMD-OPT-Shift-- │
│ ●●●●●●●●●●●●●●●●●●●●●●●●●●●●●●●●●●●●●●●    │
│ ● Kerning/Tracking                        │
│   √Increase Kern/Track amount:            │
│     By 10/200 [EM]-Space.....CMD-Shift-}  │
│     By 1/200 [EM]-Space....CMD-OPT-Shift-}│
│   √Decrease Kern/Track amount:            │
│     By 10/200 [EM]-Space.....CMD-Shift-{  │
│     By 1/200 [EM]-Space....CMD-OPT-Shift-{│
│ ●●●●●●●●●●●●●●●●●●●●●●●●●●●●●●●●●●●●●●●    │
│ ● Horizontal Scaling                      │
│   √Horizontal scale amount:               │
│     Increase by 5%.........CMD-]          │
│     Decrease by 5%.........CMD-[          │
│ ●●●●●●●●●●●●●●●●●●●●●●●●●●●●●●●●●●●●●●●    │
│ ● To Enter One Special Font Character     │
│   √Symbol Font character....CMD-Shift-Q   │
│   √Zapf Dingbat Character...CMD-Shift-Z   │
│ ●●●●●●●●●●●●●●●●●●●●●●●●●●●●●●●●●●●●●●●    │
│ ● Moving the Insertion Point              │
│   √Move to:                               │
│     Previous character.....Left Arrow     │
│     Next character.........Right Arrow    │
│     Previous line..........Up Arrow       │
│     Next line..............Down Arrow     │
│     Previous word..........CMD-Left Arrow │
│     Next word..............CMD-Right Arrow│
│     Previous ¶.............CMD-Up Arrow   │
│     Next ¶.................CMD-Down Arrow │
│     Start of line..........CMD-OPT-Left Arrow│
│     End of line............CMD-OPT-Right Arrow│
│     Start of story.........CMD-OPT-Up Arrow│
│     End of story...........CMD-OPT-Down Arrow│
│ ●●●●●●●●●●●●●●●●●●●●●●●●●●●●●●●●●●●●●●●    │
│ ● Extending the Text Selection            │
│   ● To select:                         ⬇ │
├──────────────────────────────────────────┤
│ DisplayDA 1.7 is Free ⌐1988 Bill Steinberg│
└──────────────────────────────────────────┘
```

Paul Pershing: QuarkXPress Keys, a Mac freeware desk accessory with all known QuarkXPress keyboard commands.

HERTZ [HZ]

The unit named after Heinrich Hertz and used to define frequency. 1 Hertz = 1 cycle per second.

> **DIGITAL AUDIO**

HEX [HEXADECIMAL NOTATION]

The notation of numbers using the base 16, comprising 0-9 in decimal, plus the letters A-F to represent the numbers 10-16 as single characters. (ie 0, 1, 2, 3, 4, 5, 6, 7, 8, 9, A, B, C, D, E, F). Hex is used by programmers as a convenient means of representing binary numbers, which because they use the base 2 become very long (eg decimal number 4 is equivalent to 0100 binary).

HI-8

A high-band videotape format based on the 8mm **standard** introduced by Sony, Matsushita, Philips et al in 1982 especially for use in **camcorders**. Hi-8 tapes are compact and lightweight, and because they record a higher quality image than normal 8mm tapes are used extensively for image recording or 'capture' in **interactive multimedia** or **hypermedia** programme production. However, because of their limited physical width, they are susceptible to 'drop-out' (image degradation) problems during the repetitive copying that occurs in video editing. Launched in 1990, the Sony Hi-8 cameras were aimed at consumer and professional (corporate video and bottom-end **ENG**) markets, offering superb picture quality (via a 440,000-**pixel CCD** image-sensor combined with a mosaic colour filter) together with built-in time code.

> **VIDEO FORMATS**

Sony Hi-8 Camcorder: component video in the palm of your hand.

HIGH-LEVEL LANGUAGE

A formal system of notation for describing **algorithms**, that enables programmers to concentrate on the problems a program addresses rather than the details of how a computer will carry out the instructions. Most high-level languages were originally developed to deal with particular kinds of problems. For example, **Fortran** was developed to deal with scientific and engineering problems; **C** to deal with the design of systems software. All high-level languages must be translated into **machine code** by either an interpreter or a compiler before they can be executed by a computer.

> **LANGUAGE**

HIGH RESOLUTION

Describes a display system or printer that is capable of producing well-defined characters, even in large type sizes, and smoothly defined curves in graphic images.

> **RESOLUTION**

HIGH SIERRA GROUP

A **standards** group formed in 1985 to establish data formats for **CD-ROM**. Their proposals were developed into ISO 9660, the format that allows CD-ROM discs to be used under different operating systems.

> **ISO**

HMD

> **HEAD-MOUNTED DISPLAY**

HOME SHOPPING

> **REMOTE SHOPPING**

HORIZONTAL BLANKING PERIOD

> **HORIZONTAL RETRACE PERIOD**

HORIZONTAL RESOLUTION

The number of **pixels** across a video display or computer monitor screen.

> **RESOLUTION**

HORIZONTAL RETRACE PERIOD

(Or 'horizontal blanking period'.) The time it takes for the horizontal line scan of a television screen to return to the beginning of the next scan line, and during which the electron beam in the cathode ray tube (**CRT**) is blanked out.

HOTSPOT

In **hypermedia** programmes, a part of the screen that responds to a pointing device, such as a **button** or **icon**.

HSV [HUE, SATURATION AND VALUE]

A **colour** model, used in some computer graphics applications, which must be translated into another model, such as **RGB** for screen display or **CMY** for printing. Hue refers to the actual wavelength of visible light; saturation, to the purity of the hue (ie how much the hue is adulterated with white or black components); and value, to the brightness or tonal value of the colour. The best example of an HSV colour model is Alfred Munsell's three dimensional 'global' model where value (brightness) increases on the vertical axis; degrees of saturation are represented radially, and hue is represented as segments of the equator of the globe.

HUE

> **COLOUR**

HUMAN FACTORS ENGINEERING

The art and science of designing computers and other computer-based equipment so that it is easier to use. 'Human factors' include the design of interface **hardware** – terminals, **keyboards**, personal computers – and interface **software** such as the **graphical user interface**, to ensure safety, ease of use and physical comfort.

HDTV (HIGH-DEFINITION TELEVISION)
from television
to teleputer

HDTV is the name given to TV systems that deliver around 1200 lines screen resolution. But this is only part of what 'HDTV' promises. In its ideal form, the HDTV set will be a powerful computer with a very large memory, and will connect to a fibre-optic network, with links to satellite TV, cable TV, telecommunication services such as the videophone, and other computers. As an all-digital 'teleputer', HDTV is set to be the central 'home information/entertainment' system of the twenty-first century.

By the early 1990s there were several competing HDTV systems in development in Europe, the USA and Japan, where the NHK Hi-Vision system has been extensively tested. Ultimately it will be the system that is chosen in the USA that will almost certainly determine the shape of global HDTV. It is not just a question of finding the best technological solution (though it seems clear now that HDTV will be all-digital, rather than a hybrid of digital and analog technologies). Concerns over national interests, and concern for 'backward compatibility' with current broadcast standards, have created considerable political debate. In the USA, the Federal Communications Commission (FCC) is conducting extensive tests of the six rival HDTV formats.

In Europe, the political and technical complexities that result from the sub-continent having no universal television standard (with a mix of PAL and SECAM formats) mean that HDTV development is behind that of the USA and Japan. Proposals have included a variety of 'widescreen' or 'letterbox' formats, using 16:9 aspect ratio extensions of PAL – PALplus, Clean PAL, and HD-MAC. (The latter was the intended HDTV upgrade from D-MAC, the system used by the failed BSB satellite TV broadcasting company.)

In Japan in the early 1990s, NHK was working with Japan's major electronics companies, including Sony, Toshiba and Matsushita/Panasonic, on the joint Hi-Vision Programme. They produced the first HDTV equipment, and the first broadcast HDTV programmes (in a public broadcast to 80 selected sites in Japan during the 1988 Seoul Olympics). But this initiative merely added to the confusion surrounding HDTV standards.

Regardless of the delays in the consumer sector, by the early 1990s HDTV was already being used in television and video production. HDTV production technology includes CCD cameras, HD filing systems, digital video switchers, lenses and MUSE (Multiple Sub-Nyquist Encoding) encoders, VTRs, digital framestores, laserdisc players and solid-state frame recorders – in fact all the necessary components for a complete production system. The high definition motion control work of the Polish-American director Zbigniew Rybczinski (for example in his film The Orchestra) is a testament to the creative potential of HDTV.

HDTV will be a hybrid medium, extending the user's

Sony DVW 500P Digital Betacam recorder. With the introduction of digital Betacam systems, Sony hopes to build on its established Betacam SP market. Digital Betacam is backwardly compatible with SP, and supports both 4:3 and HDTV 16:9 aspect ratios.

The Sony HDTV edit suite at Basingstoke provides 1125-line high-definition facilities for production companies and broadcasters in Europe, including editing, standards conversion and special effects with HD Ultimatte colour keying and Quantel HD Paintbox for electronic rotoscoping, retouching and caption generation.

choice and providing a variety of sophisticated control and processing functions. In an article in Scientific American (September 1991), the director of MIT's Media Lab, Nicholas Negroponte, suggests the possibility of a consumer using HDTV to choose movies from a central 'database' of 50,000 films. The selected movie would already be in digital (compressed) form, and would be transmitted to the consumer's HDTV set at very high speed, to be stored in the set's 'memory' until required, when it would be decompressed in realtime, as the viewer watched. Negroponte calls this technique 'Tell Me More' television. And it is not just movies. Negroponte suggests that entire packages of related films, videos, records, books, documentaries and interactive multimedia programmes could be ordered by the user with the help of an 'expert' guide or software agent. Negroponte illustrates this idea with an example: it takes just 80 seconds to load

some 16 hours of video and other material into the HDTV set's memory. Once there, the user can explore the material interactively.

The Media Lab, along with many other academic and corporate research laboratories around the world, is researching and prototyping many other applications for HDTV, including personalized electronic 'newspapers', surrogate travel, simulations and other hybrid 'infotainment' software. Negroponte uses Stewart Brand's term 'broadcatching' to describe how HDTV could become the central corporate and consumer mechanism by which all media is selectively 'caught', packaged and 'personalized' for direct interactive access. By combining and integrating the computer and high-definition television within a global network of high-bandwidth telecommunications, HDTV could be the technology that will bring the information revolution right into the living room.

HYPER-COMIC

An **interactive** comic or graphic novel. Ted Nelson describes the basic principle in Computer Lib/Dream Machines: 'Hyper-comics are perhaps the simplest and most straightforward hypermedium. The screen holds a comic strip, but one which branches on the student's request. For instance, different characters could be used to explain things in different ways, with the student able to choose which type of explanation he wants at a specific time.' More recently, several entertainment programmes have used the idea of an 'expanded' comic strip, building on the popularity of printed graphic novels.

Hyper-comics look set to become one of the big growth areas in **hypermedia** entertainment. Building on a large, established market that spans the teenage, student and adult sectors, they have a high 'replayability' factor, combining narrative storytelling with interactive options. Hyper-comics can also combine low production costs with highly dynamic presentation – which can include detailed illustrations, sketchy cartoons, simple solid models and wireframe animations. And since hyper-comics can be produced by a single artist or a small team working on inexpensive workstations such as the Mac, artists can retain a greater control over the aesthetics and market relevance of their programmes.

> VIDEOGAME

HYPER-MAGAZINE

An **interactive multimedia** magazine produced on **CD-ROM** or for **online** network distribution. At their best, electronic hyper-magazines combine form and content in a seamless blend of **infotainment**, **videogames**, TV or radio documentary, animation and sound. In Britain and Europe there have been several limited-edition or single-issue hyper-magazines – such as the authors' 'High Bandwidth Panning' (published as a set of seven floppy disks in 1987) and the graphic design magazine Octavo – while in the USA, the early 1990s saw the publication of several **cyberpunk** hyper-magazines.

Printed magazines specializing in hypermedia include Mondo 2000 (the first American 'cyberpunk' magazine) and Verbum, the American 'journal of computer aesthetics'. Verbum led the way with commercially-produced hyper-magazines, producing its first CD-ROM version in 1991.

> ELECTRONIC PUBLISHING

HYPERCARD

A **hypermedia** construction kit designed by Bill Atkinson and launched in 1986. HyperCard was the first really popular hypermedia application, and gave many people their first opportunity to construct their own **hypertext** and hypermedia programmes. It comprises a set of object-oriented tools for creating **cards**, **bitmap** drawings, text fields and **buttons**, and an easy-to-use but powerful **scripting** language called HyperTalk. It can support several different kinds of animation, sound and music, as well as typography. Programs created in HyperCard are called 'stacks' (from the metaphor of a stack of cards), and were originally

Infogrames: sketches of 'Chaos Control' by Frank Drevon. Like comic books, videogames are a 'hyper-comic' medium where an artist can maintain singular creative control over an entire production.

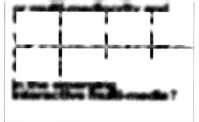

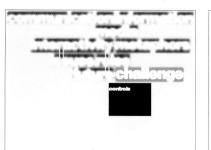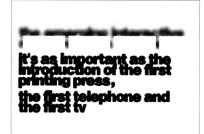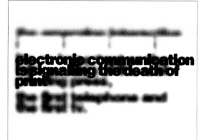

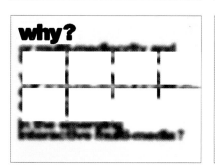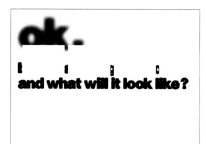

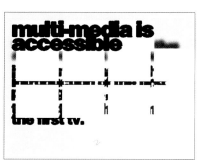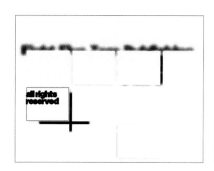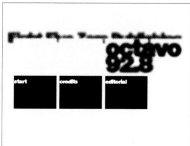

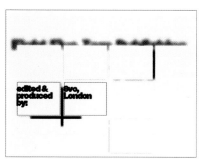

<u>Octavo</u> <u>92.8</u> <u>CD-ROM</u>: the last in 8vo's octology of
influential typographic magazines, this is an
impressive investigation of the typographer's
changing role in the world of new digital media.

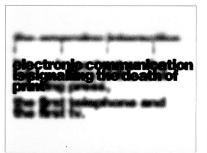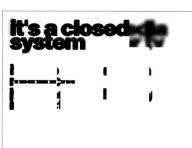

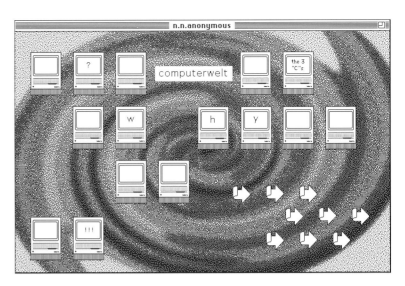

Malcolm Garrett: 'Digital Collision', the designer's thoughts on digital media, produced on and for the Apple Powerbook. Although HyperCard now supports colour and multiple windows, black-and-white stacks reach a far wider range of Mac users. This stack and others were compiled by <u>n.n.anonymous</u>, an electronic magazine available on disc and distributed as shareware on CompuServe.

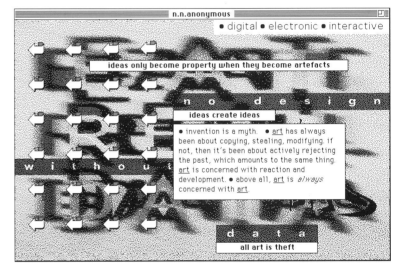

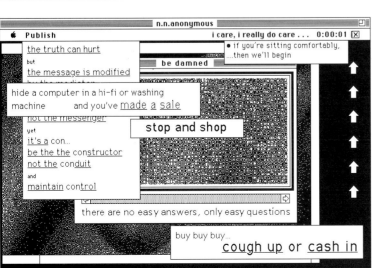

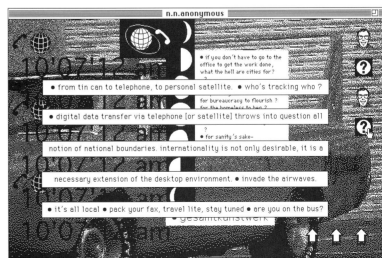

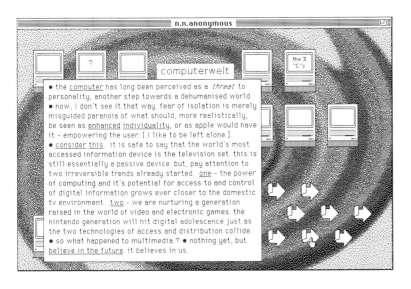

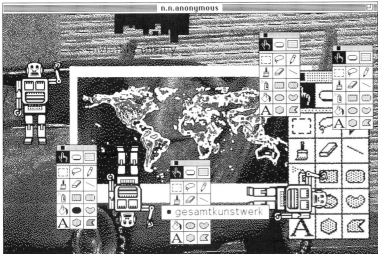

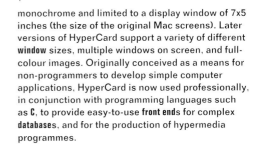

monochrome and limited to a display window of 7x5 inches (the size of the original Mac screens). Later versions of HyperCard support a variety of different **window** sizes, multiple windows on screen, and full-colour images. Originally conceived as a means for non-programmers to develop simple computer applications, HyperCard is now used professionally, in conjunction with programming languages such as **C**, to provide easy-to-use **front end**s for complex **database**s, and for the production of hypermedia programmes.

HYPERGRAM

A term coined by Ted Nelson for an **interactive** illustration, and defined by him in <u>Computer Lib/Dream Machines</u> (1974) as 'a performing or branching picture'. Hypergrams can reveal hidden parts of a picture as the user 'explores' it with a mouse pointer; produce sounds or speech when clicked on; launch an animation or video; change scale or 'zoom' in to the mouse pointer location; change image type – for example from a photograph of the human body, to an X-ray, then to a body scan, micro-photograph or medical illustration, and so on.

Hypergrams can also be activated by factors other than the user's direct input, such as the passage of time (giving different views of an illustration at different times of the day or night) or the user's previous interactions/selections, or by means of random number generation. Hypergrams can dynamically perform the roles of traditional illustrations – amplifying, commenting upon, explaining or decorating a narrative for example – and importantly, can provide the user with simple simulations or animations of complex processes. All the techniques used in illustration – such as cutaways, schematics, closeups, labelling and perspective views – have their hypergram counterparts.

>   HYPERMEDIA

HYPERLINK

In **hypermedia**, a programmed link between items of information in different sections of a programme, or in physically different locations within a **network**. Hyperlinks make it easy for the user to follow cross-references or access glossary definitions, for instance, by clicking on the **prompt** word, which is usually differentiated from normal text by colour or by typographical treatment.

> **ASSOCIATIONAL BROWSING**

HYPERMAP

An **interactive**, **digital**, multimedia map. Hypermaps enormously extend the functionality of the traditional printed map, and can include any of the features of **geographical information systems** (such as the facility to 'zoom' in to any part of the map by instant scale changes, or to find a location by means of a hyperlinked gazetteer). Hypermaps can also integrate the function of a guidebook, allowing the user to access a range of expert **guide**s (travellers, geophysicists, historians, local people) to help them 'explore' the territory. Hypermaps can also act as 'space/time' maps, in which the user can scroll back through the ages, watching the population changes in Europe during the Industrial Revolution, for example, or examining the spread of the railways or telecommunication networks as they rapidly encompassed the world.

HYPERMEDIA

A communications medium created by the convergence of computer and video technologies. The term was originally coined by Ted Nelson to describe **hypertext** systems that include multiple media – text, image, sound, animation and video. Extended by the authors to cover a variety of other computer-based applications, such as **interactive multimedia**, **videogames** and **virtual reality** systems that have some, but not all, of the elements of 'pure' hypermedia. Pure hypermedia can be characterized as having three major features: one, it is **interactive**; two, it involves a variety of combinations of multiple media, with the particular combination of media selected by the user; and three, it is formally non-linear, with no beginning, middle or end. Very few programmes meet all these criteria, which is why the authors have broadened the definition.

> **INTERACTIVE MULTIMEDIA**

>> **FURTHER READING: COTTON AND OLIVER 1993; NELSON 1987**

HYPERTALK

The **scripting** language developed by Bill Atkinson and his team for HyperCard.

HYPERTEXT

Describes a **program** that provides multiple pathways through text, enabling the user to follow existing **hyperlinks**, to link related items of text together, or retrieve linked cross-references, in a non-linear and '**random-access**' manner.

> **HYPERCARD**   > **HYPERMEDIA**

> **INTERACTIVE MULTIMEDIA**   > **XANADU**

HYPERTYPOGRAPHY

Dynamic and interactive type that combines features such as **animation**, customizable type styles and sizes, context-sensitive typefaces, 'speaking' text (text accompanied by sound), three-dimensional typefaces, etc, with the linking features of **hypertext**.

> **• HYPERTYPOGRAPHY PAGE 99**

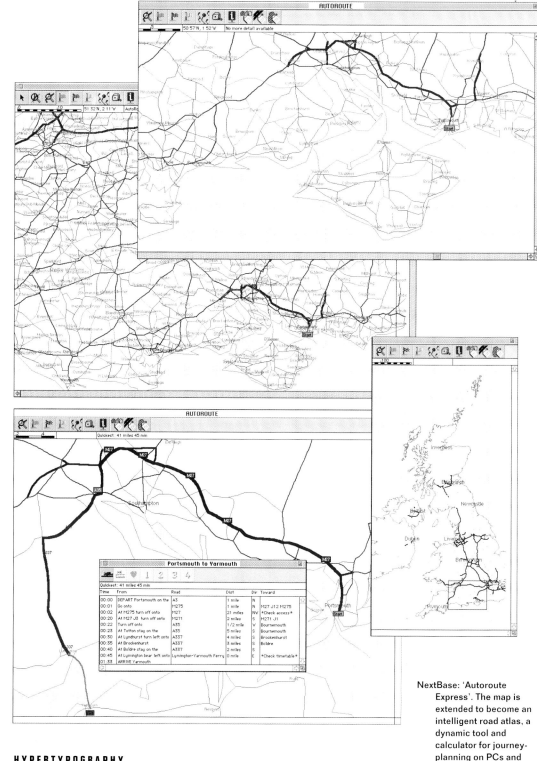

NextBase: 'Autoroute Express'. The map is extended to become an intelligent road atlas, a dynamic tool and calculator for journey-planning on PCs and Macs.

HYPERTYPOGRAPHY
the silicon Gutenberg

Just as typography is the art and design of disposing of type on a two-dimensional surface, so hypertypography is the art of disposing type through a multi-dimensional hyperspace – the cyberspace of silicon and binary memory. The cyberspace that is globally linked by copper and glass fibres, and that offers designers the means to negotiate between author and reader in all kinds of new ways. Hypertypography is multi-dimensional, and like the stereoscopic personal perspective in virtual reality, can be 'read' in different ways by the user according to the particular viewpoint defined by the 6 degrees of freedom: X,Y,Z, tilt, roll, yaw. The hypertypographer is no longer dealing with static 2-d symbols but with dynamic, intelligent textual images that trace the user's progress through an information base offering guidance and alternative perspectives. The space of hypertypography is a matrix wherein linear narrative is just one tool in a galaxy of media that offers hypertext, database, knowledge-based and expert systems. That offers speech synthesis, animation, realtime and runtime text. That offers 16.7 million colours, sounds sampled 44,000 times per second and recorded as strings of 16-bit binary numbers. That offers full-motion video digitized at 320x284 pixels with each pixel configurable through 24 bits of hue, saturation and brightness.
Cyberspace is where the computer absorbs the printing press, the tape recorder and the video. It is the space where the graphic designer becomes the hypertypographer.

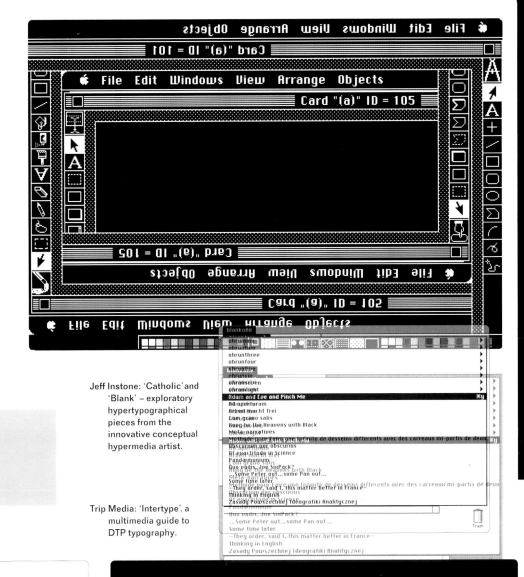

Jeff Instone: 'Catholic' and 'Blank' – exploratory hypertypographical pieces from the innovative conceptual hypermedia artist.

Trip Media: 'Intertype', a multimedia guide to DTP typography.

.bcdefghijklmno pqrstuvwxyz

normal screen display, serif face

.bcdefghijklmnopqrstuvwxyz

screen display, Marenghi face

SMALLER TEXT HAS SERIOUS PROBLEMS BECAUSE ITS VARIABLES ARE LIMITED BY PIXELS WHO EXIST AT 72 PER INCH. LIKE MOST OF US THE PIXELS JUST CAN'T EXPRESS THEMSELVES.

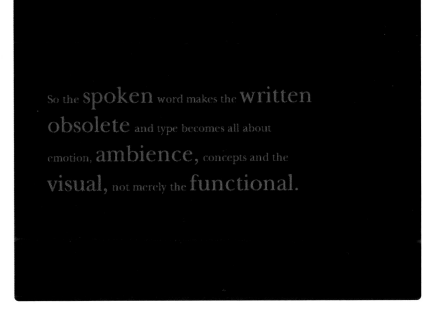

So the spoken word makes the written obsolete and type becomes all about emotion, ambience, concepts and the visual, not merely the functional.

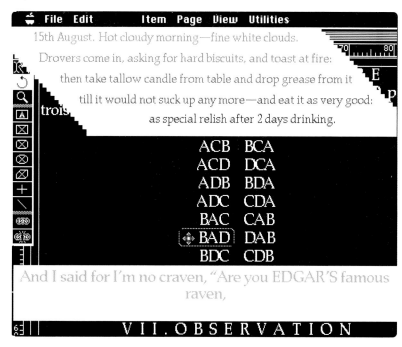

File Edit Item Page View Utilities

15th August. Hot cloudy morning—fine white clouds.
Drovers come in, asking for hard biscuits, and toast at fire:
then take tallow candle from table and drop grease from it
till it would not suck up any more—and eat it as very good:
as special relish after 2 days drinking.

trois

ACB BCA
ACD DCA
ADB BDA
ADC CDA
BAC CAB
BAD DAB
BDC CDB

And I said for I'm no craven, "Are you EDGAR'S famous raven,

VII. OBSERVATION

File Edit Item Page View Utilities

METHODE 4

a young healthy Child well nursed is at a year
Old a most delicious nourishing and wholesome
Food, whether Stewed, Roasted, Baked, or Boiled;
and I make no doubt that it will serve in a Fricasie, or a Ragoust.

A Caramel should be like a Baby's fontanelle:
all quivers and throbs.

the remaining Hundred thousand may at a year Old be offered in Sale to
the Person of Quality and Fortune, through the Kingdom, always
advising the Mother to let them Suck plentifuly in the last Month, so as
to render them Plump, and Fat for a good Table. A Child will
make two Dishes at an entertainment for Friends,
and when the Family dines alone, the fore or
hind Quarter will make a reasonable Dish, and
seasoned with a little Pepper or Salt will be very
good Boiled on the fourth Day, especially in
Winter.'

Double Gloucester; and then go on to cut the intrinsic caseous
tenuous Segments or Laminæ; and, positing such Segmer
the coquinary commodity distinguished by Culinarians
Furnus Baviæ or Dutch Oven submit the same to the F
the action of the Caloric they become mollified unto Semilic
whereupon, if we diffuse the caseous fluid on an Offula of Br
Superfices whereof hath been previously torrified, and then Season the
same with a slight aspersion of the Sinapine, Piperine and Saline
Condiments, or with Mustard, Pepper, and Salt, we shall find that
the Sapor and Fragror thereof differ in no wise from the Gust and Odour
of the Edible we had præ-attained from the Covent Garden
Cœnatorium; and, consequently, that the Welsh Rabbit is not, as the
Vulgar Pseudodox conceiteth, a species of Cuniculus vernacular
to Wales, but as was before predicated, simply a Savoury and Redolent
Scitamentum or Rarebit, which is much estimated by the Cymri or
Welsh people, who from time præ-termemorial, have been cognized as a
Philocaseous, or Cheese-loving, Nation.

"... here and QUO VADIS, JOE SIXPACK? ained castle,
looking like the remainder of a Devon PART ONE pasty, with broken forts
England, like JEFF INSTONE
mince pies, and old abbeys with no walls sticking up, looking like
cum grano salis
OBSCURIUM PER OBSCURIUS
on mouse Up

Jeff Instone: 'Quo Vadis, Joe Sixpack?' Instone describes this as 'a Humphrey Jennings/Mass Observation-style interactive textwork that explores numerous random factual and humorous observations on food and drink'. Instone authors his works in Aldus SuperCard, stretching the Macintosh interface in surreal combinations of menus and windows.

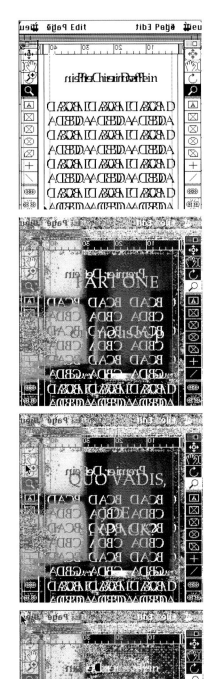

Giles Rollestone: 'Jean Baudrillard' and 'Cities unlike Towns' – images from the DreamCityScape program. Under the auspices of Colin Taylor, Robert Macauley and Mark Bowey, a wide range of exploratory hypertypography has flourished at the graphic design department of Central St Martin's in London.

The page-make-up interface assumes classical overtones in Instone's humorous hypertypography.

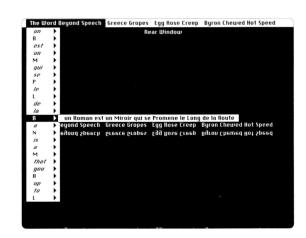

Jeff Instone: 'The Word Beyond Speech'. Instone's work comments on the maze of interconnections and the thousands of user choices available in cyberspace. Like cyberspace his hypertypography is multi-dimensional, with new meanings, new jokes and new comments emerging as a result of the user's interaction.

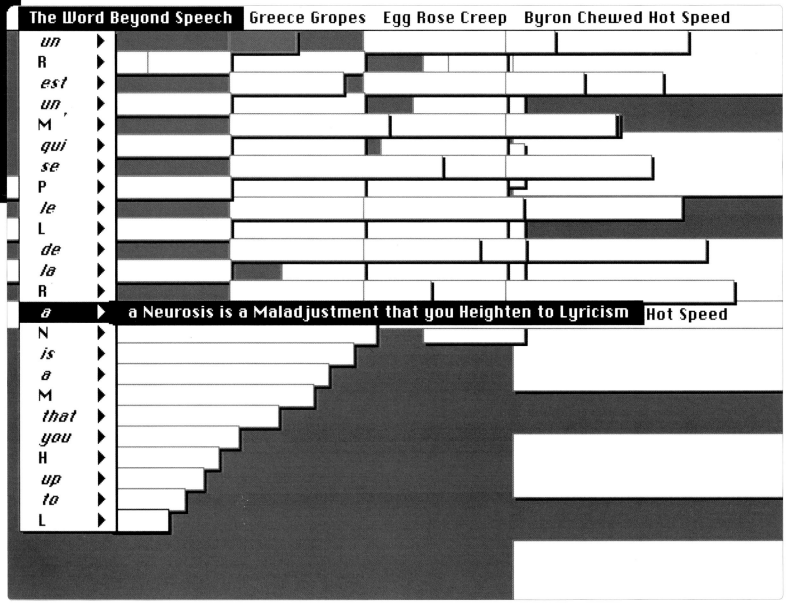

IBM

The largest computer company in the world, IBM dominated the market for **mainframe** computers from the 1960s onwards, and as a result of its market dominance, set the de facto standards for **software**, **peripherals**, and later for personal computers (PCs), well into the 1990s. Established early this century, IBM entered the computer business in the early 1950s. However, IBM proved unable to dominate the PC market in the same way that it had dominated the mainframe market. This was primarily because the computer's central processing unit **(CPU)** was made by Intel and its **operating system (MS-DOS)** by Microsoft, and both were available to other manufacturers, who competed aggressively for this market.

The information revolution that IBM helped create has entered a phase of extreme instability, characterized by a dazzling pace of technological innovation and fierce competition. IBM, which enjoyed a near monopoly in the 1970s and 1980s, is now having to rethink its strategy to adapt to these new conditions. One manifestation of this, unthinkable in earlier years, is its joint venture with Apple, the **PowerPC**. While it seems unlikely that IBM will be able to regain the dominance it once enjoyed, its expertise and financial resources mean that it will play an important role in the continuing **hypermedia** revolution. In 1993 IBM was promoting its **Ultimedia** OS/2 system for PCs.

IBM-COMPATIBLE

Describes a computer, from any manufacturer, that uses the **MS-DOS operating system**. Such computers are now more likely to be referred to as MS-DOS or Microsoft Windows computers.

> IBM

IC

> INTEGRATED CIRCUIT

ICON

A type of small pictogram incorporated into a **hypermedia** programme, computer application or **graphical user interface**. Icons can represent applications, or features within applications or programmes.

> INTERFACE   > MICON
> PICON

ICONCLASS

An iconographic classification system for images. Developed from an original idea by the art historian Henri Van de Waal, the Iconclass system was published in 17 volumes between 1973 and 1985. In 1990 a team at the University of Utrecht produced a computer-readable version, which is available in a **Microsoft Windows** application called the Iconclass Browser, to administrate image **databases** on **CD-ROM**.

> BROWSING   > NAVIGATION

IBM: Ultimedia PC. Ultimedia is IBM's range of multimedia PC components that can be configured into a wide variety of systems for particular applications. Typical specification includes 4 megabyte RAM and built-in CD-ROM drive with PhotoCD compatibility.

Icon-based tool palette.

→

IDEA MAP

A diagrammatic representation of the relationship between concepts or elements of a body of knowledge. Idea maps can be the basis of the **front end** of a **hypermedia** programme; they are also a useful device in the design of hypermedia programmes.

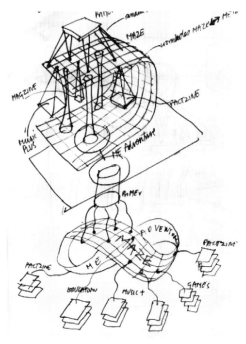

Bob Cotton: idea map. Schematics of hypermedia programme structures sometimes have to borrow from the diagrammatic visualizations of hyperspace. Here, physicist John Wheeler's sketch of his hyperspace 'wormholes' is used to describe the associative links in a hypermedia programme. The Moebius one-dimensional toroid becomes a metaphor for the non-linear nature of the new media.

IDEAL DESKTOP

A desktop computer (**personal computer**) or 'teleputer', with **network** links, that can provide **realtime** voice communications and **interactive** audio, **full-motion video** at TV quality, **videophone**, **animation** and **interactive multimedia**, **E-mail** and other data communications services, as well as personal computer applications such as **database**, word processing and graphics programs – all on the same screen. The idea of the 'ideal desktop' emerged in the early 1990s as a objective shared by computer companies, **telecommunications** and consumer electronics manufacturers. Most of the technology for such an ideal desktop is already in place; it is the final form that it will take that is the subject of both considerable speculation and enormous investment programmes. Will it be in the guise of a television set (the **HDTV** teleputer)? The **CD-ROM** drive? The personal computer? Or some new ergonomic hybrid that draws from all of these models?

> **DATA SUPERHIGHWAY**   > **FIBRE OPTICS**

IDEOGRAM

The pictographic representation of an idea. Ideograms were the second stage in the development of writing, which developed from pictograms (for example the picture of an eye representing the word 'eye'), via ideograms (the picture of an eye representing the idea of 'looking'), to phonograms (symbols representing the sound of the word 'eye').

> **ICON**

IEEE

The US Institute of Electrical and Electronic Engineers. The institute is the publisher of the IEEE standards, a set of standards and conventions for **telecommunications**, **networks** and computer processes, such as floating point arithmetic.

IFF (INTERCHANGE FILE FORMAT)

The standard **file format** for Amiga **paint programs**. Images can also be prepared in IFF format in Adobe's Photoshop (running on the Apple **Macintosh**), for export to Amigas.

> **AMIGAVISION**   > **CDTV**

IFF (INTERNATIONAL FILE FORMAT)

A **CD-i**-compatible **file format** covering compressed CD-i file types, such as CLUT4, CLUT7, CLUT8, **DYUV**, RL7, RL3 and **RGB 5:5:5**. Using Adobe Photoshop together with OptImage's CD-i plug-ins allows TGA, **PICT**, **TIFF**, **GIF** and other file formats to be converted to CD-i IFFs.

> **CD-i DIGITAL IMAGES**

IMAGE PLANE

In videographic and **interactive multimedia** systems, one of several 'layers' of images, each of which can be held in memory (or frame store) and displayed either superimposed or sequentially to create special effects such as **chromakey mattes**, **sprite** manipulation or transitional effects. **CD-i**, for example, has four superimposed planes that can contain images: the front cursor plane, two full-colour image planes, and the backdrop plane (which is also used for **full-motion video**). Part or all of an image plane may be transparent, so that the screen graphic may comprise components of all four different planes, some of which may be in motion.

> **3DO**   > **VIDEO GRAPHICS**

IMAGE PROCESSING

The use of a computer to enhance or modify an image. Image-processing techniques are widely used in **remote sensing** (satellite and spacecraft imaging), bodyscanning, electron microscopy and other scientific applications, frequently employing filtering and recolouring techniques to reveal or highlight aspects of special interest. In **video graphics** and reprographics similar techniques are used to produce the best quality for **screen** display or print reproduction.

IMAGESETTER

A **digital** typesetter that can process **page description language** files (such as **PostScript**) that contain images

and graphics as well as **digital font** information. Imagesetters output to photo-sensitive paper or film (exposed by laserprinter technology) to resolutions of between 800 and 3000 **dpi**, and can be linked directly to desktop computers running **DTP**, graphics and page make-up **software**.

IMAGING SYSTEM

Refers to equipment and software designed to digitize, compress, store, edit or retrieve images. Examples are digital **still-video cameras**; digital (film) camera systems; **scanners**; video **frame grabbers**, and digital-optical disc systems.

> **REMOTE SENSING**

Canon Ion still-video camera.

IMMERSIVE VR

Describes **virtual reality** systems using **head-mounted displays** and position-sensing **sensors** linked to the user's body, creating the illusion of being immersed in a computer-generated world.

> **AUGMENTED REALITY**   > **PROJECTED REALITY**

Virtual Research: Eyegen3 head-mounted display, incorporating earphones, position sensors and stereo-monochrome CRT displays that offer full-colour images by means of a spinning RGB colour wheel.

IN-BETWEENS

In **animation**, the images that connect two **key frame**s (the principal positions denoting where a movement begins, ends, or changes direction). In traditional cel animation, in-betweens are the responsibility of assistants to the animator, who produces the key frame drawings for the entire film. These linking sequences are produced by tracing and redrawing the frame-by-frame movements of figures and objects to provide a smooth development of the action between key frames. In **computer animation**, in-betweens are automatically created by the computer, so that a 3-d model can be moved across the screen and towards or away from the spectator by specifying the key positions at the beginning and end of the sequence, the number of frames required, the inertial effects at start and finish, the path that the object is to follow, the lensing, position and movement of the computer 'camera', and the positions and movement of the computer lighting. Even with very powerful computers, detailed animations may require several minutes of processing time per frame, and in-betweening is often performed overnight or during some other downtime.

IN-CAR INFORMATION SYSTEM

A one- or two-way communication system providing navigational and other information to drivers and passengers of motor cars. The development of mobile communication systems and portable computers has meant that the motor car can now be a mobile office. In-car information systems utilizing maps stored on **CD-ROM**, sometimes in conjunction with satellite systems to establish the precise location of the vehicle, have also been developed. Such systems not only offer navigational information, but may also offer information on restaurants, hotels and places of interest.

INDEX

In **database management system**s, a table of references to data records that is held separately from the data records. The database file management **software** can complete a search of the index much more quickly than a search among the data records themselves.

INFERENCE ENGINE

The **software** that drives a **knowledge-based system**, such as an **expert system**, and can simulate the human deductive thought processes. The inference engine uses the rules and facts contained within the knowledge base to draw logical inferences related to the problem that is being analyzed. In a hypermedia training programme, for example, the software can be used to deduce from the fact that the trainee has accessed several frames of information on a particular aspect of the courseware that the trainee might also be interested in accessing more frames on that subject, and then offer the trainee this additional option.

INFORMATICS

The art and science of processing data to produce information.

INFORMATING

Term coined by Shoshana Zuboff to describe the potential of computer technology to generate information about the underlying processes of work within an organization, thus informing and empowering the individual worker.

>> FURTHER READING: ZUBOFF 1988

INFORMATION DESIGN

The process of organizing and presenting information in optimal form for a particular purpose. Information design involves the assembly, analysis, classification, editing and presentation of information in a form that is most useful for the recipient. Designers of **hypermedia** information products can represent information in many different media, and use hierarchical, **database** and cross-referencing methods in order to provide users with different ways of accessing information in either a linear (**narrative**) or **interactive** (random-access) manner, and provide a range of interpretations of that information.

>   AUTHORING   >   DESIGN STAGE

INFORMATION RETRIEVAL

The process of recovering or extracting the required information from an information base. Information retrieval depends on three processes: the classification or indexing of information; the storing of this information in such a way that it is readily retrievable by the user; and a method of 'liaison' between the user and the storage system, so that there is as little difference as possible between the

General Logistics: TrafficMaster, an in-car information system offering up-to-the-minute details on traffic flow and hold-ups.

user's description of the information required and the description of the information as classified in the storage system.

A commonly used information retrieval system is the Dewey Decimal Index, the method of classification used in public libraries. In pictorial **databases**, the **Iconclass** system is also widely used. However, there is as yet no commonly used standard for the retrieval of **multimedia** information from databases. Such standards will become increasingly important as new interfaces based on **natural language** are used to create information retrieval systems suitable for use by non-experts.

> KNOWLEDGE-BASED SYSTEM   > STRUCTURED QUERY LANGUAGE

INFOTAINMENT

Hypermedia programmes that present information in an entertaining manner. A hybrid of 'information/ entertainment', this loose classification also includes products such as interactive atlases and encyclopedias, where the information content is presented in a variety of media 'mixes', perhaps administered by a selection of expert '**guides**' and available with commentary pitched at a number of different levels.

> • INFOTAINMENT AND EDUTAINMENT PAGE 107

INFRARED CONTROLLER

Remote hand-held controller used with **multimedia** systems, hi-fi, **videogame**, video and television systems.

INMARSAT

[INTERNATIONAL MARITIME SATELLITE ORGANIZATION]

London-based international supplier of satellite mobile **telecommunications** services, particularly aeronautical and maritime communications systems. In 1992 Inmarsat had over 28,000 terminals in use worldwide, and predicted growth of around 20 per cent per annum. Inmarsat terminals allow mobile users in both aircraft and ships to make and receive voice and **fax** calls. Personal portable systems include briefcase-sized systems that are used to send and receive secure information to and from remote and inaccessible locations. Inmarsat uses satellites in geostationary orbit above the Earth.

> GEOS   > SATELLITE COMMUNICATIONS

INPUT

Used as both verb and noun to describe the transfer of information from any source into a computer. In **hypermedia** and **virtual reality** systems, input can be by means of a **keyboard**, **mouse**, **tracker ball**, remote sensor or controller, position tracker or other form of **telemetry**, or from broadcast or narrowcast **telecommunications**.

> I/O   > OUTPUT

INSTANT JUMP

A facility in **videodisc** players to jump up to 200 frames (but normally 50 frames) within the time it takes for the screen to refresh (ie unnoticeably, with no screen **blanking**).

> INTERLEAVING   > REFRESH RATE

Satellite and groundstation, the key elements in satellite communications. Images courtesy of Inmarsat, one of the world's major suppliers of satcoms services.

INFOTAINMENT AND EDUTAINMENT
education meets
showbiz

'Infotainment' and 'edutainment' were probably the first distinct genres to emerge from the interactive media revolution that began in the late 1980s. The two terms describe a style of programme in which facts are presented in an entertaining manner, using all the capabilities of interactive multimedia systems. They differ only marginally, 'edutainment' being used to describe software designed for self-paced learning in a more structured manner. Both deal with facts, and both are aimed at the emerging 'information leisure' market created by the new interactive media.

Of course these hybrids of 'informative entertainment' and 'educational entertainment' have their precursors in older media. Originating in print genres such as popular encyclopedias, illustrated atlases and children's books, infotainment and edutainment became increasingly multimedia in form with the introduction of film and television. The film documentary and more recently the television documentary, cinema and then television news, have culminated in infotainment on a grand scale: Civilisation, Cosmos, The Ascent of Man, and thousands of more modest packages from broadcasters like the BBC and WGBH TV. Children's educational television and public service stations have produced highly popular formats such as Sesame Street. Then there are the quiz shows, ranging from Double Your Money to University Challenge, which are an abiding feature of broadcast television.

Given McLuhan's observation that 'the content of the new media is the old media', it is not surprising that hypermedia has subsumed these older genres. The range of interactive infotainment also echoes that of the broadcast media, and includes the quiz game, the documentary and the travel programme. Infotainment programmes certainly provide the bulk of the software so far produced for interactive media. From reference works such as The Guinness Disc of Records and How Things Work to travel programmes such as InterOptica's Great Cities of the World and browsable infotainment like Dorling Kindersley's Musical Instruments, the range of content is rapidly expanding.

Future infotainment and edutainment programmes are likely to use an ever greater variety of media to elucidate the idea, and to narrate or illustrate the information content. They will have less bias towards the pure textual or alphanumeric information that comprises conventional textbooks and many of the niche-market CD-ROM information discs. They may also provide a number of different ways in which the information content can be addressed. This would be partly to cater for the much wider range of abilities and experience that is to be expected in the mass consumer sector, and also a reflection of the interactive nature of the medium.

The American publishers Grolier, working with the Apple's Advanced Technology Group, have successfully demonstrated the multiple-perspective approach in their use of information guides in the 'Timetable of American History'. But this is not the only way in which infotainment and edutainment programmes set out to enrich the learning experience. Considerable work has been done on providing a means of matching the cognitive abilities of the user to the programme content, to provide the user with a choice of levels on which information can be accessed. Unlike television, hypermedia infotainment can provide a general overview and in-depth analysis, and it can span the range of levels of age, interests and educational attainment.

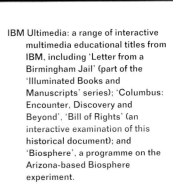

IBM Ultimedia: a range of interactive multimedia educational titles from IBM, including 'Letter from a Birmingham Jail' (part of the 'Illuminated Books and Manuscripts' series); 'Columbus: Encounter, Discovery and Beyond', 'Bill of Rights' (an interactive examination of this historical document); and 'Biosphere', a programme on the Arizona-based Biosphere experiment.

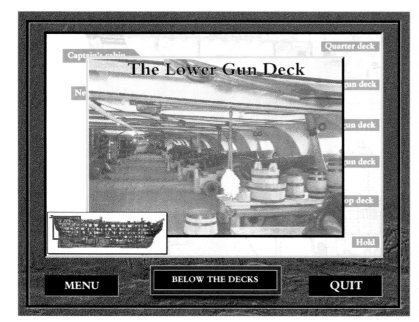

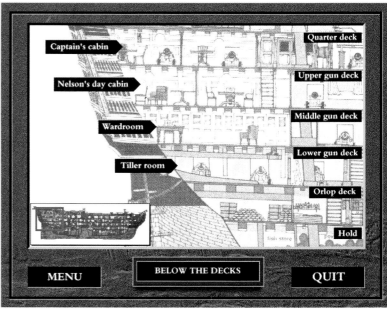

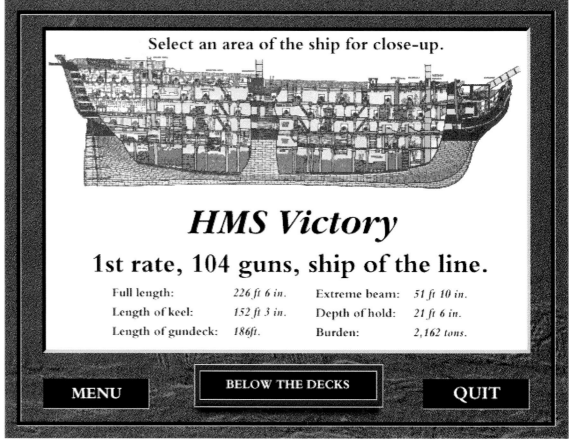

Select an area of the ship for close-up.

HMS Victory

1st rate, 104 guns, ship of the line.

Full length:	226 ft 6 in.	Extreme beam:	51 ft 10 in.
Length of keel:	152 ft 3 in.	Depth of hold:	21 ft 6 in.
Length of gundeck:	186ft.	Burden:	2,162 tons.

MENU   BELOW THE DECKS   QUIT

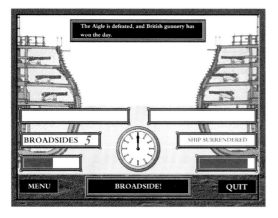

John Stevens: 'Battle of Trafalgar'. An interactive exploration of Nelson's HMS Victory and the Battle of Trafalgar, Stevens' multimedia prototype incorporates a nested series of cutaways of the Victory, linked with colour photographs of the ship, and an innovative 'battle simulator'. The progress of the battle can be viewed in a series of diagrammatic animations, and the broadside firing rate of the British and French ships compared in an 'against the clock' comparison sequence.

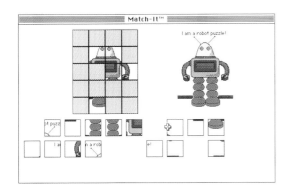

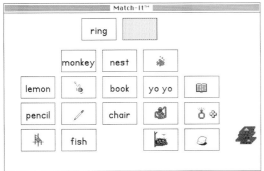

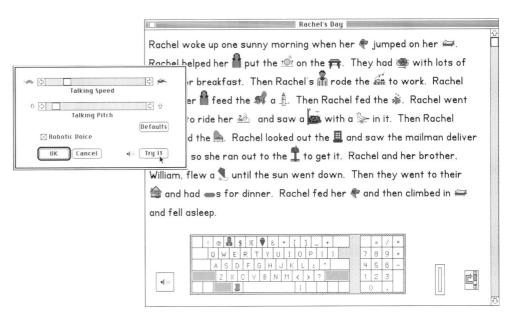

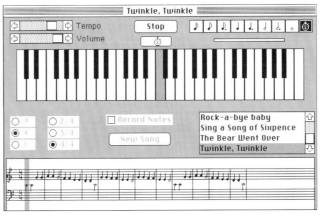

Great Wave Software: 'Kids Time'. This suite of media tools and educational puzzles for all ages incorporates a story-writing toolkit that produces instant synthesized (MacIntalk) speech, and a music composition program that records music notations from a soft piano keyboard and plays them back to the user.

Interplay Productions: Battlechess, spectacular animated chess with sound effects.

INTERACTIVE ADVERTISING

courting the interactive consumer

The concept of interactive advertising is already with us in the form of point-of-sale consoles and automatic teller machines. It may soon become a feature of interactive magazine-style programmes, hyper-comics, remote shopping services and hypermedia programmes. Such ads would offer consumers a variety of ways to explore a range of products or services, allowing them to compare and contrast different options, view the products and services on offer, and make an informed choice based on a much wider variety of information than can currently be included in press and TV advertising.

Interactive advertising is currently still in the research and development phase. So why is it important? Consider what will happen when consumers have much more control over the programmes they watch and interact with. When consumers become able to buy and watch videos and television programmes through an interactive teleputer – perhaps ordering a whole evening of entertainment and information in advance – what will happen to the advertising slots? Certainly, people may choose a cheaper programming package that includes ads, but many will want to exclude advertising altogether. So how will the broadcasters of the new media finance their productions when billions of dollars of advertising revenue is not forthcoming? And how will we receive ads, which after all can be fun as well as providing a valuable consumer service?

There are no pat answers to these questions, but consider the success of the home shopping networks in the USA, which thrive on promoting a live, marketplace atmosphere. And consider the possibility of the 'virtual mall', comprising a compendium of editorial features, single-screen ads, emotive virtual ads and virtual shopping environments echoing the style of the shopping mall. Single-screen ads, the 'classifieds' of interactive advertising, could be in database format, searchable by brand, product, price and location, and possibly including a still image, product description and price, as well as the usual addresses and telephone numbers.

Virtual shopping malls would be architectural 'walkthroughs', environments modelled in CAD and 3d computer graphic software to replicate the look and feel of a real shopping mall – but without the crowds. In the virtual mall, you always get served immediately, you are always the focus of the shop assistant's attention, you are never embarrassed by having to ask a price and never made to feel inferior when you ask the most obvious question. Virtual malls would allow you to wander through the shops and showrooms, requesting guidance, help and prices whenever you want. Or you could have the 'information' contained within the mall presented to you as a database from which you might identify a product, look at the alternatives, ask for a cost/quality 'window display' of comparable items, and so forth. At the top end of the advertising spend would be the 'mood simulations' or 'emotivations'. Transcending the pragmatic world of 'bargain hunting' and cost/quality comparisons, these virtual experiences would approach the consumer in the same way that corporate ads and top-of-the-range lifestyle advertising operate, enveloping the product or service with the stylish ambience of the Hollywood movie.

Just as current consumer ads rely heavily for their ideas and styling on the innovations of the movie maker and animator, so will emotivational interactive advertising rely on the innovations of hypermedia, VR, simulator and videogame designers. We are likely to see an increasingly seamless blurring of adverts and editorial – just as there is in newspapers, magazines, television, or in the city street itself.

Interactive advertising could certainly benefit the consumer, providing a wider range of choice, more comparative information, faster location of goods and services and on-line consumer-oriented information. It could also benefit advertisers, allowing more precise niche-targeting of consumer groups, better ways of presenting products, one-to-one pitches to target consumers, and more direct marketing opportunities. There will inevitably be a downside, however: electronic junk mail, obtrusive sponsorship of items featured in videogames and interactive movies, sleaze in the digital classifieds. As more and more information about the consumer is trawled from the cyberspace net by advertisers eager precisely to target their customers, and as pitches to individuals become highly customized,

Westminster Cable TV: 'Channel Upgrades', one of Westminster's interactive services.

privacy comes under threat. Protection could be afforded by instructing software agents to filter out junk mail, or to encrypt personal data. Policing agents could also roam the network, protecting the rights of the individual. The consumer protection societies would also have access to more precise data on products and services, and would be able to similarly market their surveys and recommendations.

By the early 1990s most of the technology necessary for interactive adverts was in place, and the infrastructure for linking home-based interactive services to regional 'hypermalls', and for the telephone, credit card ordering and purchasing of these products, was well under development. We can soon look forward to a revolution in advertising as agencies 'go digital' in their ongoing quest for new and better ways to sell their clients' products.

Informer: 'Informer Lifestyle' CD-ROM designed by Mark Bowey of Mindbath Design Associates. 'Informer Lifestyle' collates advertising research from many different sources. This CD-ROM focuses on young people's responses to ads and marketing campaigns, and provides regularly updated multimedia information for ad agencies, media buyers, product developers and marketing agencies.

Essentially they were extremely interested in the possibilities of the product, but very bored by the ad

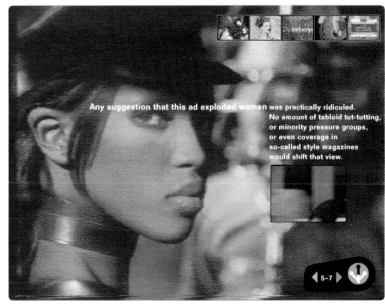

INTEGRATED CIRCUIT [IC]

The embodiment in miniature of a complete electronic circuit (comprising **transistors**, capacitors, resistors, wiring etc) on a semi-conducting substrate such as silicon. Invented by Jack Kilby of Texas Instruments in 1958 (and independently six months later by Robert Noyce of Fairchild Semiconductor), the integrated circuit was the second key breakthrough in modern electronics and **digital** computing (the first was the invention of the transistor by Shockley, Bardeen and Brattain in 1947). The integrated circuit solved the problem of the 'tyranny of numbers' – the sheer volume of wiring interconnections in electronic circuits that was setting a limit to the complexity of electronic devices. By incorporating the wiring and all the other necessary parts of a circuit within one 'monolithic' block of semiconductor material, the integrated circuit could be mass-produced. Within 25 years, annual sales of integrated circuits exceeded US $12 billion.

>   **MICROPROCESSOR**   >   **TRANSPUTER**

INTELLIGENCE

The capability of a system to modify its performance as a result of **feedback**.

INTELLIGENT

A term applied to devices (such as printers or computer terminals) that have a built-in capacity to process data.

INTERACTION

The process of control and **feedback** between user and computer (or **hypermedia** system/programme). Until recently, interaction was largely 'reactive', ie the user would do something and the computer would react (or vice versa). With increasingly 'smart' systems, however, the computer can become 'proactive', for example by 'learning' about the user. In **virtual reality** systems, interaction can take place in a virtual world where both user and computer are represented graphically and sculpturally – an 'immersive' interaction. In her book Computers as Theatre, Brenda Laurel argues that it is the user's sense of participation in the program that provides

the best measure of interactivity; she defines three useful parameters for assessing interactivity: frequency (how often interaction can take place), range (how many choices are available), and significance (does the interaction really affect matters?).

>   DRAMATIC METAPHOR   >   IMMERSIVE VR
>   INTERFACE   >   SOFTWARE DESIGN
>> FURTHER READING: LAUREL 1991

INTERACTIVE

Description of any computer-based system in which the user's input directly affects its behaviour, and its resulting output is directly communicated to the user.

>   FEEDBACK   >   INTERACTION

INTERACTIVE ADVERTISING

A concept for selling and promoting goods and services over **networks** which would allow consumers to interrogate the information provided and to specify and purchase any products they select.

>   • INTERACTIVE ADVERTISING PAGE 110

INTERACTIVE BROADCAST TV

A concept for using a combination of broadcast TV and some other form of communication link, such as the telephone system, to allow viewers to participate in programmes and to respond directly to advertising.

>   • INTERACTIVE BROADCAST TV PAGE 114

INTERACTIVE CABLE TV

A concept for two-way cable TV networks that would enable viewers to access and participate in hypermedia programmes.

>   • INTERACTIVE CABLE TV PAGE 116

INTERACTIVE ENCYCLOPEDIA

Encyclopedias were among the first **hypermedia** applications to be explored by publishers. By 1992 several book publishers had released their existing encyclopedias on **CD-ROM** and many (including Grolier and Hutchinson) had begun to exploit the **multimedia** potential of **electronic publishing**.

The simplest method of converting an existing book to an electronic format is to take the original text from the printed work, convert it to **ASCII** code if necessary (by re-keying or using **OCR scanner software**), organize it in a suitable **database** format, then construct a database **program** to administer random-access and string searches within an easy-to-use interface. Many early CD-ROM encyclopedias did just this. However, Mode 2 CD-ROMs, (**CD-ROM XA, DVI, CDTV** and **CD-i**) allow a much more 'multimedia' approach, integrating sound, **animation**, video, stills, **simulation** and adding 'hyperlinks' between associated items.

>   DIGITAL DICTIONARY

INTERACTIVE MOVIE

A concept for movies in which the viewer can determine the course of action by making decisions at key points in the narrative or choose a viewpoint of a particular character on a fixed narrative.

>   • INTERACTIVE MOVIES PAGE 117

INTERACTIVE MULTIMEDIA [IMM]

The generic term for programmes and applications that include a variety of media (such as text, images, video, audio and animation), the presentation of which is controlled interactively by the user.

>   • INTERACTIVE MULTIMEDIA PAGE 121

INTERACTIVE TV

Broadcast television with two-way communication link to give the viewer greater participation in programmes such as quizzes and debates.

>   INTERACTIVE BROADCAST TV   >   INTERACTIVE CABLE TV
>   • INTERACTIVE BROADCAST TV PAGE 114

INTERACTIVE VIDEO [IV]

A **videodisc** player (most commonly a **laserdisc** system), or in some cases a videotape recorder, linked to a **personal computer**. The user controls the programme through the computer, and views the videodisc images either on a separate television monitor or within a 'video window' on the computer monitor itself (for which the computer must have a suitable **video board**). Interactive video is widely used for training purposes.

INTERFACE

An abbreviation for 'human/computer interface' – the **hardware** and **software** through which the user interacts with a computer or **hypermedia** system. The human/computer interface has progressed through several generations, from the original 'hardware' interface (rewiring the computer to make it perform a specific **program**), through batch-processing (programs prepared as punch-cards and processed in batches), to the command-line interface (the 'C-prompt' of DOS), to the current generation of **graphical user interfaces** (such as the **Macintosh** and **Microsoft Windows**). The future promises 'immersive' interfaces exploiting **virtual reality** and simulator technologies.

>   GESTURAL INTERFACE   >   HUMAN FACTORS ENGINEERING
>   XEROX ROOMS

INTERLACE

In video systems, the method by which two video **fields** are combined to produce a single video **frame**. One field draws the even-numbered lines in the display, the other the odd-numbered lines. Fields are drawn in $1/50$ second (**PAL**) and $1/60$ second (**NTSC**). Interlace techniques provide a smoother **transition** between frames, minimizing the flicker associated with slow **refresh rates**.

>   TELEVISION STANDARDS

INTERLEAVING

Describes a method of storing audio, text and image data in alternating segments on a disc, so that each data type can be retrieved, stored in player **RAM**, and processed for simultaneous display. Interleaving is also used to provide instant **branching** options between alternative courses of action, thus keeping seek times to a minimum. The process is also widely used in **interactive video** applications, where many players have an 'instant jump' facility of 200 frames (meaning that the required frame can be located ready for display in the time it takes for the screen to refresh). To avoid any noticeable delays in an interactive sequence, images must be interleaved on the videodisc so that the move from one sequence to another requires jumps of no more than 200 frames.

> CD-i   > CD-ROM XA

INTERNET

The largest computer network in the world, with millions of users. Internet interlinks an enormous number of local networks operated by universities, research centres, government departments, non-profit and commercial organizations worldwide, and can also be accessed through 'gateways' from CompuServe and other commercial subscriber networks.

Internet's origins lie in the ARPAnet experimental network created in the 1970s by the US Government Department of Defense, in which various 'catastrophe-proof' networking options were developed. A result of the ARPAnet experiments was the Internet Protocol – a standard designed for routing data in addressed packets. The protocol was designed to let any computer communicate with any other computer, through different kinds of networks, so that in the event of a partial failure in the network, packets of data could be re-routed to reach their destination. The protocol was adopted by many academic and governmental organizations as a means of exchanging data between mainframe computers and their associated local area networks (LANs). The Internet was constructed in the 1980s by the US National Science Foundation in order to provide shared time on supercomputers for universities and research centres throughout the country, and eventually grew to encompass millions of other computer users.

> DATA SUPERHIGHWAY

INTEROCULAR [DISTANCE]

The average distance between the human eyes, about 65mm (2½ inches). This measurement is used in determining the optical spacing of stereo LCD screens in the EyePhone and similar head-mounted display and stereo viewing systems.

INTERPRETER

A computer program that translates and executes a program written in a high-level language, one line at a time. Interpreted languages run very much more slowly than languages that have been compiled into machine code. Scripting languages such as HyperTalk and Lingo are interpreted, which is why they run relatively slowly.

> ASSEMBLER   > COMPILER

INVISIBLE

In DTP, word-processing and other applications for personal computers, 'invisibles' are those features, such as letterspacing marks and 'hard return' arrows, which are not normally visible on screen, but which can be made visible by means of a menu command. In hypermedia development applications such as HyperCard and SuperCard, 'invisibles' include all those programme components, such as pop-up graphics, text panels, 'help' messages and the like, which the designer has determined will remain invisible until the user performs the action required to materialize them on screen.

I/O

In computer systems, input and output – methods of getting data into the computer (through a keyboard, touch-sensitive screen, networks, mouse, tracker ball, digitpad, video camera etc), and out of it (through a monitor, speakers, printer, recorders, disk drives etc).

IRIS

The variable aperture or diaphragm of a camera lens which opens or closes to allow more or less light to fall on the film, vidicon tube or CCD chip.

ISDN [INTEGRATED SERVICES DIGITAL NETWORK]

A set of standards for the transmission of digital data over telecommunications networks. An extension of the integrated digital network used for telephony, ISDN is designed to meet the increasing demands for the communication of interactive data, images, video and audio services, as well as the spoken word.

> B-ISDN

ISO [INTERNATIONAL STANDARDS ORGANIZATION]

Organization responsible for setting international standards for data storage, communication and display. ISO 9660 is the directory format for CD-ROM discs, allowing CD-ROMs to be used with different operating systems.

> HIGH SIERRA GROUP   > STANDARD

ISOTYPE [INTERNATIONAL SYSTEM OF TYPOGRAPHICAL PICTURE EDUCATION]

A graphic system for the presentation of statistical information, developed by Otto Neurath in the 1920s. The Isotype system used pictorial symbols to represent people, commodities etc. Neurath and his colleagues at the Isotype Institute set seminal standards for the design and display of pictorial information, influencing the work of graphic designers and interface designers.

> ICON

ITERATIVE LOOP

In a computer program, a set of instructions that are repeated until a specified condition is reached.

IV

> INTERACTIVE VIDEO

Isotype Institute: Otto and Marie Neurath's seminal use of stylized images influenced a generation of graphic designers and PC graphical user interface designers.

Urbanization of the Population

United States

1850

1930

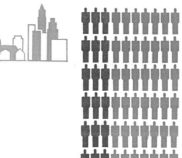

Great Britain

1850

1930

Each row of symbols represents 20 million population
red: in cities of 100,000 inhabitants and more

5

13

INTERACTIVE BROADCAST TV
nerd vs couch potato

The idea of viewer participation in broadcast television programmes has been around almost as long as television itself. Various participation methods have been used in the past, including mail-ins and phone-ins, culminating in global-scale telethons such as the Band Aid concert in 1986. Truly 'interactive' television, however, means involving the viewer in a two-way realtime dialogue with a broadcast programme. There are a number of ways to do this, including the use of ultrasonic control signals interpreted by a games console, the broadcasting of several channels of pictures that the user can choose between, and the use of simulcast FM radio signals converted to infrared signals to communicate with a console containing a portable modem.

The former system has been used by two American games manufacturers, Mattel and Axion. In 1987 Mattel demonstrated toys that were controllable by signals carried in broadcast TV programmes. Mattel's Captain Power toys were designed to work with a children's adventure programme (also produced by Mattel) called 'Captain Power and the Soldiers of the Future', a broadcast production available on videocassette. Targeted at 7- to 12-year-olds, the system allowed kids to 'shoot' at targets on the screen during special 'interactive' five-minute slots included in the broadcast programme. Axion have produced a 3-d video gaming system, 'Tech Force and the Motomonsters'. The system includes two games consoles, each operated by a child who controls up to eight small robots which can 'fight' with robots controlled by the other console. Alternatively, a single child can play against the other console while it is being controlled by ultrasonic signals carried by a broadcast programme.

The modem-based interactive systems developed by US companies such as Interactive Network (IN) and Interactive Systems Inc (ISI) are aimed at adult game show and quiz addicts. IN's system includes a keyboard/console with LCD screen containing the modem and FM receiver. During broadcast game shows viewers at home are given the chance to interact by keying answers into their console, or selecting from multiple-choice menus. This answer is then sent via the modem to IN's central computer, which is claimed to be able to deal with six million interactors a minute. When all the answers have been checked, individual scores are computed and results sent back via the FM sub-carrier to appear on the viewer's screen. The system has a 'lock-out' signal which comes into effect as soon as the correct answer has been given by a contestant in the studio, so that viewers cannot cheat.

Interactive Systems Inc have designed the VEIL (video-encoded invisible light) process, involving a terminal console with a modem and small built-in printer (for hard copy of coupons, credits and other 'prizes') that receives sub-carrier signals encoded by the broadcasters. VEIL allows viewers to become participants in games shows, again feeding their

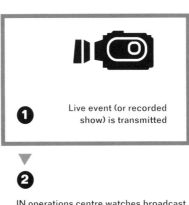

1 Live event (or recorded show) is transmitted

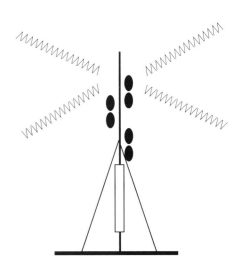

2 IN operations centre watches broadcast and enters results (or runs pre-recorded control tape for recorded shows)

8 Operations centre collects and compares results, and broadcasts winners' names within the control signal

7 If required, results are automatically transmitted via phone to IN operations centre

6 Up to four people in the home can watch the programme and play the game

3 IN operations centre broadcasts control signals on VBI, synchronized with the broadcast television

4 Home aerial receives both broadcast image and control signals

5 Control signals are decoded and retransmitted via RF link

THE INTERACTIVE NETWORK
how interactive tv works

Interactive Network: broadcast television interaction. With IN's system, viewers at home become 'doers' and can play along with game shows, participate in quizzes, respond to advertising, and predict sporting strategies and results. Interactive Network 'data jockeys' send out the game data, which is synchronized to the live or pre-recorded TV show. The signal is received at the base unit, which takes input from viewers' handsets and uses the telephone to relay scoring data back to the data jockey.

answers via modem to a central computer. Mattel used the VEIL system for the first 'one-way' interactive game show 'The Wheel of Fortune' in 1988. This allowed participants the private satisfaction of seeing their answers on screen before the studio contestants had answered.

Broadcast interaction is still in its infancy, but these nascent technologies offer the opportunity for some interesting developments, for example in electronic opinion polls, in interactive advertising, in foreign language sub-titles for movies, sub-titles services for the deaf, and for the cross-marketing of information, services or other products to mass audiences.

However, the real future for interactive television may not be in broadcast media. The high-definition systems of the near future, and the 'teleputer' hybrids of computers and television, will link into optical-fibre networks that can deliver both linear and interactive television. The broadcast wavelengths that become free when television moves to fibre distribution could then be used for 'wireless' networking for portable computers and 'personal information systems'.

QVC: interaction via the telephone on one of the USA's fastest-growing channels, now available in Britain and Europe via BSkyB satellite television. QVC brings a friendly 'market-place' flavour to home shopping, with special offers and discounts attracting a wide audience of home consumers.

Interactive Network: interactive TV controller handset. Up to four handsets can be used at the same time, encouraging family interactive play.

For Your Eyes Only
GB 1975

One of the best of Roger Moore's and Cubby Broccolli's James Bond extravaganzas. Remnants of the original story provide the anchor for an increasingly self indulgent treatment of plot.

MOVIES

Comedy
Crime
Science Fiction
Thriller
Western

POWERNET

PRINCE of PERSIA
© Copyright 1992 Jordan Mechner

Marry Jaffar... or die within the hour. All the Princess's hopes now rest on the brave youth she loves. Little does she know that he is already a prisoner in Jaffar's dungeons....

GAMES

MICROCOSM
MINDQUEST
CARICATURING
PRINCE OF PERSIA
SEVENTH GUEST

INTERACTIVE CABLE TV
one-way broadcast,
two-way narrowcast

Consumer cable television has its origins in the late 1940s, when a TV salesman in Pennsylvania erected a mountain-top aerial to improve his TV reception. His TV set was connected to the aerial by means of a coaxial cable. Reception improved enormously, and the dealer found that he could receive signals from other, more distant TV stations. The idea of cable TV was born. When the RCA corporation launched its first domestic communications satellite in 1975, operators realized that delivering TV programmes across the nation via regional satellite dish receivers and cables was cheaper than existing broadcasting techniques.

The effect of digital technologies on publishing and communications media is nowhere more profound than in the area of cable TV and telecommunications. When the basic components of media, whether they be sounds, images, video, textual information or numbers, can all be reduced to the same digital code for storage and transmission, traditional demarcations between the spheres of 'communications' and 'publishing' become eroded. In the case of telecommunications, the same networks of cables that currently support the telephone services are potentially able to carry video, text and images as well.

Telecommunications companies are currently manoeuvring to provide television and other data services, while the cable TV companies are rapidly developing phone, videophone and video conferencing services. In the late 1980s, it appeared that these services would operate within the Integrated Services Data Network (ISDN), the intention being that this would be an internationally supported standard. Action plans were developed by the RACE (Research in Advanced Communications for Europe) programme to extend ISDN to a Europe-wide broad-bandwidth network, carrying a wide variety of services in addition to interactive and narrowcast cable, phone, telex and digital fax, videophone and data communications. Fibre optics now appear to be the technology that will bond telecoms and television together.

The potential of interactive cable TV is being demonstrated by the Canadian cable operator Videotron, who schedule 12 hours a day of viewer-participation television for their Montreal subscribers. Videotron offers quiz and game shows, children's programmes, sports and news coverage, all featuring varying degrees of interactivity. In live coverage of sports events, for example, viewers can choose from a number of different camera and tape sources offering different views of the game. The company does this by narrowcasting four channels simultaneously, and featuring video windows of alternatives as insets to the main screen image. The windows can be turned on or off at will, or selected to fill the entire screen by pressing a button on the infrared remote control. When the viewer (or 'interactor') presses a button, the Videotron system

displays the selected channel without any of the tell-tale screen blanking or blips that normally accompany channel changes, so that the illusion of total viewer control over the TV editing process is maintained. The infrared remote control communicates with a 'smart' cable terminal, called 'Videoway', which switches channels seamlessly. Videoway also gives viewers the opportunity to dial up teletext, electronic mail and one-way home shopping services.

In London, Westminster Cable currently offers a limited range of interactive services, but with its advanced fibre-optic cables and video-switching technology it is very favourably placed to take advantage of the sort of interactive programming developed by Videotron. Westminster's advanced technology, produced in association with British Telecom, uses 'Switchstar' video switches which can link subscribers to a series of 12 video 'servers' (videodisc 'jukeboxes'), each carrying around 150 laserdiscs of programmes that are selectable from an on-screen menu. The jukebox is designed to be available alongside normal narrowcast and satellite programmes, 'teletext with pictures' and other interactive services.

FitVision/WBSB: a demonstration of possible home shopping, information and entertainment services for networked cable, simulating the 16:9 'letterbox' aspect ratio of high-definition television.

INTERACTIVE MOVIES
reelworld
goes realtime

Much confusion surrounds the concept of interactive movies. The idea is that the viewer can in some way become a real part of the movie, and play an active role in the plot. To a large extent, of course, this is what movie-goers have always done. Every time we watch a movie we bring a whole spectrum of cognitive tools to bear – some that we are conscious of (such as our critical faculties), and others, such as visual and aural perception, which we are less aware of. In fact any work of art, any act of cognition at all, requires considerable interactive participation. But interactive movies go one step further.

The idea of interactive movies stems from the text-based interactive fiction that appeared on computers for the first time in the mid-1970s. Interactive fiction and fantasy grew out of role-playing games, and the first interactive computer fiction, 'Adventure', was based on the game 'Dungeons and Dragons'. The 'reader' was faced with a series of branching options, which if correctly negotiated led to the treasure trove. The interface was simple: a text statement and a range of options. This kind of branching narrative contains thousands of options and permutations. Indeed, 'Adventure' was modified and extended by many of the programmers and computer hackers who played it. Because digital text requires very little storage space (one byte per letter), and minimal display technology, text-based interactive fiction is no problem for the current generation of CD-ROM-based home entertainment systems (the storage capacity of a CD-ROM is around 10 million words.)

Imagine the same branching structure applied to movies, however, where each frame of the movie requires at least 100,000 bytes. If we devised a movie with a very simple branching structure, offering the user a choice of two options after watching each one-minute segment of the film story, after just five choices we will have nearly reached the capacity of the CD-ROM, and generated over 60 one-minute film sequences. There may be over a thousand ways of viewing our interactive movie, but each unique viewing would be only five minutes long. The more choices, the shorter the movie.

Videogame adventures mostly use another kind of interactive narrative, which we could call 'interrupted linear' narrative. This involves following a linear storyline, via sets of problems, puzzles, dilemmas and other scenes where there are a number of choices to be made. The player must keep his or her on-screen surrogate in the story, and avoid being routed into some narrative cul-de-sac, or worse still, getting killed and having to start the game over again. Games like these do not have the thousands of different story routes possible in branching narratives, but they are very replayable – indeed, you have to replay, again and again, to learn how to negotiate all the obstacles.

In contrast, consider how users develop their own personal 'narrative' when engaged in piloting an aircraft in the virtual world of a flight simulator or other simulated environment. Here the choices are determined entirely by the user, and the system responds in realtime to the use of joystick or mouse. Realtime systems provide the greatest illusion of 'significance', the feeling that one's actions and interactions with a piece of software really make a difference to the outcome of the game.

Hybrid structures, combining realtime simulators, branching and interrupted linear narratives, are where most of the interest in interactive movies is now being focused. Such movies would combine the best of videogame structures – and even videogame-like media – with high-definition motion footage, graphics and animations in the style of the interactive 'graphic novel'. The success of such 'movies' will depend crucially on how well the director blends these different modes and treatments. The objective must be to marry together the narrative and different media in one seamless story space.

The shape of interactive movies will ultimately be determined by two factors – the nature of the distribution media, and the power of the hardware system. The main option for distribution media is currently the CD-ROM. These are due to double in capacity (double- and even quad-density CD-ROMs are under development), while fibre-optic networks will soon be able to deliver linear or interactive movies straight to a consumer 'teleputer'. Such systems will store software in large-capacity memory, and decompress the motion video data in realtime when required. Equipped with powerful processors, teleputers will create the conditions for a new type of interactive movie, a 'hyper-movie' that would combine virtual reality, expert systems and realtime computer graphics.

American Laser Games: 'Mad Dog McCree'. This production for the 3DO platform makes extensive use of motion video footage and heralds a new generation of videogame – the interactive movie has arrived.

Evans & Sutherland: realtime movielot simulations will play an increasing role in interactive movies as multimedia consumer players become more and more powerful.

Employing software techniques developed for movies such as Lawnmower Man and Jurassic Park, special effects programmers are already developing ideas for the creation of 'soft actors' – digital reincarnations of famous film and TV stars of the past, or of hybrids of these stars. It may not be long before soft actors appear in feature films, and very soon home-based technology could support the realtime generation of soft actors (albeit of low resolution) or indeed of the entire movie mise-en-scène. Furthermore, expert system techniques could be used to generate complex 'story arenas' through which the user may wander at will, meeting with soft actors that have distinct characters, and intentions, of their own.

Trip Media: 'BurnCycle', a prototype digital interactive movie. It may not be long before locations, sets and actors are all computer generated, but for now chromakey and other matting techniques can produce spectacular

Trip Media: 'BurnCycle'. Production shots from the chromakey studio. Real actors become synthespians floating in the alpha channel of 32-bit video. Later they will be matted into computer-generated sets.

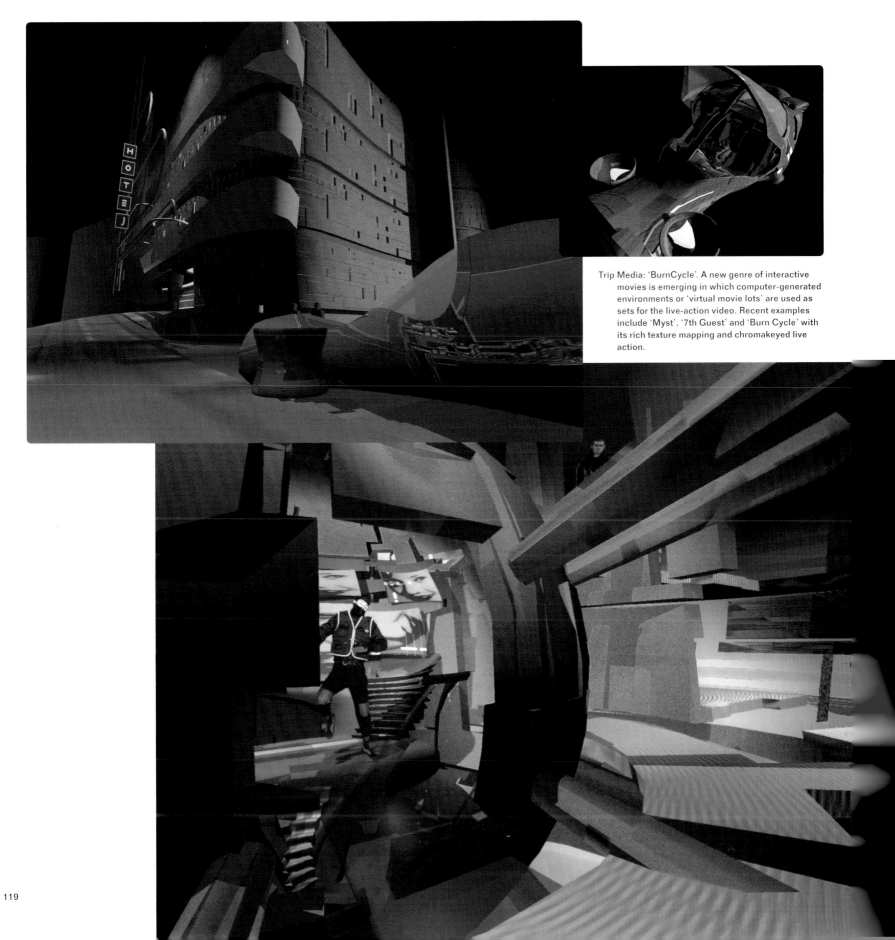

Trip Media: 'BurnCycle'. A new genre of interactive movies is emerging in which computer-generated environments or 'virtual movie lots' are used as sets for the live-action video. Recent examples include 'Myst', '7th Guest' and 'Burn Cycle' with its rich texture mapping and chromakeyed live action.

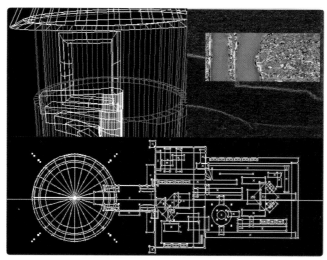

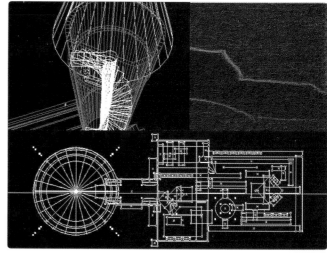

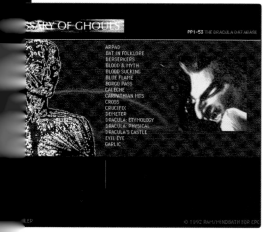

GLOSSARY OF GHOULES

PP1-53 THE DRACULA DATABASE

ARPAD
BAT IN FOLKLORE
BERSERKERS
BLOOD & MYTH
BLOOD SUCKING
BLUE FLAME
BORGO PASS
CALECHE
CARPATHIAN MTS
CROSS
CRUCIFIX
DEMETER
DRACULA: ETYMOLOGY
DRACULA: PHYSICAL
DRACULA'S CASTLE
EVIL EYE
GARLIC

GLOSSARY OF GHOULES

PP92 DRACULA DATABASE

Vampire Bat (92)

Zoological: The blood-eating bats comprise two genera (Desmodus and Diphylla) from the tropical forests of South America. Desmodus Rotundus is the most common species; it is about three inches in length, with reddish-brown fur and peculiar teeth adapted to its method of feeding; allegedly, they are able to pierce the skin and lap up the blood without awakening their victim.

‹ OVERVIEW   DIGITAL DRACULA TRAILER   © 1992 RAM/MINDBATH FOR EPC

GLOSSARY OF GHOULES

PP37 DRACULA DATABASE

Vamp (37)

Abbreviation of 'Vampire': a woman who attracts and exploits men; an adventuress. Theda Bara was the one of the first vamps in the movies; later embodiments included Rita Hayworth in Gilda, Marlene Dietrich in Blonde Venus, Greta Garbo in Mata Hari, Marilyn Monroe in Niagara and Charlotte Rampling in Farewell My Lovely. Possibly the most famous fictional vamp is of course 'Vampirella'.

‹ OVERVIEW   DIGITAL DRACULA TRAILER   © 1992 RAM/MINDBATH FOR EPC

Exploring multimedia styles of narrative interaction, Digital Dracula includes the complete text of Bram Stoker's novel, and includes a hyperlinked database, surrogate travel and adventure game interludes.

This trailer samples narrative, database and surrogate travel audio/graphic styles...

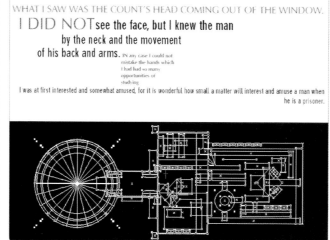

WHAT I SAW WAS THE COUNT'S HEAD COMING OUT OF THE WINDOW.
I DID NOT see the face, but I knew the man by the neck and the movement of his back and arms. IN any case I could not mistake the hands which I had had so many opportunities of studying.
I was at first interested and somewhat amused, for it is wonderful how small a matter will interest and amuse a man when he is a prisoner.

Bob Cotton and Mark Bowey: 'Digital Dracula' prototype, an experimental mix of realtime events and narrative branching, combining role-playing with infotainment.

DIGITAL DRACULA

INTERACTIVE MULTIMEDIA
the hypermedia revolution

Although one is a subset of the other, the terms 'interactive multimedia' and 'hypermedia' are often used interchangeably. Interactive multimedia resulted from the developments of computer-controlled interactive video in the 1980s, and refers primarily to videodisc and CD-ROM-based programmes that combine elements of graphics, animation, video, photographs, music and soundtracks with computer software. 'Hypermedia' describes the whole spectrum of new interactive media, spanning telecommunications, HDTV, interactive cable TV, videogames and multimedia.

The enabling technologies for interactive multimedia included fast and powerful microprocessors and dedicated co-processors to handle audio and video data; high-resolution colour CRT monitors; video digitizing and compression techniques; audio digitizing (sampling) techniques; and the mouse and other input/control devices. The availability of large-capacity data storage devices (hard disks, WORM, CD-ROM etc), and a wide range of software for image processing, computer animation, video and audio sequencing, and authoring, also represented a significant development. All these technologies were in place by the late 1980s.

Interactive multimedia design draws on a large pool of theoretical and practical work produced over the last 50 years or so. The original idea for an interactive 'memory extension' machine that would include images, text and audio, and would allow users to make 'associational links' between items of information, was outlined in some detail by Vannevar Bush as long ago as 1945. These ideas inspired many of the developments in personal computing and hypermedia that have dominated the last 25 years, including Ted Nelson's seminal writing on hypertext and hypermedia in the 1960s and 1970s, and Douglas Engelbart's development of practical hypertext systems incorporating the mouse, windows, word-processing software and electronic mail. Alan Kay's work on the graphical user interface (GUI) and the Dynabook, and the subsequent development of the GUI for the Apple Macintosh (1984), were also extremely important, as was the design of MacPaint (1984) and HyperCard (1986) by Bill Atkinson of Apple Computer.

The software and hardware systems to support 'consumer-level' interactive multimedia have been in place since the late 1980s. During the 1990s and on into the twenty-first century, publishers will be developing a wide variety of software for such systems. Many of these programmes will be information and reference 'books', or directory-style databases. Other applications include training and educational programmes; remote shopping and other information services; and a range of entertainment services.

Entertainment programmes could combine aspects of videogames and flight simulation, linear TV and feature films, interactive animated cartoons and movies. Interactive graphic novels, online magazines, customized news and periodical information services could also emerge. Telecommunications and computer facilities such as the phone and videophone, 'video-visits' and video conferencing with neighbours and friends each have a role to play, and programmes may well come to include elements of virtual reality and artificial intelligence.

Designers have already begun developing interactive entertainments. The problems are fascinating, but many are working in what is more or less an aesthetic vacuum. Certainly conventions can be imported from 'traditional' media – the grammar and syntax of film or graphic design need not be reinvented, but the basic problems of developing non-linear interactive narratives and recasting the roles of the audience/author within the new context of computer-mediated interaction and hybrid media, are far from being solved.

The new interactive media promise ever greater levels of realism. High-definition three-dimensional virtual environments, with digital sound, touch and even smell, could provide us with our own personal 'feelie' myth-scapes where we might meet real and imaginary friends, experts, guides or gurus. In this new environment of the future we could not only entertain ourselves and others but also explore the accumulated information and knowledge base of the whole human race.

Apple: 'Multimedia in Action'. One of Apple's regular CD-ROM 'newsletters' for developers, 'Multimedia in Action' covers real-world applications of multimedia in areas as diverse as education, training, point-of-information and interactive movies.

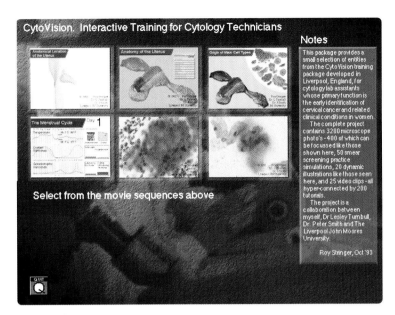

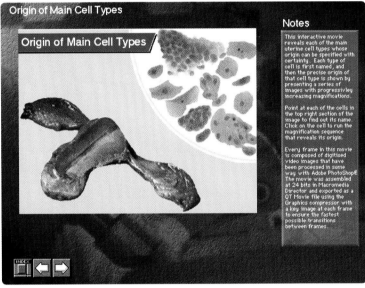

CytoVision: Interactive cytology training. A multimedia, interactive, self-paced training programme for cytology technicians, this award-winning application clearly demonstrates the role of the well-designed interface in linking together the multimedia programme contents.

Joe Gillespie/Pixel Productions: multimedia presentation for the Daily Telegraph on the future of the electronic newspaper and interactive multimedia advertising. Gillespie has been involved in the production of PDA software for Apple, and here envisages a notepad-sized PDA into which an electronic newspaper would be downloaded. This would of course feature interactive advertising as well as 'tell me more' features, animated graphics, and video and audio reports. The styling is print, the content electronic, the advertising interactive.

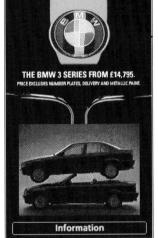

JAGGIES
Colloquial term for the 'stepping' effect that occurs when bitmapped images are displayed on a **low-resolution** monitor (or printed on a low-resolution printer), or when the image is enlarged. Jaggies can be mitigated by using **anti-aliasing** techniques.
>   BITMAP

JAGUAR
A 64-bit **RISC**-based **multimedia** system from **Atari**. Processing 64-bit data at high speed means that the Jaguar is capable of displaying **high-resolution** images and **realtime** graphic animations with high-quality sound. A **CD-ROM** bolt-on enables the system to play multimedia games, **infotainment** and **edutainment** programmes, full **CDDA**-quality audio and Kodak's **PhotoCD** discs. Jaguar's closest rival in the home multimedia/games market is **3DO**'s Interactive Multiplayer, with Sega's **Mega-CD**, Philips' **CD-i** and Commodore's **CD32** also strong competitors.

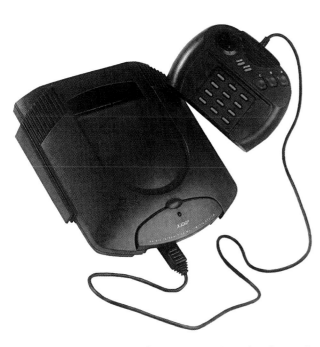

Atari: Jaguar. Superfast game-playing from Atari, with a claimed 850 million pixels per second and 64-bit processing.

JOYSTICK
A control/pointing device for computer systems, **videogames** and simulators.

JPEG [JOINT PHOTOGRAPHIC EXPERTS GROUP]
An image **compression** standard developed by the Joint Photographic Experts Group, a committee of the International Standards Organization and the **CCITT**. JPEG is a scalable algorithm offering compression factors of between 7:1 and 50:1, and is 'symmetrical' in that it compresses and decompresses in the same number of operations, and therefore the same amount of time.
>   FRACTAL COMPRESSION   >   MPEG
>   QUICKTIME

JUKEBOX
Term used to describe disc-based systems that can retrieve data from one of several discs, such as Westminster Cable's Videodisc Jukebox, which allows subscribers to select a programme from some 150 titles.
>   INTERACTIVE CABLE TV

JUMP CUT
In film and video, a **transition** that interrupts one shot to go to another that features the same scene or characters at a different time or place.

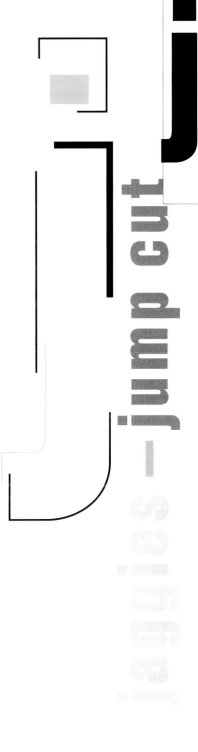

Photo-CD Index images – the hard copy that illustrates the data contents of the Photo-CD disc. These thumbnails provide a useful catalogue of the hundred or so high-definition images that can be stored on a CD-ROM.

124

KALEIDA

A joint venture between **IBM** and **Apple Computer** to develop a range of software products to enable **interactive multimedia** and **hypermedia** programmes to run on a variety of different delivery platforms. Kaleida is responsible for Script X and the Multimedia Toolkit, launched in 1993, which enable developers to produce programmes for both **Macintosh** and **Microsoft Windows** platforms. The significance of Kaleida lies in the recognition that a lack of common standards is hampering the development of interactive multimedia and hypermedia in both the commercial and consumer markets. The development of software tools that enable developers to make programmes for the widest possible market across delivery platforms respresents a considerable advance.

> OBJECT-ORIENTED PROGRAMMING

KBS

> KNOWLEDGE-BASED SYSTEM

KERNEL

The central nucleus of a **program**, **operating system** or **expert system**.

KEY FRAME

In **animation**, the drawings which describe the principal positions in a movement.

In **hypermedia** programmes, the decision points from which the user can choose to branch to another part of the programme. In **full-motion video**, the frames that are encoded in full, as reference frames for subsequent partial updating.

> COMPUTER ANIMATION
> FULL-SCREEN FULL-MOTION VIDEO
> INTERACTIVE MULTIMEDIA

KEYBOARD

An **input** device for entering text and numbers into a computer or computer-based system, by encoding an **alphanumeric** character or other symbol when a key is depressed.

Keyboards are a very efficient input device – but only if you have the necessary 'keyboard skills', ie the ability to type or at least to use two fingers fairly rapidly. Keyboards generally use the standard **QWERTY** layout which evolved with the mechanical typewriter, but other configurations are available such as the DVORAK layout which is faster and easier to use.

KILOBYTE

1024 **bytes** of data.

KIOSK

A standalone, enclosed **interactive multimedia** or **videogame console**. Kiosks are widely used in shopping malls, airports and other public venues to provide **point-of-information** programmes.

> ARCADE GAMES   > COIN-OP MULTIMEDIA

KNOWBOT

An 'intelligent software agent' or computer program that can respond to users' demands by performing simple or mundane tasks (such as searching a **database** for information) with little or no further input from the user.

> AI   > AGENT
> PERSONAL DIGITAL ASSISTANT

KNOWLEDGE-BASED SYSTEM [KBS]

Applications that can store, retrieve and analyse large amounts of information. KBSs have built-in tools for the analysis and representation of stored knowledge, and can be linked to **multimedia** or **virtual reality** systems for enhanced knowledge representation. Analysis is performed using 'IF...THEN' rules.

Knowledge-based systems are playing an important role in the management of managing (such as production scheduling, new product design and trend forecasting) and will be increasingly exploited in **database** management, training and education. By adding 'intelligence' to information processing and management, otherwise daunting tasks (such as retrieving relevant information from a vast database) can be greatly simplified.

> EXPERT SYSTEM

KODAK PHOTO-CD

A compact disc-based system for storing high-**resolution** photographic images in **digital** form. Launched by Kodak in 1992, Photo-CD allows users to have up to one hundred very high resolution images from their own negatives or transparencies encoded on CD, so that they can view them on a television set. Photo-CD is also used by graphic designers and reprographics companies for the transfer and archiving of digital images. Photo-CD discs can be viewed on **CD-i** players and other drives conforming to the **CD-ROM XA Mode 2** standards as well as on Kodak's own players.

> PHOTO-CD

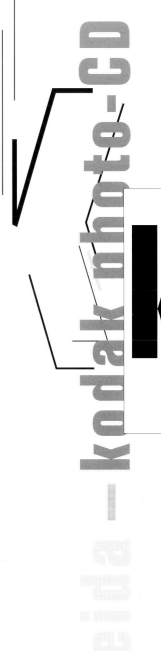

Motorola: Iridium System, providing a 'constellation' of satellites, 420 nautical miles up, for worldwide mobile communications coverage of voice, fax and data.

LAN [LOCAL AREA NETWORK]

A type of communications **network** that links computers and other devices over a limited distance, such as within a building or group of neighbouring buildings. LANs allow several users to share expensive items such as laserprinters and mass-storage facilities, or to share access to mini- or mainframe **computers**. There are several competing LAN **standard**s, some system-dependent, others capable of linking computers made by several different manufacturers. Transmission media can be **optical fibre**, **copper cable**, or radio, and the network topologies (the arrangement of the cable interconnections) include ring, star, bus and tree. By the early 1990s, LAN traffic was growing at around 30 per cent per annum (due primarily to the switch from mainframes to linked **personal computer**s for much of corporate computing), and several methods of interconnecting LANs into larger networks were being developed.

> ISDN   > WAN

LANGUAGE

Formalized system of notation for the precise description of computer programs. Computer languages evolved from basic **machine code** – which was difficult to write in and hard to debug – into **'high-level'** **language**s such as **C**, **HyperTalk** and **Lingo**.

> ASSEMBLY LANGUAGE

LAPTOP

Designation of a portable computer smaller than a 'desktop' computer but not as small as a hand-held or 'palmtop', designed to be carried around inside a briefcase. Laptops feature **LCD** colour or monochrome screens, internal hard-disks, floppy drives, and can include a modem.

> DYNABOOK   > POWERBOOK

LASER
[LIGHT AMPLIFICATION BY SIMULATED EMISSION OF RADIATION]

A device that generates an intense, concentrated beam of coherent light. A term coined in 1957 by Richard Gordon Gould, who invented the Gas Discharge Laser. Lasers are now used in a wide variety of applications, including compact disc players, laserprinters, imagesetters, **bar-code** readers, and **fibre-optic** telecommunications.

> CD-ROM
> DIGITAL-OPTICAL RECORDING
> LASERVISION

LASERDISC

A generic term for **videodisc**s and videodisc systems following Philips' **LaserVision** format, including those produced by other manufacturers.

Laser light: the data carrier at the core of the new telemedia.

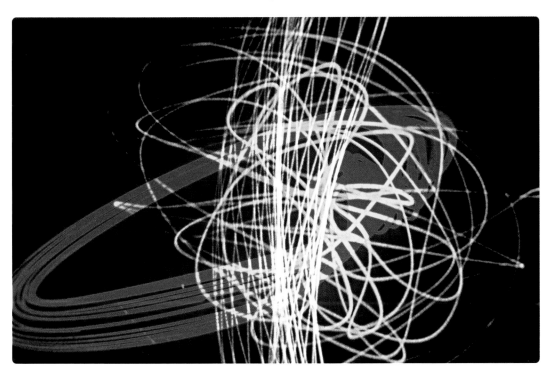

LV-ROM

LASERVISION [LV]

Interactive **videodisc** system developed by Philips. LaserVision 300mm (12-inch) discs in **CAV** mode can store 54,000 frames of **broadcast-quality** video pictures. Images are stored in **analog** format and can be displayed in full motion or in still frame within a **hypermedia** programme (running on a computer equipped with a suitable **video board**), or on a separate video monitor. In **CLV** mode LaserVision discs can store 90,000 video frames per side, allowing two hours of high-quality video.

LaserVision was a ground-breaking innovation, and gave birth to a whole industry – **interactive video** production – from which grew many of the techniques and technologies of **interactive multimedia**. However, the cost of a LaserVision player and interactive video workstations was too high for the technology to gain consumer acceptance, and consumers had to wait for interactive digital-video systems, such as Philips' **CD-i**, for use in the home. LaserVision is still widely used in training, presentation, video-wall and point-of-information applications, and is still the best system for displaying interactive broadcast-quality video within a hypermedia programme. In Japan and the USA there is a small but important market for films on **laserdisc**.

LATENCY

In **virtual reality** (VR) systems, the time lag between a user's action or movement, and the system's response. Latency is an unavoidable **artifact** of VR systems, and becomes more noticeable as response times climb above about 100 milliseconds (0.1 seconds). In this space of time, the **reality engine** (the heart of the VR system), must correlate data from the user's **position sensors**, establish the user's viewpoint, apply this information to the 3-d computer model, and finally render two views (one for each eye). The faster the user moves, the greater the latency. Faster processors will help disguise latency, but demands for more complex, higher-**resolution** virtual realities will keep pace with this, and latency is likely to be a problem for some time to come.

LCD [LIQUID CRYSTAL DISPLAY]

A flat-**screen** display technology for portable computers, **personal digital assistant**s and personal **hypermedia** systems. LCD screens work by electronically altering the polarity of light passed through a dense liquid sandwiched between two sheets of thin glass.

LED [LIGHT-EMITTING DIODE]

A **transistor** device that will emit light when an electronic current is present. LEDs are used as display lights and (in a matrix layout) for the display of **alphanumeric** characters in control panels and interfaces and as 'power' lights for consumer electronics and other video and computer hardware.

LEOS [LOW EARTH ORBIT SATELLITES]

A satellite that orbits at a height of 900-9,500 kilometres (550-6,000 miles), ie much lower than geostationary satellites (**GEOS**). Because of their relatively low orbits, LEO telecommunications services suffer less

Motorola: the 'Iridium' dual-mode portable telephone.

time-lag than other satellite voice services, and allow lighter and more portable terminals. The disadvantages include a shorter lifespan (around five years) and lower power (which means that more satellites are necessary to provide global coverage). LEOS-based telecommunications have been proposed by several groups in the USA, including Motorola with their Iridium system, TRW Space and Electronics with Odyssey, and Constellation Communications with the Aries system. These proposed LEOS systems require the launch of a number (or 'constellation') of satellites to provide global coverage.

LINEAR VIDEO

Conventional or 'passive' video, meant to be played in one continuous sequence of scenes and shots from start to finish, as opposed to '**interactive**' video, in which scenes and shots are designed to be viewed in an order determined by the user's interaction.
> FULL-MOTION VIDEO

LINGO

A **HyperTalk**-like **scripting** language for **Macromedia Director** (an authoring and animation application).
> AUTHORING

LINK

A feature of **hypermedia** programmes that allows associated items of information in different parts of a programme to be related, so that a simple mouseclick or other appropriate command takes the user from one to the other.
> HYPERTEXT

LINKWAY

Authoring language and **software** for the IBM PC and IBM-compatibles, with appropriate adapter cards, that

allows non-programmers to develop applications that combine text, colour graphics and sound, and control and display, **CD-ROM** and **videodisc** media.
> CD-ROM   > GUIDE
> ULTIMEDIA

LIT FIBRE

Popular term for **fibre-optic network** services provided by the telecommunications company that owns or manages the network, as opposed to '**dark fibre**', where network services are provided by users of the network.

LOCAL AREA NETWORK
> LAN

LOGO

A computer programming **language** for use by children, developed by Seymour Papert and his team at the Artificial Intelligence Laboratory at **MIT** between 1966 and 1968, and described in Papert's book Mindstorms: Children, Computers and Powerful Ideas. Logo was an important breakthrough, providing children with an easy-to-learn language that was also a sophisticated programming tool, capable of performing tasks like any other **high-level language**.
>> FURTHER READING: BARON 1988; BRAND 1987; PAPERT 1980

LOOP

In programming, a sequence of instructions that is repeated until some condition is satisfied.
> EVENT LOOP

LOW RESOLUTION

Describes a display system or printer that is unable to produce well-defined characters in any type size or smoothly defined curves in graphic images, resulting in type and images with jagged edges.
> RESOLUTION

LUMINANCE

In general, the measure of reflected or radiated light from a surface or light source. In video, the Y component of the signal, where UV are the **chrominance** components.

LV
> LASERVISION

LV-ROM [LASERVISION READ-ONLY MEMORY]

A 300mm (12-inch) digital-optical disc developed by Philips that combines **analog** video with **digital** data storage, first used on a large scale in the BBC 'Domesday Disc' produced in 1986. A development of the **LaserVision videodisc**, LV-ROMs can carry 54,000 video **frames** together with either 30 minutes of digital audio or 312 megabytes of data. With the advent of LV-ROM, the video and interactive authoring code could for the first time be stored on the same disc.

MAC
> MACINTOSH

MACHINE CODE
Program instructions in the form in which they will be
executed by the **CPU**.
> ASSEMBLY LANGUAGE   >   LANGUAGE
> MICROPROCESSOR

MACHINE INTELLIGENCE
> AI

MACINTALK
A synthetic speech application for the Apple **Macintosh**.
MacinTalk pronounces phonetically the words that
are typed into a MacinTalk-supported application,
such as **Macromedia Director**.
> SPEECH SYNTHESIZER

MACINTOSH
Apple Macintosh (Mac): the range of computers that
introduced the **graphical user interface** and **hypermedia** to
the mass market. The Mac is a favourite of graphic
designers, artists and hypermedia programme
developers because of its ease of use, its high
resolution and its wide range of design, **animation** and
authoring software.
Launched by **Apple Computer** in 1984, the Macintosh
featured an easy-to-use interface (based on ideas
developed by Alan Kay and others at **Xerox PARC**

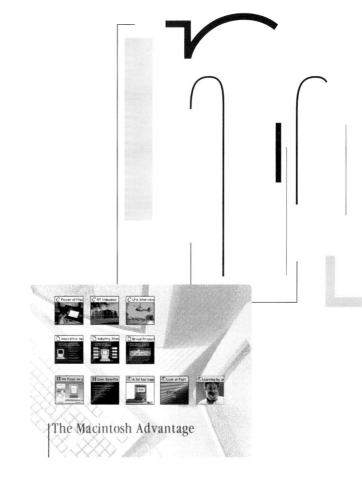

The Macintosh Advantage

Apple Macintosh. This was the computer
that brought us the first popular
graphical user interface, the first
useable paint and draw programs, the
first desktop publishing system and
the first hypermedia application. Now
it also provides a definitive suite of the
best design software for the
cyberspace media revolution.

during the previous decade), high-resolution paper-white screen, and an elegant package of 'bundled' software, including MacWrite and **MacPaint**. Since then, Apple have gone from strength to strength, introducing the first popular hypermedia authoring software (**HyperCard**) in 1986, and a range of **personal computer** products ranging from laserprinters to **scanners**, as well as high-end '**workstation**' machines such as the Quadra, **CD-ROM** drives, portables and **multimedia** computers.

> DESKTOP PUBLISHING

MACPAINT

Bitmap painting **software** for the Apple **Macintosh**. MacPaint was designed by Andy Hertzfeld and Bill Atkinson (who was later to develop **HyperCard**), and was one of the suite of **program** applications 'bundled' (supplied free) with the original Mac computer in 1984. With its easy-to-use **interface** – comprising a toolbox palette, iconic mouse pointers and painting area – MacPaint set the generic style for subsequent bitmap painting **programs**.

> PAINT PROGRAM

MACRO

In computing, a single programming command that initiates a set of commands to perform a specific task.

MACROMEDIA ACCELERATOR

An application for the Apple **Macintosh** that compresses animations created in **Macromedia Director**, saves them, and displays them at **realtime** video rates of 30 frames per second.

> COMPRESSION

MACROMEDIA DIRECTOR

An **animation** application package for the **Macintosh**. Director enables users to develop presentations and interactive **hypermedia** programmes that combine dynamic images, video sequences and sound. A development of Macromind's Videoworks, Musicworks, Zardoz and Zorro application packages, Director has become the pre-eminent **authoring** tool for **interactive multimedia**. Director is used to create finished programmes for Mac **CD-ROM**s, and as a means of prototyping programmes for other media, such as **CD-i**. Director is an ideal prototyping and presentation tool, capable of integrating complex animations, still images, motion text, 3-d model animations and motion video sequences, and combining these with sound, scripted loops and buttons. The Director scripting language 'Lingo' is similar to Apple's HyperTalk – very easy to get into and very powerful in the hands of an expert programmer.

> MEDIAMAKER

>> FURTHER READING: MACROMIND INC 1991

MAGNETIC STORAGE

Abbreviation of 'electromagnetic storage': a storage mechanism that consists of a disc, cylinder or tape coated with magnetizable material arranged into sectors or tracks. The magnetic medium rotates or 'spools' past a series of read/write heads that can read from, write to or erase data. **RAM** or **ROM** chips store **digital** data in electromagnetic form using **transistors** and storage capacitors.

> FLASH MEMORY CARD   > FLOPPY DISK
> HARD DISK   > PCMCIA
> SMART CARD

MAGSTRIPE CARD

Plastic credit, cheque-guarantee and ID cards carrying a magnetic stripe that can be used to store data. Credit cards were introduced by Diners Club in the USA in 1950. The first British card – the Barclaycard – was introduced in 1966. Magstripe cards can record on three linear tracks, and store up to 226 text characters and numbers. Card 'readers' contain a read/write head that can retrieve or modify the stored data. Despite their small memory, which limits the range of applications, magstripe cards are used in their billions. It is likely that high-security smart cards will gradually replace Magstripes in cash and transactional use.

> ATM   > PCMCIA
> SMART CARD

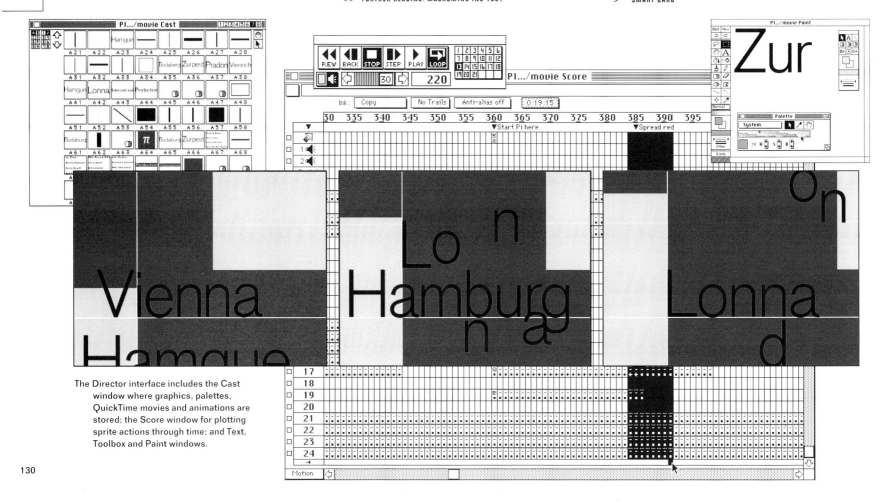

The Director interface includes the Cast window where graphics, palettes, QuickTime movies and animations are stored; the Score window for plotting sprite actions through time; and Text, Toolbox and Paint windows.

MAINFRAME (COMPUTER)

A large, centralized, multi-user computer system, requiring housing in a specially constructed environment and a specialized team to keep it functioning. Mainframes can service a wide range of user demands and modes of operation including time-sharing, batch processing and tele-processing. The late 1980s and early 1990s saw a move away from reliance on a central mainframe computer, towards **mini-computers**, on the one hand, and on the other towards distributed computing using networked personal or 'desktop' computers.

MANAGEMENT INFORMATION SYSTEM (MIS)

(Or 'executive information system'.) The adaptation of data-processing technology to provide user-friendly information for business management. MISs take a wide variety of forms; typically such systems will provide up-to-the-minute information on stock control, personnel, wages, cash-flow and so forth.
> EMERGENCY RESPONSE SYSTEM
> KNOWLEDGE-BASED SYSTEM

MANUAL

Explanatory documentation that accompanies **hardware** or **software** products. For manuals accompanying computer applications, manufacturers now have the option of publishing manuals in 'soft' (ie electronic) form, so that they can be consulted from within the software application itself. These manuals can use **interactive multimedia** or **hypertext** techniques for easy reference, and they can also provide 'context-sensitive' help and 'embedded training' (built-in lessons and demonstrations).
> ONLINE HELP

MARQUEE

The name given to the rectangular area (often denoted by flashing, dashed lines) that is created with the selection tool in **CAD**, **DTP** and **draw/paint programs**.

MASTER DISC

In **CDDA**, **CD-ROM** and **videodisc** production, an original disc from which copies can be pressed.
> CD

MATTE

In film-making and photography, an opaque mask fitted over the lens of the camera that delimits the area of the exposed picture, allowing another image to be combined with the first in a second pass of the film. Matte effects can be produced more simply in video and television production using colour-separation overlay or '**chromakey**' techniques.

MATTEL

American games company responsible for introducing several **interactive** games systems, including notably the 'Captain Power' toys. Introduced in 1987, this range included toy jet fighters with which children could interact via a broadcast television series and associated videos. The jet planes featured in the video could be 'shot down' by means of (ultrasonic or infrared) beams from the toy planes, and the children's toys could similarly be disabled by 'shots' from the television image. In the late 1980s and early 1990s Mattel produced the **PowerGlove** (in cooperation with VPL and Abrams Gentile Entertainment), a simplified version of VPL's **DataGlove**. The PowerGlove is used with some **videogame** consoles that utilize ultra-high frequency sound to determine the glove's position in the space in front of the screen. Users can 'box' with a digital Mike Tyson, trade karate blows with Ninja warriors, or interface with a variety of other 'shoot-em-up' type games.

MAZE

The maze or labyrinth is an apposite metaphor for the virtual '**cyberspace**' of computer and **telecommunication networks**, **hypermedia** programmes and **videogames**. Now used extensively in **role-playing games**, mazes have a long and multicultural history, featuring in Palaeolithic carvings, in myth and in legend, as well as in the form of calligraphic, turf and hedge mazes. The visual and metaphorical correspondences between the maze-like interconnections of silicon chips and printed circuits, and the virtual interconnections of **hypertext**, hypermedia and computer software are obvious, and graphic mazes have become a useful metaphor in the design of such software.

MD

> MINI DISC

MEDIA-CONTROL ARCHITECTURE

Apple-system **software** specifications for preparing **device drivers** (code that interfaces the **Macintosh** with various external media devices – videotape recorders, CD-audio players, videodisc players etc).
> OPERATING SYSTEM

MEDIA LAB

A facility of the Massachusetts Institute of Technology (**MIT**), the Media Lab has had a seminal influence on the direction of **cyberspace** technologies. Important areas of development have included artificial intelligence (**AI**), **interface** design, **spatial data management systems**, **computer graphics**, **digital audio**, **virtual reality**, **video conferencing**, **interactive video** and **multimedia**, **HDTV** and **networks**.
> ARCHITECTURE MACHINE GROUP

MEDIAMAKER

A multimedia presentation and **authoring** program for the Apple **Macintosh**. In MediaMaker, video, graphics, sound and **animation** can be combined and manipulated to prepare presentations and corporate videos.
> DESKTOP VIDEO   > MACROMEDIA DIRECTOR

MEDIUM

Term used to describe a means of communication or artistic expression, such as **hypermedia**, television or the book. Also describes the storage and delivery devices used to distribute **digital** data, computer **software**, **databases**, training programmes and the like.

Broadly, distribution media for digital data can be divided into two categories: physical devices and communication channels. Physical devices include **floppy disks** (of 1.4 and 2.8 megabyte capacity), **WORM** and **CD-ROM** discs of 640 megabyte capacity, and **LV-ROMs** of 1 gigabyte capacity. Other physical devices include **ROM** and **EPROM** cartridges, **flash memory cards**, **memory cards** and **smart cards** with memory capacity ranging from a few kilobytes up to several megabytes with capacities in the order of 1 gigabyte within the next ten years (ie 30 per cent larger than a CD-ROM). Communication channels include cable-based telephone and cable TV **fibre-optic** networks and computer 'wide area networks' (**WANs**) and short-range local area networks (**LANs**) which may also use wireless methods. Data distribution can also be effected by broadcast radio or TV, from terrestrial or satellite sources; and by cellular radio to portable computers, notepads and **personal digital assistant**-type personal information systems.
> CELL-NET   > DATA SUPERHIGHWAY

MEGA-CD

A **CD-ROM**-based **interactive multimedia** add-on system launched by **Sega** in 1993. The Mega-CD plugs into Sega's Mega Drive 16-bit **videogame** console, which in turn plugs into a standard television set. The Mega-CD uses two 16-bit **microprocessors**, which deliver multimedia games with high-quality **digital audio** and **digital video** from CD-ROM discs. Apart from richer graphics, video and sounds, CD-ROM-based games can offer hugely extended playing times in comparison with cartridge-based games. With the Mega-CD Sega are building on an established market of over one million Mega Drive owners, but the system does face competition from Philips (**CD-i**), Commodore (**CD32**), Panasonic (**3DO** Interactive

Mega-CD, Sega's CD-ROM bolt-on for the Mega Drive (Genesis in the USA).

Multiplayer) and **Atari** (**Jaguar**), some of which are already offering **full-screen full-motion video**, 32-bit processing, or other advanced features.
> NINTENDO

MEGABIT [MBIT]
One million **bits**.

MEGABYTE [MBYTE]
1,048,576 **bytes**, or 1,024 **kilobytes**.

MEMEX
An idea for a 'memory extension' machine described by the American scientist Vannevar Bush in an article in the Atlantic Review in July 1945. Memex was never built, but the idea of a desktop information processing system that would incorporate text, graphics and images, as well as **hyperlinks** between items of associated information, was to inspire the inventors of **hypermedia**, including Ted Nelson and Douglas Engelbart.
> ASSOCIATIONAL BROWSING

MEMORY CARD
A solid-state, portable, credit-card sized data storage system, more durable than a **floppy disk**, with much larger memory capacity and very much faster data access (read/write) times.
> FLASH MEMORY CARD   > PCMCIA
> SMART CARD

MENU
A list of choices, presented on-screen by a **program**, that allows the user to choose from a variety of alternative courses of action. Menus range from very simple text lists that occupy the entire screen, to 'pull-down' or 'pop-up' menus that appear from a **menubar** or **icon**. Such text menus can use a variety of typographic and colour-coding treatments to prioritize or classify menu items.

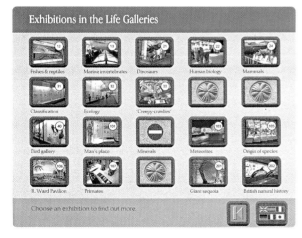

Natural History Museum: 'Wonders of the Natural World', designed by art director Brett Wickens and information designer Ian Martin using Aldus Supercard.

Hakuto International: Fujisoku memory cards.

Menus can of course be entirely visual. Imagine a menu treatment of the Beatles' Sgt Pepper album sleeve. Each of the collaged portraits on the sleeve could be a 'menu item', perhaps leading to a brief biography or a larger-scale picture of the featured person. In this way, a 'menu' can also be a collection of icons – including pictographs, motion icons etc. Of course, hypermedia designers have to consider how the user will differentiate between menu items and static (non-menu) items on a screen.
> INTERFACE

MENU-DRIVEN
Describes computer applications and **hypermedia** programmes that use **menus** of choices. Menu-driven applications avoid the user having to learn a set of commands to control the program, by providing a menu of alternatives for each stage in its operation.
> BROWSING   > INTERFACE
> NAVIGATION

MENUBAR
In **Macintosh**, **Microsoft Windows** and other similar **graphical user interfaces**, the menubar is the horizontal strip at the top of the screen that contains the **menu** titles. Menus can be revealed by pointing and clicking or dragging the menu choices from the menubar. Menubars offer the user a wide number of choices without cluttering the screen with **icon**s or lists.
> INTERFACE

MESSAGE BOX
In **authoring** and hypermedia **scripting** programs such as **HyperCard** and **SuperCard**, a small 'window' into which program commands, messages and calculations can be **input** by the user, and which can be used as a mode of **output** or **feedback** from the program. The message box is a direct method of communicating with the controlling program or with **scripts** and **objects** within that program.

MICON [MOTION ICON]
An **icon** that is animated – to attract attention, as a decorative feature, or as a way of guiding the user through a complex set of activities.
> CUECON   > INTERFACE

MICRO
> MICROPROCESSOR

MICROCHIP
(Or 'chip'.) Informal term for any **integrated circuit** on a wafer of silicon. Most commonly used in relation to **CPU**s and **RAM** chips, but also used to describe other components of computer systems.

MICROCOMPUTER
An alternative term for the **personal computer** or single-user computer; now infrequently used. The term was originally coined to distinguish personal computers from **mini-computers**.

MICROPROCESSOR
A central processing unit (**CPU**) on a single **microchip**; invented by Marcian E (Ted) Hoff in 1971, at Intel Corporation. The first microprocessor, the 4004, brought together all the basic functions of a computer on a single chip of silicon; it contained the equivalent of 230 transistors, and processed 4-bit words. Over the following two decades a series of ever more powerful microprocessors appeared. Processing power seemed to double every year, while unit prices halved. In 1976, Zilog launched one of the most popular and widely used 8-bit processors, the Z-80, and that same year, Chuck Peddle of MOS Technologies developed the 6502 – the chip that powered the Apple II. Two years later Intel launched the first 16-bit microprocessor, the 8086, and in 1979 Motorola launched their 68000 series, directly competing with Intel chips. In 1985, Intel launched their 80386 32-bit microprocessor, capable of delivering 3-4 **MIPS** (million instructions per second) while remaining compatible with software designed for its predecessor, the 16-bit 8086. The Intel 80486 followed in 1989, and the Pentium (80586) was announced in 1993.
> INTEGRATED CIRCUIT   > RISC
> TRANSISTOR   > TRANSPUTER

The Pentium chip from Intel.

MICROSOFT CORPORATION

The world's largest and most successful **software** company, responsible for a wide range of bestselling software for **personal computers**, including Word, **Windows** and Excel. Under the leadership of Bill Gates, the archetypal computer boffin turned software entrepreneur (whose genius has made him one of the richest men in the world) Microsoft is established as a central player in the creation of **cyberspace** information and entertainment systems.

Microsoft (an abbreviation of Microcomputer Software) was founded in 1975 by Gates and Paul Allen (a friend and fellow computer buff since schooldays) to promote and develop a version of **BASIC** that Gates and Allen had developed for the first **microcomputer** kit, the 8080 Altair.

Within two years, Microsoft BASIC was developed for other microcomputers, and by 1981 Microsoft had software running on – and earning royalties from – a wide range of computers, including the NEC PC8001, Japan's first microcomputer. But Microsoft's big breakthrough that year was in persuading **IBM** to let it develop the **operating system** for the IBM PC. The Microsoft Disc Operating System **(MS-DOS)** went on to become the most widely used operating system in the world – a standard on IBM PCs, and on all the **IBM-compatible** personal computers that followed.

The success of MS-DOS was followed in 1985 by **Microsoft Windows** – a **graphical user interface** that made PCs almost as user-friendly as the **Macintosh**, launched a year earlier. Through a process of continual improvement, new versions of Windows followed. Windows 3.0 (launched in 1990) was a true multi-tasking system, and **Windows NT** (New Technology), announced in 1993, has set the standard for PC interfaces of the 1990s.

Gates and Microsoft have been active proponents of **multimedia** computing since the early 1990s. Like **Apple**, and more recently IBM, Microsoft are developing windows-style interface technologies for a wide range of consumer **telecommunications**, information and entertainment systems, including multimedia **CD-ROMs**, **personal digital assistants** and interface technologies for consumer interactive television networks.

>> FURTHER READING: WALLACE AND ERICKSON 1992

MICROSOFT WINDOWS

The hugely successful **graphical user interface**, integrator and utilities software for **IBM** and **IBM-compatible** personal computers, launched by **Microsoft** in 1985. Microsoft Windows sits between the operating system **(MS-DOS)** and the applications, and provides an easy-to-use **interface** through which the user can launch programs, run utilities and switch between programs. It is a **WIMP** (windows, icons, mouse and pull-down menus) interface, the kind that was developed at **Xerox PARC** and featured on the Macintosh computers from 1984 on. Microsoft Windows is supplied with a word-processing program called 'Write', a paint program, cardfile index and several other facilities including a game, a clock and a calculator.

> WINDOWS NT

MICROWAVE

Describes wireless systems using the extremely high frequency band of the radio spectrum to transmit **analog** and **digital** data. At these frequencies signals bounce off buildings rather than going straight through them, so that generally transmitters and receivers have to be in line of sight of each other. Microwave transmitters and receivers are already an established part of national and international **telecommunications** trunk networks. In the early 1990s the technology had developed to the point where it could be used as an alternative to cable TV and conventional telephone services for domestic users. Microwave systems can have a **bandwidth** up to 300 times greater than broadcast TV and considerably better than many conventional cable TV networks. This, coupled with lower infrastructure costs because there is no need to dig up roads to lay cables, means that microwave technology is becoming a serious contender to deliver **interactive multimedia** services to the home and office.

MID-FI [AUDIO]

In **CD-i**, 'Level B' audio quality. Mid-fi is comparable with FM broadcast radio sound quality and has a bandwidth of 12,000 Hz, obtained by using 4-bit adaptive delta pulse code modulation **(ADPCM)** at a sampling rate of 37.7 kHz.

> CD-i DIGITAL AUDIO

MIDI [MUSICAL INSTRUMENT DIGITAL INTERFACE]

A **standard** for music information interchange adopted by the electronic music industry in 1983. MIDI defines both the **hardware** and **software** used to connect MIDI-compatible devices. Basically, MIDI enables many different types of electronic keyboards, samplers, synthesizers, **sequencers**, and the like to communicate effectively. MIDI add-on boards can be bought for most popular **personal computers**, with composition and sequencing software to specify timing, instruments, notes and other related information. MIDI coding is utilized in some **multimedia** editing systems.

> DIGITAL AUDIO

MIDI CONNECTOR

The 180 degree 5-pin DIN connector used on MIDI equipment.

> MIDI

MINI-COMPUTER

(Or 'mini-mainframe'.) Cabinet-sized computer, mid-way in size between a **mainframe** and a **personal computer**. Mini-computers are generally used for more specialized tasks than mainframes, and often service a **network** of workstations in a computer graphics or **multimedia** production studio.

The Microsoft Windows interface, with Bill Gates featured in a Video for Windows digital movie.

↓

MINI DISC

A 'personal listening system' launched by **Sony** in 1992, built around a recordable 60mm (2½-inch) diameter disc that offers up to 74 minutes of **digital audio** recording and playback. The system combines the audio quality and random access of disc-based digital music with the recordability of cassette systems, and presents a direct challenge to Philips' **DCC**. Pre-recorded music discs can be made using existing **CD** production facilities, while custom recordings are made on discs employing magneto-optical techniques.

> **DAT**

MIPS (MILLIONS OF INSTRUCTIONS PER SECOND)

A method of measuring the performance of a **microprocessor**. For example, the latest **RISC**-powered **personal digital assistant**s can deliver 15 MIPS (much more power than the desktop machines of a few years ago) and the RISC-powered **POWER PC** should deliver in the region of 40-50 MIPS.

MIT (MASSACHUSETTS INSTITUTE OF TECHNOLOGY)

A leading North American university particularly notable for its research into artificial intelligence (**AI**) and **robotics**, and for the work of the **Media Lab** which is based there.

> • **ARCHMAC TO MEDIA LAB PAGE 19**

MIX

In video, the **transition** effect between two shots. In audio, the combination of various tracks to produce a final soundtrack. To 'mix down' is to combine a large number of tracks into a final stereo or two-track master tape, by means of a mixing desk or digital audio software application.

> **DIGITAL AUDIO**

MNEMONICS

A means by which facts or procedures can easily be memorized. In its broadest sense, a mnemonic can be a knot in a handkerchief reminding the owner that he has to post a letter, for example. During the later Middle Ages and the Renaissance, very sophisticated mnemonic schemes were devised whereby whole bodies of knowledge could be structured within the memory, via metaphysical devices like the 'Memory Theatre' or graphical designs such as Lullian circles. In **hypermedia** and computer **interface** design, **icons**, **guides**, audio prompts, smart '**agents**' and the like serve as 'mnemonic' devices, reminding the user to perform a specific task.

MODE 1, MODE 2

The two modes in which data can be formatted on **CD-ROM**. In Mode 1, each frame of data comprises 12 **bytes** of synchronization data, 4 bytes of header information, 2048 bytes of user data, and 288 bytes of error detection and error correction code (EDC/ECC). Mode 2 has a larger user data area (2,336 bytes) with less EDC/ECC. Modes 1 and 2 can be mixed with other modes (**CDDA**, **CD-i** or **CD-ROM XA**) on the same disc, in which case the whole track must be of only one type (ie track one might be computer data, track two audio, and so on).

MODEL SHEET

In **animation**, the specification of a hand-drawn or computer-modelled character – giving details of its proportions, colouring, sound effects, 'voice', characteristic gestures and so on – used to guide the animators in their preparation of **key frames**.

> **COMPUTER ANIMATION**

MODELLING

In video, film and photography, the creative use of lighting to enhance the visual appearance of a subject, and to bring out the qualities of structure and spatial depth. In systems analysis, product development, data processing and other design-related activities, refers to the process of simulating the behaviour of complex processes (often by simplifying them). In **computer graphics**, the term is used as a shorthand for **solid modelling**.

> **SIMULATION**

MODEM (MODULATOR/DEMODULATOR)

A **digital**-to-**analog** device that links computers to the telephone **network**, and enables digital data to be modulated so that it is compatible with the analog signals carried by the telephone system. Signals are sent to a remote computer modem, where they are demodulated and the original data restored.

> **ISDN**   > **TELECOMMUNICATIONS**

MOMENTUM

In **animation**, the degree of motion in a character or object, dependent on its mass and velocity. The term is used to describe the tendency of a moving object to remain in motion.

> **MOTION BLUR**

MONITOR

Short for video or computer monitor: the **CRT** or **flat-screen** display device used for displaying a video recording, replay or edit, or monitoring the performance of a computer program or **interactive** application.

> **SCREEN**

MONTAGE

In film, video and hypermedia, the juxtaposition and interrelation of stills and motion sequences through editing, **authoring** or user **interaction**. For the first, and still the most succinct, description of the theory and practice of montage, see The Film Sense by Sergei Eisenstein.

> **SOFTWARE DESIGN**

>> **FURTHER READING: EISENSTEIN 1943**

MORPH

Computer-graphic **image processing** technique for metamorphosing one image into another. Used extensively in advertising and **video graphics**, the technique was exploited to dramatic effect in the movies Terminator 2 and The Lawnmower Man. Commercial morphing software for **personal computers** became available in 1992. 'Morph' software involves loading a 'start' and 'end' image, determining which points on the start image will relate to which points on the end image, and then specifying the number of frames required for the transition.

> **COMPUTER GRAPHICS**

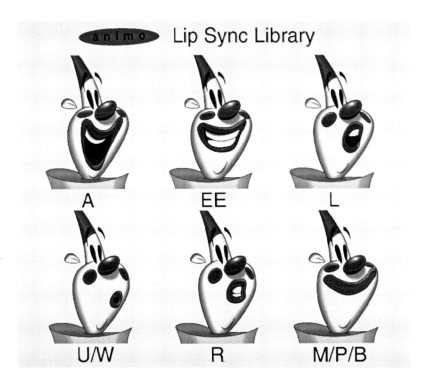

Animo Lip-sync Library, a model sheet from Cambridge Animation.

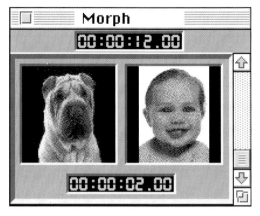

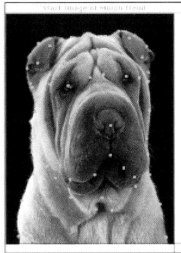

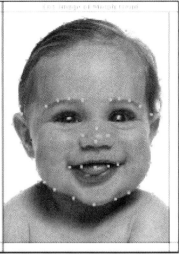

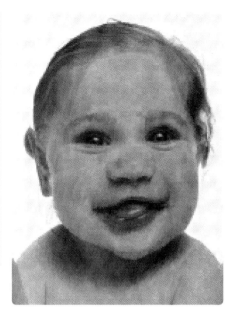

Morph: this apparently simple tool for designers has redefined the vocabulary of filmic transition effects, providing the means for a magical metamorphosis between any two objects.

MOTHERFRAME

In **hypermedia**, a main **node** or **key frame** that acts as a **menu** of choices from which the user can branch into related ('daughter') sequences or environments, or link to other motherframes.

MOTION BLUR

'Motion blurring' occurs if the speed with which a fast-moving object is captured on film or video is too slow to 'freeze' the motion of the object as it is resolved into single **frames** or **fields**. This artefact of motion pictures is used in **animation** and **computer animation** to create an effect of fast movement (a technique called 'temporal anti-aliasing').

MOTION CONTROL

The computer control of film cameras and associated equipment. Motion control allows very precise frame-by-frame control of lighting, **iris**, **mattes**, etc, so that on repeat passes through the camera, the film can be made to record different events (such as an actor talking to his own duplicated image). Alternatively, computer-generated images and animations sharing precisely the same lighting and perspective can be superimposed upon a filmed environment. Motion-control techniques ultimately derive from **rostrum camera** work, where the equipment is controlled manually. The digital control of machine tools was developed first by the US Air Force, with its APT (Automatically Programmed Tools) language. Probably the foremost creative exponent of motion control is the Polish-American film-maker Zbigniew Rybczinski, in films such as <u>Tango</u> (1980) and <u>Odessa</u> <u>Steps</u> (1987).
> COMPUTER ANIMATION   > ROBOTICS

MOTION PARALLAX

A spatial or distance cue, whereby the relative displacement of moving objects in space at a given time, gives clues as to the position of those objects. (If we are travelling on a train, for example, nearby objects such as trees and pylons appear to move faster past us than more distant objects.) Motion parallax is used in an exaggerated form in many films and computer animations, where the parallax effect is heightened by the use of extreme wide-angle lenses and physically improbable camera movements.
> COMPUTER ANIMATION   > VIRTUAL REALITY

MOTIVATIONAL FACTORS

The factors that motivate the user in a **videogame**, role-playing adventure or **hypermedia** programme. These include the quest for information or knowledge; the desire to achieve a high score; the practice of skills; and the application of knowledge, observation, memory or intelligence.
> ARCADE GAMES   > ROLE-PLAYING GAME

MOUSE

Hand-operated **input** and pointing device; a **cursor** on the computer screen moves in correspondence with the movements of the mouse on the user's desk. The mouse was invented by Douglas Engelbart during his development of the Augmentation system at the Stanford Research Institute in the 1960s. Although not commercially available until the early 1980s, the mouse was a significant breakthrough in the continuing development of a 'natural language' human-computer **interface**. Along with the lightpen, stylus and **digitpad**, the mouse provided a method of interacting with the computer that relied on gesture, and sowed the seeds for the sophisticated gesture-sensing and position-tracking systems of the 1990s, such as the **DataGlove**.
> ARC   > GESTURAL INTERFACE

MPC (MULTIMEDIA PERSONAL COMPUTER)

A hardware and software **standard**, promoted by **Microsoft**, specifying the minimum requirements for **personal computers** running **Microsoft Windows** 3.1 or above to display **multimedia** programmes. The MPC minimum **hardware** specification includes an 80286 **microprocessor**, 12 MHz processor, 2 megabytes of **RAM**, a 30 megabyte **hard disk**, **VGA** screen display, a **CD-ROM** drive with audio output, 8-bit **DAC** (digital to analog converter), an audio **synthesizer**, **MIDI** support, and a **joystick** controller.
Software standards for MPC comprise a family of file formats, collectively called **RIFF** (resource interchange file format), for text, audio, video stills and animation. The integrating **protocol** is the multimedia control interface or MCI, which governs communications between hardware, **device drivers** and software. MCI is an **ASCII** string protocol that allows **authoring** software to control the MPC hardware. MPC will run under Microsoft Windows 3.1, or **Windows NT**. By 1993, **multimedia** development tools for MPC first became available, and the system promises to deliver real multimedia capabilities to the huge number of personal computer users.

MPEG

A **standard** defined by the Moving Pictures Expert Group for the **compression** and decompression of motion-video images. The aim of MPEG was to define a standard that can reproduce TV-quality video and CD-quality audio after it has been compressed to a data rate compatible with a **CD-ROM** or **hard disk**. This requires data compression ratios well in excess of 100 to 1. MPEG uses a variety of compression techniques, including DCT (discrete cosine transform). It only stores complete data for 'key' frames in the movie, with successive frames described by the differences in the image compared with the key frame. There are two MPEG standards: MPEG-1 for data rates of up to 2 Mbit/sec and MPEG-2 (for double-density disks and multimedia networks) which supports data rates of 2-10 Mbits/sec. As a global standard, MPEG will become an important landmark in hypermedia development, opening up the possibility of true multimedia for CD-ROM-based distribution vehicles, and feature films on CD discs. The first MPEG chip for consumer multimedia players was launched by Philips for their CD-i system in October 1993.
> ISDN   > JPEG
> VIDEO-CD

MS-DOS [MICROSOFT DISC OPERATING SYSTEM]

The most widely used **operating system** for IBM and IBM-**compatible** personal computers. Developed by **Microsoft** for IBM, MS-DOS uses a 'command-line' interface, ie employing simple system 'prompts'. MS-DOS is essentially a 16-bit, single-tasking operating system, designed to run only one application at a time. In the mid-1980s Microsoft launched the **Microsoft Windows graphical user interface** for MS-DOS machines, which effectively disguises the command-line complexity of MS-DOS, and which features **multi-tasking**.

MTC [MIDI TIME CODE]

A **time code** used within the **MIDI** standard. It is used with the **SMPTE** time-code standard for synchronizing MIDI instrumentation and sequencers with video and film.

MULTI-IMAGE

Describes **audiovisual** (A/V) programmes that feature several images projected at the same time. Multi-image A/V grew out of experiments in **multimedia** events, lightshows and happenings in the 1960s, by groups like USCO, and were featured at Andy Warhol's nightclub The Exploding Plastic Inevitable. Later, multi-image performances were a central feature of the Expo 67 in Montreal, where the newly available Kodak Carousel slide projector was used in the first serious attempt to develop a non-linear, iconic method of presenting visual information. In Britain, the work of the Light/Sound Workshop at Hornsey College of Art in the late 1960s included multi-image pieces, several of which were displayed at the Museum of Modern Art in Oxford in 1968.
> VIDEO WALL

MULTI-PLATFORM

Describes computer **software** (including **videogame**, **interactive multimedia** and **hypermedia** programmes) intended for more than one **delivery system** or 'platform'. Producers often cannot recoup their development costs by producing software for a single platform, so programs are generally developed for the primary platform in a portable, 'system independent' language (such as **C**), and then adapted for use on other platforms. In hypermedia programmes, many of the design and production tasks are common, regardless of the end-user platform, and there are a wide variety of software tools for the conversion of **file formats** from one system to another. Forward-looking producers ensure that their production cycle allows for 'product re-versioning' for other delivery systems.

MULTI-SCREEN

Describes **audiovisual** (A/V) applications, that use multiple screens to create environments for slide or video presentations. Each screen in a multi-screen presentation can be serviced by at least two projectors, ensuring that an image is always present, and may display either an independent image or one that is part of a large image displayed across several screens. 'Video wall' video-monitor stacks perform a similar function to projection screens, allowing more

Sensorama, the first multi-sensory VR system, developed by Morton Heilig in the 1950s.

dynamic effects than slide-based multi-screen but with a lower **resolution**.
> MULTI-IMAGE

MULTI-SENSORY ENVIRONMENT

A real or virtual environment that combines several types of **sensors** and media; increasingly employed in theme parks, arcades, exhibition design and performance art. Incorporating elements from **flight simulation**, wide-screen and stereoscopic movies, **virtual reality** and **interactive multimedia**, multi-sensory environments can include a wide variety of sensing apparatus and multimedia feedback. Within the 'hyper' environment, movement, temperature, gesture and voice, might be sensed via infrared beams, pressure pads, video cameras etc; audio-visual feedback might include multi-screen still and motion images, multiple-source audio, ambient light modulation, and so forth.
> ARTIFICIAL REALITY   > PROJECTED REALITY

MULTI-SYNC/MULTI-SCAN MONITOR

A **monitor** that is capable of displaying signals from a range of video sources (camera, video tape recorder, **videodisc**, television, computer) and is able automatically to adjust to the different scan rates of those sources.

MULTI-TASKING

Describes computer systems that have the capability to execute more than one **program** at the same time.
> OS/2

MULTIMEDIA

Applies to works of art that incorporate the use of mixed materials (media), but more generally is used as shorthand for **interactive multimedia**.

MULTIPLAYER

A prototype consumer **CD-ROM** player, the Interactive Multiplayer™ was developed by 3DO in 1992-93.
> 3DO

MULTIPLE MASTER

A font-manipulation system devised by Adobe, in which a basic master font can be scaled, skewed, weighted, and produced in a variety of styles, all under the control of the designer. Multiple masters are designed to be 'chameleon' fonts, and Adobe have built in limits of horizontal scaling, weight and skew that preserve the unique characteristics of the font. Apart from the extraordinary design flexibility, Multiple Master fonts offer a cost saving in that a whole font family is available from a single master.
> DIGITAL FONTS

Adobe Multiple Masters: customizable fonts, providing an unlimited palette of font variations using the Myriad design matrix.

MULTIPLEX

In general, describes any system where a single device is used for multiple purposes. In **telecommunications**, describes a system that carries simultaneous signals from several sources along the same communications channel, either by frequency-division multiplexing (FDM), which divides the channel **bandwidth** into sub-channels, each occupying a small, exclusive range of frequencies; or by time-division multiplexing (TDM), which divides the channel into time slices, and assigns each time slice to a signal source.

MUSIC PLUS

A term describing a range of interactive products based on music, often in the form of **CD**s, primarily carrying digital audio music tracks, but also with the inclusion of graphics, text, video or **hypermedia** programmes to provide additional information or entertainment value.
> • MUSIC PLUS PAGE 137

MUSIC PLUS
from karaoke to the virtual nightclub

'Music plus' is the product of the convergence between digital audio music, computer graphics, and the realtime processing power of consumer interactive media systems. The term describes a range of interactive products based on music, including multimedia and 'documentary'-style interactive programmes, tools for creating or remixing music, interactive promo videos, and dynamic programmes that simulate the experience of the live performance, rave party or nightclub.

One aspect of music plus is the interactive documentary – in this context combining an opera or other musical piece with extensive annotation, such as libretti, critical notes and details of the composer in order to provide context and background. The same technique could of course be applied to retrospectives and to compilations of work by rock and pop performers.

With the introduction of full-motion video technology in 1993, the development of music plus products combining the multimedia documentary with promo videos and music tracks became inevitable. These interactive 'fanzines' aim to recreate some of the intimacy between artist and listener that used to be fostered through the medium of the vinyl album sleeve – the intimacy of shared ideas, common objectives and similar tastes. This intimacy lies at the core of live performance, and is celebrated in the best pop videos, but multimedia can provide an interactive simulation of it in providing a multi-faceted experience. Such programmes could, for example, blend video with videogames and music with morphing, or combine role-playing game techniques with the kind of surrogate performance that Thomas Zimmerman had in mind when he conceived the DataGlove.

Music plus software could also become available for the 'creative listener', providing the means to explore a wide range of musical genres. There could be introductory guides for newcomers to specialist music fields, and 'interactive companions' – multimedia reference works for fans of musical genres such as jazz, the classics or folk. Such programmes could include a discographical compilation of tracks from key composers and performers. Recorded digitally at a sampling rate equivalent to AM radio, many hours of tracks can be contained on a standard CD-ROM. Products like this would provide yet another way for the music companies to make fresh profits from their back catalogues, while offering a valuable service for the consumer.

Music plus looks likely to be a key component in breaking hypermedia products into the consumer entertainment market. A format that could combine a linear (full-motion) video of pop promos and live performances, with a multimedia fanzine, videogame-like interactive sequences, and performance simulation would undoubtedly be a winner. But the software is only half the equation –

the hardware platform would have to be as cool, as stylish and as easy to carry around as a Gameboy or a Walkman. Some of the existing TV plug-ins – machines such as Sega Mega-CD, Philips CD-i and 3DO's Interactive Multiplayer – can easily deliver software into the living room. A number of RISC-based multimedia machines may soon be competing for the potentially vast portable market. Such machines will need powerful processors for realtime animation and FMV, fast CD-ROM drives, flat, full-colour (32 bit) screens, stereo headphones and an interactive control device. There are several available technologies for portable input/output, including wired gloves and headup monocular virtual displays. Some new ideas that may be developed beyond prototype stage include wristwatch keypads, fingertip thimbles, ring buttons, badge switches and other 'wearable' accessories (NEC has done some very original R&D in this area).

Sony's Mini Disc CD format is a step towards highly portable random-access music entertainment. The launch of pen-pad personal digital systems with wireless networking, the increasing use of digital-audio broadcasting, and the rapidly expanding capacity of memory cards and smart cards – all point the way not only to new consumer music and multimedia products, but to new methods of distributing and retailing these products.

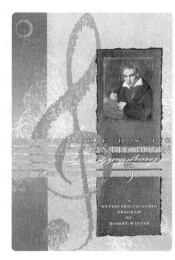

The Voyager Company: 'Beethoven: Symphony No 9', 'Schubert: The Trout' and 'Stravinsky: The Rite of Spring'. The Voyager Company is in the forefront of multimedia electronic publishing, with a large catalogue of 'music plus' titles.

Virtual Nightclub broke new ground in production financing with investors able to 'sponsor' rooms within the virtual club. Virtual environments can carry advertising in the same way as their real-world counterparts.

Prospect's Virtual Nightclub, designed by Trip Media and featuring a host of artists from Jimi Hendrix to PM Dawn. The Virtual Nightclub uses high-resolution computer animation and chromakey video to create a maze-like experience of music, video, art, fashion, conversation and music-making. Users can 'eavesdrop' on conversations between, for instance, The Shamen's Colin and cyberspace guru Terence McKenna, and other key style makers.

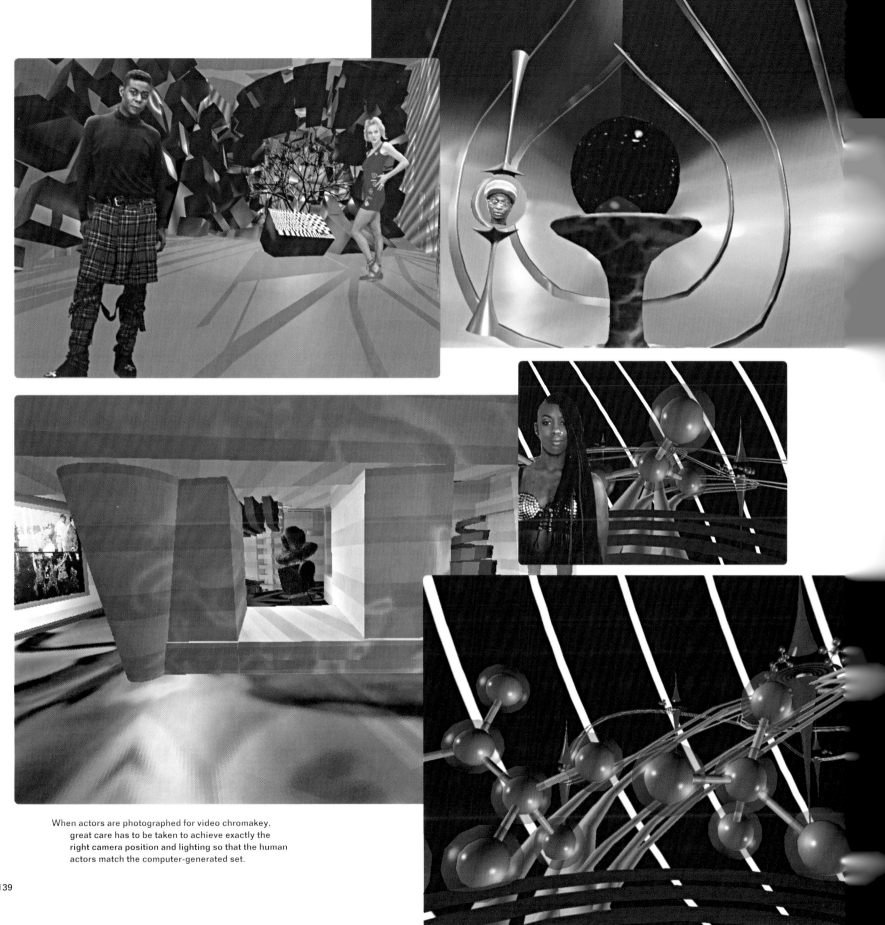

When actors are photographed for video chromakey, great care has to be taken to achieve exactly the right camera position and lighting so that the human actors match the computer-generated set.

1. movin' on up
2. slip inside this house
3. don't fight it feel it
4. higher than the sun
5. come together
6. damaged
7. stone my soul
8. carry me home

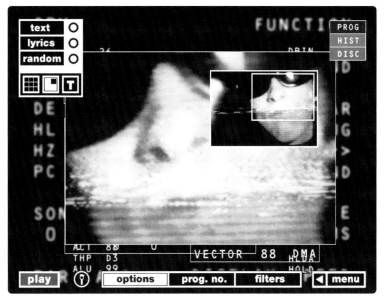

Ian Cater: 'Primal Screen', an interactive CD prototype combining fluent new wave graphics with a range of multimedia features. Produced while Cater was still a student at London's Newham Community College, it is loaded with interactive features that exploit the audio sequencing, multimedia discographical and motion video capabilities of the new generation of CD-ROM and CD-i players.

At their best 'music plus' programmes like Cater's Primal Screen prototype can be dynamic simulators as well as multi-media documentaries. With 'Primal Screen', users can remix tracks and video, design their own album sleeve, and much else besides.

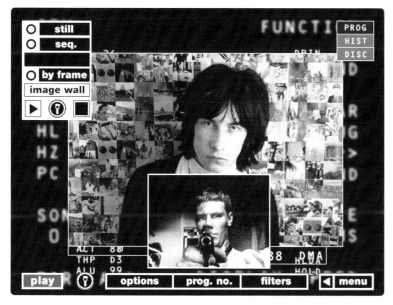

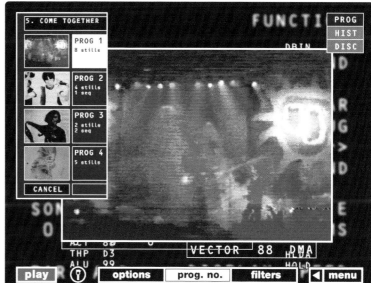

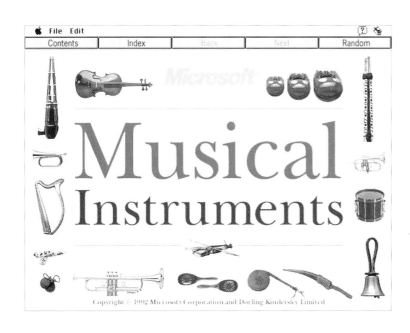

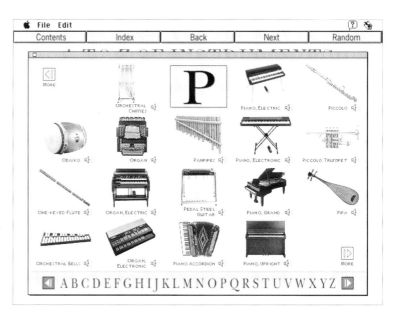

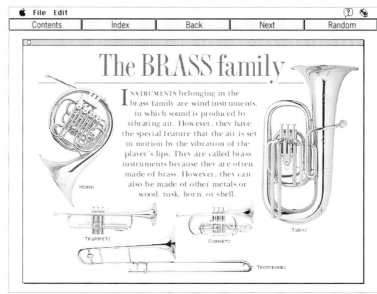

Dorling Kindersley/Microsoft: 'Musical Instruments',
educational 'music plus' on CD-ROM. This
interactive reference work on the world's musical
instruments uses high-quality illustrations and
hi-fi sound.

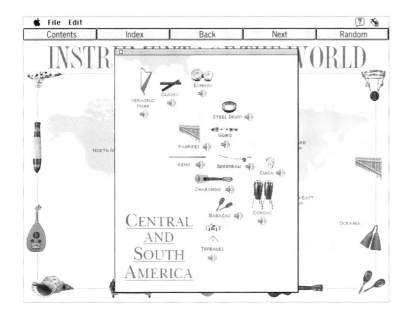

The 'Musical Instruments' CD-ROM inherits the polished graphic design style of Dorling Kindersley's printed books. The design team at DK and Microsoft have added sound and animations. 'Musical Instruments' is one of the first programmes to bridge the gap between print publishing and music.

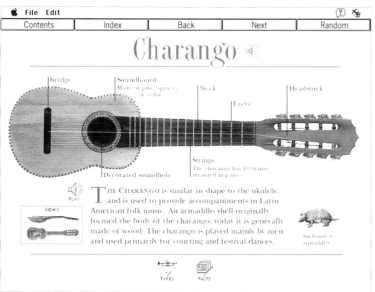

THE CHARANGO is similar in shape to the ukulele, and is used to provide accompaniments in Latin American folk music. An armadillo shell originally formed the body of the charango; today it is generally made of wood. The charango is played mainly by men and used primarily for courting and festival dances.

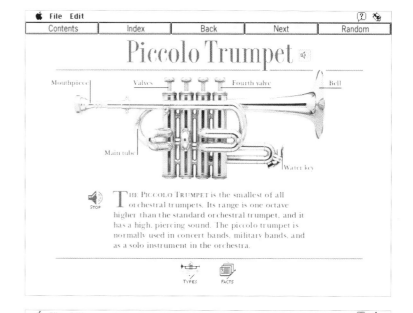

THE PICCOLO TRUMPET is the smallest of all orchestral trumpets. Its range is one octave higher than the standard orchestral trumpet, and it has a high, piercing sound. The piccolo trumpet is normally used in concert bands, military bands, and as a solo instrument in the orchestra.

THE OCARINA is a small type of flute, developed in Italy in the 19th century. When you blow into the ocarina, all the air inside vibrates, causing the sound to be produced. The larger the instrument, the deeper the note. The ocarina is a popular child's instrument in the United States and Europe, and is sometimes called a "sweet potato."

THE YUEQIN, or moon lute, is a short-necked lute from China. Inside its circular body is a fixed, metal tongue. This rattles or buzzes when the yueqin is played and enhances the tone. The yueqin is used to accompany songs, and is popular in small opera ensembles.

Steve Nelson/Brilliant Media: 'Xplora 1 – Peter Gabriel's Secret World', definitive 'music plus' CD-ROM for the Mac. Gabriel is in the forefront of the new wave of musicians who are exploring the synaesthetic nature of the digital media. Combining an interactive game, multimedia and promo videos with high-quality digital audio and elegantly designed interface graphics, 'Xplora 1' has set the standard for future 'music plus' product.

DJEMBE

A large wooden hourglass-shaped drum with a goatskin head from West Africa. It is held with a strap or between the player's knees. It is a solo instrument. Some musicians attach large metal "wings" to the top of the drum with metal rings put through a row of holes around the edge for additional resonance.

open mix

save mix

Digging Remix Tracks

duration: 07:28

BASS   DRUMS   GUITAR   PETER

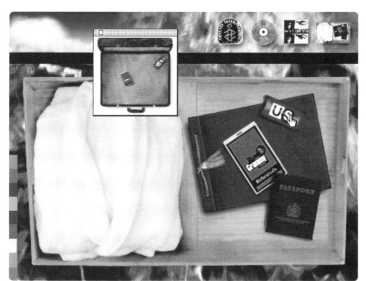

KISS THAT FROG

Jump in the water
Sweet little princess
Let me introduce his frogness
You alone can get him singing
He's all puffed up, wanna be your king
Oh you can do it
C'mon, c'mon, c'mon,c'mon, c'mon, c'mon
Lady kiss that frog
Splash, dash heard your call
Bring you back your golden ball
He's gonna dive down in the deep end
He's gonna be just like your best friend
So what's one little kiss
One tiny little touch
Aah he's wanting it so much

PETER GABRIEL 1
Released: February 1977
Catalogue: Charisma CDS 4006 (LP)/Charisma 7208 612 (Tape)/Virgin PGCDI (CD)

Humdrum
Slowburn
Waiting for the Big One
Down the Dolce Vita
Here Comes the Flood

Moribund the Burgermeister
Solsbury Hill
Modern Love
Excuse Me

DIGGING IN THE DIRT

Something in me, dark and sticky
All the time it's getting strong
No way of dealing with this feeling
Can't go on like this too long

This time you've gone too far
This time you've gone too far
This time you've gone too far
I told you, I told you, I told you, I told you,
This time you've gone too far
This time you've gone too far
This time you've gone too far
I told you, I told you, I told you, I told you

Don't talk back
Just drive the car

'Xplora 1' is dynamic infotainment as well as funky 'music plus'. The CD-ROM includes several QuickTime promo videos and is characterized by excellent sound and a smooth high resolution interface.

BLOOD OF EDEN
Bass: Tony Levin
Programming: David Bo
Additional programming
Hi hat: Daniel Lanois
12 string guitar: David R
Bridge guitar: Gus Isidor
Violin: Shankar
Doudouk: Levon Minass
Vocals: Sinead O'Conno
Lanois
Keyboard bass, keys: PC
Bridge section from a mi
Chappell

NARRATIVE

A story line or an ordered series of events.

> • NARRATIVE AND INTERACTION PAGE 148

NARROWCASTING

The provision of specialized entertainment and information programmes by means of cable **networks**, thus reaching smaller and more precisely targeted audiences than is possible with broadcast media. The expression was coined by J C Licklider of **MIT** in an appendix to the 1967 report on the future of educational television (commissioned by the Carnegie Corporation), that laid the foundation for the US Public Broadcasting System.

> BROADCASTING   >   BROADCATCHING

NATURAL IMAGES

Photographically realistic images, ie those that contain the subtle range of colours and tones associated with photographs.

> DELTA YUV   >   IMAGE PROCESSING

Natural Images: high-resolution, 24-bit digital images capture the quality of photographs.

NATURAL I/O

> NATURAL LANGUAGE

NATURAL LANGUAGE (INTERFACE)

An **interface** that recognizes commands that are given using normal speech or natural body language. Developments in interface design over the years have pointed to an increasingly 'natural' method of interacting with computers. The light pen and stylus/**digitpad** were the first **gestural interface** devices, followed by the **graphical user interface**. Gestural input has subsequently been refined through the use of the **touch-sensitive screen**, and the sophisticated manipulations possible with the **DataGlove** and **DataSuit**. The range of natural language interfaces also includes **eyeball tracking** and **speech recognition** systems, allowing a much more natural control and feedback environment, although these still have some way to go before they become general-purpose tools that are generally available.

NAVIGATION

The process of finding one's way around the contents of a **database**, **hypertext** or **hypermedia** programme. One of the main tasks of the hypermedia/**software** designer is to devise an easy-to-use system by which the user can know where he or she is in a programme, know how to go back to previous **frame**s or sequences, and know what choices are available at any stage in the programme. The user will also need to know how to record or 'tag' frames that he or she wishes to return to, and how to return to the main **menu** or section menu of the programme – all without getting lost in a myriad of windows, menus and frames.

> BROWSING

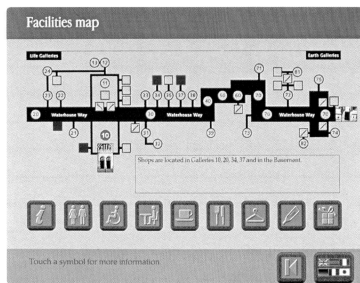

Easy-to-follow navigation aids are essential in point-of-information applications. This example is from the Natural History Museum in London.

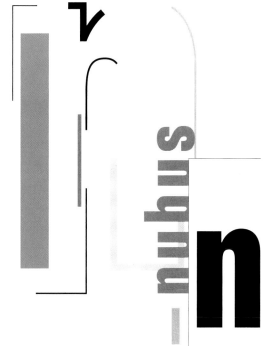

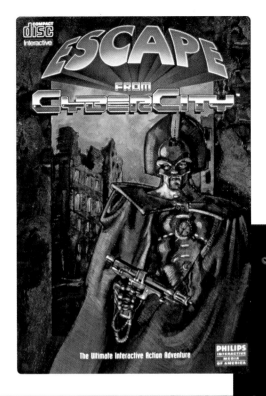

Philips: 'Escape from Cyber City' CD-i. Before the digital video cartridge, adventures like this relied on partial-motion video and animations.

NARRATIVE AND INTERACTION
new narratives for the new media

Some hypermedia practitioners have questioned whether it is possible to create interactive programmes that provide the suspension of disbelief and sense of involvement that we experience when we read a good novel. After all, how can the reader/user suspend disbelief while being forced to make creative decisions about the direction of the narrative? Such niceties are an irrelevancy to the two generations of kids who have spent in excess of US $20 billion on videogames over the last 20 years or so. They know that videogames are gripping to the point of total involvement. They also know that far from being a barrier to involvement, the intense interaction required by videogames is an essential factor in creating the involvement. As Sherry Turkle points out:

> When you play a video game you enter into the world of the programmers who made it. You have to do more than identify with a character on a screen. You must act for it. Identification through action has a special kind of hold. Like playing a sport, it puts people into a highly focused, and highly charged state of mind. For many people, what is being pursued in the video game is not just a score, but an altered state.
>
> SHERRY TURKLE, THE SECOND SELF, 1984

Videogames occupy a cultural space previously occupied by the comic strip, the chap book ballad and the fairy tale. All these forms of storytelling derive ultimately from elders and shamans who would relate their inherited tales of wonder and morality to the rest of the tribe. The telling and retelling of this lore was not simply a one-way exposition. The whole tribe could join in, asking questions, elaborating, enacting and singing incidents in the story. After Gutenberg and the invention of the printing press, storytelling increasingly became a one-way, solitary communication between author and reader. The mass media since then have all provided one-way, 'linear' communication to a passive audience. Hypermedia promises a return to an active, participating audience.

Hypermedia creates the possibility of a new kind of narrative, generated by the user within an information matrix created by the programme designer. Originally devised for the videogame, this kind of narrative is very different from the fixed storyline of a novel; it is intensely interactive, demanding frequent input from the player based on an identification with the hero and a gradually assimilated knowledge of the game's context. Such narratives often include 'interruptions' and so have a close link to the oral storytelling model mentioned above. The interruptions may be tests, explorations or problems that must be resolved by the player before the narrative can progress, they may also

Escape from **CYBER CITY**

serve to contextualize and comment upon aspects of the story, and can broaden the player's awareness of character and plot.

The discussion of interactive movies (page 117) outlines the 'combinatorial' problems that occur with the other main type of interactive storytelling, the branching narrative. Briefly, the main problem with a multimedia branching narrative is one of storage, stemming from the rapidly escalating number of scenes that have to be created in order to give the 'readers' the illusion that they have freedom to choose a particular storyline.

A solution to this problem may be to reinforce the illusion of freedom of action by 'duping' the user. Daniel Dennett, in his book <u>Consciousness Explained</u> (1991), describes a party game called 'Psychoanalysis', in which one player is sent out of the room after being told that the others are going to discuss a dream one of them has had. The objective of the game is ostensibly for the outsider to draw some 'psychoanalytic' conclusions about the dreamer through asking the group yes/no questions. In fact, what happens is that the group answers the outsider's questions arbitrarily, according to whether the last word of the question ends with a letter from the first half of the alphabet (in which case the answer will be 'yes'), or the second half (answer: 'no'). The dupe asks a series of questions that can become increasingly bizarre. Led from one (arbitrary) reinforcing answer to the next, the dupe literally invents a narrative for the hypothetical dream, entirely based on the binary (yes and no) responses of the other players. The dupe eventually comments that the dreamer must be a very sick person, much to the amusement of the other players, who point out that the dupe is the 'author' of the dream.

Could this remarkably compact and entertaining method of generating a complex storyline from a limited number of 'facts' be used as a model for hypermedia narratives? In the 1970s and 1980s, artificial intelligence (AI) researchers developed several systems in which a human user engaged in a dialogue with a computer program that was modelled on a psychoanalyst. Programs such as Racter and Eliza succeeded in suspending the disbelief of many of their 'patients', and sustained lengthy conversations using only a few simple rules, inferential logic and occasional randomness.

Or will the high-bandwidth networks of the near future offer us a different kind of 'narrative' through multi-player participative games, in which the narrative could be the result of the interactions of thousands of players? One thing looks certain: the interactive narrative media of the future will increasingly use AI and object-oriented programming techniques to create responsive environments that include 'intelligent' actors (agents) who learn from the

player, and who may have aims and sub-plots of their own. The combination of realtime systems and AI opens up the possibility of actors being able to morph into different characters, recreating and embodying the Tricksters and other shape-changers that are the stuff of myth.

>> FURTHER READING: COTTON AND OLIVER 1993; DENNETT 1993; PROVENZO 1991; TURKLE 1984

Resisting the Ultimate Dictator...

The Mythopoetics of

Cyberspace

An AI on an exponential path to omniscience. Your mission: find and destroy MNEMOSYNE.

heatshield

re-entry window

Bob Cotton: 'The Mythopoetics of Cyberspace'. This development platform for new narrative structures for interactive media movies is an 'interactive storyboard', enabling fast prototyping of ideas.

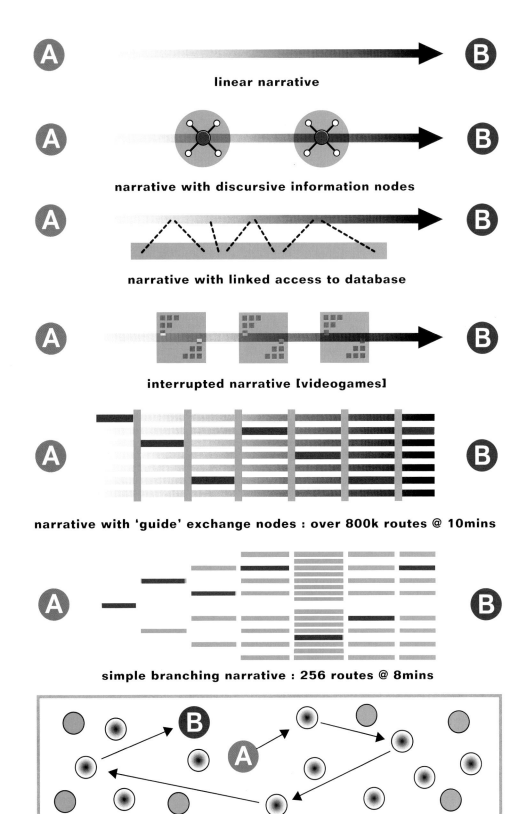

linear narrative

narrative with discursive information nodes

narrative with linked access to database

interrupted narrative [videogames]

narrative with 'guide' exchange nodes : over 800k routes @ 10mins

simple branching narrative : 256 routes @ 8mins

object oriented narrative: virtual movie lot + realtime events

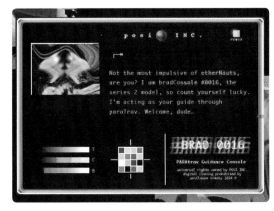

Mark Bowey: 'Quantum Realities', exploring the non-linear narrative structures combined with amorphous, neo-abstract symbolism.

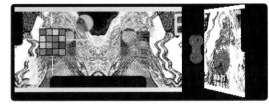

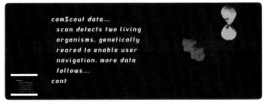

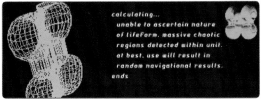

Bob Cotton: diagrams illustrating the main narrative forms of books, movies and videogames. Narrative structures for interactive movies may be a composite of these forms, or new 'object-oriented' narrative 'engines' may be developed.

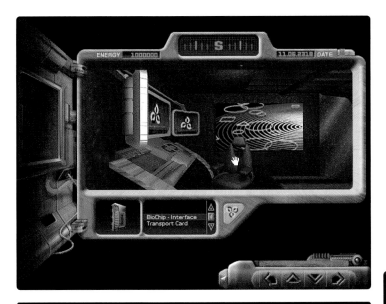

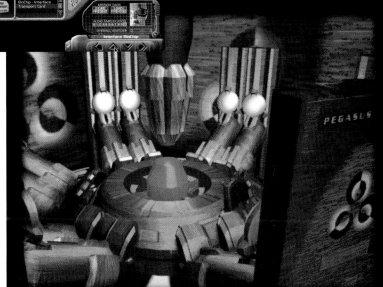

Presto Studios: 'The Journeyman Project'. Along with Presto's 'Spaceship Warlock' these were the first examples of interactive 'movies' for the Mac. Based on the model of the graphic novel, these high-resolution desktop computer graphic adventures began to explore the dramatic potential of digital media.

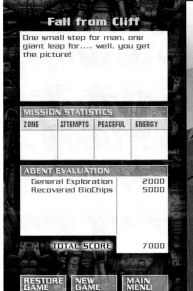

Fall from Cliff

One small step for man, one giant leap for.... well, you get the picture!

MISSION STATISTICS

ZONE	ATTEMPTS	PEACEFUL	ENERGY

AGENT EVALUATION

General Exploration 2000
Recovered BioChips 5000

TOTAL SCORE 7000

RESTORE GAME NEW GAME MAIN MENU

Cyan/Broderbund: 'Myst', featuring brilliantly rendered high-definition 3-d models linked into a virtual island construction that the user can freely explore. Developed using HyperCard and Apple's QuickTime, 'Myst' has defined the standard for interactive movie sets. Images were rendered on a Mac Quadra using Stratavision 3-d software. Offering seamless visual interaction, with ambient sound and embedded 'plots', 'Myst' is an important pointer to the future of interactive movies.

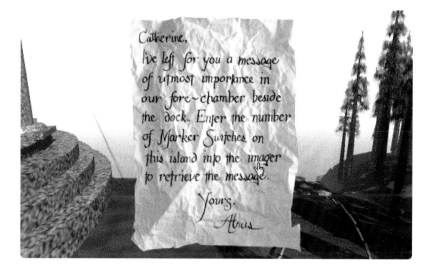

NETWORK

A system that links computers and other information/ **telecommunications** technologies together, either by cable or by 'wireless' (radio or optical means), so that they can exchange information.

> CELL-NET > DATA SUPERHIGHWAY
> FDDI > ISDN
> LAN > WAN

NETWORK TOPOLOGY

The arrangement of interconnecting transmission lines and switching **nodes** in a **network**.

NEURAL NETWORK

Describes a computer or computer **program** composed of many interconnected processing elements that operate in parallel, analogous to the way the human brain's interconnected neurons are believed to work. This may be achieved by either simulating such a process on a computer with a single **CPU** or by a computer constructed with many processors running in parallel. The advantage claimed for neural networks is that they do not require detailed programming to perform a particular function. Instead, the system can 'learn' or be 'trained' by presenting it with a series of examples and utilizing **feedback** on its performance. The major disadvantage of such systems is that the detail of the processes it uses to make discriminations and judgements are not accessible to its human controllers. Neural networks are used in a wide variety of commercial applications, including **speech** and image **recognition**, financial analysis, medical diagnosis, **database management system**, and image and signal processing.

> PARALLELISM

NEWTON

Generic name for Apple's **personal digital assistant** technology. The first Newton product, the Newton Messagepad, was launched in 1993.

> PERSONAL DIGITAL SYSTEM

NINTENDO

Japanese videogame company largely responsible for the revival and expansion of the **videogame** market. In 1992 its pre-tax profit of US $1.5 billion was greater than that of all the Hollywood film studios combined.

> • NINTENDO PAGE 155

NODE

In a **branching** programme, the main decision points or **menus** available to the user.

> CONDITIONAL BRANCHING > CONTINUOUS BRANCHING

NOISE

Unwanted signals occurring in an electronic or communication system.

> ARTIFACT

NOTEPAD (COMPUTER)

A portable computer the size of an A4 notepad. Notepad computers combine a **pen interface** (or **QWERTY keyboard**, **mouse** or **tracker ball** device) with a flat **LCD** display screen.

> DYNABOOK > POWERBOOK

NTSC
(NATIONAL TELEVISION SYSTEMS COMMITTEE)

The **television standard** used in the USA, Japan, Canada and Mexico, based on a 525-line image displayed at 30 frames per second. NTSC was the first colour television system, introduced in the US in 1954.

NUBUS

The high-speed expansion **bus** adopted by **Apple Computer** for the Mac II series.

> MACINTOSH

Apple: Newton Messagepad. The first 'personal digital assistant' from the company that christened the PDA. With the Mac, the Powerbook and the PowerCD, Apple's product stream has consistently set standards for computers. The Newton is a truly 'personal' computer – it actually learns how to be useful to you. A wide range of software is available for the Newton, including the Time Out guide to London shown here.

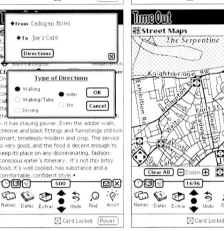
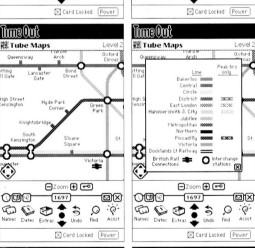

NINTENDO
gameboy of the western world

Founded in 1889 to manufacture playing cards, Nintendo has been in the games business ever since and is currently the world's most successful manufacturer of videogames. (The name means 'work hard, but in the end it is in heaven's hands'.) Nintendo's first successful move into videogames came in 1983 with the launch of the Famicom ('family computer'), a games computer that offered arcade-style graphics on a domestic television. By 1990, 40 per cent of all Japanese homes had a Nintendo system, and from 1991 to 1992 the company sold some US $2 billion worth of games hardware and software. During 1992 alone, Nintendo made more money than all the American film studios put together, netting over US $1 billion (or over US $1 million profit produced by each of its 986 employees).

The early 1980s marked the high point of the entertainment phenomenon that resulted from the first generation of videogame technology. Videogames had become the leading entertainment industry in the USA, with some US $3 billion spent on home videogames and a further US $8 billion on coin-operated arcade games. To give just one example of how videogames had come to dominate the entertainment market consider Atari's most successful game, 'Asteroids'. In one year, this game alone grossed more than the combined US earnings of the three major blockbuster movies of the 1980s: Batman, ET and Return of the Jedi.

By 1983, the first wave of videogame mania had reached its peak. Every family that wanted a videogame system had one. The technology of the first generation of microprocessors had been fully exploited; manufacturers were over-producing both systems and games, and the market had become flooded with low-quality, heavily discounted products. During 1983–84, profits dive-bombed. By 1985, industry takings had dropped substantially, and many games companies went to the wall. Surprisingly, it was in this same year that Nintendo launched its 8-bit Famicom system in the US. Backed by a US $30 million advertising campaign, Nintendo's system offered greater speed, higher resolution and a wider range of colours (16 on-screen colours from a palette of 52) than competing games systems.

But it was not superior technology alone that cemented Nintendo's success during the next few years. First of all, the company drew from its experience in selling playing cards. Over nearly one hundred years, Nintendo had successfully improved sales by adding 'entertainment value' to their cards (for example by producing cards featuring Disney cartoon characters, which were a major success with Japanese children). Understanding that entertainment value is what separates good games from bad, Nintendo's president, Hiroshi Yamauchi, applied the same approach to electronic games.

Secondly, Nintendo established a 'vertical market' for their products. Employing the successful 'razor

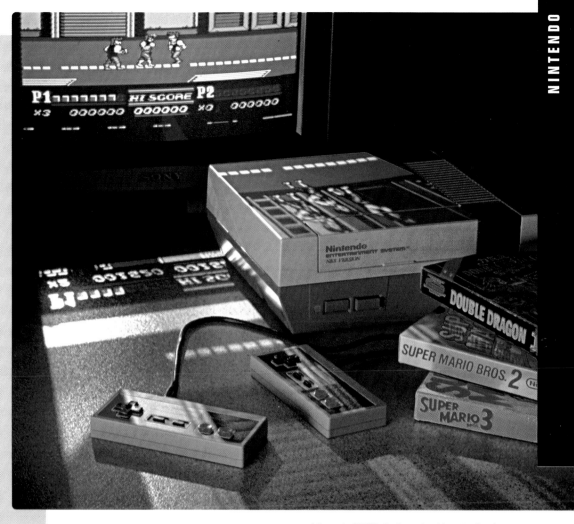

Nintendo SNES: the formula of keeping hardware prices low, and relying on profits from high-quality software, resulted in Nintendo becoming the major player in the videogames market during the late 1980s and early 1990s.

marketing' technique (buying a Gillette razor meant that you had to buy Gillette blades), the Famicom was designed so that it would only play Nintendo games cartridges. Not only did a games cartridge need a custom microchip to be installed before it would play in a Nintendo system, but Nintendo also applied rigorous quality controls, ensuring that only approved games reached the market. Furthermore, games producers were not permitted to adapt Nintendo titles for competitive games systems.

By 1993, Nintendo's main revenues derived from the sales of just three machines: the 8-bit NES (Nintendo Entertainment System), the portable, hand-held Gameboy, and the 16-bit Super NES – along with the all-important games software they run. Nintendo levies a royalty on each games cartridge sold (in 1992, this amounted to some 170 million cartridges), so far netting some US $430 million on one game (Super Mario Bros 3) alone.

In 1993, the videogame business was 21 years old, and Nintendo (as well as other games manufacturers), continued to demonstrate its commitment to developing new products for this mature market. For example, Nintendo consoles have a socket for

a modem adaptor, and already around 150,000 Japanese are using this facility to play the stock exchange with their games systems. Other possibilities include betting, home shopping and educational games (the first such title, 'Mario Paint', lets children create drawings, animation and music on their TV sets). Networked games consoles also promise new types of multi-player games, and new methods of marketing and distributing software directly to the home itself.

Games hardware is also maturing. In 1993 Nintendo's main rival, Sega, launched their Mega-CD, a CD-ROM-based system offering digital video, and 3DO and Atari both announced new RISC-based CD-ROM multimedia players. These new machines can support 'infotainment' software that combines the rich interaction of videogames with the information-carrying capacity (and low material cost) of compact discs.

Nintendo faces very fierce competition in the race to dominate the home multimedia/entertainment market. In September 1993 Yamauchi announced the company's 'Project Reality' multimedia system, to be developed in conjunction with the US computer graphics company Silicon Graphics. Project Reality machines will first be developed for the arcade market, and are due to be introduced into the home in 1995. (It should be noted, however, that past joint ventures, with Sony and Philips, have come to nothing.)

Nintendo's current dominant position in the games market may have led to a rather unhealthy arrogance. Announcing Project Reality, Yamauchi is quoted as saying: 'We don't believe in the idea of companies getting together to establish a new entertainment business. We need only one healthy, strong company as leader' (The Edge, November 1993). This attitude has led to much criticism by other games manufacturers. Referring to the company's licensing practices, 3DO's Trip Hawkins has called Nintendo the 'evil monopolist' of the games world. Hawkins has also expressed doubts about Nintendo's ability to make the step from successful toy company to market leader in the global multimedia sector.

>> FURTHER READING: PROVENZO 1991; SHEFF 1993

Nintendo Gameboy: the world's best-selling portable computer, rivalling the ubiquitous Walkman as the essential street accessory.

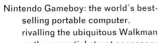

OBJECT
A discrete element. In **authoring** packages, such as **HyperCard**, describes any element that can have a **script** attached to it – for example a **button**, a **card** or a stack. In **object-oriented graphics**, describes any element, such as a circle, that can be moved independently. In **object-oriented programming**, describes the components of a **program**. In **virtual reality** systems, describes discrete three-dimensional elements that a user can interact with within that virtual environment.

OBJECT ANIMATION
In 2-d computer animations, the manipulation of objects (graphics, images, text etc) by means of **programming** or **scripting**. In **HyperCard**, **SuperCard** and similar **authoring** applications, objects that appear on the screen can be scripted to change position, scroll, invert, change size, etc, thus enabling the user to control the animation interactively. Object animation can be produced using **Macromedia Director**, with scripts written in **Lingo**.
>   COMPUTER ANIMATION   >   SCRIPT

OBJECT-ORIENTED GRAPHICS
Images composed of discrete objects, such as lines and circles, that can be moved independently. Sometimes referred to as **vector graphics**. In object-oriented graphics, images are described and stored as mathematical formulae for the vectors or directional lines that make up each one.
>   DRAW PROGRAM

OBJECT-ORIENTED PROGRAMMING (OOP)
Computer programming that uses the concept of 'objects' rather than the traditional concept of 'procedures'. In procedural programming (using languages like **Pascal** and **C**), the programmer describes functions and procedures that operate on certain types of data, and both functions and procedures are separate from the data on which they operate. In OOP, data and procedures are packaged together in an 'object'.

OOP uses five central ideas: objects (the programming entity combining data and procedures); messages (sent by one object and received and acted on by another); methods (the code in an object that tells it how to react when it receives a message with the same name as the method); classes (groups of objects with common characteristics); and inheritance (a concept related to the program's classification structure, whereby objects lower down a hierarchy of calls can 'inherit' behaviour from objects higher in the hierarchy, or from the 'root' classification itself).

Many of the ideas underlying authoring packages such as **HyperCard** and **Macromedia Director** have been adapted from OOP. For example, when a button is copied and pasted elsewhere, the **script** contained within it is also transferred. Full-blown OOP languages such as **C++** are increasingly being used to create **hypermedia** programmes because they offer a more direct modelling of the problems being dealt with, and greater programme productivity through the reuse and modifications of existing objects.
>   KNOWLEDGE-BASED SYSTEM

OCE [OPEN COLLABORATION ENVIRONMENT]
System extension module for the Apple **Macintosh**, allowing **network** users to exchange high-level data (such as formatted text, **QuickTime** movies and artwork) simply by the manipulation of **icons**. Each OCE user accesses a global mailbox from which all incoming mail can be retrieved. Mail can be in either of two directory formats: personal directories, which can be security-protected and customized; or a shared directory for general electronic mail.
>   E-MAIL

OCR [OPTICAL CHARACTER RECOGNITION]
Software that translates the shapes of scanned, printed or typed **alphanumeric** characters into character codes that can be used as text in a word-processing or other text-based application. After scanning, the characters are analysed by matrix matching and feature extraction, and when recognized, they are saved in the equivalent character code (such as **ASCII**). OCR **scanners** can recognize letterform characters in a wide range of typefaces and sizes, and where odd characters cannot be recognized, they are displayed on screen for the user to edit. Handwriting-recognition software (used in **notepad** computers with a **pen interface**) use similar matrix matching and feature extraction **algorithms**.

OLE [OBJECT LINKING AND EMBEDDING]
A feature addition to **Windows** 3.1 and **OS/2**, allowing users to create 'compound documents' that integrate tools and information from a variety of different applications and sources. Developing ideas from **object-oriented programming** and **hypermedia**, **Microsoft** have produced a system for embedding objects (graphics, soundtracks, text etc, each containing its own formatting or processing instruction) within a document, and then linking between these objects. For example, preparing a presentation document in an OLE environment would involve first setting up a 'host' document, then embedding into it the component objects – such as bar charts, diagrams, photographic images, etc. Any changes made in these component objects are automatically moved to the host document. Compound documents like this can have links to other compound documents. OLE has major implications for group working over local area and larger networks.
>   GROUPWARE   >   LAN

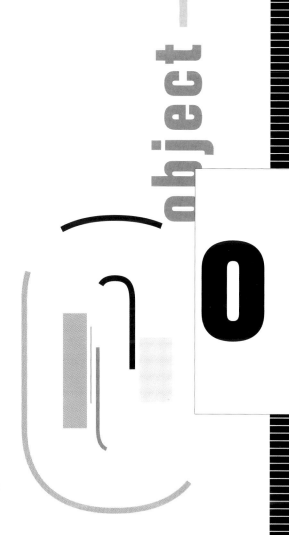

OMNIPLAYER

A machine that can play **laserdiscs** of different formats and sizes – such as analog laserdiscs, compact disc video (**CDV**), **CD-ROM** and **CD-i**.

> LASERVISION

ON-DEMAND PUBLISHING

The publishing of a customer's choice of texts from different books and documents, bound together in a composite book or compiled together in digital media such as **CD-ROM**.

On-demand publishing was pioneered over 20 years ago by the US publisher Simon and Schuster through their Ginn Press subsidiary, and implemented in the early 1990s in digital form by the educational publishers McGraw-Hill, in their Primis project. Primis allows teachers and other individuals to choose texts from the McGraw-Hill catalogue (or database of publications), add their own documentation, teacher's notes etc, and within a few days receive a laserprinted proof. On approval, the finished, bound books are printed and delivered within two to three weeks.

With the increasing importance of electronic publishing, CD-ROM, **memory cards** and even **floppy disks** have become viable media for the distribution of 'on-demand publishing' materials, and such services could be offered at even lower cost than their printed rivals, reflecting the price advantage of electronic over paper media. Electronic, customized books could be ordered and delivered over a **network**, virtually automatically. Ted Nelson envisaged just such a system over 20 years ago, and dubbed it **Xanadu**.

> ELECTRONIC BOOKS   > ELECTRONIC PUBLISHING

ONLINE

In computer systems, refers to **network** or other connections that are live and open. In video editing, refers to the final part of the editing process when working with the master tapes, as opposed to an 'offline' edit using an inferior video format, in which a cutting list (an 'edit decision list') is generated for the online edit.

ONLINE FORUM

A **network** conferencing facility where many different users can contribute to a debate on a given topic.

> E-MAIL   > GROUPWARE
> VIDEO CONFERENCING

ONLINE HELP

A text or multimedia **help system** attached to an application, that can be launched from within the application itself.

ONLINE PUBLISHING

The publication of material over a network.

> ELECTRONIC PUBLISHING   > ON-DEMAND PUBLISHING

OOP

> OBJECT-ORIENTED PROGRAMMING

OPEN COLLABORATION ENVIRONMENT

> OCE

OPERATING SYSTEM [OS]

A program that manages the resources of a computer, such as the **input/output** devices, memory, file retrieval and so forth. The operating system is loaded into the computer when it starts up, and supervises the running of other **programs** and applications.

> MS-DOS   > REALTIME OPERATING SYSTEM

OS

> OPERATING SYSTEM

OS/2

A **multi-tasking**, single-user **operating system** jointly developed by **IBM** and **Microsoft**, but now only seriously supported by IBM. OS/2 was designed to overcome some of the limitations of **MS-DOS** and to take advantage of the features offered by current and future developments of more powerful **hardware**. OS/2 has so far been overshadowed by the success of Microsoft Windows.

> WINDOWS NT

OS-9

A **multi-tasking operating system** developed for **microcomputers** using Motorola 6809 **microprocessors** in the late 1970s and **ported** to the 68000 family in the early 1980s. Its major significance today is that a modified version, called **CDRTOS** is the operating-system component of the Philips **CD-i** system.

> REALTIME OPERATING SYSTEM

OUTPUT

In computing, a term describing the information sent by the computer to a display device such as a **monitor**, or to a printer.

OVERDUB

In video and audio, the recording of new material over previously recorded tracks.

> DIGITAL AUDIO

OVERLAY

In video, **computer graphics** and **hypermedia**, the superimposition of one image over another, either by means of an **alpha channel** (or **matte**), or by overlaying a separate image window or graphics.

> VIDEO GRAPHICS

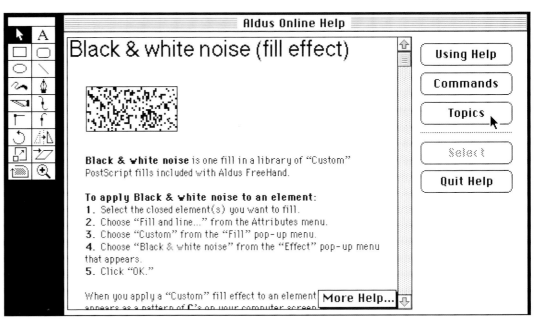

Aldus Freehand: Online Help window. Online help is much more convenient than having to use the printed manual. Generally, online help will offer fast and precise access to the required information and assistance, often in addition to browsing tools.

PACKET RADIO

A packet-switching technology for suitably equipped portable computers (with radio transmitter/receivers), packet radio facilities provide a wireless network for users on the move.

> CELL-NET > PACKET SWITCHING
> PDN

PACKET SWITCHING

A method of routing messages across a **network**. A packet-switching network consists of a number of packet-switching exchanges connected by high-speed transmission lines. When a message is sent across the network from one computer to another, a 'virtual circuit' is set up between them, and the message is split into small packets of data. Each packet contains address and sequencing information, and the exchanges are responsible for routing packets across the network, choosing the best route to allow for other traffic, storing packets until a route is clear, and making sure the packets arrive in the correct order at the correct address. Packet switching is an established technology (the **CCITT** X.25 standard) in use in many countries, and makes efficient use of the transmission capacity of large networks.

> CELL-NET > PDN
> X-SERIES RECOMMENDATIONS

PAGE DESCRIPTION LANGUAGE [PDL]

The **software** used in desktop publishing (**DTP**) and desktop graphics to provide a complete description of a page or graphic layout, which can be output to a printer or display. The great advantage of PDLs over bitmapped descriptions is that they are resolution-independent and will display or print the page described at the highest resolution of the device to which they are directed. The most popular PDL is **PostScript**, created by Adobe in the early 1980s. PostScript formed part of the first commercially available DTP system launched in 1985. Hewlett Packard have also established a PDL standard (PCL5) for their range of laserprinters.

PAINT PROGRAM

Bitmap editors where the user can manipulate colour **pixels** on the computer screen with a variety of mark-making tools, typically including 'pencils', 'paintbrushes' and 'airbrushes'.

> DRAW PROGRAM

PAL [PHASE ALTERNATE LINE]

The television standard used in the UK and Western Europe with the exception of France. PAL is a 625-line image displayed at 25 frames per second. PAL is a development of the **NTSC** system, and provides superior colour.

> TELEVISION STANDARDS

PALETTE

In some **Macintosh** and **Microsoft Windows** applications, a special kind of 'window' that always stays in the foreground of a particular application (ie it cannot be hidden by other windows). It may contain the digital representation of an artist's colour palette; or a collection of **icons** representing various painting, drawing and graphics tools; or important '**navigation**' controls that must always be present on screen. Like other windows, palettes can be moved around the screen and are **menu**-operated, with a 'close box' facility so they can be hidden when the user no longer wants them on display.

> COLOUR > DTP
> PAINT PROGRAM

PALMTOP

A small, hand-held personal computer, often with miniature **keyboard** and flat or fold-up **LCD** screen.

> PERSONAL DIGITAL ASSISTANT
> PERSONAL DIGITAL SYSTEM > PERSONAL ORGANIZER

PAN

In film and video live action, the movement of a camera pivoting through an arc horizontally. The convention has been adopted as a metaphor in some **hypermedia** programmes, where a user can pan across an image larger than that shown in the **window** or **screen**.

> MOTION CONTROL > TILT
> TRANSITION

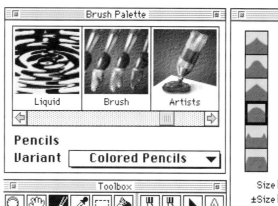
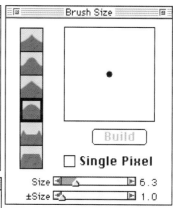

The brush palette from Fractal Design's Painter 2.0, a very sophisticated bitmap paint application that simulates a wide range of art media and substrates. Palettes such as this are designed to 'float' over the other open windows in the application, so that they are readily accessible.

PANTONE COLOUR SYSTEM

A **colour**-matching system used extensively in the graphic design and printing industries. Pantone colours are carefully graded so that exact colours can be matched throughout the design, reprographic and print process. Pantone produce a range of markers, coloured papers and films, and printing inks, as well as **software** versions of their colour system for use in graphics and **DTP** applications.

PARALLAX

> MOTION PARALLAX

PARALLEL INTERFACE

A method of sending data from one **hardware** device to another (for example between a computer and a printer) in synchronous flow along parallel lines. A parallel **interface** is much faster than a serial interface where **bits** have to be sent one at a time. Cables for parallel interfaces need to be kept as short as possible (no longer than 15 feet) because as the length of cable increases so does the danger of **cross-talk**.

PARALLELISM

A term referring to computers that use multiple processors, as opposed to a single **CPU**. Such computers are used for 'processing intensive' applications such as weather forecasting, CAD and scientific calculation, as well as the rapidly developing area of neural networks. In applications such as **virtual reality** systems, parallelism may represent the only realistic way forward. One of the factors that currently makes realistic virtual reality environments impossible is that the generation of a single image of photographic quality may take several minutes. This is because of the sheer volume of data that needs to be processed by the CPU. Computers employing thousands of processors could massively reduce the amount of time taken for such operations. The obstacle that still remains, however, is the development of sophisticated programming techniques that could take full advantage of the capabilities of parallel computers.

> NEURAL NETWORK   > TRANSPUTER
>> FURTHER READING: WILSON 1988

PARTIAL UPDATE

The refreshing of part of the screen image, rather than the whole image. New image data is added to one part of a picture that is already displayed on a monitor screen. Partial updates are used in computer **videogames**, and **videophone**, **video-conferencing** and **multimedia** systems, where motion images are required but where a limited **bandwidth** is available for the transmission of data. In early videophone systems, for example, the whole image of the user was transmitted only once, and subsequent data only updated those parts of the image that moved, such as the lips. By using partial updating combined with sophisticated image **compression** schemes, **full-motion video** can be simulated on limited-bandwidth systems such as **CD-ROM** and **CD-i**.

> MPEG   > REFRESH RATE

PASCAL

A computer programming **language** developed by Niklaus Wirth, and named after the French mathematician Blaise Pascal, who devised the first calculating machine. During the 1980s Pascal became the standard language for teaching computer programming in the US. It is now widely used as a general-purpose programming language.

>> FURTHER READING: BARON 1988

PC

> PERSONAL COMPUTER

PCM

> PULSE-CODE MODULATION

PCMCIA
(PERSONAL COMPUTER MEMORY CARD INTERNATIONAL ASSOCIATION)

An association that currently includes over 180 computer companies, formed to define a global **standard** for the format and hardware interface of **memory cards**. The standard defines the physical size of the cards, the interconnecting pin arrangements, and what can be achieved with them. The main aim is to allow memory cards to work in the widest

EO Communicator. The pen provides a more 'natural' interface with pad- and pocket-sized portable computers and personal digital assistants.

range of machines – including portable and **palmtop** computers, **personal organizers** and **personal digital assistants**, and hand-held **videogame** machines. In 1991, the PCMCIA standard was made compatible with the memory card format recommendations of the Japanese Electronics Industry Development Association (JEIDA).

PCMCIA cards will function in both memory-card and 'smart-card' applications, ie serving as memory storage for small computers, or as smart-card add-ons that not only provide extra memory but can embody additional 'smart' functions.

> PERSONAL DIGITAL SYSTEM

PDA

> PERSONAL DIGITAL ASSISTANT

PDL

> PAGE DESCRIPTION LANGUAGE

PDN (PACKET DATA NETWORK)

A set of **protocols** for the transmission of data over the public switched telephone network. In the UK, British Telecom have offered the Packet Switch Stream Service since 1982, and Mercury the PDNS (previously Mercury 5000). Most PDN services allow users dial-up access to X.25 networks in other countries – such as Telenet and Tymnet in the US.

> CELL-NET   > NETWORK
> PACKET SWITCHING   > X-SERIES RECOMMENDATIONS

PEN INTERFACE

An interface designed to allow users to operate 'notepad'-style computers as naturally as they would use a pencil and paper notebook. Pen-based computers are controlled by a special pen that is sensed by the computer. Users write directly onto the **screen**, and handwriting-recognition **software** converts handwriting to **ASCII** text. Formatting, editing and typographical commands can be given by using familiar gestural marks like underlining, scratching out and encircling words. Drawings and text can easily be integrated. Other computer functions are controlled by means of notebook-style interfaces, which resemble an electronic 'Filofax' and allow the user to select desired applications or **files**.

Pen interfaces are an important breakthrough in personal computing – another step towards the ideal **Dynabook** system described by Alan Kay. By taking advantage of the fact that many more people know how to write with a pencil or pen than know how to type, and by providing a device that can be held in one hand (while the other hand holds the pen), pen-driven devices promise to extend the power and usability of the computer still further.

> OCR   > PERSONAL DIGITAL ASSISTANT
> PERSONAL DIGITAL SYSTEM

PERIPHERAL

Describes hardware attached to and under the control of a computer. Examples include external **hard disks**, **CD-ROM** drives, **scanners**, **videodisc** players, **modems** and printers.

> WORKSTATION

PERIPHERAL VISION

The edges of a human's visual field. Our view of the world is delimited by an angle of vision measuring about 175-185 degrees horizontally by about 145-155 degrees vertically, and of this wide field or 'cone' of vision, only a relatively small central area is in focus. However, the peripheral (out of focus) area plays an important role in providing visual cues as to our position and movement vis-à-vis the outside world, a fact exploited in wide-screen movies, flight simulators and **virtual reality (VR)** systems. The more an image is of a scale that involves our peripheral vision, the greater the illusion of presence, of 'being there' in the projected image.

Flight simulators and VR systems create this illusion in two ways: by projecting an image encompassing a wide field of vision onto curved 'wraparound' **screens**, and by situating the observer close to these screens. Thus in flight simulation, the pilot's view from the simulator cockpit or flight deck is completely filled with the image, and in VR systems, the screens are placed right in front of the eyes, where again they fill the field of vision.

With **HDTV** flat-screen systems – potentially large enough to cover an entire living-room wall – the notion of the home as a simulator which can be programmed to display any kind of 'decor', or clad with any kind of 'natural' pictures, becomes a possibility. This new kind of 'soft furnishing' may eventually be used to display therapeutic and mood-enhancing programmes, or to whisk us off to sail round Cape Horn or watch the dawn from Everest.

> FLIGHT SIMULATION > MULTI-SENSORY ENVIRONMENT
> SENSORAMA > SIMULATION

PERSISTENCE OF VISION

A phenomenon of human vision whereby discrete events are perceived as continuous motion, resulting from the inability of the retina to follow and signal rapidly changing intensities. For example, a light flashing at a rate of more than about 50 flashes per second appears to be a steady brightness. Films are projected at 24 frames per second, but a three-bladed shutter raises the flicker rate to 72 flashes per second, giving the illusion of a smoothly moving image. In television and video, the frame rate is 25 frames/sec in the UK (30 frames/sec in the US), but flicker is reduced by separating each frame into two **field**s, each comprising alternate horizontal lines. These fields are interlaced, so the screen is never blank, and they are refreshed alternately, raising the flicker rate to 50 flashes/sec (UK) and 60 flashes/sec (US). Without persistence of vision, films, **animation**s and television would not create the successful illusion of movement that they do.

> COMPUTER ANIMATION > LATENCY

PERSONAL COMPUTER

Generic term for single-user computers based on a **microprocessor** with all the **hardware** and **software** required for an individual to work autonomously. Term first coined by Alan Kay in the early 1970s when the majority of computer users worked on terminals connected to large, centralized multi-user systems.

PERSONAL DIGITAL ASSISTANT (PDA)

A pocket-sized device that combines the functions of personal organizer, 'palmtop' computer and cell communications terminal or **modem**. The name was first popularized in 1992 by John Sculley, then CEO of Apple Computer, when he announced Apple's plans for their Newton PDA.

> CELL-NET > PERSONAL DIGITAL SYSTEM
> • PERSONAL DIGITAL ASSISTANTS PAGE 163

PERSONAL DIGITAL SYSTEM (PDS)

A hybrid personal cell-phone and pocket computer announced by **IBM** in 1993, the PDS contains personal organizer and **telecommunications** applications (such as dialling automatically from an organizer entry) and takes **PCMCIA** slot-in **memory card**s and **smart card**s offering a range of extra functions. These include AM/FM radio with recording/playback facilities, Global Positioning System (**GPS**), digital camera, digital **fax** and a range of **electronic book** products.

> PERSONAL DIGITAL ASSISTANT

PERSONAL ORGANIZER

A hand-held or '**palmtop**' computer specifically designed as a replacement for conventional personal organizer systems, such as the Filofax or Lefax. Personal organizers typically include a calculator, diary, notepad, address book, calendar, etc, and feature a small **LCD** screen, **alphanumeric** keypad, **port**s for transferring data to and from personal computers, and **memory card**s for storage. **Integrated circuit** or 'smart' **card**s may also be used to carry extra functions such as spreadsheets and **database**s.

> DYNABOOK > PERSONAL DIGITAL ASSISTANT
> PERSONAL DIGITAL SYSTEM

PERSPECTIVE SYSTEMS

Systems or projections used in image-making to create realistic illusions of depth. There are several systems in wide use in illustration, **computer graphics** and **videogames**, including **vanishing-point** (linear) perspective, **aerial perspective**, and isometric, axonometric and vertical-oblique projections. Most computer graphics that aspire to photographic realism use vanishing-point perspective, together with depth-intensity cueing or 'fogging' – techniques that simulate aerial perspective.

Used in conjunction with **motion parallax** and interposition, vanishing-point perspective provides all the clues necessary to give a very real illusion of spatial depth in **computer animation**. But achieving relatively realistic 'realtime' animations requires powerful processors. Until the early 1990s these were only available in commercial flight simulators and expensive workstations. Realtime animation is an essential ingredient of videogames, and up to now programmers here have either opted for very simple **solid modelling** (with very little detail) or adopted the 'parallel' perspective systems of isometric, axonometric and vertical-oblique projections. These provide depth clues by means of a fixed 'grid' of orthogonals (distance lines), which means that they are infinitely extendable – vast backgrounds can be created, and the scene altered by scrolling across the projected space. In isometric projection (a projection approximated in many Roman, Byzantine and Persian paintings, and especially in Japanese woodcuts of the eighteenth century) objects are represented with verticals and lines drawn at an angle of 30 degrees to the horizontal. Axonometric projections use horizontals drawn at 45 degrees, and vertical-oblique adds the top and front views of

Electronic Arts: 'Road Rash' for 3DO. With the latest generation of RISC-powered multimedia computers and games consoles, realtime animation and simulation using realistic images are possible for the first time on personal systems.

objects. These projection systems are far easier to compute than vanishing-point perspective, and until recently formed the mainstay of videogame spatial illusions.

IBM (Portsmouth): oblique projection in wireframe.

PHONG SHADING

An improvement on the **Gouraud shading** technique, developed by Bui-Tuong Phong. Phong shading uses a more detailed calculation that is sensitive to the directional effects of specular highlights.

> COMPUTER GRAPHICS   > RENDERING ENGINE

Phong shading: example by Peakash Patel.

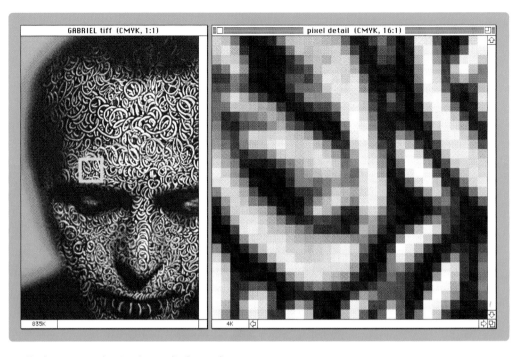

Desktop paint applications have a display resolution of around 72 pixels per inch, and users can 'zoom in' to alter individual pixels.

PHOTO-CD

A **CD-ROM**-based **standard** and system developed by Kodak and Philips. Photo-CD discs store photographic resolution images for display on an ordinary television set.

> • PHOTO-CD PAGE 164

PICON

Pictorial or picture **icon**: a small but elaborate, often full-colour, illustration representing a feature within a **graphical user interface**, or **software** application (such as a **hypermedia** programme), and indicating the location of a **button**.

> MICON   > TRICON

PICS

A **file format** for the **Macintosh** that allows the import and export of sequences of **PICT**-quality images. Used extensively in **animation** and 3-d **modelling** applications.

> COMPUTER ANIMATION   > MACROMEDIA DIRECTOR

PICT/PICT2

A standard image-data **file format** for the storage and exchange of graphics on the Apple **Macintosh**. Routines for the creation, display and printing of PICTs are built in to the Mac system, so that an application need contain no special graphics-processing routines in order to incorporate a PICT file generated in another application. PICT2 extends PICT with more support for colour.

PIE

Apple Computer's Personal Interactive Electronics Division. PIE has four main, interrelated areas of activity: Newton technology, **telecommunications**, publishing, and interactive multimedia **personal digital** assistants. Apple's decision to establish PIE as a separate division has a wider significance as part of a growing recognition by a number of computer manufacturers that computer **hardware** and **operating systems** are increasingly becoming 'commodities', ie goods where the decision to buy is made predominantly on the grounds of price. The convergence of communications media is seen as an opportunity to move into more profitable areas of activity, where the expertise of computer companies can earn higher returns.

PIXEL [PICTURE ELEMENT]

The smallest unit of the computer **screen**. On a black-and-white (1-bit) screen the pixel is either white or black. On a colour (8-bit or 24-bit) monitor, pixels can be any colour from a choice of hundreds or even millions of colours. The number of colour choices available depends on the pixel 'depth', ie how many **bits** are available to describe the colour values at any pixel. Pixels are also the measure of **resolution** of the screen (as in 72 pixels/inch).

> PIXEL ASPECT RATIO

PIXEL ASPECT RATIO

The width-to-height ratio of a screen **pixel**. In many systems (such as the **Macintosh**) the screen pixel is square, but some systems have non-square pixels, and allowances have to be made in preparing images where the aspect ratio is critical – for example in circles, squares and other symmetrical geometrical figures.

> ASPECT RATIO

PLANE

> IMAGE PLANE

PERSONAL DIGITAL ASSISTANTS

cyberspace in your palmtop

What happens when the electronic personal organizer, the cellular telephone, the hand-held videogame machine and the palmtop computer are squeezed together into a single, pocket-sized portable system? Firstly, the idea needs to be given a suitable name. Apple's president (and then CEO) John Sculley came up with the first attempt. Latching onto the digital base of all the hitherto disparate systems that would come together in the new machines, Sculley labelled them 'personal digital assistants' – a term that also implies a system with some built-in 'intelligence' – and announced Apple's first PDA, the Newton. Since then, we have had the 'teleputer' (although this term was first used to describe the television/computer hybrids of the future), IBM's 'Personal Digital System' and Amstrad's 'Pen Pad'.

Typical features of the new PDAs were rapidly established. In 1994, these included a low power-consumption, high-speed RISC-based microprocessor; a flat-screen pen interface and handwriting recognition software (because you can't easily use a QWERTY keyboard with one hand holding the computer); memory card slot (for industry-standard PCMCIA cards); a connector (or infrared device) for sending data directly to a desktop computer and a modem to connect the PDA to the telephone. Some PDAs will not have all of these features; some may have many more. By slotting in different memory or 'smart' cards, for example, the PDA could be transformed into an electronic book, fax machine or radio receiver. Apple's Newton prototype offers short-range infrared communications for transmitting data to other Newtons, or (through an AppleTalk network) to a desktop computer. In due course PDAs may well offer a range of more exotic extras, including videophone services and global positioning systems.

Some PDAs could lean towards the cellular phone market, others towards the personal organizer or palmtop computer sector, while others may integrate the functions of personal radio and tape recorder. The American communications giant AT&T is firmly committed to the cellular phone approach, identifying voice communications as the critical component in its PDA developments. AT&T plans to create a platform that will handle all forms of message systems, including paging, fax, modem and voice. Indeed, all kinds of new wireless services are likely to grow up around the PDA. AT&T's Personal Communications Services (PCS) currently offer a variety of voice and data communications, from pagers to E-mail and 'broadcast fax' (fax messages sent to hundreds or even thousands of recipients). Other PCS facilities include information services (from Reuters, Dow Jones, Associated Press etc), and a system for obtaining abstracts of articles from dozens of subject categories, delivered directly to the PDA by electronic mail.

Outside the corporate sector, the consumer success of PDAs will depend upon a number of factors. Manufacturers will need to provide easy-to-use interfaces and applications software inside pocket-sized and affordable hardware systems. Success may also depend on widespread establishment of the necessary digital-cellular phone and/or packet-switched radio networks, with affordable service charges. The phenomenal growth of cellular phones during the 1980s indicates that people like to communicate on the move. PDAs can offer a much wider spectrum of communications services, combined with diary, address book and notebook facilities. By the end of the decade, they could well be ubiquitous.

APPLE'S PDA

A range of 'intelligent' products from Apple Computer (and manufactured under licence by Sharp), was heralded by the introduction of the Newton – a hand-held device combining desktop computing power (equivalent to an Intel 486 PC), handwriting-recognition 'pen' interface, and flash memory card storage. The Newton, which is networkable and can send or receive faxes, measures around 190x110mm (7x4 inches) with a folding lid cover for its combined screen/writing surface of approx 140x90mm (5x3 inches). The Newton represents a significant breakthrough and launches Apple into the wider consumer-information electronics market. It also introduces 'intelligent assistance' techniques, with which the user can note down a name and telephone number, for instance, to be 'read' automatically by the Newton and recorded in its digital address book. Apple's aim was to provide an easy-to-use device that would use its own 'initiative' to 'understand' typical things that the user does. Newton's 'intuitive' interface is designed specifically to appeal to consumers with no previous experience of computers; but computer-literate users can also connect the Newton to their personal computer to exchange data.

PDAs promise to become more and more sophisticated. With the Newton, Apple has already produced an interface that recognizes cursive writing (as against characters merely drawn individually). Other developments for this type of product might well include voice input (for voice operation, memo recording, and perhaps in due course a speech-recognition system to convert spoken language to text files), and cellular telephone capability.

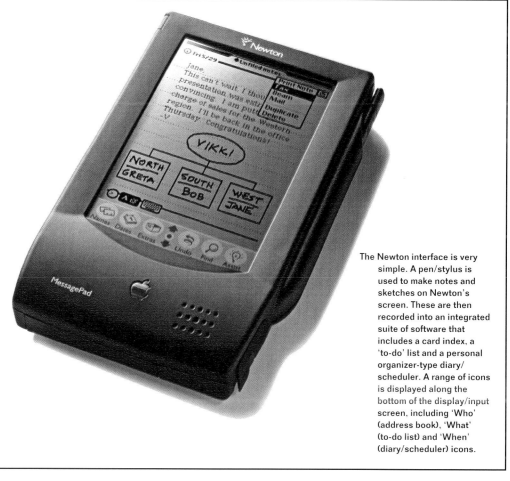

The Newton interface is very simple. A pen/stylus is used to make notes and sketches on Newton's screen. These are then recorded into an integrated suite of software that includes a card index, a 'to-do' list and a personal organizer-type diary/scheduler. A range of icons is displayed along the bottom of the display/input screen, including 'Who' (address book), 'What' (to-do list) and 'When' (diary/scheduler) icons.

PHOTO-CD
snaps on TV

By the early 1990s several digital photographic systems were on the market. These ranged from reasonably priced still-video cameras from companies such as Canon and Logitec, to sophisticated digital backs for professional camera systems such as the Nikon and Hasselblad. The technology involves delivering a digital image file to an electromagnetic storage system (floppy or hard disk); the image file can then be processed and edited with image-processing software such as Adobe Photoshop. The problem with these direct-to-disk systems is that the cheaper cameras suffer from a very low (below VHS-quality) resolution, while the professional high-resolution systems are very expensive. What was needed was a low-cost bridge between conventional photography and the computer. Enter Kodak with Photo-CD.

Kodak's idea is a very simple one – when you take your exposed roll of film to be developed and printed, you can also order a Photo-CD disc. As well as supplying normal colour prints or slides, the outlet will scan these images and store them as high-resolution files on a special CD. At home, the disc is inserted into a Photo-CD player and the images viewed on a TV set.

Some players can 'zoom' into selected areas of the image. The Photo-CD disc is a special 'multi-session' format that allows up to one hundred images to be added to the disc at different times. Images are stored at a number of sizes, including thumbnails (small reference images), screen-size for viewing, and high-resolution for printing or for retouching on a personal computer.

As well as special Kodak Photo-CD players, Photo-CD discs can also be played in many CD-ROM drives and other systems such as Philips' CD-i, the Atari Jaguar and the 3DO Multiplayer. In fact, with endorsements by most of the major computer, reprographics, communications and consumer electronics companies, and growing popularity with consumers, Kodak Photo-CD appears to have become the de facto standard for high-resolution imaging systems. Kodak scanning prices are not only cheaper than conventional high-resolution scans; the system is also an excellent archiving medium, as once recorded, image files cannot be erased, and each disc has its own reference number, making filing and retrieval easy. Photo-CD discs are designed to have a lifetime of about 50 years (roughly the same as negatives), and so provide very compact storage.

For photo libraries and archives, Photo-CD provides several security features, including ownership and copyright references, the ability to place a 'watermark' (such as the word 'proof') over images, and the ability to encrypt high resolution images to prevent unauthorized use. For the print reprographics business, Photo-CD offers a low-cost scanning and file interchange medium as an alternative to conventional, expensive high-resolution scanning techniques.

Kodak has developed three main versions of the Photo-CD format: the standard disc stores up to one hundred images (approx 6 megabytes per image); Photo-CD Catalog discs store up to 6000 thumbnail images, and are aimed at the photo library and archive market; and the Portfolio Photo-CD stores up to 800 images, and has multimedia capabilities, with images, text, graphics, sound, and authoring software to create interactive applications.

Portfolio Photo-CD should find many applications outside the consumer market, including corporate multimedia presentations, and the production of low-cost slide lectures and courseware for schools and colleges. Already used in a number of applications from engineering to data storage, Photo-CD is destined to bring low-cost CD-ROM publishing much closer to the desktop.

In the consumer sector, Photo-CD brings together the snapshot and the television, and includes applications such as photo 'family tree' software and special celebration presentation kits. More creative applications include programmes such as the 'Caricaturing' CD-i, in which photographs of the famous can be digitally distorted into caricatures. The Caricature disc contains a few hundred photos of stars, politicians and sports celebrities, and by slotting in a personal Photo-CD disc, caricatures of family members can even be made, and then saved on a VHS tape.

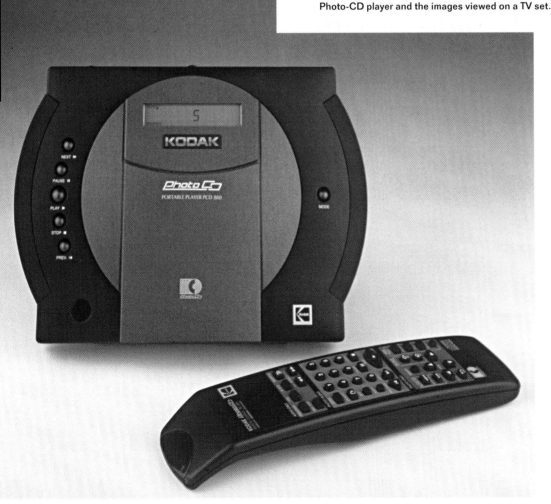

Apple PowerCD, a Photo-CD-compatible CD-ROM drive from Kodak. Note the consumer-electronic styling, a radical shift from the anonymous boxes of earlier drives. Photo-CD is both a consumer product and a professional tool for reprographics, imaging and archiving. Bringing photography into the television age, this portable Photo-CD drive can be plugged into a monitor or an ordinary television set.

PLAYSTATION

Generic term for a computer-based entertainment system. Typically, a playstation might include a TV set or **monitor**, **personal computer** with **CD-ROM** drive or **interactive multimedia** system, and stereo system. Future playstations may be built around TV sets with on-board computers (such as some of the proposed **HDTV teleputers**), or around powerful multimedia devices. Whichever particular hybrid of technologies emerges, it is likely to feature considerable processing power and powerful memory, **network** connections for high-bandwidth information and entertainment systems, a high degree of interactivity, and perhaps some form of simple stereo **head-mounted display** or visor.

> IDEAL DESKTOP   > WORKSTATION

PLV

> PRODUCTION-LEVEL VIDEO

POI

> POINT OF INFORMATION

POINT OF INFORMATION [POI]

Describes **interactive multimedia** systems located in museums and other public spaces that provide information about what can be seen and its location, and often providing detailed information.

> • POINT OF INFORMATION PAGE 166

POINT OF SALE [POS]

Describes electronic advertising, promotion and vending systems available at points of sale such as stores and shopping malls.

> ATM   > EPOS
> POINT OF INFORMATION

POLYGON

In **computer graphics**, a two-dimensional element defined by a list of vertices and possibly a fill pattern, used to define the surface of solid models.

You need a Macintosh equipped with a PowerPC processor to run this application.

[OK]

PowerPC: IBM RISC system/6000. Powerful chips offer fast rendering of high-resolution computer graphics, opening up the possibility of desktop virtual reality and other realtime simulators, and the prospect of full-screen full-motion video. In 1994 Apple launched their PowerPC upgrades for most Mac computers.

PORT

A socket in a computer system through which an **input/output** device or **peripheral** may be attached.

PORTED

Describes software that has been developed on one computer system and transferred or translated to run on another system. For example, a computer game originally developed to run on an **IBM** or **IBM-compatible** computer may be 'ported' to run on an Apple **Macintosh**. Code that has been ported rather than rewritten cannot take advantage of any special features of the system to which it has been transferred.

POS

> POINT OF SALE

POSITION SENSOR

Technology that tracks the location of a headset, **DataGlove** or other object in 3-d (X,Y, Z coordinate) space. Position sensors are used extensively in **robotics** and **virtual reality** systems.

> BIOSENSOR   > DATASUIT
> HEAD-MOUNTED DISPLAY

POST-PRODUCTION

The final stage in the production of a film, video or **interactive** media programme. In film and video, this is the stage when material is edited into its final form, when colour grading takes place and when optical or video effects, captions, titles, subtitles, credits and so forth are added. In interactive media production, this is the stage where the **software** is thoroughly tested and debugged.

> AUTHORING   > PRE-PRODUCTION

POSTERIZE

Image-processing technique for converting a digitized, continuous-tone (colour or monochrome) **bitmap** image to a smaller number of tones or colours.

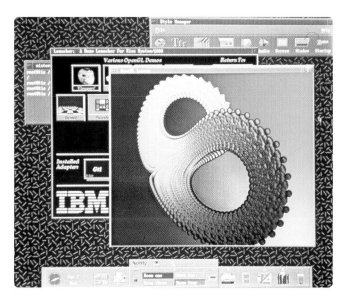

POSTSCRIPT

A popular **page description language** introduced by Adobe Systems in the mid-1980s.

POWERBOOK

A range of **laptop** computers produced by **Apple**. The first truly portable, notepad-sized **Macintosh**, the Powerbook was designed in conjunction with the consumer electronics giant **Sony** and is a masterpiece of stylish, user-friendly engineering, with a built-in **tracker ball**, ergonomic **keyboard** and backlit **LCD** screen.

POWERGLOVE

A gesture and position-sensing glove for interfacing with **videogame** consoles, developed by a consortium comprising Abrams Gentile Entertainments, VPL (the developer of the **DataGlove**), and **Mattel**, and manufactured by Mattel. Instead of the expensive fibre optics used in VPL's DataGlove, the PowerGlove uses strips of plastic printed with electrically conductive ink. These strips line the glove, and finger flexing alters the conductivity of the strips. Ultrasonic technology, rather than magnetic **position sensors**, is used to track the PowerGlove's position in space.

POWEROPEN

The **multi-tasking**, multiple-user **operating system** developed for the **PowerPC**, and based on **Apple**'s A/UX **Unix** and IBM's AIX Unix operating system. Through its 'applications binary interface' (ABI), PowerOpen can emulate DOS, IBM and Apple Unix and Mac functions, as well as run native PowerPC applications.

POWERPC

A hybrid **personal computer** that can run **Macintosh**, **MS-DOS** and **Unix** software, developed by **Apple**, Motorola and IBM and based around a reduced instruction set or **RISC** chip. The Motorola PowerPC RISC chip is a development of IBM's RS/6000 chipset, and runs a version of Unix called **PowerOpen**. The PowerPC runs Macintosh and DOS applications under **emulation**. The PowerPC has the potential to become the standard personal computer, because it has the capability to run **software** from the three major platforms in a powerful RISC-based machine, and offers **workstation** power of around 56 **MIPS** (millions of instructions per second).

PRE-PRODUCTION

The stage in the development of a film, video or **interactive** media programme before the actual production of images, sounds etc. During this stage, the design of the programme is developed on paper, through **storyboard**s and **flowchart**s. An interactive prototype may be produced, and the entire production is scheduled and budgeted. Researchers are employed to locate and clear rights on any necessary archive pictures or films, subject experts or writers are called in to produce **courseware** and content material, and the production manager assembles a team of specialist production personnel.

> AUTHORING   > POST-PRODUCTION

POINT OF INFORMATION
silicon salesman to telemedia terminal

The idea of providing additional information to amplify the personal experience of visiting a particular location or event has been with us for a long time. For many centuries this information was provided by a human guide – an expert who would accompany the visitor, guiding them through the significant points of interest – or by a printed guide book or pamphlet. With the introduction of low-cost portable tape recorders, the audio guide has supplemented the human guide and the guidebook.

Although the book and audio tape are essentially linear, they can and do encourage a considerable amount of interaction from the user. For example, the exemplary audio guide to London's Westminster Abbey contains a simple code that tells the user when and where to listen to the tape, and when to pause the tape in order to move to a new point of view. Books work in the same way. Both are eminently portable, but both are restricted in the range of information they can convey. While the audio tape might play us some music by the famous composer whose tomb we are viewing, and the book show us a reconstruction of the ruined building we are visiting, it takes an interactive multimedia system to combine these media, and to add dynamic animations, 3-d reconstructions, video footage and a comprehensive database.

Integrating all this information into one interactive system provides something that is superior to tapes, books – even to fallible human beings. It also means that users can have personal control over where and when they access more information, and indeed, what kind of extra information they want. What is more, interactive multimedia systems can present such a complete and authoritative guide that they can provide the means for the surrogate 'exploration' of remote sites for people who cannot make a personal visit.

Of course, the book and the videotape can be used and viewed 'offline' (away from the actual location), but the interactive nature of CD-based systems, and the fact that they feature the panoply of modern media, as well as the speed and accessibility of the computer database, create something quite unusual in the history of publishing. Combining in one system both simulation and information, the interactive CD-ROM can 'package' much more of the experience of visiting an abbey, a museum or a gallery than can a book or tape. Those institutions who have ventured into electronic POI are of course aware of the publishing potential of the new media.

In the mid-1990s, the CD-ROM was the only interactive publishing medium to consider, with an 'installed base' of perhaps several million players. By the end of the decade, however, the potential of the new telemedia networks of copper, cable and fibre optics will be exploited. The concept of publishing takes on a new meaning when people can connect 'live' to a POI resource at any time. For example, the possibility is thus created for continuous updates to the information base. Current and special exhibitions can be featured in a way that extends the market for such events far beyond their usual audience. The exhibition becomes publishable and broadcastable, open 24 hours a day to an audience of millions.

This information revolution has important consequences for the more overtly commercial world of electronic point of sale (EPOS) and mail order. Soon it will no longer be necessary to print vast, expensive catalogues, with all their problems of production, storage, distribution and currency, since it will be possible to distribute them electronically through the broadband network. Current developments in retail provide another example of the convergence that has characterized digital media. The actual point of sale is expanding far beyond the high street or the mall, and may theoretically continue to do so until there is a point-of-sale terminal in each and every home. Here, catalogue information can merge with customer education, advertising and sales incentives, and the customer may 'window-shop' across a range of competing products and prices.

When the demarcations between the store, the catalogue, the advert and the checkout disappear, and the retailer becomes a publisher, a range of opportunities are created. The retailer could become involved in distribution (both traditional and electronic – eg of books, records and films), in entertainment (as in home shopping channels), and in advertising – both as a creator of interactive ads, and in providing the infrastructure through which the many manufacturers featured in their electronic catalogue could advertise. In institutional terms, the POI producer or museum could become a publisher of interactive information relating to its primary assets – a publisher of catalogues, guides, archives and research. Special exhibitions could be packaged electronically to extend their appeal to a global audience.

The future of POI and EPOS also looks likely to include the use of ubiquitous chips for the 'object-oriented' multimedia captioning and labelling of artifacts, the use of smart cards in personal digital assistants for customized guides and, inevitably, an increasing employment of virtual reality techniques to amplify the experience of online remote shopping.

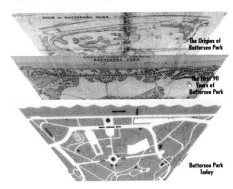

Working Knowledge Transfer: 'Battersea Park and Pump House Interactive Console', a multimedia POI system for visitors to London's Battersea Park, covering the history and development of the park in images, graphics and video. The programme was designed by Clive Richards, Brian Kriss and David Seymour, with graphics by Graham Howard of Art of Memory.

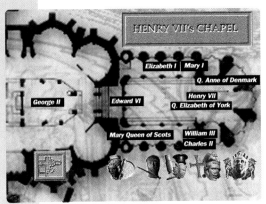

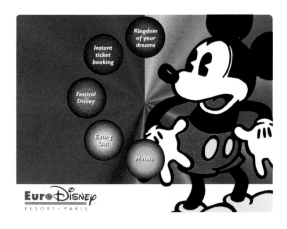

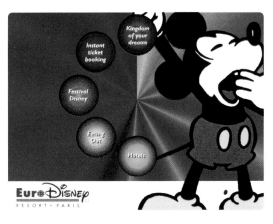

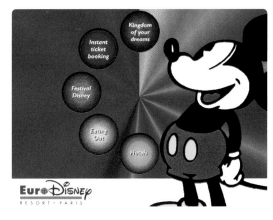

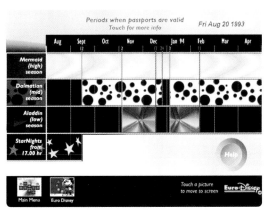

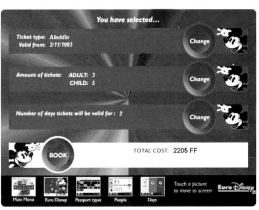

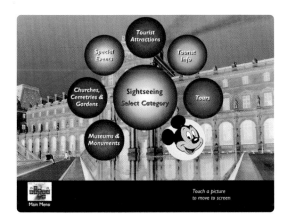

©The Walt Disney Company

IN.form: Euro Disney POI system designed by Andrew White. Combining the immortal Disney characters with a user-friendly multimedia guide and booking system for Euro Disney, the programme was produced on the Apple Macintosh and converted for the PC-based touchscreen delivery platforms using ToolBook.

Fit Vision/Sophie Roberts: prototype interactive multimedia guide to Westminster Abbey. Users can explore the Abbey with or without the assistance of expert guides. This programme incorporates motion video as well as an extensive database of the Abbey, its contents and context.

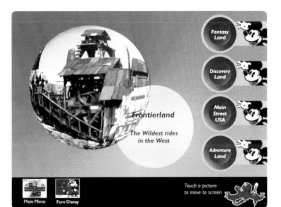

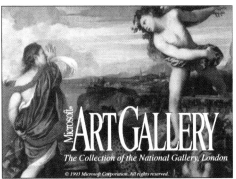

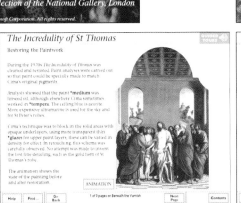

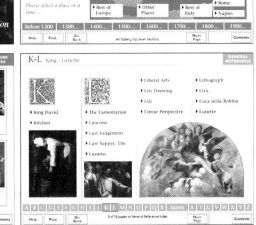

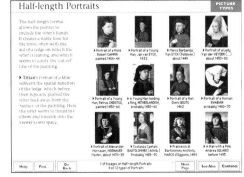

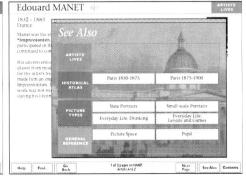

Microsoft: 'Art Gallery', the CD-ROM version of the innovative POI installation at the National Gallery in London. 'Art Gallery' repackages the point-of-information programme for normal-size (640x480 pixels) Mac or PC screens. Increasingly, POI material will reach a much wider audience through electronic publishing on CD, and soon through the broadband networks of the data superhighway. Original design and production for the POI system were by the National Gallery and Cognitive Applications.

'Regency Town House', a museum POI installation that recreates Regency Brighton. Users can experience the sights and sounds of the early nineteenth century.

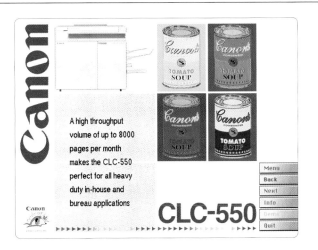

Joe Gillespie/Pixel Productions: 'Canon CLC'. This point-of-information programme for Canon provides users with an easy-to-use and informative demonstration and explanation of Canon's laser copier/printer and scanner system.

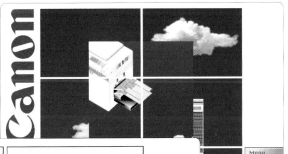

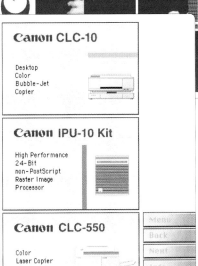

PRO-SUMER

A semi-professional user (consumer) of media technology. Examples are video makers who use **camcorders** and **desktop video** systems, and musicians who use **synthesizer** and **sampling** systems.

PRODUCTION-LEVEL VIDEO [PLV]

The asymmetrical **compression**/decompression mode in Intel's digital video interactive (**DVI**) that relies on **mainframe** computer processing to compress digital video data by ratios of between 120:1 and 160:1. Compressed data can be decompressed in **realtime** by a desktop PC equipped with a DVI chipset or expansion board. Using PLV, up to 72 minutes of **full-screen full-motion video**, with an image size of 256x240 **pixels** and displayed at 30 **frames** per second, can be stored on a **CD-ROM**. PLV-compressed data can also be stored on **floppy disk**, **hard disk** or **flopticle**.

> REALTIME VIDEO

PROGRAM

A set of statements and instructions designed to enable a computer to perform a specific task or series of tasks. The term refers to both the source program (the code the programmer writes) and the object program (the code that is executed by the computer). Special programs called compilers are used to translate source code (generally written in a **high-level language** such as **Pascal** or **C**) into object or low-level **machine code**.

> LANGUAGE   > PROGRAMMING
> SCRIPT

PROGRAMMING

The process of preparing a set of instructions for a computer in order to make it perform a particular activity. The main steps in programming are: firstly, to understand the problem and to develop a logical plan (or **algorithm**) for its solution; secondly, to write the instructions in a suitable programming **language** or code; and thirdly, to run, test and correct (or 'debug') the **program**.

> SCRIPTING

PROGRAMMING LANGUAGE

> LANGUAGE

PROJECTED REALITY

A **virtual reality** system that combines a live performance or a video image of the participant with a projected computer environment. One of the earliest projected realities was Videoplace, developed by Myron Krueger around 1975.

> ARTIFICIAL REALITY

PROLOG

A **high-level language** developed for computer-aided theorem-proving, but now an important language for AI research and applications. Prolog is not suitable for general purpose programming, but excels at dealing with applications involving logical relationships such as **expert systems** and **natural language** databases. Prolog was selected by Japan's Institute for New Generation Technology as the programming language for the development of 'fifth-generation' computers – 'smart' computers that would understand natural language, and cope with voluminous amounts of information.

> LANGUAGE
>> FURTHER READING: BARON 1988

PROMPT

A message displayed by a computer system to signal a course of action to the user.

> INTERFACE

PROTOCOL

In **telecommunications** and networking, a set of **standards** for exchanging **digital** information between computers or terminals. Protocols are established by equipment manufacturers and by international standard organizations, such as **ISO** and **CCITT**.

PROTOTYPING

An approach to developing a **software** application or **hypermedia** programme by producing working models (prototypes) demonstrating aspects or features of intended products that can be tested and evaluated. Prototypes allow the designer to test the structure, content, presentation and interface of a hypermedia programme, and to solve the problems of **navigation** through the information space of the programme. Hypermedia prototypes may be produced in **authoring** applications, in software toolkits such as **HyperCard** or **SuperCard**, or in **interactive** animation programs like **Macromedia Director**.

> PRE-PRODUCTION

PUBLIC DOMAIN SOFTWARE

Copyright-free **software** that is circulated on **floppy disk** or available from **network** bulletin boards.

> BBS   > SHAREWARE

PULSE-CODE MODULATION [PCM]

A technique for converting analog signals into **digital** form. PCM is used in many applications, importantly in **telecommunications** to convert telephone speech into digital code, and in the production of audio **CD**s. For 'telephone speech' quality, the analog signal is sampled at 8 kHz (8,000 samples per second), and 8 bits are used to record the amplitude at each sample point, resulting in a bit-rate of 64 kilobits per second. CD-quality music is produced by sampling the audio signal at 44.1 kHz and using 32 bits per sample, resulting in a bit-rate of 1.4 megabits per second.

> ADPCM   > CDDA
> DIGITAL AUDIO

The Vivid Group: Mandala™ projected reality system. Users can 'step into' and control a virtual video environment, enjoying full-body interaction with no cumbersome head-mounted hardware or digital gloves to get in the way.

Q CHANNEL

One of eight subcode channels (labelled P-W) on
compact disc audio (**CDDA**), the Q channel contains
the main control and display information (identifying
tracks, indexes and running times) and the absolute
playing time. Channel P simply separates musical
tracks, while channels R-W are used to encode data.

QUANTEL

British manufacturer of computer-graphic and videographic systems, such as the Video Paintbox,
Graphics Paintbox and Harry. Quantel systems are
central to many broadcast television studios and
audiovisual and video facilities houses throughout
the world.

> COMPUTER GRAPHICS   > VIDEO GRAPHICS

QUANTIZE

The process of converting an analog quantity into a **digital**
quantity. For example, in **pulse-code modulation**, the
analog signal is 'sampled' several thousand times
per second, and a digital value is recorded that is
equivalent to the amplitude of the analog signal at
each of the sampling points.

> SAMPLING RATE

QUICKDRAW

A set of drawing routines built into the **Macintosh** system
(as part of the 'user interface toolbox') and available
to every Macintosh application.

> QUICKTIME

QUICKTIME

A set of **standards** or **protocols** for dynamic (time-based)
data handling (including image and audio
compression/decompression) for the Apple **Macintosh**.
QuickTime is a software extension of the Macintosh
operating system, enabling the Mac to play audio,
animation and video files without additional **software** or
hardware, and allowing compressed video sequences
to be decompressed and displayed at **realtime** rates
on the computer **monitor screen**.

Introduced in 1991, QuickTime allows any application
(such as a word-processing, **E-mail**, animation or
presentation package) to support dynamic data by
means of a standard **file format** called 'Movie', which
can contain synchronized sound, video or animation
in any combination; it also provides a standard
method for interfacing with video **peripherals** (video
tape recorders, **videodisc** players, etc). 'Movie' files
can be cut and pasted (just as images or text can
be transferred) through a range of Macintosh
applications. Apple have also extended the **PICT** file
format to include automatic image compression and
decompression.

A number of image compression **algorithms** are used to
compress and playback video and animation clips,
and the 'compression manager' theoretically allows

the use of any compression algorithm. The
video compressor can display 24-bit video (with
accompanying sound) in a small **window** (approx 100
x150 **pixels**) at 25 or 30 **frames** per second. The
animation compressor uses **run-length encoding**
techniques to compress computer-generated
animations.

> FULL-MOTION VIDEO   > JPEG
> MPEG

QUIZ GAMES

Computer-based question-and-answer games. General
knowledge quizzes have always been popular
parlour games, and many books of questions and
answers are still published. Ever since the invention
of the boardgame Trivial Pursuit by Scott Abbott and
Chris and John Hainey in 1971, and its subsequent
rise to become the bestselling boardgame of the
1980s, **videogame** designers have been trying to
develop electronic quiz games that might emulate
its success. The advent of **interactive multimedia**
technology, such as **CD-i** and **DVI**, promises quiz
games of television quality, with a wide range of
question formats, including questions based on
photographs, paintings, video and film excerpts, and
music and voice clips. Such games will combine the
professional styling of TV games shows with the
personal interaction and sociability of videogames.
In 1991, Commodore released a version of Trivial
Pursuits on its multimedia **CD-ROM** system, **CDTV**; and
the same year Ace Coin Equipment announced its
new 'Genius Machine', a trivia quiz supported by
multimedia data stored in compressed DVI form on
CD-ROM.

> ARCADE GAMES

QWERTY

The standard organization of **alphanumeric** characters on
a keyboard.

> KEYBOARDS

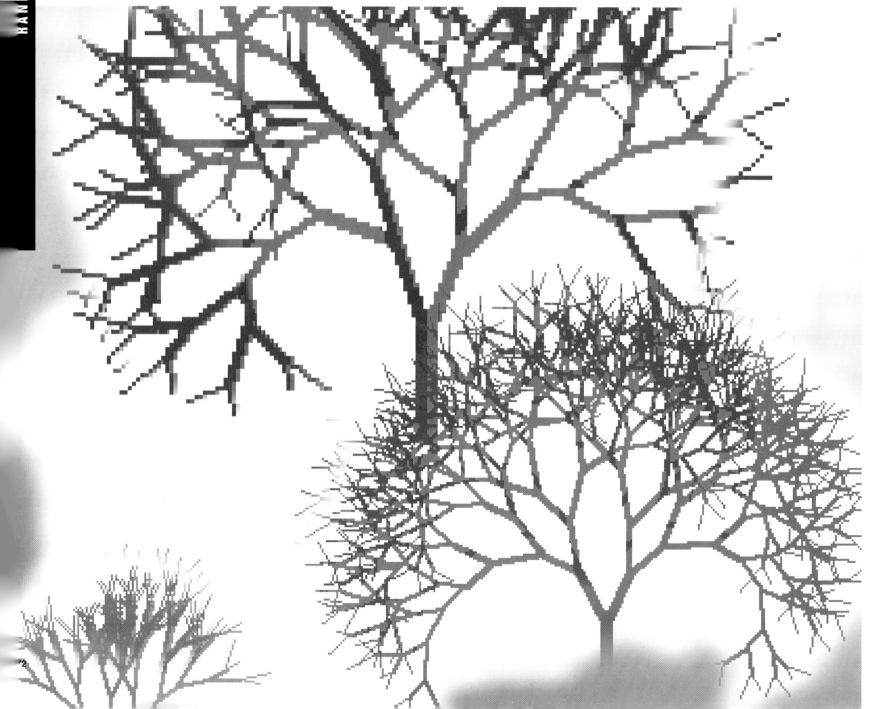

Broderbund: 'KidPix'. A milestone in interactive software, this children's painting program makes extensive use of random number generation to surprise and delight. Here, each time the tree tool is used, a different tree is generated in realtime.

RADIOSITY

A computer graphic rendering technique for accurately simulating the effect of radiant or reflected light generated by objects within a scene. In a computer-generated 3-d model, several light sources can be specified, and radiosity techniques are used to determine the effect of these light sources when they are reflected from matt or glossy surfaces onto other surfaces in the model (such as a red table casting a pink glow onto an adjacent white wall). The techniques for radiosity were derived from scientific studies of radiant heat transfer and illumination engineering.

> COMPUTER GRAPHICS   > RAY TRACING

RAM (RANDOM-ACCESS MEMORY)

Data storage that can be 'written to' and 'read from'. In computers, RAM is volatile, temporary storage that is used to run **program** applications.

> ROM

RANDOM ACCESS

A general term referring to non-sequential media, such as **hypermedia**, that do not have a physical beginning, middle or end.

IBM (Portsmouth): ray tracing using an IBM RISC system/6000.

RANDOM NUMBER GENERATOR (RNG)

A computer **program** that produces random numbers, or selects one number at random from a prespecified range or list of numbers. RNG functions are used in many innovative ways in **hypermedia** and **software** program design, typically to provide non-repeating 'default' sequences for display when a programme is not being used (for example in arcade **videogames** and **point-of-sale** hypermedia programmes, where random sequences from the game or shopping catalogue are displayed on a monitor to attract new customers). Broderbund's 'KidPix' painting program for children makes use of RNG to provide a wide variety of images (such as **fractal image** 'trees') through the use of one painting tool.

> AUTOPLAY   > DEFAULT

RASTER IMAGE FILE FORMAT

> RIFF

RAY TRACING

A computer graphic rendering technique for the realistic simulation of shadows, and the reflection and refraction of light in an image. Ray tracing is very demanding of computer processing time, and it is often used to render just those particular objects in a scene, such as drinking glasses and mirrors, where these attributes are most needed.

> COMPUTER GRAPHICS   > RADIOSITY

READ/WRITE MEDIA

Electromagnetic or digital-optical storage on which data can be written (copied to) or read (copied from).

> CD-R
> HARD DISK
> WORM
> DIGITAL-OPTICAL RECORDING
> WMRM

REALITY ENGINE

A computer system designed to generate 3-d virtual worlds in sound and vision. A typical system combines a powerful **microprocessor**, two graphics processors (for stereo imaging), and **digital signal processors** for stereo sound.

> VIRTUAL REALITY

REALTIME

In human-computer **interface** design and **simulation** systems such as **virtual reality**, 'realtime' means systems that exhibit no discernible delay between **input** and **output** – between user action and system response. Typically this means a response time of less than 50 milliseconds.

> FLIGHT SIMULATION
> REALTIME ANIMATION
> LATENCY
> SIMULATION

REALTIME ANIMATION

Images computed and displayed at such a speed as to give the illusion of natural movement – this is ideally around 25 **frames** per second, but frame rates of over 15 frames per second are acceptable as 'realtime'. Realtime animation speeds depend on the complexity of the image being processed from model data, and the speed of the processor. Military and commercial **flight simulation** systems use powerful **mainframe** computers to provide very high **resolution** images displayed at frame rates of 25 frames per second through videobeam projectors. In non-realtime 'frame by frame' animation, each image is computed over a period of minutes (or even hours for complex images on desktop computers), before it is recorded to **hard disk**, film or videotape.

> COMPUTER ANIMATION
> SIMULATION
> PERSISTENCE OF VISION
> VIRTUAL REALITY

REALTIME OPERATING SYSTEM

A **multi-tasking operating system** for **multimedia** systems, which allows the precise synchronization of **digital** audio and video, and user **interaction**. In **multimedia** applications, both video and audio data need to be played at exactly the same speed as they were recorded, in exact synchronization. The application must also respond to interactive actions of the user, and this means that the system must be aware of the exact playback point of the audio and video. Exact timing must be kept, while the system is simultaneously delivering the considerable volumes of data necessary for **full-motion video**, monitoring and responding to user **interaction**, updating the screen **interface**, and running the application program. Realtime operating systems were designed to handle this multiplicity of tasks, so that there is no discernible delay for the user.

> CORTOS

REALTIME VIDEO (RTV)

The mode in Digital Video Interactive (**DVI**) that provides symmetrical, **realtime** video image **compression** and decompression. RTV is produced directly on a **personal computer** equipped with a DVI chipset or expansion boards. It provides a lower level of quality than **production-level video** and is used for programme development and prototyping.

REAR PROJECTION

> BACK PROJECTION

RED BOOK

The CD-audio (**CDDA**) **standards** document that is published by Philips and **Sony**, containing the technical specification for **base-case** CD players and disc formats.

REFRESH RATE

The time it takes for the computer or **hypermedia** system to display an image on the **monitor** screen. Refresh rate depends on a number of factors, including the speed of the computer's processor, the speed of the transfer of data from storage medium to processor, and the size and **resolution** of the image to be displayed on the monitor.

> CRT

RELATIONAL DATABASE

Describes a **database** that is based on the mathematical theory of relations, and that is structured as a series of two-dimensional tables that can be manipulated by mathematical and algebraic (**Boolean**) operations. Each record or 'entry' is made up of a list of connected items (such as a person's name, address, age, gender, etc), and any subset of these items can easily be retrieved. So, for example, the user might ask the database to retrieve all the records for women aged 36 or over, or all the records sharing the same postcode or zipcode. The relational model was developed by EF Codd of **IBM** in the early 1970s.

> DATABASE MANAGEMENT SYSTEM

REMOTE SENSING

The collection of data from a distant source, by airborne, satellite or spacecraft apparatus, which is then transmitted to a computer for processing. Images that are useful for weather forecasting, land-use surveys, pollution monitoring and mineral prospecting are now gathered using remote sensing techniques.

> • REMOTE SENSING PAGE 175

REMOTE SERVICES

The **interactive** access to services that are mediated by a remote computer – for example cable TV 'home shopping' services or automatic teller machines (**ATMs**).

> • REMOTE SHOPPING PAGE 177

REMOTE SHOPPING

(Or 'home shopping'.) Describes services that allow customers to 'shop' from home, viewing store catalogues or even enjoying '**surrogate travel**'

experiences around 'virtual' stores, and ordering their requirements via telephone and credit card.

> INTERACTIVE ADVERTISING
> • REMOTE SHOPPING PAGE 177

RENDERING ENGINE

A **software** or hardware/software system for the creation of shaded surfaces in 3-d **computer graphics**. Early rendering systems involved describing the surface of 3-d 'wireframe' objects in terms of sets of **polygons**, then applying smooth-shading techniques (such as **Gouraud** or **Phong** shading) to produce a smooth surface. Current rendering systems incorporate a variety of techniques, including **ray tracing**, **radiosity**, **texture mapping** and bump-mapping.

RESOLUTION

Measure of the detail in an image or sound. Images are measured in **pixels** (dots) per inch, and in the number of **bits** used to describe the colour values (or **greyscale**) at each pixel. Audio is measured in the number of samples per second, and the number of bits used to **quantize** those samples.

> SAMPLING RATE

RETRIEVAL ENGINE

A **program** or subroutine that provides faster and easier access to items of data in large data collections, such as **CD-ROM**.

> KNOWLEDGE-BASED SYSTEM

RGB (RED, GREEN, BLUE)

The primary additive colour system used in **computer graphics**, television and video applications. RGB signals provide the best quality displays, as signals are used directly by the cathode-ray tube (**CRT**) to control the output of the three electron guns that together scan the phosphor-coated **screen**. RGB images are clearer than those produced by **composite video** or broadcast signals.

> CMY
> HSV
> COLOUR

RGB 5:5:5

An image-encoding technique used in **CD-i**: the red, green and blue (**RGB**) colour components of each **pixel** are each **quantized** and are represented by five **bits** of information. This gives a maximum of 32,768 colours, and a data size of 210 kilobytes for a normal **CD-i** screen resolution of 384x280 pixels. RGB 5:5:5 encoding is used for complex graphics and illustrations.

> CD-i DIGITAL IMAGES

RIFF (RASTER IMAGE FILE FORMAT)

A digital image **file format**, more efficient than **TIFF**, that records **greyscale** values allowing RIFF images to be edited in detail.

RIFF (RESOURCE INTERCHANGE FILE FORMAT)

A set of **file formats** for **MPC** (multimedia personal computer) defined by **Microsoft** for audio, text, video (graphics) stills and **animation** files. Text is encoded

in **RTF** format, audio in the **MIDI** file format, or as digitized sound in the WAVE format, which caters for mono or stereo sound encoded as (**pulse-code modulation**) data at 8 or 16 bits per sample. **Sampling** rates include 11 kHz ('voice quality'), 22 kHz (FM-radio quality), and 44.1 kHz (CD-audio quality). Image file formats include **Windows** metafiles, BMP (**bitmap**) and RIFF DIB (device independent bitmap) for still images and graphics, and MMF (multimedia movie format) for animations and motion video.

RISC (REDUCED INSTRUCTION SET CHIP)

A **CPU** designed to execute only the most frequently used programming instructions. The instructions left out must be carried out by combining the ones that remain. The result is that the most frequently used instructions are processed more quickly than in a CISC (a complex instruction set chip), but the ones that are left out execute more slowly. The overall result of this design strategy is CPUs with considerably increased processing speeds. A further benefit is that such CPUs, being simpler, are cheaper to design and manufacture.

First developed by **IBM** in the mid-1970s, this concept has now been adopted by a number of manufacturers. RISC chips are used in **workstations** and **personal digital assistants**, and may replace CISC technology in **personal computers**, as increasingly they become multimedia communication devices requiring very fast processing speeds.

> 3DO   > PERSONAL DIGITAL SYSTEM
> POWERPC

RLE

> RUN-LENGTH ENCODING

ROBOT

A programmable, electro-mechanical device, linked to a computer, consisting of mechanical manipulators, and more recently, sensors. The term is derived from the Czech words meaning 'serf' and 'obligatory work', and was first used by Karel Capek (1890-1938) in his short story, Opilec (1917), and then in his play RUR (Rossum's Universal Robots) (1921).

Robotic systems have been developed for Moon landing and exploration, for deep water oil-pipeline maintenance, for nuclear power plant inspection, for bomb disposal and other similar tasks. The first robot designed for industrial use was the Unimate, produced by Unimation Inc in 1962. The most popular of these early robots, the Unimation 2000, was capable of moving its arm in several directions, and opening and closing its gripper (hand).

Second-generation robots, such as those introduced by Hitachi and Cincinnati Milacron in the early 1980s, were much more sophisticated, with precision picking and placing, and more delicate gripping. The use of these robots revolutionized industrial practice, especially in the automobile industry, where they were used for welding, spraying and similar operations.

In the mid-1980s, a third generation of robots – such as Automatix's RAIL series, Unimation's PUMA, and **IBM**'s 7535 and 7565 – were equipped with some

REMOTE SENSING
multispectral
earthwatch

Remote sensing is used to monitor and map the Earth's surface at a number of different scales, through a range of sensors operating in the visible and infrared areas of the electromagnetic spectrum. The collected data is transmitted to a host computer on the Earth's surface, and a variety of filtering and image-processing techniques are used to convert it into meaningful images for a wide variety of uses.

Using devices such as 'multispectral scanners' (optical instruments for measuring the varying intensity of electromagnetic radiation reflected from the Earth's surface) and 'thematic mappers' (which operate in the visible and infrared), satellites provide regular data updates while orbiting the Earth once every hundred minutes or so. Orbits are polar, at a height of 800-1000 km (50-60 miles approx) above the surface. The NASA Landsat, for instance, has two sensing systems that scan a strip 185 km (115 miles) wide on each orbit and construct an image of the surface beneath as the satellite travels its orbital path. This data is used in an ever-increasing number of applications, from weather and agricultural forecasting to land usage, mineral surveying and pollution monitoring.

The French Spot satellite, launched by Espace in 1986, uses a sensor capable of collecting data from several different directions, from which three-dimensional images can be reconstructed, and heights derived from the various features shown. Spot can determine heights to within 5 metres (16 feet) of accuracy, and detect details down to 10 metres in size.

Data from Landsat and Spot satellites can be supplemented by microwave data from the European ERS-i satellite, imagery from the British UoSAT 5 Earth Imaging System, and recently available data from the former Soviet Union. The US National Oceanic and Atmospheric Administration also operates satellites, and supplies free data to developing countries.

NASA has led the way with the development of artificial satellites, manned space vehicles and remote sensing technologies. We owe the vision of the 'Whole Earth' to NASA.

The amount of data transmitted by remote sensing satellites is huge. Some images cover an area of approximately 100x100 nautical miles and include some 48 million pixels, each described by 24 bits of data. In an average 'pass' of the satellite from horizon to horizon it may transmit as much as 100 gigabytes of information, requiring large memory stores and mainframe processing power. However, to make data more accessible to countries with limited resources – and incidentally to independent companies and even home personal computer users – scientists at Los Alamos National Laboratory in New Mexico have developed sophisticated filtering software that reduces data to amounts that can be easily and efficiently handled by a desktop computer.

Meteorological data has been available to anyone with a Mac and a suitable satellite dish for some time now. This system allows you to sit in front of your own computer and view the world live 'from orbit'. This extraordinary development is only the beginning: satellite images could eventually be used to update a 'realtime atlas', to feed in to a 'World Game' simulator (such as that described by the American visionary Richard Buckminster Fuller), or to provide the truly global locations for a terrain- and map-based videogame.

Remote Sensing has already proved to be a powerful tool in the business of accurately recording and forecasting the weather. Over the last two decades the equally important task of mapping the world's geophysical resources – one of the first steps towards effective planetary management – has begun. These natural 'information resources' could be extended to benefit the entire world. The role that software can play in this task is of key importance. The next few years might see the further development of user-friendly image processing and expert system software, specifically designed to allow all the countries of the world to access the mass of data derived from remote sensing.

intelligence, containing general-purpose computers with vision and/or tactile sensing systems. Robots like these are controlled with specialized programming languages, such as IBM's AML, which allow the robot to make decisions based on changes in their working environment – for example, to find and identify particular machine parts regardless of their orientation, and to use them in complicated assembly tasks.

ROBOTICS

The science and technology of the design and manufacture of **robots**. As a discipline it lies across the boundaries of artificial intelligence (**AI**) and mechanical engineering. All the disciplines of artificial intelligence come together in robotics, including machine intelligence, machine vision, pattern recognition, decision-making, natural language understanding and **expert systems**. These component disciplines are rapidly maturing, and over the next 20 years or so robotics look set to spread from the factory production line to the farm, the school-room and the home.

> ROV   > TELEPRESENCE

>> FURTHER READING: MINSKY 1988

The SHADOW biped walker: a prototype domestic robot designed by David Buckley. Already ubiquitous in the manufacturing area, robots will soon impact on the domestic scene, taking over a wide range of household tasks.

ROLE-PLAYING GAME [RPG]

A game in which the players assume fictional identities within a map-, maze- or terrain-based adventure or quest. Role-playing is now the basis for a number of **videogames** and **virtual reality** environments.

> • ROLE-PLAYING GAMES PAGE 178

ROM [READ-ONLY MEMORY]

Software that is physically embedded in a storage device in a permanent form that cannot be erased or written to. Parts of a computer's **operating system** may be stored in ROM, which, unlike the software stored in **RAM**, will not be lost when the power is turned off.

ROOMS

> XEROX ROOMS

ROSTRUM CAMERA

A camera mounted on a rostrum (camera copy stand) for the purposes of cel, collage, or model **animation**; for video digitizing (frame grabbing); or for capturing stills, graphics or 3-d objects onto film or video. Rostrum cameras can be very sophisticated, with the rostrum platen or bed moving in several directions, and with these movements, as well as camera operations and lighting, all under computer control.

> FRAME GRABBER   > MOTION CONTROL

> ROTOSCOPE

ROTOSCOPE

A technique for creating **animations** by tracing live-action film or video sequences. Invented by the Fleischer brothers in 1915, the technique was used by them in a full-length animated feature, Gulliver's Travels (1939), and resurrected by Ralph Bakshi for his adult

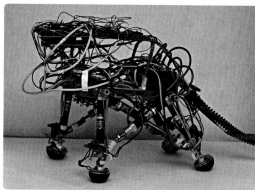

Technology Applications Group (TAG): Igor quadruped walking robot, designed for research in machine learning and motion experiments.

animated features Fritz the Cat and The Lord of the Rings in the 1970s. In the 1980s rotoscopy was used by video artist Annabelle Jankel in the pop promo for Elvis Costello's Accidents Will Happen, and the technique has been exploited by other animators and video artists, using **video graphics** technology.

In its simplest form, a rotoscope back-projects live action film images frame by frame onto a ground glass screen, where the artist can trace off the required movement and detail onto a cel. In videographic rotoscopy, the images are digitized into a paintbox system (such as a **Quantel**), and worked on directly by the animator before being saved to disk.

ROV [REMOTELY OPERATED VEHICLE]

Telematically controlled vehicles which are used in many kinds of hazardous situations, such as bomb disposal, nuclear pile maintenance and deep sea operations. Submarine ROVs have been used extensively in the exploitation of the North Sea oil fields, and more spectacularly, in the exploration of the wreck of the Titanic by the Woods Hole Oceanographic Institute (1986). Here, the ROV (named 'Jason Jnr') was controlled by cable from a submarine, and successfully operated at depths of 4000 metres (13,000 feet).

> ROBOTICS   > TELEPRESENCE

RPG

> ROLE-PLAYING GAME

RS 232

A **standard** specified by the US Electrical Industries Association (EIA) for the electrical connections or **interface** for serial communication between **personal computers** and printers or other **peripherals**.

> SCSI   > SERIAL INTERFACE

RTF [RICH TEXT FORMAT]

A text **file format** created by **Microsoft**, that retains some formatting information (margins, tabs, fonts and font styles etc) along with the text data. RTF is recognized by a number of word processors.

> PERSONAL COMPUTER

RTV

> REALTIME VIDEO

RUN-LENGTH ENCODING [RLE]

One of the earliest image-**compression** techniques, still used in **multimedia** systems such as **CD-i**. RLE uses two-byte codes, where one byte identifies the colour, and the other byte the number of **pixels** that are to be set to that colour. RLE is useful for images made up of flat colour areas, such as cartoons, schematics, diagrams and two- or three-colour graphics, but is less effective for photographic or 'contone' images, because its efficiency depends on long stretches of repeated data.

> CD-i DIGITAL IMAGES

REMOTE SHOPPING
the magic mall

Imagine your own private shopping mall, one that changes instantly to include only the range of goods and products that you are interested in, one in which you are always the only customer, one that is always open and full of assistants to help or advise you. Entering the mall, you indicate that you are interested in a new car and you select the price range. Instantly, the mall becomes a collection of car showrooms, featuring all the current models that fall within that price range – together with any special offers on more expensive models. You can look at any of the cars, in any colour, and with any combination of features, and then watch videos of the car on the road. It may even be possible to sit behind the wheel, call up all the comparative data on a group of cars of the same style, colour and price range, read reviews from the car magazines, or see a video review clipped out of a broadcast motoring programme.

This sophisticated 'virtual reality' kind of home-shopping service is not yet available, but millions of armchair shoppers in the USA are already well on the way towards the magic mall. Two cable TV companies, QVC (Quality, Value and Convenience), operating from Pennsylvania, and HSN (Home Shopping Network), based in Florida, already offer home-shopping services to millions of North Americans. HSN pioneered television home shopping in 1982, and QVC has been operating since 1987. Between them they earned more than US $2.2 billion in revenues in 1992. Already home-shopping services are available via satellite in the UK and Europe. With the increased fibre-optic cabling of the USA, Europe, the UK and Japan during the next decade, these services are set to become much more interactive, and therefore more personalized.

The potential of home shopping is very strong, whether it is distributed via interactive disc 'catalogues' or provided as a service by telecommunications, satellite and interactive cable TV companies. The catalogue mail-order business is worth US $70 billion in the USA alone, and interactive television home shopping is likely to be qualitatively superior to its postal counterpart, as well as quicker and easier. Remote shopping software may be like having a multimedia, three-dimensional Yellow Pages on your television set. And above all, it will probably be free to the end-user, just as most mail-order and discount store catalogues are. The ordering of goods and payment for them may be by phone and credit card, or eventually by smart card inserted into the home multimedia system. In the longer term, remote shopping may even become a social activity: telecommunications systems running multi-participant virtual reality software could create shared venues offering social interaction as well as shopping and other services.

FitVision/WBSB: 'PowerNet' home shopping and services prototype simulating the 16:9 aspect ratio of high-definition TV. Future cable and broadband fibre-network services will be highly interactive, offering services such as home shopping, interactive advertising, telebanking and ticket booking services.

QVC Channel: Home Shopping. The cable channel QVC offers 'armchair' shopping combined with the 'live' feel of home selling parties and interaction via the telephone.

ROLE-PLAYING GAMES

the genesis of the videogame

Role-playing games (RPGs) grew out of wargaming – the reconstruction and simulation of battles using miniature toy soldiers, tanks, ships etc, and fought on a tabletop 'map' or model landscape – and rely on the same elaborate sets of rules governing what can and cannot be done. These 'rules of engagement' specify the potential of each unit in terms of fire power, manoeuvrability etc, and dice are used to simulate the chance factors of real-life military engagements.

Spurred by the phenomenal success of JRR Tolkein's trilogy The Lord of the Rings after the paperback publication in the late 1960s, many wargamers began to add fantasy elements to their medieval battles, and rules began to appear for games including dragons, magical swords and other fantastic creatures and artifacts. In 1974, two wargamers in the United States, Dave Arneson and Gary Gygax, collaborated in the production of a fantasy wargame they called 'Dungeons and Dragons'. It became the first and probably the most popular of the role-playing games. Published as three boxed booklets by Gygax's company Tactical Studies Rules, Dungeons and Dragons was enormously successful, and became the focus for a whole industry of games, toy models, magazines and conventions. The concept has since been successfully adopted for numerous computer videogames and virtual reality environments.

RPGs involve the (human) players controlling a set of (fictional) characters within an adventure story or quest (generally a treasure hunt). The abilities of each character within the game are represented numerically, with points for intelligence, strength, magical powers, weapons, healing and so on. The referee or 'Dungeon Master' (DM) often spends a considerable amount of time preparing the game 'campaign', drawing maps and diagrams of the series of situations, in which the characters' skills will be more or less balanced with the range of difficulties they will face. The DM considers this to be part of the fun of RPGs, and many will spend several days preparing a game scenario for their players. For the players, the fascination of role-playing games lies partly in solving the problems set by the Dungeon Master, partly in nurturing the growth and development of their assumed characters or roles, and partly in the social interaction that takes place during play.

During the mid- to late 1970s 'Dungeons and Dragons'-style role-playing games began to appear as programs on mainframe and mini-mainframe computers at universities and research centres throughout the USA and Europe. The first was probably 'Adventure' (written by two students at Stanford University), in which players are confronted with the textual descriptions (at first printed out by the computer, then later displayed on a monitor screen) of a series of caves or rooms. Players then type in what they wish to do (leave the room, pick up an object, and so forth), and the computer responds by either letting them continue, or by restricting their options because, for example, they failed to collect the correct tool some frames previously.

Computer role-playing games (CRPGs) currently cannot aspire to be nearly as rich and as interactive (in the sense of true person-to-person social interaction) as conventional RPGs. CRPGs allow the user (player) to create a persona with which they can identify, and to accord this persona with attributes that can be determined statistically, but during the game itself, the player has very limited freedom to choose direction and tactics.

By the early 1990s, the first commercial 'virtual reality' RPG, 'Legend Quest', had appeared. Designed to run on W Industries' 'Virtuality' machine, 'Legend Quest' is a VR game for four players, each of whom adopts an 'avatar' personality (or 'digidentity') – a computer-generated character that the player can select and customize. A database of 18 characters is available, including a human, dwarf or elf, of either sex, each of which by profession can be a wizard, a thief or warrior. The player's moves are tracked and recorded in a database, which also keeps track of the avatar's attributes and progress. The four characters search for wealth and knowledge, and meet monsters whose responses are based on learning techniques developed in artificial intelligence research. With different human players, and different responses from the monsters they meet, the game is never played the same way twice.

Three years before the publication of William Gibson's novel Neuromancer, a novella by the American writer Vernor Vinge introduced the world to the idea of the virtual cybernetic space of computer and telecoms networks. The story True Names (1981) describes the adventures of role-playing gamers in this new cyberspace. Vinge speculates on the importance of the metaphor of role-playing, arguing that the magical vocabulary of the role-playing game is much more appropriate to the new virtual reality than are the 'data structures' and 'communications protocols' of corporate computing. The role-playing game metaphor has also been visualized in the Disney movie Tron (1982) and in Neal Stephenson's novel Snow Crash (1992), as well as in numerous other cyberpunk texts.

By providing both the means and the metaphor for people to personalize their telematic experience of cyberspace, the role-playing game looks set to remain a central feature of the developing telemedia that will characterize the twenty-first century.

Cryo: 'Dune'. Frank Herbert's award-winning sci-fi adventure was published in 1965, and since then has inspired a cult following. Cryo's role-playing game, published by Virgin, combines stills, video, animation, digitized music and speech.

Anglia TV: 'Knightmare'. Juliet Henry Massy plays Gwendoline of the Green in this 'watch as they interact' role-playing game. 'Knightmare' makes extensive use of chromakey and 3-d computer modelling to situate the participants in a wide range of fantasy locations.

Anglia TV: 'Knightmare'. A 'disagreement' on the quest through the electronic maze – 'over the shoulder' cyberspace adventure on broadcast television. Anglia has pioneered this genre, combining interactive role-playing fantasy with video graphics and virtual reality technologies.

SAFE AREA
> VIDEO SAFE

SAMPLING
> AUDIO SAMPLING

SAMPLING RATE
The number of times per second that an analog signal (such as a sound wave) is analyzed so that it can be converted into a **digital** signal.

> ADPCM
> AUDIO SAMPLING
> DIGITAL AUDIO
> PULSE-CODE MODULATION
> QUANTIZE

SATELLITE COMMUNICATIONS
Telecommunications and **broadcasting** systems using Earth-orbiting satellites to transmit their signals.

> • SATELLITE COMMUNICATIONS PAGE 180

SATURATION
The amount or strength of the hue present in any **colour**. Saturation describes the degree to which the hue has been 'diluted' with white. Fully saturated blue is pure, solid blue, while desaturated blue will be a pastel 'sky blue'. Colours for TV and **video graphics** should not be fully saturated, as intense colours tend to 'bleed' across the screen.

> CHROMINANCE
> CMY
> LUMINANCE
> RGB

SCAN
The process of digitizing an image by means of a desktop **scanner**, or high-resolution drum scanner (in pre-print reprographics).

SCAN CONVERSION
The process of converting television (**interlaced**) video signals to computer (non-interlaced) **RGB** signals and vice-versa.

> VIDEO BOARD

SCANNER
Hardware for digitizing images, ie converting **analog** values to **digital** samples. Desktop scanners generally offer **resolutions** of between 300 **dpi** and 600 dpi, while professional pre-print drum scanners are capable of thousands of dpi.

> FLATBED SCANNER
> OCR

SCENE GENERATOR
In **virtual reality** and **simulation** systems, the system that generates images from stored 3-d model data in response to the user's actions. In the mid-1960s, Ivan Sutherland realized that rather than employing physical models and cameras to create realistic scenes for flight simulators, the computer could be used. In 1968 he teamed up with David Evans, forming Evans & Sutherland to develop electronic scene generators and flight simulators. In a scene generator, the set of data describing the physical world – the airport or landscape – is held in memory. As the controlling computer receives positional data from the simulator cockpit controls, it calculates the viewpoint of the pilot, and draws or 'renders' the scene to be displayed in the cockpit windscreen. Considerable computing power is required for this task, as to promote an adequate sense of realism in the simulated experience, the scene must be re-calculated and re-rendered in **realtime**, ie at rates of 25 frames per second.

> FLIGHT SIMULATION
> SKETCHPAD

SCREEN
Area on which visual information from a computer, **hypermedia** or television system is displayed. This may be a cathode-ray tube (**CRT**) phosphor-coated glass screen, a liquid-crystal display (**LCD**), or the reflective screen of a videobeam or optical projector.

> • THE SCREEN PAGE 181

Sony: Jumbotron video screen. This kind of massive video screen points the way towards the wall-to-wall 'soft information furniture' that will be a feature of the broadband telemedia of the next century.

SCREEN CAMERA
Software that allows the user to 'grab' a whole **screen** or part of the current screen display and save it in an image **file format** such as **PICT** or **TIFF**.

SCRIPT
A computer program written in a **scripting** language, such as **HyperTalk** or **Lingo**.

➡ ➡

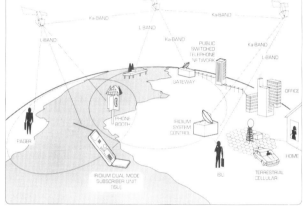

SATELLITE COMMUNICATIONS
global village and telematic nomad

We are so accustomed to receiving live television images from around the world, it is easy to forget that this is a relatively recent development. The first international television hook-up connecting all five continents was not until 1967. The occasion was the epoch-making 'One World' programme devised by the BBC. This 125-minute programme featured live black-and-white transmissions from 18 countries around the world, and was broadcast to an audience of around 500 million people in over 30 countries. The main British contribution was the live performance by the Beatles of 'All You Need Is Love'. The show was iconic proof of the 'Global Electronic Village' forecast by Marshall McLuhan, and a realization of Arthur C Clarke's visionary paper on the possibilities of artificial satellites published in Wireless World magazine as long ago as 1945. In 1985, some 18 years after 'One World', Bob Geldof's 'Live Aid' was watched live by over 1500 million people in 160 countries. The technology that made these global television programmes possible is the communications satellite.

Echo-1, the first communications satellite, launched in 1960, was merely a passive reflector. Orbiting at an altitude of 1610 kilometres (1075 miles), it was a 30-metre (100-foot approx) aluminium-coated Mylar balloon that reflected any signal beamed at it, but at greatly reduced power. After Echo-2, later satellites (including the famous Telstar launched in 1962), were 'active' – they received signals from ground stations, amplified them, and re-transmitted them to ground stations in other parts of the world.

Satellites are governed by Kepler's laws of planetary motion. The higher the satellite, the slower it orbits. Satellites in low orbit move quickly across the sky, making it more difficult for ground stations to track them. Echo-1, for example, at an altitude of 1610 km, orbited the Earth every two hours. However, at an

Motorola Iridium System. The Iridium telephone connects users to local cell nets or to satellites overhead, which relay voice, paging, data or fax messages around the world to groundstations, and on to the recipients. A 'constellation' of 66 low Earth orbit satellites (LEOS) provides 24-hour global coverage.

altitude of 37,500 km (23,300 miles), the orbital period is 23 hours 56 minutes. A GEOS satellite at this altitude, positioned over the equator, will maintain a constant position relative to the Earth's surface (with a 4-minute time lag due to the Earth's rotation around the sun). As few as three satellites orbiting at this height can provide global communications links.

This 'geostationary' or 'synchronous' orbit offers satcoms operators several advantages. For example, ground stations can point continuously at the same spot in the sky, and the satellite's antennae can be very precisely positioned for the best reception and transmission. Satellites in high orbits are less subject to decay (with lifespans of 10-12 years), and are in the Earth's shadow less frequently (satellites are powered by solar cells, and lose power in the dark). Furthermore, the equatorial orbit offers coverage between latitudes 60 degrees north and south, reaching most of the populated world. The disadvantages of geostationary orbit include the greater power required for re-transmission, and the time delay caused by the signal having to travel a

greater distance. This time-lag amounts to between 0.5 and 1 second, depending on the number of satellite links required. While time-lag is not very important in one-way broadcasting, it can be an irritation with two-way voice communications, and is too slow for interactive services.

By the end of the decade, new 'low Earth orbit satellites' (LEOS), such as Motorola's projected Iridium system, should radically cut time-lag, and furthermore will require less powerful transmitters and receivers. Dish sizes may come down to pocket size, and within a few years, portable personal digital assistants (comprising personal computer, modem, telephone, messaging system and so on) should be able to link with any other PDA/personal phone anywhere in the world. For the true technophile, the mobile 'telematic nomad', 'satcoms' could provide a complete communications, news and information system. For the home, satcoms promise new methods of shopping – selecting and downlinking music, video and interactive information and entertainment from the vast databases of the world's media output.

SCRIPT X

An object-oriented scripting language developed by **Kaleida**, the **Apple/IBM** joint multimedia venture. Script X is designed to cope with the increasing proliferation of data types and formats in multimedia applications, and to provide a single data description language to run programmes over an extensive range of hardware and software environments. Available for the **Macintosh**, **Windows**, **MS-DOS** and **OS/2** operating systems, it will run on the **PowerPC** platform.

SCRIPTING

The process of programming using a scripting **language**. Scripting is a 'very high level' (nearly plain English) approach to programming, and offers non-programmers an easy route into developing their own applications or **authoring** hypermedia programmes, and an introduction to thinking 'algorithmically' (or logically) – the necessary precursor to programming in languages such as **Basic**, **Pascal** or **C**.

> HIGH-LEVEL LANGUAGE   > HYPERTALK
> LINGO   > SCRIPT X
> TELESCRIPT

SCROLLING DEVICES

Interface devices, such as scroll bars, that allow the user smoothly to move text and images within a screen **window**, so that a much larger 'virtual' area can easily be contained and viewed within a small window on the monitor screen.

> MACINTOSH

SCSI [SMALL COMPUTER SYSTEMS INTERFACE]

(Pronounced 'scuzzy'.) A high-speed communications interface system, allowing fast data transfer between **personal computers** and external **peripherals** such as **hard disks**, **scanners**, **WORM** drives, etc. SCSI transfers data in parallel (**bits** are sent alongside each other down separate wires, rather than serially down one wire), at a speed determined by the **CPU** of the host computer (and of course the data transmission speed of the external device). Up to six external SCSI devices can be 'daisy-chained' together, but each must have its own electronic ID number or SCSI 'address', which establishes a priority of use (the higher SCSI addresses being given priority).

> PARALLEL INTERFACE   > SERIAL INTERFACE

SCSI-2

A **SCSI** specification that allows data-transfer rates of between 10 megabytes per second and 40 megabytes per second.

SEARCH

In **database** software, the act of looking for an entry, keyword or phrase. Searches may use several keywords strung together and qualified by **Boolean operators** such as 'and', 'or' or 'not'.

SEARCH TIME

The time it takes to process an enquiry and retrieve an item of information from a **database**.

> SEARCH   > SEEK TIME

SEBAS
[SONY ELECTRONIC BOOK AUTHORING SYSTEM]

Authoring software for the development of 'electronic books' for the Sony **Data Discman**. SEBAS consists of a set of software tools for **MS-DOS** computers. The general procedure for authoring electronic books is to prepare the text as an **ASCII** file, mark the text for chapter, paragraph, keyword or other 'searchable' items using **SGML** tools, then employ the SEBAS tools to create indices through which the user can locate these items, and to generate a complete, integrated electronic book data file. This file is then tested using emulator software, and formatted using **ISO** formatter software for mastering onto **CD-ROM**.

SECAM [SEQUENTIAL COULEUR À MÉMOIR]

Sequential colour with memory: a 50 Hz, 625-line broadcast television system developed in France, and used in France, Eastern Europe and some countries in the Middle East and North Africa. The three primary colour signals are sent sequentially, unlike **PAL** and **NTSC**.

> TELEVISION STANDARDS

SECTOR

In electromagnetic disks, and in digital-optical discs such as **CD-i** and **CD-ROM**, the smallest addressable unit of information (the unit that can be 'read from' or 'written to' in a single operation). In CD-i a sector is 2352 bytes long.

> FLOPPY DISK   > HARD DISK

SECTOR ADDRESS

In **CD-i** and **CD-ROM**, the address information that forms part of the sector header, expressed in minutes, seconds and sector number.

SEEK TIME

In a **hard disk**, **CD-ROM** or **laserdisc**, the time taken for the read heads to locate and retrieve the required data from a disk.

> SEARCH TIME

SEGA

A Japanese **videogame** company second only to the market leader **Nintendo**. From Autumn 1990, when they launched their Mega Drive 16-bit system at a street price US$30 lower than Nintendo's Super

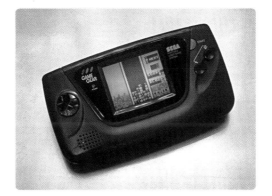

THE SCREEN
cyberspace through the looking-glass

'The screen is where the interpersonal, interactive consciousness of the worldmind is emerging. The screen is where the perceptual wetware groks the informational output of the cyberware. The screen is where minds of tomorrow will mirror themselves, meet each other, enter the universe of information and knowledge. The screen is the window into the info-worlds that are already evolving into the hyperweb conceptualized by Ted Nelson (1974), the Matrix predicted by cyberpunk bard William Gibson (1984).

TIMOTHY LEARY, 1988

The screen is the central technology that spurred interactive computing in the 1960s by creating the possibility of the command-line interface, and which in the 1970s and 1980s gave us the graphical user interface for personal computers. The evolutionary shift from using the screen merely for the display of alphanumerics, to utilizing the power of the cathode-ray tube (CRT) for the display and interactive control of graphics, came with the invention of the Sketchpad by Ivan Sutherland in 1963. Sketchpad enabled users to control a computer by directly drawing on the CRT screen with a light pen. Later, with the development of the digitpad, mouse, the video camera and scanner, the screen became a sophisticated visual interface, providing interactive multimedia programmes with full-colour animation, video, stills and high-resolution text and graphics.

Screens are currently developing in two ways: they are getting big enough and flat enough to substitute for real windows in our living room; and they are becoming much smaller – small enough for us to use in hand-held games consoles, wristwatch computers, active badges and stereo eyephones.

Bigger screens may not just provide us with bigger images. The change could be of a different order, for as screens become large enough to fill our peripheral vision completely, our sense of distance from the image display could dissolve. Imagine a room in which the walls are covered more or less completely with HDTV-style flat screens, the image contents of which could be controlled through a pocket-sized computer. Such 'soft' decor could create the illusion of 'being' anywhere: the North Pole for the Northern Lights, a tropical beach or an orbiting satellite, at the touch of a button.

Small screens are already a feature of eyephones and similar head-mounted displays. These devices provide the 'wrap-round' illusion of presence by being placed right in front of our eyes, with each screen displaying a slightly different (stereoscopic) view of the computer-generated images that we are seeing. Small-screen technologies are vital to the promised revolution in personal simulators, that could provide education, entertainment, sports and sex simulations in the interactive, multimedia, virtual 'telepresence' world of the next century.

NES, Sega has been challenging Nintendo's dominant market position. Sega has both launched the latest technologies ahead of Nintendo, and undercut Nintendo's prices.

Sega also adopted Nintendo's enormously successful strategy of supplying systems that can only play their own proprietary cartridges. Strict control of **software** for the company's own games systems means that the problems of quality control and over-supply (two reasons for the crash of the first-generation videogame market in 1982-3) are solved: both Nintendo and Sega are guaranteed a cut of the profits on each game sold for their respective systems. In 1993, Sega launched the **Mega-CD (CD-ROM** player) in the UK, after very successful sales in Japan. Sega also announced a low-cost **head-mounted display** that will interface with Mega-CD systems.

> **3DO**
> **CD32**

> **CD-I**
> **JAGUAR**

SEGUE

In radio **broadcasting**, the device by means of which two disparate tracks or news items are linked. Sometimes used in **hypermedia** programme design to describe the mode of transition between one user choice and another.

> **AUTHORING**

SEMANTIC (DATA) COMPRESSION

Expression coined by Nicholas Negroponte to describe the extraordinary compression of meaning that human beings can achieve in their gestural, spoken and written language. He gives the example of a wink: 'During a dinner party, you might wink across the table at a close friend. By applying a slightly perverted measure of bandwidth, we can claim that your wink delivers a mere one bit. Yet that bit carries an enormous amount of information; if asked, you might need more than 100,000 bits to explain the content of the message to a stranger. In a real sense, you achieved data compression in excess of 100,000 to one. With that degree of compression, we could send high-definition television (HDTV) over telephone lines.' (Products and Services for Computer Networks', Scientific American, Sept. 1991). In an interview in Stewart Brand's book, The Media Lab: Inventing the Future at MIT, Negroponte talks about the importance of semantic data compression: 'Analogy is a wonderful way to think of semantic data compression: this signal is like that signal, and you got that signal already. It is a dramatic class of bandwidth compression that will start to emerge in computer science.'

> **BANDWIDTH**
> **MEDIA LAB**

> **COMPRESSION**

SENSENET

One of the '**cyberpunk**' terms for the combined **telecommunications** and computer **network**s that are gradually enveloping the planet. Science fiction authors such as John Brunner, Vernor Vinge, Bruce Stirling and William Gibson have envisaged a world where people would have multi-sensory interfaces with such a network, via body **sensor**s or even physical 'cranial implants'. The 'SenseNet' thus becomes a McLuhanesque physical/metaphysical extension of the human sensorium.

> **CYBERSPACE**

SENSOR

Devices for collecting data on physical properties, such as movement, colour, humidity, temperature, noise level, position, etc, and for feeding this data into computer systems. In **virtual reality** systems, sensors are the physical devices – including **head-mounted displays**, wired gloves, suits, force balls, etc – that return positional and attitudinal data.

> **BIOSENSOR**
> **PROJECTED REALITY**

> **DATAGLOVE**
> **TELEMETRY**

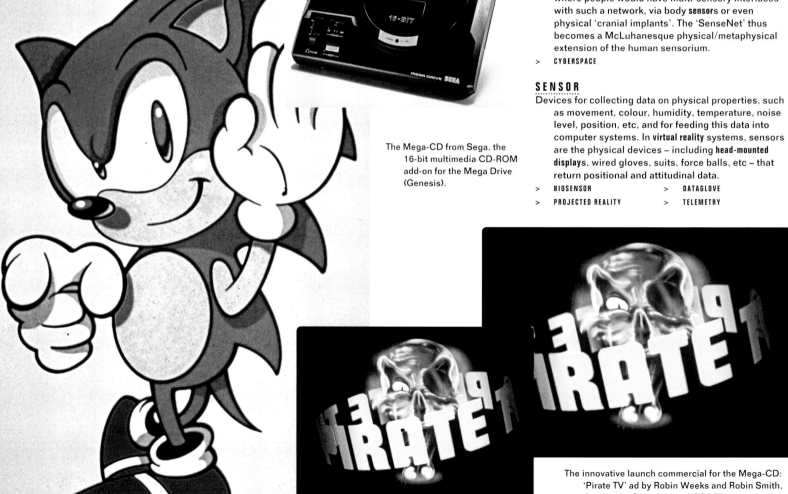

The Mega-CD from Sega, the 16-bit multimedia CD-ROM add-on for the Mega Drive (Genesis).

The innovative launch commercial for the Mega-CD: 'Pirate TV' ad by Robin Weeks and Robin Smith, directed by Steve Lowe of RSA Films.

SENSORAMA

The first experimental multi-sensory 'virtual reality' engine. Invented in the 1950s by the cinematographer Morton Heilig, it used film loops, stereo sound, smells, wind and other effects to create the illusion of motorbiking through downtown Brooklyn. Heilig decided to take the existing Cinerama wide-screen system to its logical conclusion, and develop a projection system for images that would extend to completely fill the viewer's peripheral vision. Despite commercial setbacks with this system, Heilig went on to patent an arcade single-user console system he called 'Sensorama'. The first simulator designed for entertainment, Heilig planned to put Sensorama 'Experience Theatres' in every coin-op arcade in the USA. However, the system was never mass produced and was a mechanical cul-de-sac. It ignored the two most powerful technical developments of the time – television and the computer.

> ARCADE GAMES   > MULTI-SENSORY ENVIRONMENT

SENSORY IMMERSION

> IMMERSIVE VR

SEQUENCE

A unit of a film or video programme. In film and video, a programme is made up of a number of sequences, and each sequence made up of a number of scenes. Scenes can be further broken down into shots, which describe each part of the film or video that is recorded in one continuous run of the camera. All these component parts of a film or video are assembled together to form a narrative chain of events in the eye of the viewer.

> INTERACTIVE MOVIE   > MONTAGE
> NARRATIVE

SEQUENCE EDITOR

Software that allows sequential information to be edited and reordered.

> SEQUENCER

SEQUENCER

Computer software that records the events and gestures of an electronic musical performance (the keys that were played, and the timing and duration of the notes), but not the sounds themselves. Sequencers were the first software applications to exploit the potential of the MIDI protocol, which sends digital data between electronic musical instruments, computers and other equipment. The sequencer can 'play' these instructions back to the original musical instruments, controlling the keyboard, synthesizer or drum machine to create the original 'first generation' sound afresh. By means of a computer running a sequencer program, and a MIDI keyboard synthesizer, drum machine, sampler and tape recorder, a complete sound recording studio can be built on the desktop. Sequencers present musical information as graphics on the monitor screen – either in rectangular blocks, or as musical notation displayed on a time grid. Components can be copied or cut, and pasted into new sequences, as well as edited and processed to alter other MIDI parameters, such as pitch bend and aftertouch.

> CD-MIDI

SERIAL INTERFACE

A method of transferring data from one hardware device to another (for example between a computer and a printer) in a sequence of bits sent one at a time, with all the bits contained in one byte or file transmitted in single stream. The serial interface is one of two main methods of transmitting data to and from computers, the other is the parallel interface.

> SCSI

SERVER

A computer attached to a network of other computers which provides a particular service to those computers; or software that provides a service to other software applications within a single computer. For example, a print server can be software that manages the printing of files from several different applications, or may be a dedicated computer that controls an imagesetter or laserprinter.

SFX (SOUND EFFECTS)

Recorded or synthesized sounds added to a soundtrack to increase dramatic impact. In film and video, 'natural' sounds (wind, rain, a door slamming, etc) are recorded, edited and mixed down to a stereo track containing the main narrative and music. 'Generated' sounds include instrumental, sampled and synthesized effects.

> AUDIO SAMPLING   > DIGITAL AUDIO
> SYNTHESIZER

SGML (STANDARD GENERAL MARKUP LANGUAGE)

A method for marking or 'tagging' text for processing by various software programs (such as typesetting programs), used by the American Association of Publishers and other bodies. 'Tags' are codewords and symbols that are inserted or 'embedded' in the text to identify the type of text material that follows them, such as sub-heads, captions, body text, footnotes etc. They may also be used to identify a keyword, phrase or graphic, so that it can be indexed and searched for by a user in a database program.

> DTP   > ELECTRONIC BOOK
> ELECTRONIC PUBLISHING   > SEBAS
> STRUCTURED QUERY LANGUAGE

SHAREWARE

Copyrighted software that is distributed freely, usually via network bulletin boards (BBS). Shareware is a 'trust' system: users are asked to pay a small fee directly to the author if they find the software useful, and delete it from their system if they do not.

> COPYRIGHT   > PUBLIC DOMAIN SOFTWARE

SHOT

In video, film or photography an image or sequence of images made in one set of exposures through the camera. The smallest unit of the editing process after a single frame. The closest equivalent in hypermedia would be the screen or the card.

> SEQUENCE

SHUTTER GLASSES

Stereo viewing glasses for virtual reality and other 3-d computer-generated images. One of several solutions to the problem of providing low-cost stereo vision for head-mounted displays.

> STEREOSCOPE

SIMULATION

The process of modelling and representing an activity, environment or system on a computer.

> TELEPRESENCE
> • SIMULATION AND FLIGHT SIMULATION PAGE 184

SIMULATION MANAGER

In a virtual reality system, the central, core software that controls the devices and resources necessary to create the 'virtual' environment. Simulation manager software enables the user or programmer to determine the nature of the virtual environment: it controls the various input and output devices, the various 'objects' within the virtual world, and the simulation itself, providing viewpoint, modelling and rendering data. It also provides programming tools and libraries of routines, and a scripting language that calls those routines.

SKETCHPAD

The first interactive, realtime computer graphics system, invented by Ivan Sutherland in 1962, which marked the beginning of computer-aided design (CAD) and laid the groundwork for the new art and science of computer graphics and flight simulation. Sketchpad was a revolutionary system in that for the first time an artist could sit at a display monitor, and using a light pen, create drawings directly on the screen. Drawings could be saved in many different versions, then combined together using copy and paste techniques. The Sketchpad software incorporated object-oriented programming, featured icons, and was driven directly from the screen display. In contrast to the existing time-consuming 'batch processing' method of computer programming, Sketchpad allowed realtime interaction with the computer (a mainframe TX2, one of the first transistorized computers).

> OBJECT-ORIENTED GRAPHICS   > SIMULATION

Ivan Sutherland, founder of Evans & Sutherland.

→ →

SIMULATION AND FLIGHT SIMULATION
modelling reality
in realtime

'Simulation' is the process of modelling and representing the behaviour of a system on a computer. The system is modelled in such a way as to mimic the original as closely as possible, so that when new data is introduced the reactions of the model can be used in a predictive way. Spreadsheets are the most ubiquitous example of computer simulation. Financial systems, such as production budgets or profit and loss accounts, can be modelled in a spreadsheet application, and parameters changed to produce a wide range of forecasts.

An intrinsic part of simulation is the 'visualization' or illustration of the often complex systems being simulated. Visualization brings the power of computer graphics and computer animation to simulator software. Visual images and animations can supplement numerical data output and provide users with an easily comprehended visual display and tools for complex data analysis. It is easier to spot overall patterns of profit and loss by looking at a graphic bar-chart than it is by wading through multiple columns of numbers.

According to Robert Shannon in Systems Simulation: The Art and Science, 'Simulation is the process of designing a model of a real system and conducting experiments with this model for the purpose either of understanding the behavior of the system or of evaluating various strategies for the operation of the system.' Simulation provides one of the most powerful problem-solving tools ever invented. There are two main types of simulation: discrete simulation, which mainly deals with queuing systems (such as customer-flow through supermarket checkouts), and continuous simulation, which models systems that change continuously through time (such as ballistics and flight simulation). Hybrid simulation software, which copes with both sets of problems, is also available.

Simulation techniques are used in hundreds of different fields, including emergency response systems, air-traffic control, aircraft design and ambulance dispatching. A variety of visualization tools – such as graphic diagrams or photo-realistic movies – are available, depending on what computer power is available to the user. For example, realtime military and commercial flight simulators need mainframe computing ability, but you can still enjoy a flight simulation program on your personal computer, even though it uses relatively crude images.

Visual simulations may be programmed for complex chemical or electronic research; for training purposes, as in flight or driving simulators; for entertainment, education, sports or sex in hypermedia or virtual reality (VR) systems, or for design work using computer-aided design (CAD) software. Computer simulations provide solutions to problems that would otherwise be either impossible or impractical to obtain. For example, with a CAD system an architect or interior designer can create three-dimensional photo-realistic models and plot

various views or sequences of views, which simulate walks around or through 'virtual' buildings. In most CAD systems, these animations are recorded frame-by-frame (to videotape, or to a digital animation file format), and replayed at 15-25 frames per second to simulate the 'walkthrough'.

In flight simulators, powerful computers generate these images in realtime, so the image display instantly responds to the trainee pilot's cockpit controls. By recomputing the changing views of the virtual landscape every $1/25$th of a second, and displaying these views on wide-angle screens, the simulator pilot is enfolded in a truly interactive visual environment. Further realism is added by appropriate sound effects, and by the use of hydraulics, which synchronize the physical movement and orientation of the cockpit with the realtime display.

The ability to produce realtime, interactive simulations is a unique attribute of the computer, and one that takes us far beyond the confines of the TV or movie screen. Simulation is set to play an increasingly important role in the development of the information and entertainment media of the next century.

Flight, maritime and space simulations. Evans & Sutherland's Image Generation hardware can produce 24,000 texture-mapped surfaces in every frame of realtime simulation.

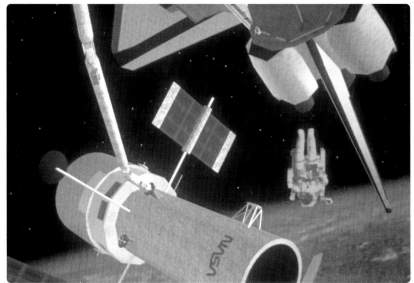

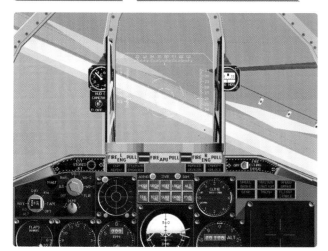

Hughes Rediffusion Simulation: Concept 90 Simulator, a training simulator for Atlanta's Delta Airlines. Hughes also produces a 'leisure simulator', based on the same technology, to provide all kinds of simulation experiences for consumer entertainment in arcades and theme parks.

Namco: 'Air Combat'. Between the desktop PC and the military and corporate flight simulators are the custom-built arcade models. With programs in ROM, arcade consoles like this example from Namco provide highly realistic realtime flight experiences.

A10 Attack: flight simulator for the Mac. 'Fully featured' flight simulators for personal computers cannot offer the resolution of military and commercial simulators – but they are around £1million cheaper.

SMALLTALK

One of the first **object-oriented programming** languages and environments. Developed by Alan Kay's team at **Xerox Parc** in 1972, it was the result of Kay's search for a suitable programming environment for his **Dynabook** computer. While now only used by a few enthusiasts, it has had a considerable influence on current developments in computing. Most major **software** developers now use object-oriented programming methods, employing languages such as C++ which incorporate many ideas from SmallTalk. The **graphical user interface** used in the Apple **Macintosh** and **Microsoft Windows** is directly derived from the SmallTalk programming environment.

SMART CARD

A credit card-sized data storage unit containing a **microprocessor** and several megabytes of memory.

> ATM   > MAGSTRIPE CARD
> PCMCIA
> • SMART CARDS AND MEMORY CARDS THIS PAGE

SMPTE

[SOCIETY OF MOTION PICTURE AND TELEVISION ENGINEERS]

A body that sets **standards** for video and film technologies. The SMPTE **time code** standard is used to synchronize audio and video sequences.

> MIDI

SOFT ACTOR

A computer-generated or computer-rotoscoped anthropomorphic image representing a human actor. Soft actors (also called 'synthespians', 'virtual actors' or 'vactors') can be produced by a variety of **digital** image-processing techniques, including a combination of **digital video**, 3-d modelling, **chromakey** image matting, **texture mapping** and **computer rotoscoping**. Soft actors will increasingly be a feature of movies and television films – initially for crowd scenes (soft actors can easily be replicated and repositioned) and for dynamic sequences that are beyond the scope of physical or filmic special effects, and later for the creation of hybrid characters, the stuff of myth and fantasy literature. Soft actors will also play a key role in **interactive movies**, in **virtual reality** simulations and in **multimedia** videogames.

> COMPUTER ANIMATION   > COMPUTER GRAPHICS

SMART CARDS AND MEMORY CARDS

memories made of silicon

The technology that is changing the face of personal finances, information and entertainment is based on solid-state memory – data stored on a chip. The memory chip is embodied on a cartridge that is about the same size as a credit card. These cartridges come in two main types: the memory card, which just stores data, and the 'smart' card, which has built-in processing power as well as memory.

Portable 'palmtop' and pocket-sized computers, such as Personal Digital Assistants and similar systems, require a much more compact data storage mechanism than the floppy disk or hard disk of their larger desktop cousins. The memory card, with its super-fast access times and storage capacity of several megabytes or more, is the preferred medium. In 1992, memory cards could store up to 16 megabytes, with projected capacities increasing beyond 64 megabytes – even up to a gigabyte by early next century (about one-third more data than a current CD-ROM).

Memory cards contain a memory chip (ROM, EPROM, flash memory or similar device), housed in a plastic container only just thicker than a credit card, with a pin connector to plug into the computer or consumer electronics product. The pins are of different lengths, with power and earth (ground) pins the longest, to ensure that these connections are made before any data is transferred to or from the card.

The first widespread application of memory cards was in the mid-1980s in consumer electronic products, especially videogame consoles. Sega's memory card contained a single ROM chip which, with its 32-pin connector, provided a relatively indestructible method of distributing games software. Around this time, Fujitsu introduced a 38-pin card with an 8 kilobyte EPROM for use with various office machines (as fontcards for laserprinters, number storage for fax machines etc).

In 1989, in order to develop a world standard for pin connectors and card formats, the Personal Computer Memory Card International Association (PCMCIA) was formed by leading electronics and chip manufacturers. During late 1989 and early 1990, the PCMCIA published a 68-pin standard for memory cards, an important milestone in the development of pocket computers. The PCMCIA standard has been adopted by many of the videogame, personal organizer and PDA manufacturers. The IBM Personal Digital System provides a good example of how a basic system can be extended with memory cards.

Smart cards are data storage cards with an onboard microprocessor as well as memory. Smart cards can store several megabytes of data, providing enough memory to record all of the information on your account, and the processing power to record withdrawals and deposits. Smart cards are gradually changing the face of high-street banking, introducing everyone to the idea of 'digital money'.

The smart card's predecessor was the standard magnetic-stripe (magstripe) card. Magstripe cards were introduced in the mid-1960s, but it took about 15 years for them to be accepted by the major credit-card companies. Following this 'product development' period, the magstripe card gradually became the standard transaction method, and from 1980 to 1990 about 1 billion of them went into circulation. If smart cards were to follow the same development cycle, they should be in widespread use by 1996, and by the first decade of the twenty-first century they could be the standard method of transacting personal business.

Smart cards were originally developed in France in the mid-1970s as credit cards for use with the telephone system, to eliminate the cost of collecting coins from payphones. Throughout the 1980s they were refined and tested in many customer trials conducted by credit-card companies and banks. By the late 1980s smart cards were in widespread use in Japan in the form of 'retail premiums': supermarket bonus schemes in which phonecards were given away free with large purchases. Customized cards were even used as wedding gifts. In 1991, the UK discount company Argos announced 'premier points' – a smart card scheme – at Mobil petrol stations. Customers collect credits on a personal smart card every time they buy petrol, and the points are redeemable against goods purchased at any Argos store. The use of smart card technology means that customers do not have to collect stamps or tokens on paper, and they have a highly portable electronic record of their credits.

Smart cards are more reliable and encode more data than magstripes, but they are still relatively expensive and have a shorter battery life. 'Super Smart cards' (tested in the early 1990s in Japan) have three-year batteries and a small keypad to make the card independent of an in-store 'reader'. Smart cards look set to change the face of portable computing and telecommunications technologies, especially in the field of interactive information and entertainment. But the average person will probably first use smart cards in supermarkets and stores as an extended form of cash, giving regular, and large-spending, customers bonus credits or 'shopper points'. The transfer of information could be two-way, with the shopper's card receiving credits and recording debits, while the store card-readers record purchases for input to stock-taking systems, and record the customer's name and address for market research, targeted promotions, and so on.

In due course smart cards look likely to be widely used as general credit cards, and as 'cash' cards in automatic teller machines (which themselves will offer a much wider range of customer-targeted services), and for personal medical records, educational attainments, and similar applications where personal data-storage is necessary.

SOFTWARE DESIGN
the aesthetics of cyberspace

'Software should be simple, hot and deep.'
MOTTO OF ELECTRONIC ARTS

Why simple, hot and deep? Because designing interactive software for the mass market is very different from designing software for the computer-literate PC owner. First of all, consumer interactive software has to be very easy to use (simple). Secondly, it should fully optimize the hardware it is played on (hot), and thirdly, it should offer the user much more than is immediately obvious, encouraging and rewarding exploration (deep).

The art of consumer software design is only some 20 years old. The pioneers were the videogame designers of the early 1970s, people like Nolan Bushnell, Al Alcorn and Ted Dabney (who together designed 'Pong', the very first consumer entertainment software), and Trip Hawkins (the founder of Electronic Arts, and the inspiration behind 3DO). But before the appearance of videogames, much work had already been done on interactive software design, notably by Douglas Engelbart and his team at the Augmentation Research Centre, and by Ivan Sutherland in his Sketchpad project at the University of Utah.

Later in the 1970s Ted Nelson published his famous treatise on interactive computing and software design, Computer Lib-Dream Machines, and Myron Krueger began his exploration of software environments that were responsive to natural gestures. By the early 1980s, Alan Kay and his colleagues at Xerox PARC had developed the WIMP graphical user interface that was to define personal computing in the 1980s and 1990s. But these developments were initially only of import in the relatively small marketplace of personal computing. By 1980, the videogame business was already in its second incarnation and going platinum, returning profits running into billions of dollars. Manufacturers achieved these profits by designing, producing and marketing games that were consistently fulfilling the teenage audience's desire for software that was, in Trip Hawkins' words, 'simple, hot and deep'.

Arcade games like 'Pong' were the first example of computers being used for pure entertainment. Even before computers, arcade games such as pinball machines had demanded a high level of interaction. The new videogames speeded this up, providing interaction with greater frequency, greater range and deeper significance. These were the three main criteria of interactivity identified by another software guru, Brenda Laurel, who started as a videogame designer. In Computers as Theatre (1991), Laurel lists her criteria for assessing interactivity, with 'frequency' meaning how often you interact, 'range' meaning the number of choices you have, and 'significance' meaning how much of what you do really affects the outcome.

Very few videogames designers have been forthcoming about their art. This is partly due to the commercial

Cyan/Broderbund: 'Myst'. One of the coolest of the first generation of 'interactive movies', 'Myst' is a masterpiece of 3-d narrative, combining smooth and seamless authoring with astute use of HyperCard and QuickTime.

Presto Studios: 'The Journeyman Project'. From the same team that developed 'Spaceship Warlock', 'Journeyman' pushes the idea of the interactive graphic novel to its logical conclusion, with high-resolution 3-d graphics pointing the way for future interactive movies.

Realworld: 'Xplora 1 – Peter Gabriel's Secret World'. Setting the standard for 'music plus' multimedia, 'Xplora 1' seamlessly combines video, sound and graphics within an absorbing game environment.

Maxis: 'Sim City 2000'. The ultimate city-simulator, 'Sim City' is a strategy game that is 'simple, hot and deep' – deep enough for users to spend hundreds of hours probing the parameters of civic management and town planning.

pressures of a highly competitive business, partly to the accent on marketing rather than design, and partly to the rather rigid labour structures in the industry. Apart from Brenda Laurel, the other major exception is Trip Hawkins. In an interview in Byte magazine in 1983, Hawkins defined his criteria for successful consumer software: it must be simple. This means easy and quick to get into, with only simple controls at first, gradually adding more complexity as the game progresses. Similarly, the player must have just enough context to start the game, with more context and additional, or subsidiary, goals added later.

According to Hawkins, the software must also be hot. It must optimize the use of the hardware in the delivery system (the microprocessor, memory, colour, sound and video capability of the console or computer). Secondly, it must optimize interactivity (in Laurel's terms 'frequency and range'), and thirdly, (increasingly important in multimedia software) it must optimize the use of component media – the video, animation, simulation, graphics, music and sound that make up the programme.

Finally, software must be deep. It must have depth in terms of the levels of operation and play, with numerous modes and permutations to explore. It must be deep in terms of information, with plenty of relevant data organized in hierarchies for the user to explore, and presented in a variety of media. And software must be deep in terms of the quality and depth of experience it offers. It must fulfil, or even transcend, its initial promise. It should satisfy, surprise, enrich, excite and inspire.

Software designers in the cyberspace entertainments of the 1990s are applying the insights of Laurel and Hawkins to a wide variety of consumer interactive media, including software for arcade virtual reality machines, such as W Industries' Virtuality system. But perhaps the most ambitious to date are the multiple-participant virtual worlds created by Chip Morningstar and F Randall-Farmer of Lucasfilm. Their ground-breaking Habitat project (begun in

1985) was immensely ambitious in scope, with an online system supporting a 'population' of thousands of users in a single, shared cyberspace – a virtual township in which users could 'communicate, play games, go on adventures, fall in love, get married, get divorced, start businesses, found religions, wage wars, protest against them, and experiment with self-government'.

Habitat used simple iconographic comic strip-style visuals, within which users communicated through voice bubbles and text, moving their on-screen characters (or 'avatars') by means of a keyboard or mouse. Morningstar and Farmer sum up their experience of Habitat by stressing that the 'sharedness' of the environment was more important than the display technology used, or the quality of the computer graphics. Multi-user environments such as Habitat (and its latest incarnation Club Caribe) demand ever more skills from designers. As the creators put it:

> We have come to believe that the most significant challenge for cyberspace developers is to come to grips with the problems of world creation and management. Cyberspace architects will benefit from study of the principles of sociology and economics as much as from the principles of computer science.
>
> **MICHAEL BENEDIKT [ED], 'THE LESSONS OF LUCASFILM'S HABITAT', CYBERSPACE: FIRST STEPS, 1992**

Cyberspace and virtual reality are complex, realtime environments. Designing good software for them will require a much greater degree of multi-disciplinary teamwork than that needed for single-user videogames or other consumer software. But cyberspace is by definition a world of multiple users, and bringing it to life will be the work of the software architects of the 1990s.

>> FURTHER READING: HAWKINS 1983; LAUREL 1991; MORNINGSTAR AND RANDALL-FARMER 1992

SOFTWARE

The programming code or data components of a computer system (as opposed to **hardware**). The term is now used to cover the broad range of **digital** and analog media – such as music, films and animation – that form the software of computer-based hardware systems such as **CD-i**, **CD-ROM** and **networks**.

SOFTWARE DESIGN

The process, methods and techniques of designing computer programs and interactive multimedia and hypermedia programmes.

> • SOFTWARE DESIGN PAGE 187

SOLID MODELLING

A **computer graphics** 3-d model that has been rendered with surface shading, light sources, and perhaps **texture mapping**, as opposed to a **wireframe** or vector model which is rendered only in lines.

SONY CORPORATION

One of Japan's leading and most innovative consumer electronics companies. Formed by Akio Morita and Masuru Ibuka in 1947 (as Tokyo Tsushin Kogyo – later changed to Sony), Sony started by making rice cookers and heating pads. In the 1950s, Sony produced the first successful pocket-sized transistor radios and Japan's first reel-to-reel tape recorder, and the 1960s the company rapidly expanded on the back of the television boom. From the early 1960s, with Norio Ohga in charge of Sony's Design Centre, Sony became synonymous with cool, elegantly designed high-tech products. Since 1970, when Sony, JVC and Matsushita launched the U-Matic videotape format and range of video recorders, Sony have released a succession of innovative professional and consumer electronic products, including the phenomenally successful (and much copied) Walkman (1979), the Mavica still-video camera (1981), Betamovie, the first camcorder (1982), **CD-ROM** (with Philips, 1983), the HiVision **HDTV** format, the digital video recorder and 8mm video (1985), the Video Walkman (1988), **DAT** recorders (late 1980s), the **Data Discman** (1990) and the **Mini Disc** recordable CD system (1993).

Sony is committed to continuing their philosophy of fostering the kind of 'one-to-one' relationship between people and machines that they demonstrated with the Walkman, and are exploring this philosophy for children (with the 'My First Sony' range), and for adults (with portable **multimedia** systems extending the Data Discman format). But Sony is not restricting itself to hardware. Like the other major players in the media melting pot of the 1990s, Sony knows the importance of software to the success of its products – not least because of the lesson it learned during the videotape format wars of the 1970s (when Sony's superior Beta technology lost to JVC's VHS because more movies were available on the VHS format). Looking forward to the HDTV and multimedia future, Sony have already bought CBS Records and Columbia Pictures Entertainment Inc, and are developing HDTV tape formats for wide-screen home-view movies that match the resolution of the cinema.

SPATIAL DATA MANAGEMENT SYSTEM (SDMS)

An experimental audiovisual **database** management system developed by the **Architecture Machine Group** (later the Media Lab) at MIT between 1977 and 1979. The system was influenced by the observation that human beings seem to find it easier to remember things if what is being remembered is linked to a spatial location. This idea has a long tradition going back to the memory systems developed in Classical Greece and the Renaissance, which used mental

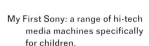

My First Sony: a range of hi-tech media machines specifically for children.

'floor plans' to store parts of a speech or poem and retrieve them by mentally 'walking through' an imaginary building.

The SDMS prototype system utilized large wall-size screen displays on which images, text and graphical **icon**s could be displayed. The user could issue commands through a small touchpad, or use a **joystick** to 'fly through' a two-dimensional representation of the database structure. By 1979, SDMS screen 'objects' could be browsed through and juxtaposed into new relationships by means of gesture (finger pointing, with the hand position-tracked by a sensor) and **natural language** (spoken commands). Pointing at an area of the screen would move a screen cursor to that position, and spoken commands such as 'Put that' (identifying the image with the cursor over it), 'there' (moving the finger/pointer to a new position), would move the image to the place indicated. Icons included a calculator, calendar and telephone, which represented corresponding utility programs.

The spatial data management systems explored by MIT laid the groundwork for future generations of 'memory' machines. Using **virtual reality** techniques, such machines will provide virtual 3-dimensional structures onto which information can be mapped. Large collections of information can be represented using 3-d maps, architectural models or indeed virtual cityscapes. The user will be able to navigate around such collections of data much as in the real world we find our way around a library or a museum. Such 'memory machines' will feature the entire range of database search mechanisms, as well as **hyperlinks**, knowledge trails, and semi-intelligent '**guides**' and '**knowbots**'.

> **BROWSING**   > **MNEMONICS**

SPEECH QUALITY

Digital audio sampled at a low **resolution**, and providing a recording that is better than 'telephone quality' and comparable to AM radio quality. In **CD-i**, this is 'Level C', the fourth level of audio quality, using 4-bit **ADPCM** at a sampling frequency of 18.9 kHz to achieve a **bandwidth** of 8.5 kHz.

> **CD-I DIGITAL AUDIO**   > **SAMPLING RATE**

SPEECH RECOGNITION

(Or 'voice recognition'.) The ability of a computer system to understand and act upon an **input** command spoken in a '**natural language**' such as English. Two main problems have been faced by teams developing speech recognition: how to recognize continuous speech (as opposed to single spoken commands), and how to overcome the wide range of variations in voice, accent, intonation, dialect and so on that exist in any one language. Current speech-recognition software has to be 'trained' to recognize a range of simple spoken commands from a single user. Speech recognition is becoming increasingly important – both in the control of hand-held portable communication/computing systems like **personal digital assistant**s, and in the development of 'hands-off' systems (for instance those for the visually impaired or for situations where visual attention is required elsewhere, such as **in-car information system**s.) In the longer term, speech recognition will also play a major role in the development of automatic translation systems, eventually allowing us to telephone anywhere in the world and converse in our native language.

> **AI**   > **SPEECH SYNTHESIZER**

SPEECH SYNTHESIZER

A device enabling 'voice response' from a computer system to the human user. Typical speech synthesizer **software** for **personal computer**s (such as MacinTalk) takes a text word, interprets the pronunciation by means of an index of phonemes, correlates an appropriate signal via a table of correspondences, and 'pronounces' the word through an audio synthesizer.

> **AUDIO FEEDBACK**   > **INTERACTION**

SPRITE

Small screen image under program or interactive control, widely used in **videogame**s. Sprites are small blocks of **pixels** that can be moved around the screen very quickly and can represent **alphanumeric** characters, cursor shapes, directional arrows or graphics that form part of a user **interface** or videogame animation. Graphic 'animation' components in **Macromedia Director** are also called sprites.

> **CURSOR**

SQL

> **STRUCTURED QUERY LANGUAGE**

STACKWARE

Generic name for interactive programmes developed using Apple's **HyperCard** application. The introduction of HyperCard (which was 'bundled' free with every Macintosh computer for some years) led to the development of a market for **hypermedia** programmes, and a wide variety of commercial stacks, **shareware** and public-domain stacks became available on bulletin boards (**BBS**) and via shareware disks. Apple's decision to launch HyperCard, and to feature it as standard **software** for the Mac, can be seen in retrospect as having precipitated the **interactive multimedia** revolution of the early 1990s.

STANDALONE

Software created in an **authoring** program or similar **software** construction kit that is then configured to run independently of the mother program. **Hypermedia** programmes configured in **SuperCard**, for example, can be made into standalones automatically. The standalone loses the editing features of the mother program, but otherwise retains all the end-user functionality of the original. A 'runtime' version of the mother program's code is embodied within the standalone, and standalones can be run on computers that do not have the mother program installed.

STANDARD

A formally or informally agreed technical specification allowing, for example, equipment from different manufacturers to work together. The fact that any **CD** audio disc can be used in any CD audio player is due to their both having been manufactured using common standards. Similarly, international telephone calls are only possible because of formal international agreements on common standards. The great number of incompatible multimedia computing standards that currently exists is one of the major obstacles to the development of a mass consumer market for **hypermedia** and **interactive multimedia** programmes.

STEP FRAME

In video and **interactive video**, the facility to move through a sequence of video images frame-by-frame (forwards or backwards), either under direct interactive control or automatically. Step frame techniques can be used to help in the analysis of a video live-action sequence, and as a means of viewing a set of elapsed-time images or individual stills in a kind of 'slide show' mode.

> **ELAPSED-TIME RECORDING**

STEREOSCOPE

A device for viewing pairs of images that are taken at slightly different angles and viewed by each eye exclusively, so that the combined image gives an impression of depth and solidity. Stereoscopy techniques play an important role in **head-mounted displays** and viewing devices for **virtual reality**, and have been explored since the 1830s, when Charles Wheatstone produced the first stereoscope for viewing geometric patterns in three dimensions. Stereo cameras utilize either two lenses (spaced at the average **interocular** distance) arranged so as to expose two frames simultaneously, or a prismatic beam-splitting device in front of a single lens, recording two images side-by-side on a single frame. The stereo photographic prints are viewed through a special device that has two eye-pieces, so that when combined the stereo images provide an illusion of 3-d.

Stereo techniques have also been used for moving images, the main systems being anaglyph (red/green or red/violet colour separations, viewed through corresponding filters in front of each eye, and discovered by Louis Ducos du Hauron in 1891) and Polaroid (stereo images filmed and viewed through polarizing filters). Other methods for 3-d cinematography include lenticular systems (projecting two images simultaneously onto a screen that is made up of cylindrical refracting elements or 'ridges', similar to stereo postcards) and time-based, or 'time-multiplexed' systems involving the sequential interleaving of left-eye and right-eye images. Using electronic shutters, each eye is presented with the correct view alternately and sequentially, the sum of the two views creating the 3-d illusion. This latter technique is used in stereo goggles and similar head-mounted displays that use peizoceramic (PLZT) viewing glasses to switch very rapidly between right- and left-eye views, and in the current **LCD** glasses for 3-d simulations and **virtual reality** systems.

> **CONVERGENCE**   > **EYEPHONE**
> **SHUTTER GLASSES**

STILL

A static image, originally a single frame clipped from a motion picture sequence, and now generally used to describe photographs and other images intended to be viewed independently or held on screen for some period of time. A 'stills sequence' is a sequential display of still images, generally with some added linking device such as an audio (music) track or voice-over commentary.

> SHOT   > STILL FRAME

STILL FRAME

A single frame from a motion picture sequence that is displayed repeatedly as a motionless image, a technique used in **interactive video** programmes played from **videodisc**. Still frames can be used to arrest action for dramatic effect, to freeze motion for purposes of analysis, or to provide an image which may serve as a background for a graphical **menu**, a graphic overwrite, voice-over commentary, music, or set of superimposed linking **buttons**.

STILL-FRAME AUDIO

In **interactive video** and **multimedia**, a method of displaying a single image on screen while accompanying audio is played. One of the techniques for producing this effect is to load the image data into **RAM**, while the audio data is read from disc in **realtime**.

STILL-VIDEO CAMERA

A camera that records images electronically rather than optically. Images can be stored as analog video signals on a **floppy disk**, or more commonly, as **digital** signals. Many digital still-video cameras, such as the Dycam, can transfer digital images directly into **personal computers** such as the **Macintosh**, ready for editing, **image processing** or incorporation into **hypermedia** programmes. Another still-frame video camera, the Canon RC-251, records up to 50 images on a two-inch **floppy disk**, and has an imaging system based on a charge-coupled device (**CCD**) with a resolution of 40,000 **pixels**.

> IMAGING SYSTEM

The Logitech Fotoman Plus digital camera produces up to 32 digital image files per session. These are stored in the camera's RAM and can be directly downloaded into a PC or Mac for image processing.

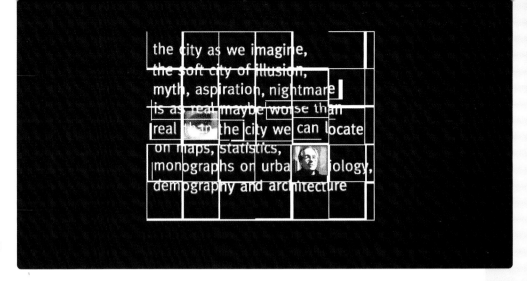

Giles Rollestone: 'DreamCityScape', virtual graphic poetry with an intuitive interface exploring urban film, game and music culture. This kind of freeform authoring, stretching the envelope of GUI design, flourishes in the streetwise environment of the best art and design schools.

THE STREET
testbed for the new media revolution

Alan Kay has remarked that the future of a successful technology is to become mundane. The place technology becomes mundane is on 'the Street'. The Street is the melting pot where consumer culture meets the lifestyle of 'the Edge': the place where the Walkman and the Gameboy thrive alongside the ghetto-blaster and hi-tech trainers; the place where the new cyberspace media will be adopted and adapted to the needs of real people. And like the Edge, the Street is also a metaphor for everyday life – the almost invisible world of inventiveness, creativity and adaptation, where people find their own ways of getting by: the chaotic, messy place where we actually live. It is here that technology and media live or die, flourish or disappear.

Some of the most startlingly inventive uses or misuses of technology take place on the fringes of society, on the Edge and on the Street. For example, the hi-tech products of the pharmaceutical industry are persistantly misused for pleasure by the drugs culture. Drug dealing with a mobile phone, and couriers on mountain bikes, are uses that manufacturers never originally had in mind. Rave promoters also use a whole battery of technology to quickly assemble and disassemble a party for thousands of people.

Jacques Vallee in The Network Revolution (1984) wrote of his experiences with Chip Tango and the Midnight Irregulars, a community of teenage hackers who roamed freely over the global network of computers. 'Teenagers who take orders for dope over the 50 Kbite lines of MEGANET are telling us more about our future than all the final reports, seminars on distributed management, and scholarly symposia published under the aegis of prestigious professional organizations like IEEE, ACM ... For Chip Tango and his friends are humans who have already adapted to the digital society and have bent it to suit their requirements.' In a phrase that could have jumped out of a cyberpunk novel, Chip Tango talks of how, when moving around MEGANET (probably in reality ARPANET) he '"attaches his consciousness" to a particular process'. For Chip Tango and his contemporary equivalents, the world of cyberspace and hypermedia, which most of us view with a mixture of excitement and trepidation, is their playground. A playground as familiar to them as swings, roundabouts and slides are to us.

Of course, the use and misuse of technology and media in the world of drug culture, hackers and the pop underground looks far from mundane when viewed from the respectable reaches of society. But it is the culture that looks exotic and strange. From inside, the technology has become mundane: just another part of everyday life.

The Street is a much wider context than the exotic fringe of the Edge. It is what goes on in homes, workplaces and public meeting places. VHS beat Betamax on the Street, because, although it was a less sophisticated technology, the content available on VHS video tapes was what people wanted. They wanted to be able to watch films at home, at a time convenient to them. There is a whole new medium of communication being developed on the Street through the use of camcorders to record events, to send videos of those events instead of letters, and to provide home-made entertainment. Another example is the culture of the fax, which is developing into a global network for the distribution of jokes, gossip and personal messages.

The Street is more than 'The Market' – as in 'let the market decide' – because people do not simply make choices between one product and another. They invent and improvize uses that are often far from the imaginings of their producers. Those people professionally concerned with hypermedia and cyberspace, who can develop an empathy for the ecology of the Street, are those who are most likely to prosper in the turbulent, destructive, creative times of their passage from the glamorous and new to the mundane.

>> FURTHER READING: VALLEE 1984

STOP-FRAME RECORDING

The film and video technique of recording a live-action sequence by taking a series of **frames**, with each frame separated by a time interval of a few seconds, so that when the final sequence is displayed at motion video rates, the action appears fragmented and speeded-up. Essentially the same process as **elapsed-time recording**, stop-frame can be a powerful dramatic device.

STORAGE CAPACITY

The amount of data that a storage medium can hold, measured in **byte**s.

> CD-ROM   > FLOPPY DISK
> HARD DISK

STORYBOARD

A series of drawings and instructions describing a proposed **audiovisual** presentation, film, **hypermedia** sequence, **animation** or video. Storyboards are used at the **pre-production** or **design stage** to sketch out an entire linear video or film sequence, with pencil or marker visuals to indicate the locations, scenes and camera angles, together with a written description of the action, its duration, lighting, camera movements, music and sound effects, voice-over, and the transitional effects necessary to progress from one scene to another. Storyboards are essentially a shorthand method of describing a video, allowing the director to visualize each scene and creatively to develop his or her ideas before major production expenses are incurred. Storyboards may be prepared from a previously written script or screenplay, but sometimes the script will be written to follow the visual action described in the storyboard.
Crude thumbnail sketches are often sufficient for 'working' storyboards (intended to be supplemented by a verbal description), but for presentation storyboards prepared for a client, professional illustrators specializing in marker visuals are often employed.

> AUTHORING   > COMPUTER ANIMATION

STREET, THE

A metaphor for everyday life and the way that people adapt and use technology in their lives which may be very different from the way that the producers of that technology envisaged.

> • THE STREET PAGE 190

STRING-SEARCHING

In **database** and **hypermedia** programs, the process of searching the database or hypertext by keying in a name, word or phrase (a 'string' of characters). Multiple criteria searches can use Boolean expressions such as 'and', 'or' and 'not' to link several strings together

> BOOLEAN OPERATORS

STRUCTURED QUERY LANGUAGE [SQL]

A **standard** adopted by the American National Standards Institute (ANSI) as a language for interacting with **relational database**s. SQL is not a language to be used directly by the average end-user. SQL commands

SURROGATE TRAVEL
around the world in 80 nanoseconds

The idea of visiting foreign countries with none of the physical discomforts of actual travel has been with us since ancient times. In the last few hundred years, the book has replaced the magic carpet as the most common vehicle for 'surrogate travel'. Guided by an author's textual trail, we suspend disbelief and in the eye of our imagination wander the streets of Shang-hai, Paris or Buenos Aires. The author is our expert guide, drawing our attention to places of interest, and providing the context that enriches and informs our imaginary visit.

Following the development of interactive video systems in the late 1970s, the full power of the computer and television is now available for modern armchair travellers. The first surrogate travel programme was the Movie Map, produced by the Architecture Machine Group (ArchMac) at MIT in 1979. The Movie Map consisted of hundreds of video clips taken from a car driving around the town of Aspen, Colorado. Sequences were shot and edited to include a large number of options for the user to branch left or right at every road junction, and then encoded in analog format on laserdisc. Users controlled the sequence of images, effectively 'travelling' around the town at will. They could also use a 'season knob' to control the season and a 'time knob' to see historical photographs, and were able to call up 'microdocumentaries' on many of the buildings. In 1979, this was a breakthrough in interactive media and a revolutionary glimpse of the future.

The same technique is used now, by recording images to laserdisc or encoding them as full-motion video sequences on CD-ROM. The introduction of video boards in the mid-1980s means that now the controlling buttons can be superimposed on the video imagery, which is displayed on the computer monitor itself rather than on a separate screen. Disc storage space can be optimized by shooting video at low frame rates, or at stop-frame recording speeds of 1-2 frames per second. As the user wanders, apparently freely, around the town or city, items of special historical or cultural interest can be highlighted with buttons that call up extra sequences or stills, along with a voice-over guide, text and architectural drawings.

The idea of surrogate travel has been extended with the creation of 3-d computer models of cities – such as the surreal cityscape created by artist Matt Mullican at the New York Museum of Modern Art in the late 1980s. Using computer animation techniques, Mullican constructed a fantasy environment that alluded to dozens of different architectural and fine-art styles. The same methods can be used in interactive movies and videogames, in which virtual cities can be constructed using the whole gamut of modelling techniques, live action footage, hand-drawn animation and chromakey video.

Given a complete and detailed computer model of a city, the programme producer has a virtual 'movie lot'

High-resolution realtime simulation from Evans & Sutherland, the company that pioneered electronic scene simulation for flight training.

Media Design Interactive: 'London, The Multimedia Tour'. Multimedia brings a range of audio and visual experiences to the interactive exploration of a foreign city.

which can be customized, just as traditional movie lots were. The basic city can be 'dressed' for different periods and different seasons, or modified for entirely different movie genres. Different animations can be generated from this model, deploying the entire range of cinematographic techniques. In other words, a single model can service several games or interactive movies. Because the model is digital it can easily be distorted and transformed into a 'metaphysical' environment: an expressionist set for The Cabinet of Dr Caligari, Piranesi's Carceri or a topological paradox by Escher, for example.

In the near future, we might see surrogate travel programmes that will allow the user a much greater degree of freedom to move around the modelled environment. The processors that drive home teleputers and HDTV systems may well be powerful enough to support highly realistic realtime computer graphics. Further to this, fibre-optic networks may encourage a kind of social 'virtual visiting' between families and friends who could swap home videos with live online voice-overs, or engage in a wedding or other celebration, by means of video-conferencing techniques.

must be embedded within programming languages or 'hidden' inside prompt-driven, **menu-driven**, or **graphical user interface**s.

SUBROUTINE

A self-contained set of **program** instructions that are subsidiary to the main program, and can be called repeatedly from any part of the main program, as and when needed. Subroutines are used to save storage space (the subroutine is written only once, rather than repeated throughout the main program), and to make programming easier and quicker (by utilizing pre-programmed subroutines, or subroutines that form part of the computer's operating software). A collection of subroutines is called a 'library'.

> LANGUAGE   > PROGRAMMING

SUPER-BIT MAPPING (SBM)

An extension of the **Red Book** CD-audio standard that provides a means by which studio digital recordings using 20-bit words can be successfully transformed into 16-bit CDDA without the normal losses in quality, retaining subtle changes in sounds. Super-Bit Mapping was announced by **Sony** in 1993.

> CDDA   > DIGITAL AUDIO

SUPERCARD

A hypermedia **authoring**/software development application from Aldus, for developing, prototyping and creating **standalone** software applications on the **Macintosh**. SuperCard uses a superset of Apple's HyperTalk scripting **language** (called SuperTalk), and is a **software** development package rather then merely an authoring tool. It shares with **HyperCard** an easy-to-use scripting language, and component 'cards' (objects that can contain graphics, images, animations, text, buttons and so forth). Cards are organized into **windows**, which are parts of a SuperCard 'project'. Unlike first-generation HyperCard, SuperCard is an 8-bit (256 colour) program, supporting multiple windows of varying sizes and styles, and giving users access to the complete range of Macintosh interface devices, such as pull-down **menus**, **dialogue box**es and resources. Designed by Bill Appleton (who also programmed Course Builder and World Builder) and developed by Silicon Beach Software, SuperCard was launched in 1989.

SUPERCOMPUTER

A general term used to describe the largest, fastest and most powerful computers, designed to process complex scientific applications, weather forecasting, weapons research and geological exploration, as well as very high resolution **computer graphics**, **computer animation** and **flight simulation**. The first generation of supercomputers were produced by a number of manufacturers, including Cray Research and the Control Data Corporation in the USA, and Hitachi and Fujitsu in Japan.

In the 1990s, supercomputing means parallel processing **(parallelism)**, as opposed to the traditional sequential processing of data. Most supercomputers, like the 'connection machines' made by the US company

Thinking Machines Inc and the GigaCube made by the German firm Parsytec, use a multi-processor architecture designed for parallel processing. Thinking Machines' CM-5 is built by linking tens, hundreds or even thousands of processing units together. Each board contains a powerful SPARC processor and 8-32 megabytes of dynamic **RAM**, and links to other boards by means of three very high speed communications networks for control, data and system diagnostics. Parsytec's GigaCube contains 64 Inmos **transputers**, linked with special routing **microchips** to deliver a **bandwidth** of around one gigabyte per second. Machines like this will be developed to deliver teraflop performance – able to perform one billion (US: one trillion) floating point operations per second. Supercomputers offering this kind of performance are so expensive as to be a major national resource, and in the USA plans are underway to link these resources into a high-speed supercomputing network (**Data Superhighway**s), providing remote access to supercomputers for users all over the country.

Most computer users already enjoy the kind of power in their desktop **personal computers** that would have put the first generation of **mainframe** computers to shame. The latest desktop machines, such as the **RISC**-based **PowerPC**, and even games consoles powered by RISC chips, boast performances that just a generation ago would have been considered to be in the supercomputing league.

SURROGATE TRAVEL

The simulation of a place, such as a town, in a **hypermedia** programme or **virtual reality** system, giving the user a sense of being able freely to explore that environment.

> • SURROGATE TRAVEL PAGE 191

SVHS (SUPER VHS)

A videotape format, launched in 1987, with a higher bandwidth than standard VHS, giving a resolution of 400 lines in contrast to the 260 lines of **VHS**. Tapes and cassettes are the same size as VHS, but while VHS tapes can be played on SVHS equipment, the two formats are not 'backwardly' compatible.

> HI-8   > U-MATIC

SYNCHRONOUS

A process in a computer that is linked to the main clock of the computer. For example, if music and sound are to be precisely synchronized in a **multimedia** programme, the **software** controlling both must use synchronous processes.

SYNCHRONOUS TRANSMISSION

Data transmission method widely used in **telecommunications**. Information is transmitted as a continuous string of characters, preceded and followed by a synchronization (sync) character to align the clocks at the sending and receiving mechanisms. Contrasted with asynchronous transmission where each character is transmitted separately (sandwiched between start and stop **bits**, at rates of up to 2400 bits per second), synchronous

transmission can achieve bit rates of up to 9600 bits per second over a conventional public telephone network.

> NETWORK   > PACKET SWITCHING

SYNTHESIZER

A device for creating and generating sounds and music electronically. The first synthesizer, the MiniMoog, was invented by Robert Moog (in collaboration with the composers Herbert A Deutsch and Walter Carlos) in 1965. Developments in electronic music-making can be traced back to the first electric organ, designed by the Frenchmen Coupleux and Givelet in 1930, and the electromagnetic organ – designed by the famous Laurens Hammond in 1935. That same year Adolph Rickenbacher (working with George Beauchamp, Harry Watson and Paul Barth) designed the Electro Vibrola Spanish Guitar. This was followed in 1947 by the first modern electric guitar designed by Paul Bigsby. The electric guitar business began properly with Leo Fender marketing the Broadcaster in 1948, followed by the Telecaster in 1950. During the early 1950s, experiments in purely synthesized music were carried out at the University of Bonn, and an electronic sound studio was built at a West German radio station. Early synthesized music technology comprised a disparate range of generators and filters, and it was Moog's genius to bring all these components together in one small unit. Walter (now Wendy) Carlos was one of the first to play classical music on a synthesizer. His album Switched On Bach (1968), recorded on a Moog, became a million seller.

> SAMPLING

SYNTHESPIAN

> SOFT ACTOR

SYSOP (SYSTEM OPERATOR)

The person responsible for managing and supervising a **network**.

SYSTEM 7

Operating system software for the Apple **Macintosh** released in 1990, containing many new features, including virtual memory (using spare **hard-disk** space), built-in networking (Personal AppleShare), TrueType font support, and inter-application communication, as well as a host of smaller improvements in the Macintosh interface.

TABLE OF CONTENTS
> TOC

TAG IMAGE FILE FORMAT
> TIFF

TALIGENT
An **Apple/IBM** joint venture to produce an object-oriented **operating system**, which can be used by both companies and licensed to others.
> KALEIDA
> OBJECT-ORIENTED PROGRAMMING
> POWERPC

TAPE STREAMER
An electromagnetic **digital** tape cassette system adopted for data storage. Tape streamers are a cheap storage medium for archiving data, but suffer from slow seek and retrieval times because of their linear, non-random access nature.
> BACKUP   > WMRM
> WORM

TBC
> TIME-BASED CORRECTOR

TELECINE
The system for transferring film to video. A complete telecine installation is called a telecine chain.

TELECOMMUNICATIONS
The transmission and reception of information from point to point, via wire, radio, microwave or satellite.
> SATELLITE COMMUNICATIONS
> • TELECOMS PAGE 195

TELECOMS
> TELECOMMUNICATIONS

TELECONFERENCING
A meeting, discussion or debate conducted over a computer **network**. Until the early 1990s teleconferencing was largely text-based. The more widespread use of **personal computers** with **multimedia** capabilities, and the development of communication channels such as **ISDN**, make the rapid development of multimedia teleconferencing likely to be a feature of the next decade.
> VIDEO CONFERENCING

TELECOTTAGE
A method of bringing information technology to rural areas in a shared local resource. Typically this might comprise **personal computers**, laserprinters, **modems**, **fax** and desktop publishing (**DTP**) facilities. Word processing, **E-mail** and spreadsheet software might also be included.

TELEMATIC NOMAD
Description of a person who takes advantage of portable information and **telecommunications** technology to work 'on the move'. Typically, a telematic nomad might use a **personal digital assistant**, electronic personal organizer, **palmtop** or **laptop** portable computer, and a **modem** and cell-phone to link to **E-mail** or other services, or direct to a central office. The advent of **LEOS** (low Earth orbit satellite) communications will provide global communications coverage at consumer prices.
> GROUPWARE   > TELEWORKING

TELEMETRY
The recording of measurements or other data taken by meters or other instruments at remote sites (for example meteorological data from unmanned weather stations) by automatic transmission to a central computer system.

TELEPRESENCE
A term coined by Marvin Minsky in 1979, to describe the technology of remote-control tools for dealing with nuclear, chemical and fire hazards and emergencies. (He attributes the idea to Robert Heinlein, whose 1940 novel <u>Waldo</u> describes telerobotic control.) Also used to describe the psychological experience resulting from a user's immersion in a **virtual reality** or simulator environment, or from the feeling of 'being in two places at the same time', when controlling and seeing through the 'eyes' of a remote **robot**.

TELEPUTER
Systems that are a hybrid of television and computer – such as proposed **HDTV** systems, or the '**ideal desktop**' envisaged by consumer electronics, telecommunications and computer manufacturers.

TELEROBOTICS
Describes robotic systems that are controlled from a distance.
> ROBOTICS   > TELEPRESENCE

TELESCRIPT
A **scripting** language developed by General Magic, designed to control messaging and **E-mail** for both desktop and portable computers, and for communications devices like **personal digital assistant**s. Telescript serves as a set of messaging **protocol**s in both the portable device (host), and the desktop computer or other on-line device, working with a communications application also developed by General Magic, and called 'Magic CAP' (Communications Application Platform). Designed to allow mobile users freely to communicate with any other Telescript-compatible device, Telescript uses customizable 'software **agents**' that can be programmed to retrieve particular information for

turing machine—

t

→

particular applications (for example, collecting notes on a meeting filed on the office computer and inserting them in your diary on your PDA in time to brief you for the next meeting), and that can actually 'learn' from the user's habits over a period of time. **Apple** will use Telescript for their Newton PDA, and AT&T have adopted it for their EASYMAIL on-line information system. **Sony**, **IBM** and Matsushita also support Telescript.

> CELL-NET

TELETEXT

An information service utilizing spare capacity within the broadcast television signal for the transmission and display of information on adapted television sets. Teletext systems are essentially 'one-way' services: information is broadcast, picked up and stored by decoders in specially adapted television sets, and then retrieved and displayed by the user on demand.

> VIDEOTEX

TELEVISION STANDARDS

National and international standards for television **broadcasting**. There are currently three main standards in use around the world: **NTSC**, **PAL** and **SECAM**, and efforts to resolve a global standard for **HDTV** were still in progress in 1993.

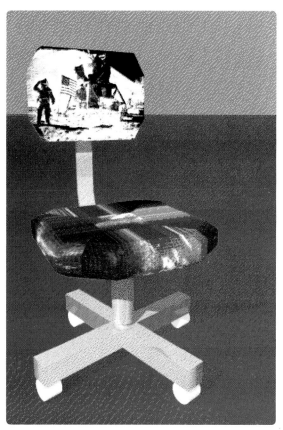

Texture mapping: example by Peakash Patel.

TELEWORKING

(Or 'remote working'.) The facility conferred by modern computing and **telecommunications** technologies that allows people to work from home, and still be in direct contact with a central office. Teleworkers use **personal computers** linked to their central office via a **modem** and telephone network. They can work individually, using appropriate **software** (DTP, programming, word processing etc), or in a team of people, some of whom may also be working from home, using **groupware** software.

TEXTURE MAPPING

A computer graphic rendering technique invented by Ed Catmull at the University of Utah, by which **2-d** graphics and images can be 'mapped' onto 3-d objects and surfaces. Texture maps can be created from any 2-d image, such as a digitized photograph, painting or pattern, or created by using a **software** procedure (a special **program** that generates textures like velvet or leather). Texture mapping is used to create photo-realistic 3-d images without increasing the geometric complexity of the 3-d model. For example, a basic model of a room can be clad with texture maps of wallpaper or images of Persian carpets, and paintings or photographs can be mapped onto rectangular surfaces to provide wall decorations or the views from windows. A variety of texture mapping that provides the illusion of a 3-d surface is called bump mapping.

> COMPUTER GRAPHICS   > RADIOSITY
> RAY TRACING

THREE-DIMENSIONAL COMPUTER GRAPHICS

The use of computers to create virtual 3-d models, and to display images of those models from different viewpoints.

> COMPUTER ANIMATION   > COMPUTER GRAPHICS
> SIMULATION   > VIRTUAL REALITY

TIFF [TAG IMAGE FILE FORMAT]

A widely used graphics **file format** developed jointly by **Microsoft** and Aldus as a format for **DTP** and **scanner** applications.

TILT

In video and film, the action of moving the camera in a vertical arc – in contrast to a '**pan**', in which the camera is swivelled horizontally.

TIME CODE

In video, the frame-by-frame timing information recorded on a spare audio track to facilitate editing. The standard time code is **SMPTE**, which gives each frame a unique number. Time in SMPTE is specified in frames per second, and a SMPTE-to-MIDI converter, which translates the music timing divisions of MTC to the video frame timings of SMPTE, guarantees frame-accurate sound synchronization.

TIME-BASE CORRECTOR

Device that corrects electronic and mechanical errors in a video system (eg a video tape recorder or other non-synchronized source), and produces a stable,

synchronized signal. In **desktop video** suites, time-base correctors are often built in to the VTR or **camcorder** hardware.

TIME-LAPSE RECORDING

> ELAPSED TIME RECORDING

TOC [TABLE OF CONTENTS]

In compact discs, the subcode information that defines the type and number of tracks on the disc. The TOC is incorporated in the Q subcode channel of the lead-in area of all CDs, and includes the sequential number, beginning and end points, track length and type (ie audio or data).

> CDAD   > CD-i
> CD-ROM   > Q CHANNEL

TOKEN RING

A method of controlling the information traffic (or 'packets') sharing a single **channel** on a local area network (**LAN**). The token (a short series of **bits**) circulates continuously, passing from computer to computer around the **network**. When a computer receives the token it is free to transmit one or more packets of information on the network. Other computers have to wait until they receive the token before transmitting. Token-based systems can also broadcast and multicast messages. They operate at speeds of between 4 and 16 megabits per second. Token-passing is used on both ring and **bus network** topologies, defined by ISO 8802/5 and 8802/4.

> NETWORK TOPOLOGY   > PACKET SWITCHING

TOUCH-SENSITIVE SCREEN

(Or 'touchscreen'.) An **interface** technology that allows users to point at the **screen** with their finger and control the computer or **hypermedia** programme that is being displayed. Touchscreen monitors use surface acoustic-wave, infrared or capacitance-sensitive sensors that are superimposed over the screen display. **Menu** options, **icons** and other interface **buttons** are overlaid with 'touch-sensitive' areas, so the user can choose an option directly, with a finger, rather than using a mouse or other pointing device.

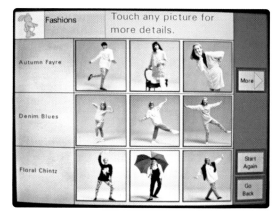

POI system from IBM Nottingham for 'Pride and Joy' shops.

TELECOMS
connecting the global village

BT Madley Exchange: BT are leaders in digital compression techniques that optimize the use of international cable and satellite bandwidth. BT's compression and switching technologies will be core components of future high-band telemedia networks.

Until recently, most people would have described a telecommunications company (or a 'Telco') as one that managed a telephone system. Indeed, this is still an accurate description: telephone traffic or 'voice traffic' makes up about 90 per cent of the average Telco's business. Increasingly, however, it is in the other ten per cent of their business that big profits can be made. Earnings from fixed-line voice traffic are only increasing at the low rate of around five per cent a year, while much larger growth – in the order of 25-35 per cent – is taking place in cellular phones and data traffic. Hybrid personal digital systems (that combine the features of cellular phone and personal organizer) create the possibility of a potentially huge market for data and voice communications services, such as messaging and paging. And non-mobile data traffic includes a range of services such as data networks, leased lines, information systems, and high-bandwidth systems such as B-ISDN.

As telecommunications utilities are deregulated, Telcos face increasing competition from companies who pipe television into the home, or wire services into the office. Consequently, Telcos are increasingly concentrating on this spectrum of non-voice communications. Nynex, one of the US phone companies created when the Bell telephone monopoly AT&T was split up in 1984, predicts that by the year 2000 voice traffic will make up only 60 per cent of its income, the other 40 per cent being made up of the range of services indicated above. The UK telecommunications giant BT (formerly British Telecom) shares the same strategic aims – its recent purchases have included the US data network Tymnet, and 25 per cent of a Japanese data network. In June 1993, BT also announced a global telecommunications partnership with MCI, North America's second largest long-distance telecoms carrier. The logic is clear: it is the 'services' sector that holds the key to future profitability.

These services are based on the central asset of the Telcos, the network of copper and fibre-optic cables that link homes and offices into the global network of the telephone system. This network can be used to deliver services, as well as to carry voice traffic; parts of the network can be leased to private clients (banks and insurance companies, for example), and in addition the Telco can manage private networks for their owners.

Most of the telephone network is made up of twisted-pair copper wires, which have a limited bandwidth compared with the coaxial cables used by cable TV companies. But compression techniques will soon enable copper wire to carry as many as four video channels of reasonable quality, so copper is far from dead. Indeed, all our homes are connected via copper cable to the wider telephone network. However, the latest infrastructure of telecommunications networks uses fibre-optic cables, which have a very high bandwidth, and can carry as many as 500,000 conversations, or 5000 video channels. Fibre currently provides the main arterial system for the Telco, and will be increasingly employed in major international links, such as the Trans-Atlantic fibre cable, opened in 1988.

Home infotainment via the telecoms network appears to be right on our doorstep. Recently introduced products such as the videophone and 'smart' phone, make use of major advances in compression technology. The videophone offers consumers more intimate telephony, while the smart phone combines the ease of use of the telephone with the benefits of computer networking. Smart phones will provide services such as electronic banking, bill-paying, E-mail and personal faxes, and eventually the possibility of more elaborate applications for the home and office such as groupware, remote shopping and distance learning.

In the 1990s we are witnessing an unprecedented convergence of interests as the giant media, electronics, computing and telecommunications companies jockey for position in the race to bring interactive information and entertainment services into the home. By the early years of the new millennium, the telecommunications companies will be more than merely the providers of voice telephony. They will be competing with cable TV to supply video-on-demand, extending their radio and satellite communications services, providing electronic data interchange and video conferencing services for business clients, and operating computer/phone networks.

BT Oswestry Telecommunications Centre: monitoring the world's telecoms traffic via a 'war room'-scale interface into the cybernet.

Touch-sensitive screens are used extensively in **point-of-information** hypermedia systems, and have been introduced in some **laptop** portable computers. The chief advantage of touch-sensitive screens is ease of use, especially for novice users unaccustomed to pointers like the **mouse** or **tracker ball**, but they are relatively expensive to purchase, and screens require regular cleaning.

> GESTURAL INTERFACE

TOUCHSCREEN
> TOUCH-SENSITIVE SCREEN

TOUR
In complex **courseware** or otherwise 'information-rich' **hypermedia** educational or **infotainment** programmes, a predetermined, structured pathway allowing the user to survey the subject matter at a variety of levels of depth, from overviews to detailed specifics. Tours are a form of structured **browsing**, whereby students or casual users can be introduced to the subject matter within an information-based programme at an educational level that best suits them. Hypermedia designers and computer-based training authors have developed several sophisticated ideas for tours, including allowing the user to choose from a variety of 'guides' – subject experts who present tours through particular aspects of the subject matter in a style that users select as being most appropriate for them. In this way, tours allow users to choose from a variety of different perspectives on the same information base.

TRACKER BALL
An **input** device for **personal computers**, **videogame consoles** and other **interactive** systems, consisting of a small, heavy ball housed within a control box. The user rolls his or her hand across the ball to control the position of a screen **cursor**. A tracker ball is in effect an inverted **mouse**.

TRACKING
In computer-aided learning (**CAL**) and **hypermedia**, the recording of the route (or track) that a user takes through a particular information base or **courseware** package. This information is recorded as a set of **frame** addresses that record the user's path, and can also include the amount of time spent 'reading' each frame, or performing the activity embodied in constituent frames of the programme. Tracking is used for navigation (eg the user can 'back-track'), to provide data for an **inference engine**, and to record a student's activities for assessment purposes.
In digital typesetting and page make-up, software, 'tracking' allows the designer to alter the amount of spacing between letters.

> BROWSING   > DISTANCE LEARNING

TRANSISTOR
The switching device using semiconductors created in 1948 by John Bardeen, Walter Brattain and William Shockley of Bell Labs (for which they were awarded the Nobel Prize in 1956). Transistors replaced thermionic valves as switching devices in

computers, and gave birth to the micro-electronics business. The first transistor radios were produced by Sony in 1955.

> INTEGRATED CIRCUIT   > MICROPROCESSOR
> TRANSPUTER

TRANSITION
In film and video, the change from one shot or scene to another. The main transition techniques include the **cut** (first scene is abruptly replaced by the second scene); the **dissolve** (the first scene is faded out while the second scene is faded in) and the **wipe** (the first scene is 'pushed' off the screen by the second scene). Transition effects created digitally are widely used in video **post-production**, on systems such as the **Quantel** Harry digital effects suite. Transition effects are also frequently employed in **multimedia** systems (such as **CD-i**, where several digital transition effects are stored in the system **ROM**), and in desktop video sequencer/editors and authoring systems. Typical digital transition effects include dissolves by **pixels** or by pixel blocks, Venetian blind shutters, 'barn door' opening and closing, zooming in and out, and 'scrolling wipes'.

TRANSPARENCY BIT
In **CD-i**, the **dedicated** bit that controls the overlay transparency in the **cursor** and **RGB** planes.

> ALPHA CHANNEL   > CHROMAKEY
> IMAGE PLANE   > MATTE
> VIDEO GRAPHICS

TRANSPUTER
A **RISC** processor, with its own memory and communication links, developed for parallel processing; often described as a computer-on-a-chip, the transputer represents a major breakthrough in computer technology which has yet to be fully exploited. Designed by Ian Barron of Inmos in 1983,

Caplin Cybernetics: QTIO. Plug-in board with Inmos transputer for MicroVAX.

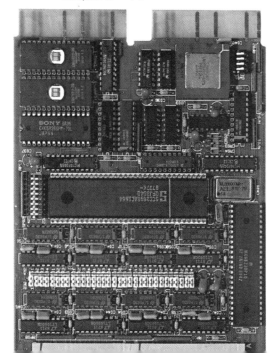

the T800 transputer went into mass production in 1987, delivering a performance 12 times that of the Intel 80386 microprocessor launched just two years earlier. Transputers are used in **supercomputers** such as the Meiko Computing Surface, a scalable personal supercomputer that Intel used to compress **full-motion video** data in its development of **DVI**. ('Scalable' means that the computer can contain just four transputers, or be enlarged to contain many hundreds.) One of the largest Meiko computers is the Edinburgh University Concurrent Supercomputer, which contains 600 transputers, together with an additional 64 Intel i860 microprocessors.

TREATMENT
A term originating in the film industry for a short written description of the style and content of a proposed idea for a movie. Now used for similar documents outlining ideas for **hypermedia** programmes.

> AUTHORING

TREE STRUCTURE
The structure of a **branching** programme schematized as a central sequence (the trunk of an inverted tree) with options represented as branches.

> FLOWCHART

TRICON [THREE-DIMENSIONAL ICON]
An **icon** produced as a 3-d object that is animated and recorded as a sequence of pictures. When clicked with the mouse or other pointing/**input** device, the tricon runs through its short animation, providing positive feedback for the user.

TROJAN HORSE
A term used by **hackers** to describe software written to help transport a computer **virus** from one computer to another. A Trojan Horse is designed to appeal to the user as a 'must have' piece of entertaining **software**. When the software is run, it spreads a virus into the user's system.

TURING MACHINE
An abstract general model for a logical machine, devised by Alan Turing in his 1936 paper 'On Computable Numbers...'. The Turing Machine comprises an infinitely long tape, divided into squares, each of which can be blank or contain a symbol; a **scanner** designed to display only one square at a time and to read, write or erase the contents; and a set of instructions (a **program**). In this machine, only four steps are possible: to move the tape one square to the left or right, alter the symbol in the exposed square, or stop. Turing proposed that the 'program' (the machine's instructions) could be embodied on the same tape as the 'data' (the symbols in the squares). Such a machine would be a 'universal machine' – able to simulate all other computing machines, merely by changing the **software** (the instructions on the tape).

>> FURTHER READING: HODGES 1983

U-MATIC

Three-quarter inch video tape format introduced by **Sony**, JVC and Matsushita in 1970. In the 1970s U-Matic was considered of high enough quality for corporate video programmes, but it was later superseded by U-Matic SP (Superior Performance), now one of the standard professional video formats, alongside Beta SP, **D1** and D2.

> VIDEO FORMATS

UBIQUITOUS CHIP

A very low cost **integrated circuit** chip designed to control an appliance, sense its state and communicate with other **microchip**s or computer-controlled devices via wireless or cable. The brainchild of Mike Markkula (one of the co-founders of **Apple Computer**), whose 'Neuron' chip is made under licence by Motorola and Toshiba, the ubiquitous chip will eventually be cheap enough to use almost anywhere. Markkula's company, Echelon, has developed **network** management products that are capable of maintaining networks with several hundreds – or even thousands – of **node**s. Each node could be a ubiquitous chip, monitoring a device or appliance. In the home, for example, ubiquitous chips open up the possibility of complete home-control systems, where domestic appliances, communications, entertainment media, heating, alarm systems, air conditioning and the like could be controlled by a central **personal computer**. Such systems would offer huge savings in energy and provide a high level of security and convenience. The devices would even be able to 'talk' to each other – for example by automatically turning off the central heating in a room where the window has been left open.

> MICROPROCESSOR   > UBIQUITOUS COMPUTING

Active badge from Olivetti Research Lab, one of a range of 'ubiquitous' devices that could become a feature of tomorrow's corporate personal communications systems.

UBIQUITOUS COMPUTING

The idea that computing power can be integrated within commonplace business items such as name tabs, notepads, chalk boards, notice boards and the like, so that the 'computer' itself becomes invisible and all we are aware of is an enhanced functionality, is emerging from development work at Xerox Palo Alto Research Centre (**Xerox PARC**). Mark Weiser, head of the Computer Science Lab at PARC, writing in <u>Scientific</u> <u>American</u>, uses the example of the electric motor as a technology which is thoroughly ubiquitous, yet almost completely invisible (he points out that the average automobile has 22 electric motors on board). Under Weiser's direction, scientists at PARC are developing a range of products that could become the key components of ubiquitous computing, including the PARC Tab – a 'smart' badge of 70x80mm (2¾ x 3¼ inches) that has three control buttons, audio output, an infrared communications device, and a pen interface. A larger, page-sized pad is driven by two **microprocessor**s, has four megabytes of **RAM**, a paper-white, high-**resolution screen** with a pen **interface**, and a high-speed radio link for networking to other pads and desktop computers. Elsewhere, researchers at Olivetti Labs are developing 'active badges' and similar devices, thet will bring ubiquitous computing to the office.

>> FURTHER READING: WEISER 1991

ULTIMEDIA

The **multimedia** PC system from **IBM**, based on an Intel 80386 **microprocessor**. The system includes a minimum specification of: 4 megabytes of random access memory (**RAM**); a **SCSI** (hardware interface) controller; **CD-ROM** extended architecture (XA) disc drive; 160 megabyte SCSI **hard disk**; **XGA** graphics; CD-quality audio; 2.88 megabyte floppy drive; microphone and internal high-quality speaker; and a front control panel that includes volume control and sockets for microphone and headphones. Ultimedia is IBM's answer to **Microsoft**'s **MPC** (Multimedia PC) specification. Its support for the **CD-ROM XA** format (which enables the system to play discs that share many of the features of **CD-i**, including synchronized audio and visuals) opens up the possibility of Ultimedia machines being able to read Kodak **Photo-CD** and eventually even CD-i discs.

UNIVERSE

In a **virtual reality** system, the entire environment in the current simulation, ie including **sensor**s, **object**s, viewpoints, lights and sounds, etc.

UNIX

A **multi-tasking**, multi-user **operating system** developed in the early 1970s at AT&T's Bell Laboratories. Originally designed for **mini-computer**s with many terminals,

→

UNIX is now the operating system used in most workstations, often with a graphical user interface. It is an extremely powerful operating system giving the experienced user a very high level of control, and for this reason is the preferred development environment for many software engineers.

> POWERPC

USER GROUP

An association of users of particular software or computer systems. Such user groups meet to discuss problems, exchange experiences, tips and hints, and can act as pressure groups on behalf of software consumers.

USER INTERFACE

The means by which the user controls a computer system and/or computer software. The user interface includes the hardware for input and output (such as a mouse, keyboard or monitor screen), and software (such as prompts, menus, windows, icons and so forth. Graphical user interfaces, such as the Macintosh interface and Microsoft Windows, are becoming the dominant user interface for personal computers.

USER LEVEL

In HyperCard, the level of access allowed to the user. Access can be restricted to browsing (being able to view information and sounds without altering them in any way), or may allow various degrees of text editing or input, right up to level 5, which allows full scripting and editing of the stack itself.

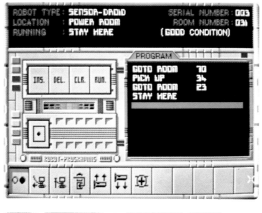

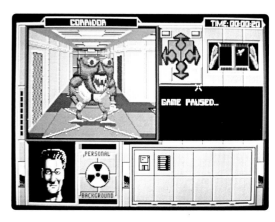

Gremlin Graphics: 'Federation of Free Traders' and 'Space Wrecked'. The videogame led the way in the exploration of 'consumer-friendly' interface design.

Cyan/Broderbund: 'Myst'. Freeform 3-d interfaces literally disappear – in this interactive movie, the user can explore the entire screen image in a quest to discover the narrative secrets embodied in it.

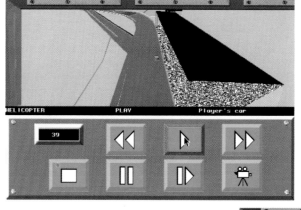

Konami: 'Bill Elliot's Nascar Challenge', a national stock-car racing game. Users can choose the car and set-up, choose the racetrack and 'film' their 500 mile races, either from inside the car or from an overhead virtual helicopter. Nascar is one of America's most popular spectator sports.

VACTOR (VIRTUAL ACTOR)

> SOFT ACTOR

VALIDATION

The testing of a **multimedia** programme before final
debugging and mastering. The term derives from
computer-based training (CBT) where it was used to
describe the user-testing of **courseware** before final
revisions were made.

> AUTHORING

VANISHING-POINT PERSPECTIVE

(Or 'linear perspective' or 'artificial perspective'.) The
system of representing 3-d space on a 2-d plane,
formalized by Leon Baptista Alberti and Filippo
Brunelleschi in Florence in the fifteenth century.
Vanishing-point perspective describes objects or
scenes from a particular (monocular) viewpoint,
and is the perspective system that most closely
replicates the human visual experience, providing
us with a geometrical mechanism for computing
photographically 'realistic' scenes in **three-dimensional
computer graphics**, **CAD** or **virtual reality** applications.

> PERSPECTIVE SYSTEMS

VCR (VIDEOCASSETTE RECORDER)

A device for recording or playing a videocassette;
generally refers to **VHS**, **SVHS** or **Hi-8** consumer or
'prosumer' tape decks. The control that the VCR
brought to people over what, when and how they
watched television, makes it an important precursor
to **hypermedia**.

> VTR

VDP (VIDEO DISPLAY PROCESSOR)

Special VLSI (Very Large Scale Integration) chipset for
the decompression and processing of **realtime** video,
used in Digital Video Interactive (**DVI**).

VECTOR DISPLAY

A display-screen technology in which the images are
made up of straight lines (vectors) rather than the
'raster' (dot) scan of a television or monitor screen.
Vectors are repeatedly redrawn at a rate fast
enough to avoid screen flicker. Vector displays
can incorporate hardware to perform dynamic
functions – such as scaling, perspective
transformations and rotations.

> COMPUTER GRAPHICS

VECTOR GRAPHICS

A rendering technique in 3-d computer **modelling** and **CAD**
in which the model is described by vectors (lines)
and flat planes of colour. Simple vector models (such
as those used in car and flight simulator games can
be manipulated in **realtime** on many **videogame consoles**
and **personal computers**.

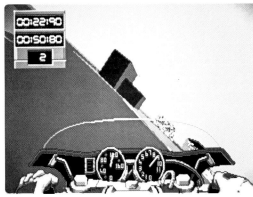

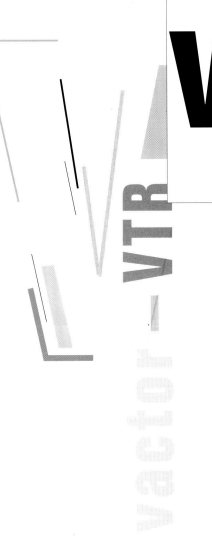

Gremlin Graphics: 'Team Suzuki'.
A racing car sim in vector
graphics – the fast-filled
polygon models are drawn in
vanishing-point perspective
and displayed in realtime.

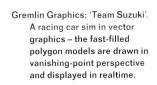

VERTICAL RETRACE PERIOD

In television and video, the time between each vertical field scan of the screen.

> CRT

VGA [VIDEO GRAPHICS ARRAY]

A display standard for computer monitor screens (and also an expansion board that implements the standard) introduced by IBM with its PS/2 range. Graphics modes include 256 colours (or 64 greys) at 320x200 pixels, and 16 colours at 640x480 pixels. Super VGA (SVGA) adds 640x480 and 800x600 displays in 16,256 and 32,768 colours.

> CGA
> EGA
> XGA

VHS [VIDEO HOME SYSTEM]

The domestic half-inch video format developed by JVC, and launched in 1975. VHS is now the dominant home video format, with more then 80 per cent of sales. Super VHS (SVHS) was launched in 1987.

> VIDEO FORMATS

VIDEO BOARD

Expansion boards for personal computers that allow the display of still and motion video images on a computer monitor screen. Video boards come in a variety of specifications, and variously allow users to connect their computers to a video source (VCR, camera or broadcast video); play live video on their screens; digitize ('framegrab') video images (and more recently video sequences); and overlay or superimpose computer-generated text and graphics on the video image. Interactive video, video 'multimedia' presentations, video conferencing, desktop video (DTV) editing and video graphics have all been made possible by video boards.

> INTERACTIVE MULTIMEDIA

VIDEO-CD

A CD-ROM-based digital video format announced by Philips in 1993. Video-CDs will conform to a new White Book CD-ROM standard, and use MPEG data compression to store up to 72 minutes of full-screen full-motion video on a single CD. The introduction of this format means that it is possible to use a single CD drive to play audio discs, multimedia discs, videogame discs, Photo-CD discs and video-CDs.

> CD-i
> CD2X

VIDEO CONFERENCING

The linking together of individuals and groups by means of telecommunications networks and video technology, so that people in remote locations can participate in 'meetings' where one or several or the participators is 'present' in the form of a live video link displayed on video monitors. Video conferencing is now an acceptable cost-effective alternative to actual meetings, especially considering the financial and productivity costs of air travel and hotel accommodation, though set-up costs are still high. A soundproof video conferencing studio is necessary, equipped with lighting, microphones, cameras and monitors. Video and sound signals are sent via the

Olivetti: Pandora networked multimedia for computer workstations.

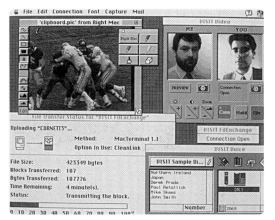

Northern Telecom Europe: VISIT video for personal video conferencing and the intimacy of face-to-face communication.

telephone network, using a video CODEC to encode signals in digital form.

Video conferencing, with stop-motion images and sound, requires at least the 128 kilobytes per second promised by current ISDN standards (112 kilobytes per second in the US), and for rapid refresh-rate video links, a data-transfer rate of 384 kilobytes per second (or higher) is needed. Video compression techniques such as MPEG can reduce the amount of data transmitted, but high-quality video conferencing really requires fibre-optic cabling, and many corporate users have installed their own dedicated optical networks to provide this facility. In 1993 several 'desktop' video conferencing systems were launched for personal computers, linked by LAN or telecommunications networks.

> VIDEOPHONE

VIDEO FOR WINDOWS

A software video file format introduced by Microsoft in beta form in late 1992, as a response to Apple's QuickTime. In early 1993, SuperMac launched their popular VideoSpigot board in a PC version for capturing and compressing Video for Windows files. The VideoSpigot will digitize 30 frames per second at a standard window size of 160x120 pixels, with 15 frames per second at 320x240 pixels. Playback for Video for Windows is not hardware-assisted, and speeds and window sizes depend on the power of the computer's CPU.

> DESKTOP VIDEO
> MICROSOFT WINDOWS

Microsoft's digital video software for Windows, like Apple's QuickTime, is a software-only compression and decompression application.

VIDEO FORMATS

The dominant format for consumer video-cassettes, with over 80 per cent of the market, is VHS (Video Home System), launched by JVC in October 1975 and marketed from 1976. The success of VHS was largely due to the availability of pre-recorded software (ie films), and it was this factor that led to VHS dominating the market over Philips' V2000 and Sony's technically superior 'Betamax' in the 'format wars' of the mid- to late 1970s. Other 'consumer' formats include VHS-C and 8mm (for camcorders); and the higher quality (semi-professional) formats: Super VHS (SVHS) and high-band 8mm (Hi8). Videotapes for broadcast-quality video and corporate video include Sony U-Matic SP, Beta SP, D1 and D2 formats.

VIDEO GRAPHICS

Graphics produced for television or video, generally using a caption generator or digital 'paintbox' system like the Quantel.

>> FURTHER READING: MERRIT 1987
> • VIDEO GRAPHICS PAGE 201

VIDEO GRAPHICS
digital media and electron beams

Video graphics for television and audio-visual presentations are produced by three main technologies: 3-d computer graphics and computer animations produced on mainframes or powerful workstations; animated graphics and digital motion video sequences edited and processed on a system such as the Quantel Paintbox; and titles and captions produced by means of a caption generator. Generally, 3-d computer graphic animations are produced by specialist facilities or production houses, rather than in-house at the TV studio. These sequences are recorded to digital videotape, which can then be edited or mixed with other video sources, stills or graphics using a Paintbox-type system. 3-d video graphic effects can also be produced on the Quantel for example, which can take video images and wrap (texture-map) them on to three-dimensional objects, spin or rotate them in space, or distort them into other shapes. 'Cypher', the caption-generator extension to the Quantel, includes a library of over 1400 digital fonts that have been specially designed for video display (that is, they are anti-aliased, and come in suitable sizes for normal TV viewing).

Video graphics of one form or another make up some 10 per cent of total programming time in broadcast television. For example, each channel has a station ident (an animated logotype identifying the broadcasting company), each programme has a titles and credits sequence, interval graphics, trailers and station announcements. News, current affairs and documentary programmes utilize graphics extensively to display charts, graphs, maps and diagrams. In addition to this are the extensive video graphics used in advertisements, which with much higher budgets per second than other broadcast material, frequently break new ground in the use of computer animation and videographic special effects, such as morphing, motion control and multi-image sequences.

Apart from broadcast television, video graphic techniques are used in audio-visual material for presentations, promotions, training and other commercial applications. Increasingly, video graphics for these applications are generated with desktop video (DTV) systems based on workstations or personal computers. Such systems provide an accessible entry level into video graphics, typically including a video board for digitizing video and stills from tape and camera sources, and sequencing and editing software with a wide variety of digital transition effects. On the Macintosh, DTV systems such as the Avid Media Suite can be used in conjunction with animation software like Macromedia Director and 3-d computer graphics and animations applications such as Infini-D.

With the advent of CD-ROM systems supporting digital full-motion video (FMV), video graphics are coming to play an increasingly important role in the production of interactive multimedia. FMV systems are already in use in coin-op multimedia consoles such as the bar and pub quiz games produced by Ace Coin. A number of major consumer electronics companies announced FMV systems in 1992 and 1993, including Philips with CD-i, Sega with Mega-CD and 3DO with the Interactive Multiplayer. All these systems are designed to plug into standard television sets, and the software they run quite naturally will be assessed against the high production values of broadcast programmes. Designers and producers of interactive FMV software therefore increasingly will strive for television-quality video graphics.

Quantel: Hal. An update of Quantel's popular Harry, Hal is a digital video compositor capable of handling 7½ minutes of broadcast-quality motion video in RAM and offering the user tools for the limitless multilayering of images, for colour correction, colour keying, digital special effects and stereo digital audio. Hal is used for the production of high-quality title sequences, commercials, trailers and promos.

Quantel: Dylan, Quantel's random-access disk-storage technology effectively integrates a range of SCSI disks into one large 'intelligent' array. This allows long sequences of digital video to be stored for 'non-linear' editing.

Quantel: Henry, a concurrent editor for multilayering video with a suite of pen-operated, random-access techniques for fast and flexible digital video editing.

Quantel: Desktop Paintbox. Using the Apple Macintosh computer as a peripheral server, the Desktop Paintbox provides exceptionally fast image-processing.

Quantel: Domino, Quantel's digital film/optical special effects technology. Domino effectively provides film-makers with the same image-manipulation tools that video producers have become used to over the last ten years or so.

Electric Image: 'Global Warming'. The blend of colour keying, large projection screens and set construction produces a dynamic mix of 'hard' and 'soft' images.

The Frame Store: Children's TV titles. The Frame Store combines video and computer-generated images to create composite sequences for a wide range of broadcast television and corporate video programmes.

The Frame Store: manipulating video images and texture mapping them in realtime to computer graphic models provides intricate and spellbinding titles sequences for broadcast television.

English & Pockett: idents for Anglia TV and London Weekend Television, from one of the most innovative videographic design groups in the world. This kind of work is produced on high-end equipment like the Quantel.

VIDEO-ON-DEMAND

In consumer interactive media cable **networks**, a service that offers users the choice of hundreds or even thousands of movies for 'soft rental' viewing at home. A variety of '**video server**' technologies for video-on-demand services were under development in 1993, including data **compression** and multiple-channel broadcasting.

VIDEO SAFE

In video, the 'safe text' area (expressed in **pixel** coordinates) that allows designers to plan screen layouts to account for the anomalies in consumer TV sets, the differences in **aspect ratio** between transmitted image and set, and maladjustment of sets. By limiting important graphic information to the safety area, designers are assured that this information will be visible on all domestic television sets or monitors. A good rule of thumb is to allow a 1 1/10 total screen size 'border' on all sides, so that a 576 line x768 pixel image would have a top and bottom border of 76 lines and left and right border of 57 pixels.

> AUTHORING

VIDEO SERVER

A technology that stores a number of video feature movies either in analog form (ie on **laserdisc** or tape), or in digital **full-motion video** form (on **hard disk**, **WORM**, or **CD-ROM**), to provide a 'video-on-demand' online service for **interactive cable TV** networks. Considerable development work is underway in this area, with the aim of creating video servers that can store thousands of films and potentially serve millions of clients.

VIDEO WALL

A display system comprising a rack of nine or more video monitors connected to either a **laserdisc** or **digital video**/tape-based system and controlled by a computer. Different images can be displayed simultaneously on all screens, or one image can be displayed over two or more screens to give a large 'wall'-size display. Video walls are used extensively in exhibition work, product launches, shop window and **point-of-sale** applications.

> MULTI-IMAGE   > MULTI-SCREEN

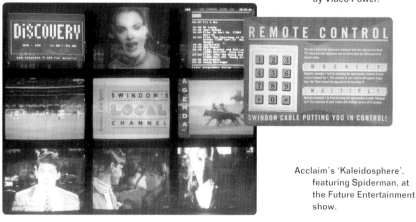

Video Power: 'Hendrisphere' from the 'On The Road Again' tour – a dynamic video wall configuration.

Video Power: part of the 36-screen 'Winter Cyclorama' in the Olympic Museum, Lausanne.

Video walls have proved their effectiveness in exhibition displays, product launches and shop window point of sale. This display for Britain's Swindon Cable is by Video Power.

Acclaim's 'Kaleidosphere', featuring Spiderman, at the Future Entertainment show.

VIDEOGAMES
seminal cyberculture

Videogames, the first consumer interactive media, are a major cultural phenomenon. And because they are aimed at the youth market (8- to 18-year-olds), videogames have become controversial, just as previous youth media, like rock'n'roll and comics, did. Much of the criticism (for instance, that the games are sexist and violent) may be well founded, but what is important here, as Marshall McLuhan recognized with TV, is that it is not the content but the 'medium' that is 'the message'. The content of the games may change, maturing and diversifying as the market grows. Videogames can just as easily mirror the real world and real-world goals (such as educational qualifications), as they do the artificial fantasy worlds of Super Mario and Sonic. As Eugene Provenzo points out in <u>Video Kids: Making Sense of Nintendo</u> (1991), current games 'are pointless relative to most educational, social, and cultural needs. One does not become a professional videogame player.'

The real change that is taking place is in the adoption, on a worldwide scale, of interactive computing itself. Following McLuhan, Philip Meggs has suggested that videogames are the harbinger of a more general cultural trend:

> In general, games often function as society's early warning system: they cushion culture shock by allowing people to prepare for future upheavals. Playing cards printed from woodcuts in late Mediaeval Europe enabled illiterate citizens to learn counting, symbol-recognition, and cognitive skills on the eve of the typographic revolution. In the same sense, the videogame phenomenon acclimated citizens to the impending computer revolution.
>
> PHILIP MEGGS, 'WILL VIDEOGAMES DEVOUR THE WORLD...?', <u>PRINT</u>, VOL XLVI:VI

Videogames, with pointless content or otherwise, illustrate the increasing fascination with controllable, programmable computing machines. Using the mytho-poetic language of the comic strip and the animated cartoon (instead of the structured corporate style of the graphical user interface), and exploiting the power of the narrative, the puzzle and the quest, videogames have proved to be a totally absorbing medium. What is more, in promoting a sense of control over the complex micro-worlds that can be embodied in the cyberspace of the microprocessor, videogames are succeeding in teaching 'computer literacy' to millions more children than lessons in MS-DOS or Basic ever did.

The first computer games originated in North American universities in the 1960s and 1970s. 'Spacewar' was developed in 1961 at the Massachusetts Institute of Technology (MIT) by a student, Steve Russell, working at MIT's Project MAC; and 'Adventure' was invented by two students at Stanford University in the early 1970s. Spacewar was based on E E 'Doc' Smith's 'Lensman' series of science fiction novels, while 'Adventure' was a text-based 'interactive

fiction', featuring a dungeon-like environment, where the player wandered through a series of caves in pursuit of treasure, encountering traps, monsters and puzzles. These mainframe computer games inspired Nolan Bushnell, who was a graduate student at MIT, to develop games that would run on smaller, standalone machines, designed for installation in games arcades.

Bushnell's success with 'Pong' (the table-tennis game) in 1972, his subsequent creation of the computer/games company Atari, and the proliferation of arcade games that followed, primed the market for videogames, computer games written for then newly available micro- or 'personal' computers, and the specialized or 'dedicated' games consoles that followed. By far the most successful games system – the 'Walkman' of videogames – is the Nintendo Gameboy. Within two years of its launch in 1989, the Gameboy was the market leader in hand-held consoles.

Videogames can be classified into several groups: adventure games, puzzle games, featuring animated graphical and logical puzzles; role-playing games (based on board- and map-structured games); racing games (mainly car races); shoot-'em-ups (videogames following the style of arcade games like 'Space Invaders'); strategy games (wargame-type scenarios using extensive graphic maps and isometric scrolling landscapes); sports simulations (covering a wide range of sports from snooker and golf to kick-boxing and sumo wrestling); 'beat-'em-ups; and machine simulations (flight, tank or submarine simulators). In addition, a large number of games are hybrids of these categories, such as Maxis' 'Sim City', or develop hypertext/hypermedia ideas of linked and branching narratives, such as Activision's 'Cosmic Osmo'.

The market for games systems can essentially be split into three: console machines that plug into a television, such as Sega's Mega Drive and Nintendo's Entertainment System and Super NES; PC-based games – including the Commodore Amiga, Atari ST and IBM-compatible games systems; and hand-held systems – predominantly Nintendo's Gameboy and Sega's Game Gear.

The future for videogames looks very exciting. The huge bandwidth of fibre-optic networks promises more virtual reality games – where users can meet the avatars of their friends, and compete in a variety of surreal environments. The application of AI techniques will bring games with artificially intelligent protagonists, or with characters (or objects) that intelligently adapt to the user's game-playing. Generally we will see an increasing use of multimedia, high-resolution video and simulations. The 3DO Interactive Multiplayer, Atari's Jaguar and Sega's Mega-CD point the way here.

Sega: Mega-CD and Mega Drive. The popular Mega Drive (Genesis in the US) has been a major contender in the 16-bit console market. With the addition of the Mega-CD bolt-on, it signalled Sega's introduction into the multimedia games market. In 1994, the two machines were repackaged as the Multi-Mega (CDX in the US).

Atari: Jaguar. Atari's 64-bit machine, designed to compete with the new generation of 32-bit-plus multimedia games engines, is equipped with no less than five microprocessors for ultra-fast high-resolution games.

Tomy: Barcode Battler. This innovative games machine scans product bar codes to determine the player's game points or 'battling data' for their role attributes as 'Warrior' or 'Wizard' players. In the same manner as role-playing games, points are accorded for life duration, and defence and attack expertise.

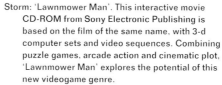

Storm: 'Lawnmower Man'. This interactive movie CD-ROM from Sony Electronic Publishing is based on the film of the same name, with 3-d computer sets and video sequences. Combining puzzle games, arcade action and cinematic plot, 'Lawnmower Man' explores the potential of this new videogame genre.

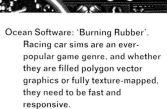

Ocean Software: 'Burning Rubber'. Racing car sims are an ever-popular game genre, and whether they are filled polygon vector graphics or fully texture-mapped, they need to be fast and responsive.

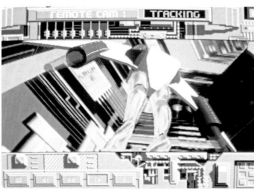

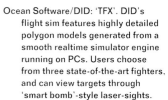

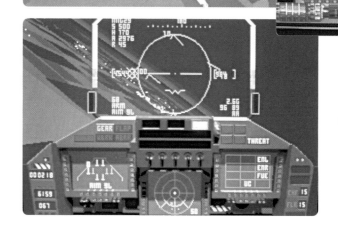

Ocean Software/DID: 'TFX'. DID's flight sim features highly detailed polygon models generated from a smooth realtime simulator engine running on PCs. Users choose from three state-of-the-art fighters, and can view targets through 'smart bomb'-style laser-sights.

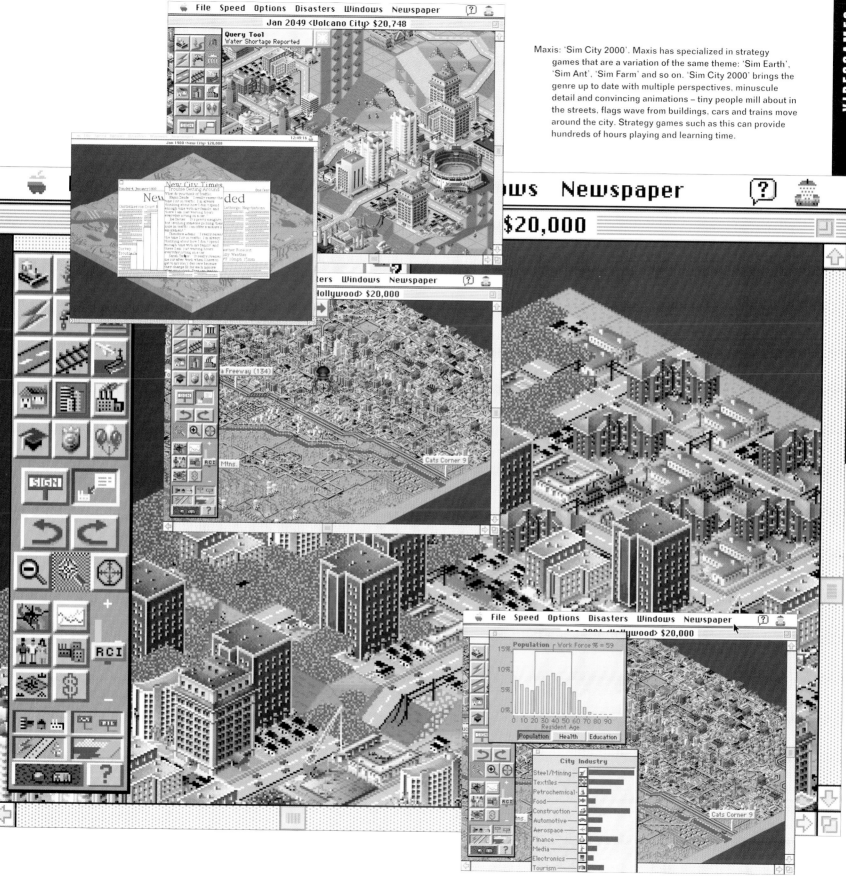

Maxis: 'Sim City 2000'. Maxis has specialized in strategy
games that are a variation of the same theme: 'Sim Earth',
'Sim Ant', 'Sim Farm' and so on. 'Sim City 2000' brings the
genre up to date with multiple perspectives, minuscule
detail and convincing animations – tiny people mill about in
the streets, flags wave from buildings, cars and trains move
around the city. Strategy games such as this can provide
hundreds of hours playing and learning time.

VIDEODISC

Discs that store analog video signals. Although there have been several electromagnetic videodisc formats, the dominant technology is now optical (where the video signal is read from the disc by means of a laser), such as Philips' **LaserVision** system. Laserdiscs are available in two 300mm (12-inch) formats. **CAV** (constant angular velocity) discs store one video **frame** per track, and can store a maximum of 54,000 frames per disc. CAV discs are used for **interactive video** applications, and as well as the normal play/fast forward/reverse and frame-by-frame stepping, they offer rock-steady stills, and 'instant jump' facilities between frames within 200 or so tracks of each other. **CLV** (constant linear velocity) discs are used for linear movies and video programmes, and offer around 60 minutes of motion video per side.

> LASERVISION

VIDEOGAME

A game produced for a coin-op arcade system, a **personal computer** or for a dedicated console, hand-held games system, such as those produced by **Nintendo** and **Sega**.

> ARCADE GAMES   > • VIDEOGAMES PAGE 205

VIDEOPHONE

A telephone that allows users to view each other on small video screens. In the early 1970s, Bell Laboratories were the first to develop and market a videophone, called the 'Picturephone'. Early videophones like this were too expensive, and showed very poor quality slow **refresh-rate** video. With the advent of **digital** telecommunications, new standards of digital video **compression** and data transmission, and the falling costs of camera and screen technologies, the latest generation of videophones offers clear video images with relatively smooth motion. For example, the AT&T videophone uses a compression **chip** which compresses and decompresses images using

Relate 2000 Videophone. This is BT's first commercial videophone, using compression techniques to allow two-way voice and video links over standard twisted-pair cables.

discrete cosine transform techniques. With this chip, images can be compressed using either **JPEG**, **MPEG** or CCITT H.261 (videophone) standards. The AT&T videophone transmits colour images at ten **frame**s per second over standard telephone lines. Videophone technology for the home will doubtless follow the lead of private corporate videophone networks, and expand to include video answerphone facilities and possibly small-scale or 'desktop' **video conferencing** and other on-line services. AT&Ts Smart Phone, for example, includes a **touch-sensitive screen** and programmable keys for functions like checking a bank balance; systems also exist for 'videophones' that appear in a window on the screen of a **personal computer**, and use **ISDN** lines, allowing viewers in different locations to view the same images and data while seeing each other in video windows.

> GROUPWARE

VIDEOTEX

A two-way information service connecting a computer system to specially adapted television sets or **personal computers** via normal telephone lines. Originally called 'viewdata', videotex was invented by a British Telecom (BT) engineer, Sam Fedida, in 1970. BT's Prestel service provides travel and transport information, and BT leases space in the Prestel **database** to other information providers to distribute corporate and product information to clients and dealers.

> TELETEXT

VIRTUAL

In computing, refers to a **simulation** of a process or device. For example, the term 'virtual memory' refers to a technique whereby a **hard disk** can simulate the behaviour of **RAM**, albeit at a considerably slower speed. Using virtual memory a computer with, say, 2 megabytes of RAM and a hard disk with sufficient free space could run a program requiring 8 megabytes of RAM. The term '**virtual reality**' is used in this sense, referring to a simulation of reality rather than something very nearly real.

VIRTUAL PRIVATE NETWORK [VPN]

Network facilities that have all the functions and facilities of a private network, but that exist as circuits leased from a public telephone **telecommunications** utility or company (telco). The VPN, which can link a client's offices in several locations – even internationally – is maintained by the telco. The client pays the telco for the maintenance of the network, and enjoys the advantage of telco services, network flexibility, and much lower costs relative to creating and operating their own network. The telcos benefit by increasing market share, reducing network costs, and supplying a variety of information, **EDI**, **E-mail**, video **conferencing** and other services.

VIRTUAL REALITY [VR]

The simulation of reality through **realtime** 3-d modelling, position-tracking and stereo audio/video techniques. VR systems break away from the convention of the user/screen **interface**, and surround

users with a 'realistic' computer-generated environment. Users can directly participate in simulations of processes at any scale, calling up linked **hypermedia** information and explanation when they need it.

> ARTIFICIAL REALITY   > AUGMENTED REALITY
> IMMERSIVE VR;   > PROJECTED REALITY
> • VIRTUAL REALITY PAGE 209

VIRTUAL SEX

A concept for a **virtual reality** system where, through the use of **biosensors** and bio-stimulators, an individual can have a sexual encounter with a simulated being that exists only within the system, or with one or more other individuals acting through simulated bodies of their choice.

> • VIRTUAL SEX PAGE 212

VIRTUAL THEME PARK

A **network** of **virtual reality** consoles or systems that offer a variety of simulations, including multi-participant games. Unlike their physical namesakes, virtual theme parks do not require acres of real estate, but instead provide their users with intense 'hands-on' **interactive** experiences in the private space of a VR console. For example, the 'BattleTech' Centres run by Virtual World Entertainments accommodate participants in dozens of 3-metre (10-foot) long control pods known as 'BattleMechs'. The BattleMech cab is modelled on a military tank simulator, and is represented as being the control unit for a giant robot warrior. It contains a control panel, interface screen and a view screen showing the simulated world outside the cab. Players compete in teams, and are able to communicate with each other to coordinate tactics. Other virtual theme park games include racing-car simulators, flight and sports simulators, and super 3-d **videogames** played in a variety of virtual worlds.

> ARCADE GAMES

VIRTUALITY

A **virtual reality** 'leisure system' from W Industries. Virtuality systems are available in a variety of different configurations for arcade, night club, bar and theme park installations. Systems are driven by a powerful custom-designed high-performance computer, 'Expality'. This multi-processor design provides full-colour stereoscopic **realtime animation**s in response to the user's movements, and CD-quality multi-channel sound. Both **CD-ROM** and **hard disk** are used for mass storage of **databases** and **digital audio** data, and the multiple TMS 34020 and MC68030 processors draw 30,000 transformed, clipped, and shaded **polygons** per second onto a high-**resolution** 1,024x768 pixel screen.

The user interfaces via a **head-mounted display**, the '**Visette**', and different **consoles** allow sit-down or stand-up virtual participation. Launch software included: VTOL, a Harrier jump-jet simulator; Total Destruction, a stock-car racing simulator; Exorex, a 'robot-warrior-versus-cyberdroids' virtual battle; and Dactyl Nightmare, a 'cyberspace entertainment experience'.

VIRTUAL REALITY
cocooned in realtime

Virtual reality (VR) is a revolutionary technology that attempts to promote a complete suspension of disbelief in a computer simulated experience. The user's dominant senses (visual and aural) are fed with high-resolution images and stereophonic sounds derived from a computer model. The screen image is inescapable as it is displayed right in front of the user's eyes, in stereo, and moves with the user. Each movement produces a new set of images, recomputed and displayed in near-realtime, of the point of view which would be seen if the spectator was actually within the computer-generated model. Realistic sounds are also used, with intensity and directional cues employed to persuade users that they are in a credible environment. Participants can also use special gloves to manipulate virtual objects, leading them to adopt a kind of primitive sign language as they move through cyberspace.

Virtual reality systems vary in levels of sophistication from desktop VR, based on a personal computer equipped with add-on processors which display the virtual environment on a standard monitor, to fully 'immersive VR' systems, where visors and other devices give the user the illusion of being 'within' the virtual world. Between these two extremes are 'translucent' visor systems and cantilever systems such as the boom display system developed by the Fake Space Labs in Palo Alto, California. By taking the weight of monitors on a cantilever boom, the participant can easily manipulate the high-resolution stereo monitor.

There are four main components of a VR system. The most visible components are the stereo-optical visors and position-sensing gloves, which are sometimes called 'effectors'. Other effector technologies include the 3-d mouse, wands, suits, cantilever devices, and biosensor bracelets and headbands. These effector technologies provide position-sensing, orientation, biofeedback sensors and audio-visual feedback from the VR system. Effectors interface with the 'reality engine' – the heart of the VR system. This comprises the computer system and the sound and video processors that supply the effectors with the sensory data – stereo realtime visuals, stereo positional audio and force feedback. The hardware system is driven by the 'application': software that defines the structure and context of the simulation, and determines the rules that govern interaction between the user and the objects in the virtual world. The application draws on what has been called 'geometry', the fourth component. This is the stored data that describes the three-dimensional computer graphics structures of the virtual world and the objects within it.

In the early 1990s VR entertainment systems were running videogames, role-playing adventure games and flight and sports simulations. VR systems were also under development or already in use in a variety of other fields, including scientific research, human factors design, conferencing, education and information retrieval. Combined with interactive

multimedia or hypermedia informational systems, high-definition television and high-bandwidth telecommunications networks, VR promises to develop into the most powerful medium of communication and education/entertainment simulation yet devised. Virtual reality looks set to help define the shape of future media, whether through total immersion in virtual worlds, or by means of holographic techniques that will bring elements of surreality to our 'real' world.

>> FURTHER READING: BENEDIKT 1992; HELSEL AND PARIS-ROTH 1991; PIMENTEL AND TEIXEIRA 1993; RHEINGOLD 1991

Virtuality: Virtuality Standup Console. VR has become a successful arcade attraction, with a range of coin-op role-playing games. Virtuality (formerly W Industries) leads the way with polished consumer entertainment applications of VR.

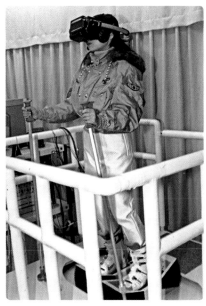

NEC: VR Ski system. Protective rails are necessary to protect users from harm when they are transported into a surrogate mountain scape.

Division CDK: Cyberspace Developer Kit.

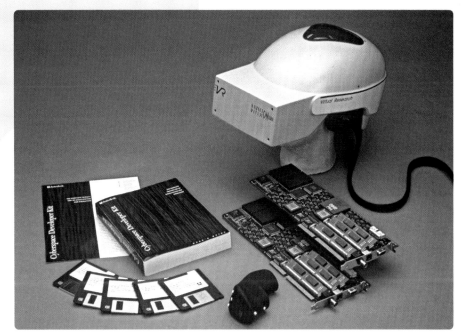

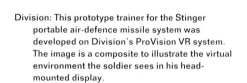

Division: This prototype trainer for the Stinger portable air-defence missile system was developed on Division's ProVision VR system. The image is a composite to illustrate the virtual environment the soldier sees in his head-mounted display.

Division: one of the leaders in VR hardware, Division manufactures head-mounted displays and virtual world generators for a variety of training, scientific, simulation and leisure applications.

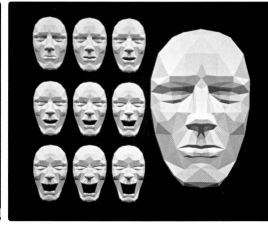

Dimension International: desktop VR applications allow PC owners to explore the virtual world of the microchip. Users can customize virtual actors or 'synthespians' to inhabit cyberspace.

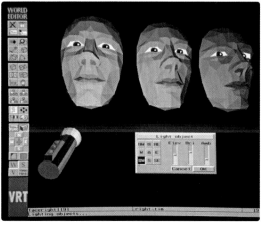

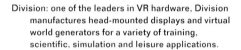

ANYONE
CAN BE A STAR

INTERACTIVE
MUSEUM EXHIBITS

TORONTO

317 Adelaide Street West - Suite 302
Toronto Ontario Canada
M5V 1P9
TEL: (416) 340-9290

The Vivid Group: 'Mandala'™ projected reality system. These images of an interactive 'virtual world technology' from the Canadian virtual artists The Vivid Group were grabbed from their demonstration video. 'Mandala' VR participants need no special head-gear – they interact in a freeform style reminiscent of Myron Krueger's 'Videoplace' experimental environments.

This exciting development opens up the possibility of new virtual entertainments combining dance, athletics, Tai-Chi and other physical sports, such as archery and fencing.

PARIS   TORONTO

INTERACT
BETWEEN CITIES

SAVES   MISSES

TOTAL
SIMULATION

VIRTUAL-TOUCH

VIRTUAL
WORLDS

POWER   55

NICK ARCADE

INTERACTIVE
GAME SHOWS

INSTANTLY

MOVE
TO THE BEAT

TO YOUR
MOVES

ENTER
WITH MA

SIGHT

YOU CONTROL

THE VIRTUA
WORLD REAC

YOU ARE
THE ARTIST

DRAW
A PICTURE

NO PHYSICAL
RESTRAINTS

NO TECHNICAL
KNOWLEDGE

DREAM UP
NEW REALITIES

VIRTUAL SEX

soft core and soft machines

The first 'virtual sex' experiment was probably a US government-funded project called 'Intersex', carried out at the University of Tokyo in the 1960s. The aim of the Intersex project was to develop a system that would enable US military personnel stationed abroad to enjoy a simulated sexual experience without the risk of venereal disease.

The project involved taping the responses of female volunteers (on video and audio tape), and using these as audio-visual stimulation for the male subject. Considerable work was done on the use of pheronomes (the natural scents produced during sexual activity), and sensory stimulants such as coloured lights, vibrators and artificial perfumes. The implications of Intersex were that anyone could have their sexual responses taped and experienced remotely by any suitably equipped member of the opposite sex. Funding was withdrawn when the government realized the process could severely threaten the institution of marriage, and encourage virtual promiscuity on a large scale.

More recently, with the advent of computer networks and virtual reality systems, Ted Nelson's concept of 'teledildonics' has been revived. Nelson coined the term in 1974, to describe a system patented by How Wachspress, which was capable of converting audio signals into tactile sensations. VR enthusiasts use the term to describe the possibility of special 'feelie' suits, that would be wired with tactile sensors (yet to be invented), geared to enable you to touch virtual objects or bodies and receive a realistic impression of their surface textures. Combined with remotely captured or generated images and sounds relevant to the virtual partner, such 'teledildonic' suits could provide a sort of surrogate sexual experience.

Partners very distant from each other could connect their teledildonic apparatus via computer or high-band ISDN networks, and enjoy the experience of virtual sex with no fear of disease, and without necessarily feeling the need for any further social commitment. It is worth mentioning, however, that even without the simulated experience of virtual sex, couples that have never met each other physically actually have 'married' as a result of relationships formed over computer networks. In one case, the wedding ceremony and reception were attended electronically by stay-at-home guests from all over North America.

While sensory-immersive virtual sex is still a thing of the future, there has been considerable concern in the UK and USA over the availability of digital pornography on network bulletin-board systems. Young children have access to these via their home computers and modem connections. They can download pornographic stills and animation clips of material that is otherwise only available in 'adult' magazine shops and back-street video stores. It is difficult to monitor this activity, and police and other regulatory forces are making considerable efforts to educate parents and teachers about the dangers of unsupervised network access. Soft- (and not so soft) core pornography is already widely available in disc form, including some videogame-style programmes such as 'Mac Playmate' and 'Virtual Valerie' from designer Mike Saenz.

Whatever one's personal feelings about virtual sex and digital pornography, the techniques that make such products possible are the subject of considerable research and development. Biofeedback technologies such as those being developed at Stanford University (where researchers are developing a system called 'Biomuse' that uses electrical signals from the brain and muscles to control a music synthesizer) and Ultramind's 'Relax Plus' (in which users control computer software by means of alphawaves), in combination with Immersive VR techniques, may result in the kind of sexual pleasure-machine enjoyed by the comic-strip heroine Barbarella in the famous Roger Vadim film.

>> FURTHER READING: RHEINGOLD 1991

Reactor: 'Virtual Valerie 2'. Chicago-based software house Reactor has been in the forefront of soft-core multimedia role-playing games. 'Virtual Valerie' is a bestselling title on Apple CD-ROM.

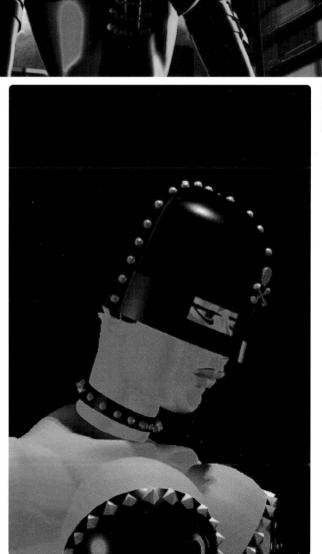

Reactor: 'Donna Matrix'. A 3-d modelled dominatrix-style synthespian from Reactor Software. Computer 'actors' like this will become increasingly realistic, and will soon be generated in realtime VR systems.

Reactor: 'Virtual Valerie: The Director's Cut', a more intimate version of the successful CD-ROM title.

'Future Sex' magazine: the very latest in exotic erotica. This issue is devoted to cybersex, and features a wide range of teledildonic apparatus.

VIRUS

A computer **program**, modelled on biological viruses, that replicates itself by attaching itself to other computer programs, and demonstrates its presence either harmlessly or in a damaging way. Viruses are activated under conditions specified by the author of the virus – on a particular time or date, or when a particular command is enacted – and can cause catastrophic damage, interfering with, erasing or corrupting data files. A virus is usually contracted via **floppy disk** or through **modem** connections. Special anti-virus or 'vaccine' **software** can be installed to check for the presence of a virus and destroy it. The first viruses on personal computers were probably on the Apple II in the early 1980s, but it was not until 1988 that they became a generally recognized problem, featured on the covers of magazines such as Time and Business Week. In November of that year, Robert Tappan Morris, a student at Cornell University, introduced a virus into the **Internet** network. His virus was intended as a harmless experiment, designed to exploit several weaknesses in the **UNIX** source code, but the virus was itself flawed and a programming error resulted in the virus propagating much more rapidly than he had intended. A large part of the Internet was infected, causing several large campus and research lab **LANs** to close down, and the issue of computer viruses was elevated to one of considerable national and international importance.

> HACKER   > TROJAN HORSE
>> FURTHER READING: HAFNER AND MARKOFF 1991; STOLL 1989

VIS [VIDEO INFORMATION SYSTEM]

A **CD-ROM**-based interactive home entertainment system from Tandy, launched in the US in 1993. Powered by an Intel 80286 **microprocessor**, and comprising a CD-ROM drive and infrared hand-held remote controller, the 16-bit VIS plugs into a standard television monitor. The VIS runs under Modular Windows – a cut-down version of the popular personal computer interface that requires much less **RAM** – in 512 kilobytes of RAM. Special chips provide extra support for video colour and **resolution**. VIS is one of a number of competing interactive media systems, including Philips' **CD-i**, the **3DO** Interactive Multiplayer, Atari's **Jaguar**, and Commodore's **CDTV**.

VISETTE

An audio/visual **interface** visor used by W Industries' '**Virtuality**' arcade **virtual reality** consoles. Visette features a stereo viewing system using colour **LCD** screens coupled with 'infinity' optics, CD-quality stereo audio, a microphone, and a position-tracking **sensor** that also monitors the angle at which the player holds his or her head.

> EYEPHONE   > HEAD-MOUNTED DISPLAY

VOCODER

An audio device for breaking up speech into energy bands that can be processed independently. Used for special sound effects, **digital audio** techniques can now be used to produce similar effects.

VOICE RECOGNITION

> SPEECH RECOGNITION

VR

> VIRTUAL REALITY

VTR [VIDEO TAPE RECORDER]

A device for recording or playing a videotape, either reel-to-reel or in a cassette. Generally refers to professional tape decks.

> VCR

Tandy VIS system.

WALK-THROUGH

A term used to describe computer **animation**s created to show how a building or other architectural scheme will look from the viewpoint of someone walking through it. Also refers to **realtime** systems that display scenes from user-selected points in a computer architectural model.

> SURROGATE TRAVEL

WAN (WIDE-AREA NETWORK)

A computer **network** that interconnects terminals at many sites over very large (national and international) distances, using existing telephone networks. An early example of a WAN was the Advanced Research Projects Agency Network (**ARPAnet**), set up by the US Defense Department in 1969. ARPAnet used mini-mainframe computers as 'packet switches', which were connected by dedicated telephone lines capable of carrying data at 50 kilobits per second. ARPAnet linked scientists, researchers and academics in universities and research centres throughout the US, providing an electronic forum by which **databases**, **software** and **E-mail** could be exchanged. ARPAnet grew into **Internet**.

The development of broadband integrated services digital network (**B-ISDN**) promises to extend wide-area networking to encompass millions of international users and provide voice, video and data communications through the same connections. Such integrated networks would open the possibility of video parties (as well as more formal **video conferencing**), **remote shopping** and **surrogate travel**, and provide the distribution medium for all kinds of entertainment and education software, including video, music, books, games and **interactive multimedia** entertainments. B-ISDN networks could eventually link wireless local area networks (**LANs**), allowing '**cell-net**' multimedia communications between mobile individuals; realtime electronic newsgathering (**ENG**); personal emergency services, and the like.

> DATA SUPERHIGHWAY   > PACKET SWITCHING

WAVEFORM

The graphical representation of a sound in terms of air-pressure over time, or audio signals as voltage over time. Sound digitizing or 'sampling' applications for computers display the captured **waveform** as a graphic display, which can be viewed at various **resolutions**, processed with tools that amplify, reverse, echo etc, and that allow precise editing.

> SAMPLING RATE

WAVEFORM TABLE

In digitally synthesized music, the series of numbers (quantized samples) that describe a **waveform**.

> QUANTIZE   > SAMPLING RATE

> SYNTHESIZER

NEC Corporation: wearable PC.

WEARABLE COMPUTER

Personal computers, electronic organizers and **personal digital assistants** that can be worn as an accessory – as a bracelet, headband, shoulder bag, etc. Wearable computers require new methods of **input**, and new user-interface design. Many of these methods are derived from **virtual reality** research, including **speech recognition**, single-handed **keyboards**, **DataGloves**, **eyeball tracking**, **eyephones** and monocular eye-screens.

WELL [WHOLE EARTH 'LECTRONIC LINK]

A network started by the <u>Whole Earth Catalog</u> (founded by Stewart Brand, who also wrote the definitive first account of the MIT Media Lab), the WELL is one of the US networks most popular with writers, cyberpunks, programmers, virtual reality and multimedia developers.

> INTERNET

WETWARE

Cyberpunk slang for human beings and other animals (as opposed to computer hardware and software).

WHITE BOOK

Document specifying the CD-ROM standard for Video-CD, published by Philips and JVC in March 1993. Video-CD discs will store 72 minutes of full-motion video compressed under the MPEG-1 standard.

WILD TRACK

A sound-track that is not synchronized with the screen images – ie a background or atmospheric sound, or a voice-over commentary.

> OVERDUB

WIMP

[WINDOWS, ICONS, MENUS, POINTERS, OR WINDOWS, MOUSE, PULLDOWN MENUS]

Term used to describe the first generation of popular graphical user interfaces, such as the Macintosh interface and Microsoft Windows.

WINDOW

Part of a hypermedia or computer graphical user interface that provides the user with a frame through which an application, file or part of the programme contents can be viewed.

> MACINTOSH   > MICROSOFT WINDOWS

NEC Corporation: wearable PC terminals. Design prototypes from the Advanced PC Design Centre in Tokyo. These include the Wearable Data Terminal (above) with its neck-mounted computer and CD-ROM drive, and a forearm console, which incorporates a bar-code scanner. The Porto Office backpack (below, and previous page) contains the computer and memory device which links a keyboard and screen display at the wrist with a speaker and earphones at the head.

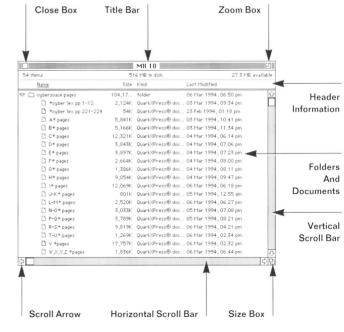

Close Box | Title Bar | Zoom Box

Header Information

Folders And Documents

Vertical Scroll Bar

Scroll Arrow | Horizontal Scroll Bar | Size Box

WINDOWS
> MICROSOFT WINDOWS

WINDOWS NT [WINDOWS NEW TECHNOLOGY]
An updated version of the Microsoft **graphical user interface**, Windows NT shares many of the features of **Microsoft Windows** Version 3.1, but is geared to run on modern 32-bit processors like the Intel 80386 and 80486, as well as on non-Intel chips, such as the MIPS R6000 RISC. It is 'backwardly compatible', allowing application programmes for Windows, **MS-DOS** and character-based **OS/2** programs to run under it on suitable machines.

WIPE
In film and video, a **transition** effect whereby the one image is progressively covered by another, in effect 'wiping' over it. **Digital** versions of the wipe are available in **animation** and presentation software and include various directional effects.
> VIDEO GRAPHICS

WIRED GLOVE
A generic term for gloves that incorporate flexing and position sensing, for use in computer **interface**, **arcade games** and **virtual reality** applications.
> DATAGLOVE   > POWERGLOVE

WIREFRAME
In **three-dimensional computer graphics** and computer-aided design (**CAD**) applications, wireframes are models described by lines or vectors, as if they were models made of wire, rather than being fully shaded 'solid models'. In **computer animation** and architectural '**walk-throughs**', wireframes are used to create the equivalent of animation 'line tests' – prototyping the animated movements in **realtime** – before the expensive and time-consuming process of rendering takes place. Wireframes can be processed to remove hidden lines, so that a more realistic scene is produced.
> COMPUTER GRAPHICS

WIRELESS NETWORK
Describes a collection of computers or other communication devices that are connected together by infrared, radio or microwave links rather than by cables. Cellular radio networks are an essential ingredient of mobile telecommunications and in conjunction with LEOS satellites are set to provide worldwide mobile coverage.
> CELL-NET

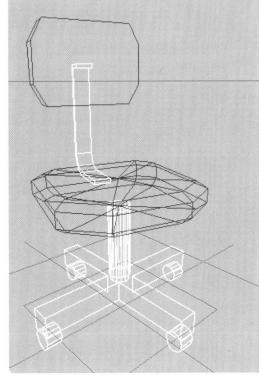

Wireframe model: example by Peakash Patel.

WMRM [WRITE MANY, READ MANY TIMES]
An optical disc system that uses lasers of two strengths to write/erase the data, and to read it.
> WORM

WORKSTATION
Originally referred to an 'intelligent terminal': one of a number of terminals attached to, and allowing shared access to, a **mainframe** or mini-mainframe computer. These terminals had on-board memory and powerful processors, with a variety of **input** and **output** devices (**keyboard**, digit pad, light pen, **screen** etc), and linked the user through a fast **network** · to mainframe processing power. Nowadays, 'workstation' can refer to any desktop or tower (floor-standing) machine with sufficient **RAM** and processing power for computation-intensive tasks – such as **CAD**, **computer graphics** and **virtual reality**.
> PLAYSTATION

WORLD GAME
An idea proposed by Richard Buckminster Fuller in which data on the world's physical and human resources would be embodied in a vast computer **simulation** of the planet. This 'Earth resources' simulator would be used to run strategies proposed by different political, economic and social groups in a continuing competition to discover 'how to make the world work'. The world game computer would configure the world simulation **software**, extrapolate the results of competing theories, and display the outcome on a giant 60-metre (200-foot) diameter globe of the Earth. Fuller imagined these 'mini-Earths' suspended high in the air over major cities around the world. He calculated that at about 200 feet up, the globe would float like an artificial satellite, relaying the state of the world game to the population – a constant reminder of the fragility of 'Spaceship Earth'.
>> FURTHER READING: FULLER 1971

WORLD VIEW
In three-dimensional computer graphics, the workspace display in which objects can be disposed on the Cartesian 'world coordinates' and viewed from different user-controlled orientations, prior to defining eye- or camera- positions for still-image or animation rendering. In desktop modelling programs, objects are prepared within a set of four linked windows, showing front, side and top views, as well as a reference perspective image, before viewing in the 'world view' window.
> COMPUTER GRAPHICS

WORM [WRITE ONCE READ MANY TIMES]
An optical disc system used for **backup** and **archiving** of digital data. 'Write once' discs are available with storage capacities of up to around one gigabyte (1,000 megabytes). Files can be copied to them, and retrieved from them, but when the disc is full it cannot be erased or reused. Once recorded, optical discs are immune from electro-magnetic interference, and are therefore considerably safer as **archive** media than magnetic disks.
> WMRM

WYSIWYG [WHAT YOU SEE IS WHAT YOU GET]
Software that represents graphics and typefaces on screen in close approximation of the final printed result.
> ADOBE TYPE MANAGER   > DIGITAL FONTS
> DISPLAY POSTSCRIPT

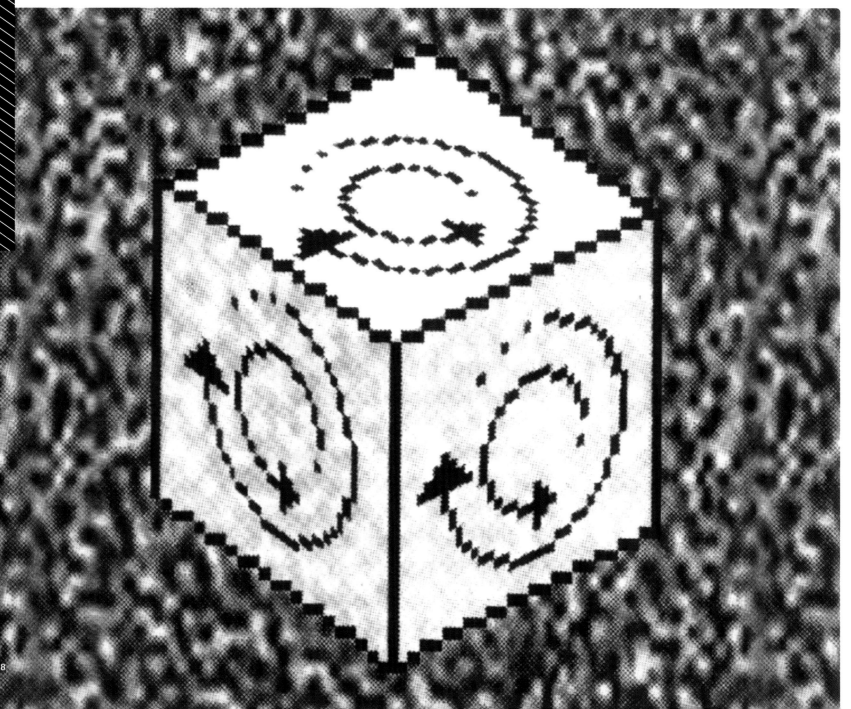

X-AXIS
The horizontal axis of Cartesian (X,Y, Z) spatial
coordinates.
> CARTESIAN COORDINATE SYSTEM

X-SERIES RECOMMENDATIONS
Recommendations endorsed by the world's
telecommunications authorities (through the **standards**-
making body **CCITT**) relating to data communications
over public data **network**s. The recommendations
include standard guidelines on transmission speeds,
modes of operation for user devices and interfaces
between networks. For example, the X.25 CCITT
recommendation is a standard that specifies the
interface between a computer or other user device
and a **modem**, for exchanging packets of data through
a **packet-switching** network.

XANADU
An experimental hypermedia/storage management
system devised by Ted Nelson for the non-linear
exploration of textual and other information. In its
ideal implementation, Xanadu would provide users
with **hypertext** links to all the books (and eventually all
the pictures, movies, videos and computer
programs) in all the world's libraries and museums,
and would 'make you part of a new electronic
literature and art, where you can get all your
questions answered and nobody will put you down.'
>> FURTHER READING: NELSON 1974

XCMD (EXTERNAL COMMAND)
A program that can be added to a **HyperCard** or **SuperCard**
application to provide additional functions, or to
control **hardware** such as **videodisc** or **CD** player.
> XFCN

XEROX PARC
(XEROX PALO ALTO RESEARCH CENTER)
The Xerox Corporation's research and development
centre at Palo Alto, California. Xerox PARC has been
a powerful influence on the development of
cyberspace technologies since the early 1970s, when
a number of computer scientist stars – including
Alan Kay (see **Smalltalk** and **Dynabook**), and John
Warnock (founder of Adobe Corporation), began
work on developing an **interface** for **personal computer**s
that would be truly 'personal' – a **graphical user
interface** that incorporated ideas from Douglas
Engelbart's **ARC** developments, and used windows
and the **mouse**. The PARC interface was to sow the
seed for the enormously successful **Macintosh** and
Microsoft Windows 'WIMP' interfaces of the 1980s. In
the 1990s, Xerox scientists at PARC and at the
EuroPARC in the UK are developing a wide range
of new computer-based technologies, including
the '**Xerox Rooms**' interface, and personal information
products based on the idea of **ubiquitous computing**.

Xerox PARC: three of the developers of the Xerox
Rooms interface – Jock MacKinley, Stew Card
and George Robertson. PARC is still in the
forefront of interface design.

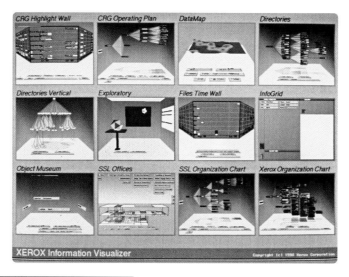

XEROX Information Visualizer

Copyright (c) 1990 Xerox Corporation

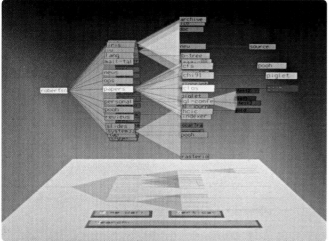

Xerox Rooms 'Information Visualizer' from PARC. Xerox PARC broke new ground in human-computer interface back in the late 1970s and early 1980s with their 'WIMP' interface design. The 3-d constructs of the 'Information Visualizer' define PARC's vision of a user interface suitable for the personal multimedia computing of the next decade, where masses of information will need to be retrieved, stored, manipulated and understood.

XEROX ROOMS [INFORMATION VISUALIZER]

A three-dimensional human-computer interface developed at Xerox PARC. The 'Information Visualizer' (or 'Rooms') is based on PARC's research into how people use their computers. It centres on the idea of task-oriented clustering of information – based on the fact that people prefer to form 'clusters' of software and data for performing specific tasks, and like to access these clusters as quickly and efficiently as possible. In Rooms, PARC has organized the interface as a metaphor for a set of interconnected virtual rooms (in both two and three dimensions), which users can 'enter' in order to work on their graphics, databases, spreadsheets etc. Rooms are connected by 'doors' (the back door takes the user back to the room previously occupied) which the user can travel through. Or the user can 'jump' to another room by using an overview, ie a window which shows several rooms at the same time.

Just as 'windows'-based graphical user interfaces extended the screen space available to computer users beyond the actual physical space of the screen, by allowing overlapping windows, and by providing windows onto information spaces that were much larger than the screen size, so Rooms allows users to extend the screen into a much larger virtual 3-d space. Using the metaphor of interconnected rooms makes navigation between and through these spaces much more intuitive than the act of finding one's way through a complexity of overlapping windows of varying sizes. Rooms makes extensive use of images and realtime animation of 3-d objects to extend the screen's information-carrying potential and provides several ways of creating and viewing informational models in 3-d. A 3-d model can be rotated to reveal extra information, or can reveal structures and relationships that 2-d graphics are unable to. The first commercial application of Xerox Rooms was 'Rooms for Windows', released in April 1992, which supplements the Microsoft Windows interface.

XFCN [EXTERNAL FUNCTION]

A computer program that can be added to a HyperCard stack or SuperCard project designed to report a result back to the controlling program.
> XCMD

XGA

A display technology developed by IBM as a replacement for VGA (video graphics array), and offering 256 colours at 1024x768 pixels. XGA forms part of IBM's Ultimedia specification.

X,Y,Z COORDINATE SYSTEM
> CARTESIAN COORDINATE SYSTEM

Y-AXIS

The vertical axis in Cartesian (X,Y,Z) space.
> CARTESIAN COORDINATE SYSTEM

YELLOW BOOK

The document defining the CD-ROM standards, developed jointly by Philips and Sony.
> MODE 1/ MODE 2

YUV

In video, the luminance (Y) signal, and the two chrominance signals (U and V).

YUV ENCODING

A video encoding system that takes advantage of the fact that the human eye is less sensitive to colour variations than to intensity (luminance) variations. Each picture line contains luminance (Y) information encoded at full bandwidth, with (on alternative lines) the chrominance (U and V) signals encoded at half bandwidth.
> DELTA YUV

Z-AXIS

The 'depth' axis in Cartesian (X,Y,Z) space.
> CARTESIAN COORDINATE SYSTEM
> Z-BUFFER

Z-BUFFER

In three-dimensional computer graphics, a 'depth-buffer' algorithm, devised by Ed Catmull in the mid-1970s to solve the problem of hidden-surface removal for complex smooth-shaded objects. The Z-buffer requires two arrays (areas of memory, or 'buffers') to hold depth and intensity values for the scene to be rendered, and functions by examining each pixel-sized surface fragment, deciding which pixels will fall within the screen area, and then computing the depth of that point in space, and the amount or intensity of light at that point.
> COMPUTER GRAPHICS

ZOOM

In video and film, 'zoom in' and 'zoom out' specify camerawork which uses a zoom (variable focal length) lens. 'Zoom in' increases the focal length of the lens, giving a reduced angle of view and increasing the size of the subject in the frame. 'Zoom out' decreases the focal length of the lens, giving a wider angle view but diminishing the size of the framed subject. Zoom is also used to describe the facility in computer graphics software to increase the size of a part of the image (usually centred on the cursor position) for bitmap or spline editing.

A

Ackerman, Diane. A Natural History of the Senses. London: Chapmans, 1990.

Ambron, Sueann and Hooper, Kristina (eds). Interactive Multimedia. Redmond, Wash: Microsoft Press, 1988.

B

Bar Code Systems Inc. A Guide to Bar Codes. USA: 1988.

Barnsley, Michael and Sloane, Alan D. 'A Better Way to Compress Images'. Byte, Jan. 1988.

Baron, Naomi S. Computer Languages: A Guide for the Perplexed. Harmondsworth: Penguin Books 1988.

Bass, Thomas A. The Newtonian Casino. Harlow: Longman, 1990.

Bateson, Gregory. Mind and Nature: A Necessary Unity. London: Fontana, 1979.

Baudrillard, Jean. 'The Ecstasy of Communication' in Post-Modern Culture edited by Hal Foster. New York: Bay Press 1983.
'The System of Objects' in Design After Modernism edited by John Thackara. London: Thames and Hudson 1988.

Benedikt, Michael (ed). Cyberspace: First Steps. Cambridge, Mass: MIT Press, 1992.

Bester, Alfred. Golem 100. London: Pan Books 1981.

Biedny, David and Monroy, Bert. The Official Adobe Photoshop Handbook. New York: Bantam Books, 1991.

Blankenship, Loyd. Gurps Cyberpunk: High-tech/Lowlife Roleplaying Sourcebook. Steve Jackson Games Inc., 1990.

Boden, Margaret A. The Creative Mind: Myths and Mechanisms. New York: Basic Books, 1991.

Brand, Steward. The Media Lab: Inventing the Future at MIT. New York: Viking Penguin, 1987.

Bruner, Jerome. Towards a Theory of Instruction. New York: W W Norton, 1966.

Brunner, John. Jagged Orbit. New York: Arrow, 1972.
The Shockwave Rider. London: Methuen, 1988.
Stand on Zanzibar. New York: Ballantine, 1969.

Bukatman, Scott. Terminal Identity: The Virtual Subject in Post Modern Science Fiction. Durham and London: Duke University Press, 1993.

Burroughs, William S. Nova Express. New York: Grove Press, 1964.
The Soft Machine. New York: Grove Press, 1966.

Bush, Vannevar. 'As We May Think', Atlantic Monthly, August 1945. Reprinted in Macintosh Hypermedia Vol 1. Michael Fraase, Scott Foreman and Co, 1990.

Buxton, Bill. 'The 'Natural' Language of Interaction: A Perspective on Non-Verbal Dialogues' in The Art of Human-Computer Interface Design edited by Brenda Laurel. Reading, Mass: Addison-Wesley, 1990.

C

Chaput, Thierry. 'From Socrates to Intel: The Chaos of Microaesthetics' in Design After Modernism edited by John Thackara. London: Thames and Hudson, 1988.

Coates, Nigel. 'Street Signs' in Design After Modernism edited by John Thackara. London: Thames and Hudson, 1988.

Collier, David and Cotton, Bob. Designing for Desktop Publishing. London: Quarto, 1989.

Cooley, Mike. 'From Brunelleschi to CADCAM' in Design After Modernism edited by John Thackara. London: Thames and Hudson, 1988.

Cotton, Bob and Oliver, Richard. Understanding Hypermedia. London: Phaidon Press, 1993.

Culhane, Shamus. Animation: From Script to Screen. London: Columbus Books, 1989.

D

Dawkins, Richard. The Blind Watchmaker. Harmondsworth: Penguin Books, 1988.

Deken, Joseph. Computer Images: State of the Art. London: Thames and Hudson 1983.

Dennett, Daniel C. Consciousness Explained. Harmondsworth: Penguin Books, 1993.
'Thinking with a Computer' in Images and Understanding ed. Barlow, Blakemore and Weston Smith. Cambridge: Cambridge University Press, 1990.

Dick, Philip K. Do Androids Dream of Electric Sheep? London: Grafton, 1968.
The Simulacra. London: Methuen, 1977.

Dubery, Fred and Willats, John. Perspective and other Drawing Systems. New York: Van Nostrand Reinhold, 1972.

E

Eames (Office of Charles and Ray). A Computer Perspective: Background to the Computer Age. Boston: HUP 1990.

Edge magazine. 'An Audience with: John Waldern' in Edge 4, January 1994.
'CD-ROM: The Truth' in Edge 2, November 1993.
'Game Over' in Edge 3, December 1993.
'Network Television' in Edge 2, November 1993.
'Sex and Violence' in Edge 2, November 1993.
'VR The Next Step' in Edge 3, December 1993.

Eisenstein, Sergei M. The Film Sense. London: Faber and Faber, 1943.

➡

Evans, Christopher. The Mighty Micro. London: Victor Gollancz, 1979.

F

Fisher, Scott S. 'Virtual Interface Environments' in The Art of Human-Computer Interface Design edited by Brenda Laurel. Reading, Mass: Addison-Wesley, 1990.

Foley, J. D. and Van Dam, A. Fundamentals of Interactive Computer Graphics. Reading, Mass: Addison-Wesley Publishing Company, 1982

Foster, Hal (ed). Post-Modern Culture. New York: Bay Press, 1983.

Fraase, Michael. Macintosh Hypermedia. Glenview, III: Scott, Foreman and Co, 1990.

Franco, Gaston Lionel (ed). World Communications: New Horizons, New Power, New Hope. Le Monde Economique International Publications, 1984.

Fuller, Richard Buckminster. I Seem To Be A Verb. New York: Bantam, 1970.
Inventory of World Resources (World Game Series). Carbondale, III: 1971.

G

Geake, Elisabeth. 'Computer Games Make Learning Virtually Irresistible' in New Scientist No 1816, April 1992.

Gibson, William. Burning Chrome. London: Grafton, 1988.
Count Zero. London: Grafton, 1987.
Mona Lisa Overdrive. London: Grafton, 1988.
Neuromancer. London: Grafton, 1986.

Gombrich E H. Art and Illusion. Oxford: Phaidon Press, 1960.

Greenberg, Donald and Marcus, Aaron & Schmidt, Alan H & Gorter, Vernon. The Computer Image: Applications of Computer Graphics. Reading, Mass: Addison-Wesley Publishing Company, 1982

Greenberger, Martin (ed). On Multimedia. Santa Monica: The Voyager Company, 1990.

Greenfield, Patricia Marks. Mind and Media: The Effects of Television, Videogames, and Computers. Cambridge, Mass: Harvard University Press, 1984.

Greiman, April. Hybrid Imagery. London: Architecture, Design and Technology Press, 1990.

H

Hafner, Katie and Markoff, John. Cyberpunk: Outlaws and Hackers on the Computer Frontier. New York: Simon and Schuster, 1991.

Halas, John and Manvell, Roger. The Technique of Film Animation. London: Focal Press, 1959.

Hanhardt, John G. Video Culture: A Critical Investigation. New York: Peregrine Smith Books in association with Visual Studies Workshop Press, 1986.

Hardison, O B. Disappearing Through the Skylight: Culture and Technology in the Twentieth Century. New York: Viking, 1989.

Haraway, Donna 'A Cyborg Manifesto: Science, Technology and Socio-Feminism in the 1980s' in Simians, Cyborgs and Women. New York: Routledge, 1989.

Hawkins, Trip. 'Shaping Consumer Software', in interview with Phil Lemmons and Barbara Robertson in Byte, October 1983.

Helsel, Sandra K and Roth, Judith Paris (eds). Virtual Reality: Theory, Practice and Promise. London: Meckler, 1991.

Hirschfeld, Thomas P (ed). Interactive Multimedia: When Worlds Converge (Investment Report). New York: Salomon Brothers June 1993.

Hodges, Andrew. Alan Turing: The Enigma. London: Hutchinson, 1983.

Hoffos, Sharpless, Smith and Lewis: CD-i Designer's Guide. New York: McGraw Hill, 1992.

Hofstadter, Douglas R. Godel, Escher, Bach: An Eternal Golden Braid. New York: Basic Books, 1979.

Holmes, J Eric. Fantasy Role Playing Games. London: Arms and Armour Press, 1981.

J

Jankel, Annabel and Morton, Rocky. Creative Computer Graphics. Cambridge: Cambridge University Press, 1984

Jones, Jon Chris. 'Softecnica' in Design After Modernism edited by John Thackara. London: Thames and Hudson, 1988.

K

Kay, Alan C. 'Computer Software' in Scientific American, Vol 257, No 3. September 1984.
'Computers, Networks and Education' in Scientific American, September 1991.
'User Interface: A Personal View' in The Art of Human-Computer Interface Design edited by Brenda Laurel. Reading, Mass: Addison-Wesley, 1990.

Krueger, Myron W. Artificial Reality. Reading, Mass: Addison-Wesley, 1983.
Artificial Reality II. Reading, Mass: Addison-Wesley, 1992.
'Videoplace and the Interface of the Future' in The Art of Human-Computer Interface Design edited by Brenda Laurel. Reading, Mass: Addison-Wesley, 1990.

Kurtenbach, Gordon and Hulteen, Eric A. 'Gestures in Human-Computer Interaction' in The Art of Human-Computer Interface Design edited by Brenda Laurel. Reading, Mass: Addison-Wesley, 1990.

Kurzweil, Raymond. The Age of Intelligent Machines. Reading, Mass: MIT Press, 1990.

L

Lambert, Steve and Ropiequet, Suzanne. CD-ROM: The New Papyrus. Redmond, Washington: Microsoft Press, 1986.

Lambert, Steve and Sallis, Jane (eds). CD-i and Interactive Videodisc Technology. New York: Howard W Sams and Co, 1986.

Lansdown, John. 'Understanding the Digital Image' in Images and Understanding ed. Barlow, Blakemore and Weston Smith. Cambridge: Cambridge University Press, 1990.

Larsen, Judith K and Rogers, Everett M. Silicon Valley Fever: Growth of High Technology Culture. London: George Allen and Unwin, 1985.

Laurel, Brenda (ed). The Art of Human-Computer Interface Design. Reading, Mass: Addison-Wesley, 1990.

Laurel, Brenda. Computers as Theatre. Menlo Park, CA: Addison-Wesley, 1991.
'Interface Agents: Metaphors with Character' in The Art of Human-Computer Interface Design edited by Brenda Laurel. Reading, Mass: Addison-Wesley 1990.
'On Dramatic Interaction' in Verbum 3.3. San Diego: 1989.

Leary, Timothy. 'The Interpersonal, Interactive, Interdimensional Interface' in The Art of Human-Computer Interface Design edited by Brenda Laurel. Reading, Mass: Addison-Wesley, 1990.

Leonard Brett. 'VR Goes to Hollywood', interview with R U Sirius in Mondo 2000 No 6.

Levy, Steven. Artificial Life: The Quest for New Creation. London: Jonathan Cape 1992.
'Brave New World' (Jaron Lanier and VR) in Rolling Stone 580, June 1990.
Hackers: Heroes of the Computer Revolution. Dell, 1984.
Insanely Great: The Life and Times of Macintosh – the Computer that Changed Everything. New York: Viking, 1994.

Lodge, David. 'Narration with Words' in Images and Understanding edited by Barlow, Blakemore and Weston Smith. Cambridge: Cambridge University Press, 1990.
'The Novel as Communication' in Ways of Communicating edited by D H Mellor. Cambridge: Cambridge University Press, 1990.

Lowenstein, Otto. The Senses. Harmondsworth: Penguin Books 1966.

M

MacroMedia Inc. MacroMedia Director: Interactivity Manual. San Francisco: MacroMedia, 1991.

Mandelbrot, Benoit. The Fractal Geometry of Nature. New York: WH Freeman and Co, 1977.

Matthews, W H. Mazes and Labyrinths: Their History and Development. New York: Dover Publications, 1970.

McClellan, Jim. 'From Here to Reality', The Face, December 1989.

McLuhan, H Marshall. Understanding Media. New York: New American Library, 1964.
War and Peace in the Global Village. New York: Bantam Books, 1968.

Meggs, Philip B. 'Will Videogames Devour the World? (And Some Related Questions)' in Print, Vol XLVI:VI.

Mellor, D H (ed). Ways of Communicating. Cambridge: Cambridge University Press, 1990.

Merrit, Douglas. Television Graphics: From Pencil to Pixel. London: Trefoil, 1987

Minsky, Marvin. The Society of Mind. London: Pan Books, 1988.

Moorcock, Michael. The Condition of Muzak. London: Fontana, 1976.
A Cure for Cancer. London: Fontana, 1968.
The English Assassin. London: Fontana, 1972.
The Final Programme. The Jerry Cornelius Quartet. London: Fontana, 1965.

Morningstar, Chip and Farmer, S. Randall. 'The Lessons of Lucasfilm's Habitat' in Cyberspace: First Steps edited by Michael Benedict. Cambridge, Mass: MIT Press, 1992.

Mountford, S Joy and Gaver, William W. 'Talking and Listening to Computers' in The Art of Human-Computer Interface Design edited by Brenda Laurel. Reading, Mass: Addison-Wesley 1990.

Museum of Modern Art. Information Art: Diagramming Microchips. New York: Museum of Modern Art, 1990.

N

Negroponte, Nicholas. The Architecture Machine. Cambridge, Mass: MIT Press, 1970.
'The Noticeable Difference' in The Art of Human-Computer Interface Design edited by Brenda Laurel. Reading, Mass: Addison-Wesley, 1990.
'Products and Services for Computer Networks' in Scientific American, September 1991.
Soft Architecture Machines. Cambridge, Mass: MIT Press, 1975.

Nelson, Ted. Computer Lib – Dream Machines. Redmond, Wash: Tempus Books of Microsoft Press 1987; originally published 1974.
'The Crime of Wizzywig' in Mondo 2000, August 1989.
'The Right Way to Think About Software Design' in The Art of Human-Computer Interface Design edited by Brenda Laurel. Reading, Mass: Addison-Wesley, 1990.

Newman, W. M. and Sproull R. F. Principles of Interactive Computer Graphics. New York: McGraw-Hill, 1979.

Niven, Larry. Ringworld. London: Victor Gollancz 1972.
The Ringworld Engineers. London: Victor Gollancz, 1980.

Noake, Roger. Animation: A Guide to Animated Film Techniques. London: MacDonald & Co, 1988.

O

Oren, Tim (et al). 'Guides: Characterising the Interface' in The Art of Human-Computer Interface Design edited by Brenda Laurel. Reading, Mass: Addison-Wesley 1990.

P

Pagels, Heinz R. The Dreams of Reason. New York: Simon and Schuster, 1988.

Palfreman, Jon and Swade, Doron. The Dream Machine: Exploring the Computer Age. London: BBC Books, 1991.

Papert, Seymour. Mindstorms: Children, Computers and Powerful Ideas. New York: Basic Books, 1980.

Penrose, Roger. The Emperor's New Mind. London: Vintage, 1990.

Penzias, Arno. Ideas and Information. New York: Simon and Schuster, 1989.

Philips IMS. The CD-i Design Handbook. Reading, Mass: Addison Wesley, 1992.

Pickover, Clifford A. Computers and the Imagination. Stroud: Alan Sutton Publishing, 1991.
Computers, Pattern, Chaos and Beauty. New York: St Martin's Press, 1990.

Pierce, Mark Stephen. 'Making Fun' (Videogame Design) in Verbum 3.3, 1989.

Pimentel, Ken and Teixeira, Kevin. Virtual Reality: Through the New Looking-Glass. Windcrest, 1993.

Pohl, Frederick.
Beyond the Blue Event Horizon. London: Victor Gollancz, 1980.

Poundstone, William. The Recursive Universe. Oxford: Oxford University Press, 1985.

Preston, J M (ed). Compact Disc-Interactive: A Designer's Overview. Deventer, Antwerpen: Kluwer, 1987.

Provenzo, Eugene F. Video Kids: Making Sense of Nintendo. Cambridge, Mass: Harvard University Press, 1991.

R

Reichardt, Jascia (ed). Cybernetic Serendipity: The Computer and the Arts. London: Studio International 1968.

Rheingold, Howard. Virtual Reality. London: Secker and Warburg, 1991.

Rossotti, Hazel. Colour: Why the World isn't Grey. Harmondsworth: Penguin Books, 1983.

Roszak, Theodor. The Cult of Information. London: Paladin, 1988.

Rucker, Rudy. Software. New York: Avon, 1982.
Wetware. London: New English Library, 1989.

S

Schwartz, Peter. The Art of the Long View. New York: Doubleday, 1991.

Sculley, John and Byrne, John A. Odyssey: From Pepsi to Apple. London: Collins, 1988.

Shafer, Dan. Hypertalk Programming. Indianapolis: Hayden Books, 1988.

Sheckley, Robert. Mindswap. London: Victor Gollancz, 1966.

Sheff, David. How Nintendo Zapped an American Industry, Captured Your Dollars, and Enslaved Your Children. New York: Random House, 1993.

Sherman, Barrie and Judkins, Phil. Glimpses of Heaven, Visions of Hell: Virtual Reality and Its Implications. London: Hodder and Stoughton, 1992.

Shirley, John. Eclipse. New York: Bluejay, 1985.
Eclipse Corona. New York: Popular Library, 1990.
Eclipse Penumbra. New York: Popular Library, 1987.

Simmons, Dan. Hyperion. New York: Doubleday, 1989.

Sipe, Russell. 'Whose turn to Play God?' (Videogames) in Verbum 3.3, 1989.

Sladek, John. The Müller-Fokker Effect. New York: Carroll and Graf, 1974.

Sless, Peter. Learning and Visual Communication. London: Croom Helm, 1971.

Stephenson, Neal. Snow Crash. New York: Bantam, 1992.

Stirling, Bruce (ed). Mirrorshades: A Cyberpunk Anthology. London: Paladin, 1988.

Stirling, Bruce. Islands in the Net. New York: Legend/Arrow Books, 1988.
Schismatrix. New York: Ace, 1985.

Stoll, Clifford. The Cuckoo's Egg. London: The Bodley Head, 1989.

Swain, Bob. 'Pixel Tricks Enrich Flicks' in New Scientist No 1841, October 1992.

T

Thackara, John (ed). Design After Modernism. London: Thames and Hudson, 1988.

Turkle, Sherry. The Second Self: Computers and the Human Spirit. New York: Simon and Schuster, 1984.

V

Vallee, Jacques. The Network Revolution: Confessions of a Computer Scientist. Harmondsworth: Penguin Books, 1984.

Vince, John. Dictionary of Computer Graphics. London: Frances Pinter, 1984.

Vinge, Vernor. Across Realtime. New York: Baen Books, 1991.
True Names and Other Dangers. New York: Baen Books, 1987.

W

Waldern, Dr Jon. 'W Industries', interview in Black Ice, Issue 1, January 1993.

Weiner, Norbert. Cybernetics: or Control and Communication in the Animal and the Machine. Cambridge, Mass: MIT Press, 1948.

Wilson, Greg. 'Computing in Parallel' in New Scientist, 11 Febuary 1988.

Winograd, Terry and Flores, Fernando. Understanding Computers and Cognition: A New Foundation for Design. New York: Ablex Publishing Corporation, 1986.

Wright, Karen. 'The Road to the Global Village' in Scientific American, March 1990.

Y

Youngblood, Gene. Expanded Cinema. London: Studio Vista, 1970.

Z

Zuboff, Shoshana. In the Age of the Smart Machine: The Future of Work and Power. New York: Basic Books, 1988.

the cyberspace lexicon